Praise for

Underminers

How incredibly helpful, that Keith Farnish has given me a new word to describe how I act in the world. Here I thought I was a crank, a doomer, a scold, a Cassandra, a downer, a bummer, a fearmonger, just because I want to help rid the world of a culture that is systematically killing off the life of this planet. That's what that culture tells me, anyway. Turns out I'm an Underminer! Sounds like a noble profession to me. It even comes with an instruction manual now. How about that!

—T.S. Bennett, writer & director, *What a Way to Go: Life at the End of Empire*

Take a social animal (that's us) and deprive it of its band or tribe (something industrial society does so well) and you get two results: alienation and asocial behavior on one hand, and extreme conformism and docile obedience on the other. Neither is particularly fulfilling. Farnish's book teaches us the bag of tricks by which we can free ourselves and restore our humanity by reconnecting with others.

—Dmitry Orlov, author, *Reinventing Collapse* and *The Five Stages of Collapse*

Every now and again a book claws its way through the cracks in the concrete slabs of greenwash, timidity and shallow thinking, and — gasping for air — demands our fullest attention. Farnish's latest book, *Underminers*, is one of those rare few. *Underminers* challenges us to face the perfect storm of social, ecological and personal crises we are facing with a genuinely realistic perspective and a deeper understanding of their causes. It's a must-read for anyone who wants to engage with the world they see before them with integrity and honour, and who wants to do whatever they can to save the exquisite beauty of the world that still remains.

—Mark Boyle, author, *The Moneyless Manifesto* and *The Moneyless Man*

Keith Farnish has been a thorn in the side of the Machine for many years. If this book alerts others to the ecocide that industrial civilisation continues to unleash on the natural world, and gives them some ideas for resisting it, it will be a job well done.

—Paul Kingsnorth, director, The Dark Mountain Project

Whether in the external world or the inner one, undermining is no small feat. *Underminers* provides us with both inspiration and instruction in how to heal the many layers of our disconnection, and I highly recommend it as a necessary tool for transforming the old model of civilization into a creative construct for inter and intra-connection.

—Carolyn Baker, author,
Navigating The Coming Chaos: A Handbook For Inner Transition and
Collapsing Consciously: Transformative Truths For Turbulent Times
CarolynBaker.net

underminers

a guide to subverting the machine

keith farnish

Cover design by Diane McIntosh.
Original cover photo by Horst Kiechle, used with kind permission.

Printed in Canada. First printing September 2013.

Paperback ISBN: 978-0-86571-754-1
EBook ISBN: 978-1-55092-545-6

Inquiries regarding requests to reprint all or part of *Underminers* should be addressed to New Society Publishers at the address below.

To order directly from the publishers, please call toll-free (North America) 1-800-567-6772, or order online at www.newsociety.com

Any other inquiries can be directed by mail to:

New Society Publishers
P.O. Box 189, Gabriola Island, BC V0R 1X0, Canada
(250) 247-9737

New Society Publishers' mission is to publish books that contribute in fundamental ways to building an ecologically sustainable and just society, and to do so with the least possible impact on the environment, in a manner that models this vision. We are committed to doing this not just through education, but through action. The interior pages of our bound books are printed on Forest Stewardship Council®-registered acid-free paper that is **100% post-consumer recycled** (100% old growth forest-free), processed chlorine free, and printed with vegetable-based, low-VOC inks, with covers produced using FSC®-registered stock. New Society also works to reduce its carbon footprint, and purchases carbon offsets based on an annual audit to ensure a carbon neutral footprint. For further information, or to browse our full list of books and purchase securely, visit our website at: www.newsociety.com

Library and Archives Canada Cataloguing in Publication

Farnish, Keith, author

Underminers : a guide to subverting the machine / Keith Farnish.
Self published in 2012.

Includes bibliographical references and index.
ISBN 978-0-86571-754-1 (pbk.)

1. Anarchism. 2. Political ecology. I. Title.

HX833.F37 2013 320.5'7 C2013-902744-0

Disclaimer

THE AUTHOR, PUBLISHERS, DISTRIBUTORS AND RETAILERS accept no responsibility for the outcomes of any activities carried out by anyone else as a result, direct or indirect, of reading this book. If you are not prepared to take responsibility for your own actions, then you should not be undermining. The author is an Underminer and is responsible for his own actions.

The essays contained within this book do not imply the contributors' agreement with the contents of any other part of the book. Though juxtaposed with the relevant sections of the book, the essays are individual and collective works separate from those of the author and as such should not be considered an endorsement of the author's own writing.

The cover image is derived from an original photo by Horst Kiechle. Sincere thanks for permission to use this awesome example of tree roots undermining the urban landscape.

— Keith Farnish, 2013.

Contents

Acknowledgments

WRITING THIS BOOK WAS AN OFTEN LONELY, usually difficult, process that found its greatest joys in the connections I was able to make, old and new, with those who could help the project along its way (and keep me sane). Over those more than two years, I was kept busy in so many other ways by my wonderful family, the friends I have made here in the part of the world I love and the things that matter so much more than sitting in front of a computer tapping at bits of plastic.

For the times I did manage to tap bits of plastic, the following people helped enormously and are still helping me, although, as the disclaimer says, they might not agree with everything that's in this book:

Ana Salote, "B," Ben DeVries, Bob Black, Carolyn Baker, Cory Morningstar, Dave Pollard, David Edwards, David McKay, Depaver Jan Lundberg, Dmitry Orlov, Eoin Cox, Guy McPherson, Helen Mulley, Janaia Donaldson, Jeff Mincey, Mark Boyle, Mike Bonanno, Nicky Hager, Paul Kingsnorth, Peter Bauer (Urban Scout), Richard Reynolds, Sharon Astyk, Stephanie McMillan, Tim Bennett and various members of Anonymous.

Introduction

HOW CAN SOMETHING SO CONNECTED BE SO DISCONNECTED? I ask myself this question sitting in a library a few miles from my home in the borders of Scotland, wirelessly hooked up to the Internet providing me with access to just about every piece of information ... the civilized world considers to be of consequence. There was a pause in my writing there because the phrase that so nearly reached my fingertips was "every piece of information of any consequence" — literally a much more satisfying expression but so far from the truth. What I am able to access via the corporate-controlled routers, switches and servers that comprise the Internet may be close to all the information Industrial Civilization has gathered in its short tenure on Earth, but it is a closed, self-perpetuating network as disconnected from the real world as its individual components will be from each other when the current eventually ceases to flow.

It was nearly four years ago that what I thought would be my *magnum opus* was first published in book form. Not that I expected to sell a great number of copies of *Time's Up!* but I did expect something to come of it. Maybe it did; maybe I've been looking in the wrong places, or perhaps the work that came about as a result is hiding in the cracks and beneath the floorboards of public awareness. There is no doubt that anything that has the potential to destabilize the Culture of Maximum Harm, as Daniel Quinn so accurately calls Industrial Civilization, needs to be protected. Nevertheless, the question that has come back to me by email, letter, word of mouth and, indirectly, through the comments and thoughts on many blogs and forums, is one that suggests I am far from finished in my writing. That question is, "What can I do?"

This book is a response to that question.

It is not the definitive response; it's barely an adequate response, given the level of emotion with which some people have phrased the question, but it is the best I can do for now. It is also a big personal risk. Over the past couple of years my life, and that of my family, has changed. We have moved to a place where connections with the real world, with fellow human beings and the rest of nature abound; so life has changed for the better. We would love things to stay this way, but know they cannot and will not, as the environment nature created and nurtured crumbles under the boot of civilization, and the energy that feeds the machine starts to sputter out. The publication and distribution of this book's content is a risk to our circumstances but reflects the nature of the situation we are increasingly going to experience. It is also something I have to do. Undermining is something we are all going to have to take a part in if we are once again to take control of our own destiny.

And that raises the question of what undermining is. The simple definition is as good as any: removing that upon which something depends for its strength. If you want to make a house fall down, then start removing bricks from its base; eventually, if you remove enough bricks, the house will tumble to the ground. If the house is tall or top-heavy, then you will need to remove fewer bricks. If the house already has weak foundations, or poor construction, then you might not have to remove many bricks at all. The same principle applies to anything you wish to undermine: a wall, a political party, a corporation, an entire set of principles by which a population carries out its daily life.

The way in which Industrial Civilization keeps us attached to its principles — such as the belief that economic growth is a good thing or that it is necessary for a few people to tell the majority how to live or that having a well-paid job is a natural human aspiration — is by ensuring civilized people are kept disconnected from anything that might provide them with an alternative view of what life is really about. This disconnection from the real world is achieved through what I call the Tools of Disconnection. If we stay attached to the underlying principles of Industrial Civilization, then we have little chance of surviving the next century as a viable species; and as long as we remain disconnected from the real world that is almost certain.

The way to return civilized humanity to a state where long-term survival is a real possibility is to reject the principles of Industrial Civilization and live as though we wish to have a future. The way to achieve this is by undermining the Tools of Disconnection. That is what this book aims to do, not merely in words, but by fostering an entire generation of people who are willing to go beyond the superficial rhetoric of the mainstream environmental organizations, a generation of people who are ready to take risks in order to return humanity to a connected state.

We are the Underminers, and this is our time.

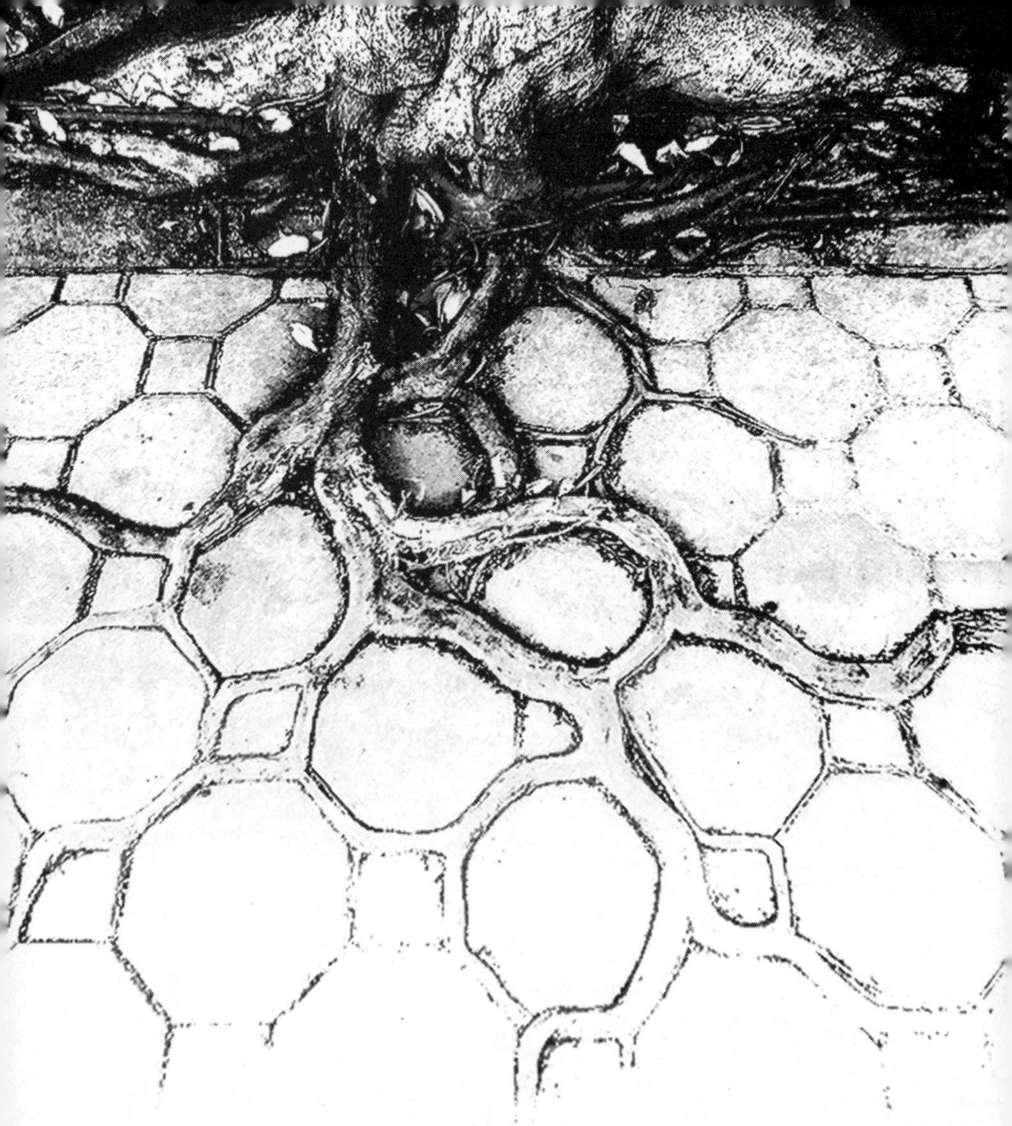

PART ONE

Groundwork

What makes us human is we do things that
go beyond the simple need to survive.

What makes us civilized is not knowing when to stop.

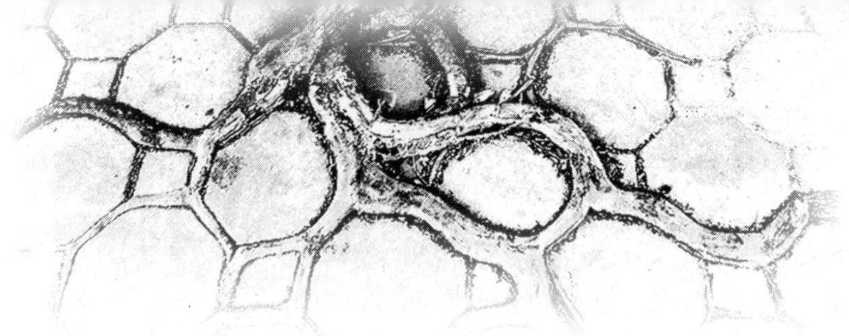

CHAPTER ONE

Shake Yourself From Sleep

I CAN'T REMEMBER ANYTHING UP TO THE AGE OF THREE. Some people say they can, but I'm not so sure — it's surprising how easy something said about you or a photograph in an album can become embedded as a "memory." The first real memory I have, rather than one replicated by Kodak, was of a rainstorm.

Between the ages of two and eighteen I lived in the English seaside town of Margate. In the first ten years or so of our time there — an exquisitely blissful time of life when worrying was something other people did — we ran first a guest house and then a slightly more grandly titled "hotel." The guest house, one of hundreds of small and medium-sized accommodations that served the once teeming masses of East Kent holidaymakers, was located on one of the many streets that run perpendicular to the oceanfront road, leading inland toward the main shopping street. Behind our modest establishment was a concrete yard in which stood a small motor home. There may have been more to it than that, but details often get forgotten when you are three. The occasion is lost to me, but some kind of late-night party was taking place and for the sake of a good night's sleep, I had been moved, along with my older sister, into the motor home. Sleep didn't pass over me like the shadow of a cloud crossing the evening sun; this night the rain was pouring down, drumming a mighty tattoo upon the metallic roof. Things start to become unclear, but at some point I must have complained of a headache, for which I was administered a paracetamol[1] tablet — maybe just a half. Shortly after, sleep took me and the memory faded.

It's very rare that I get headaches, and usually nothing that a night's sleep can't resolve (with a slight sense of irony); nevertheless, when one does start really punching its way through my anterior cortex, paracetamol is my analgesic of choice. I can't honestly say that the rainy night in the caravan is the reason for this, but someone in the world of advertising can probably give me an opening here. Let's just say the way we perceive the world, and subsequently behave in it, is dominated by the messages we receive in our developmental years:

> It is relatively easy for producers and retailers to begin a relationship with children as future consumers.... One of the basic behaviours parents teach children is to go into the marketplace and satisfy their needs through certain products and brands. In effect, children learn to find need-satisfying objects and stick with them.[2]

Make of that what you will, and I'm sure you already have your own opinions on the power of advertising, but for anyone who sees commercials as a fairly harmless enterprise — a sort of wallpaper behind the furniture of television programs — never forget that advertising exists to make people want things they otherwise would not have bought. To put it another way: advertising creates need out of nothing.

There is, of course, a corollary of global proportions to the dancing pixels on the television screen, the glowing billboards that flit-flit-flit past as you ride the escalator, the glossy sheets that fall from the pages of the newspaper and in your mailbox: a corollary of death that comes to the victim as easily as passing a new iPhone through the bright red beams of a barcode reader. Perhaps a little twinge of anguish as your bank balance clicks downward and into barcode-scanner red. Maybe even the tiny recognition that the person who assembled your purchase lies sprawled in the suicide nets that a factory in China installed to prevent further public embarrassment after a high number of employee suicides drew media attention.

How nice of them to save us from too much guilt.

By the time you read this, the iPhone might seem as quaint as the Walkman, the ZX Spectrum or the Raleigh Grifter: at least if you grew up in the 1970s in the same kind of environment as I did. Take a couple of moments to replace these with favorite items from your youth; then disassociate yourself from them so they just became objects from someone else's past — it's difficult, isn't it? The memories ooze through: making up compilation tapes to listen to on the bus, writing adventure games in Basic that would never be completed, pulling half-hearted wheelies along the beach, taking care not to startle too many old ladies. The bitter white tablet that eased my headache, probably through the warm blanket of placebo, takes its place on that treadmill that is your civilized life.

I had a Walkman, a ZX Spectrum, a Raleigh Grifter, because that's what people had at the time — because that's what was advertised and gradually, through a process of mental osmosis, became a necessary cultural artifact. But I never had a DAT player, a Commodore 64 or a Muddy Fox BMX. For me, those things hold memories but little meaning. Alliance to a particular item is a personal thing; in commerce it drives rivalries between companies and increases sales, breeding brand loyalty that is the lodestone of consumer success. Once you have brand loyalty — and what a powerful cultural grip *that* is — then you have the consumer by the balls (metaphorical or otherwise), and thus iPod becomes iPhone becomes iPad becomes iLife.

And, yes, iLife does exist.

Replace toys and gadgets with clothing, home furnishings, places to live, movies to see, food to eat, jobs to do, parties to vote for, lifestyles to embrace — the whole construct of civilized life is a series of discrete packages that may change their contents from time to time, but as entities they are so fundamental to modern culture that without them we feel as if we may as well not exist. From the first blip on the TV screen we experience as babies we have been mentally programmed: the only escapes we have in the civilized world are dreamless sleep — and death.

There are times in life when you have to risk offending someone. Where I live now there is a fairly high proportion of church-goers compared to the town we moved away from in 2010. Religiously it doesn't compare with anything like a typical southern US town, and is positively heathen if viewed alongside Tehran, Manila or Salt Lake City (although I can't see the occupants of these three places ever coming to an agreement over what "heathen" means), but nonetheless the question of religion is discreetly shooed to the back of the room as soon as it is raised, because I don't actually have any. Pushed as to whether I would be attending a church service, for instance, I may say, "No, I'm not religious at all," and perhaps sense a thin veil falling between the questioner and me. That veil becomes more akin to a fortified security fence with barbed wire and snipers in a place where religion is ... well, the religion.

I can steer clear of Tehran, Manila and Salt Lake City pretty easily, but mention that you aren't a Consumer or a Voter or a Citizen just about anywhere in the industrialized world, and the snipers will be quietly releasing the safety catches. And so, perhaps with the opening salvo of this book, and certainly in the next few sections, most people reading this will not exactly be sympathetic to what I have to say.

> The gunman's call for draconian measures to be implemented to lower global population and destroy civilization echoes the eco-fascist propaganda of people like author and environmentalist Keith Farnish, who in a recent book called for acts of sabotage and environmental terrorism in blowing up dams and demolishing cities in order to return the planet to the agrarian age.
>
> "The only way to prevent global ecological collapse and thus ensure the survival of humanity is to rid the world of Industrial Civilization," writes Farnish in the book, adding that "people will die in huge numbers when civilization collapses". Farnish's call for violence, "razing cities to the ground, blowing up dams" provides a deadly blueprint for nutcases like Lee to follow.
>
> Farnish explains his desire to see rampant population reduction in the name of saving the planet, with rhetoric chillingly similar to that contained in Lee's online screed.[3]

Quite a dramatic interpretation of what I actually wrote, but the message here is clear: "Don't mess with our way of life." Now that's odd because the writer, Paul Joseph Watson, would be among the first to complain about anything that suppresses human liberty — like corporations telling people what to eat and how to dress, perhaps — but as a 28-year-old, living in a large English city, brought up in an era when greed was most definitely good, Watson expresses a view that mirrors the feelings of virtually every politician, every corporate executive and close to every ordinary human being who has felt the irresistible pull of consumerism in the formative years. People don't like to hear that almost everything they have ever believed in is wrong, and they will do everything in their power to retain those beliefs.

Which makes me a heretic, at best.

But I suspect you have got this far because part of you thinks there is more to making the world a good place to live in than buying the right brand of shoes. You might think politicians don't have our best interests at heart when they say that businesses need the freedom to grow, or that Bill Gates's reason for promoting genetically modified food is perhaps not because he can't stand to see people go hungry or that Al Gore is not entirely devoted to the idea of reducing greenhouse gases to the kind of levels that would actually stabilize the climate.

It doesn't take much of an effort to be a cynic; but to *really* question everything you may have previously held as true is, for most civilized people, a step too far. It challenges your loyalties. It denies your personal experiences. It makes a mockery of who you think you are.

It undermines you.

I apologize for the inconvenience, but all I want to show you is the truth — and that is most definitely the last time Al Gore will be playing a part in this story.

Undermining in Context

Some time ago I wrote a book called *Time's Up*!, which still underpins everything I have subsequently written, including this book. The three primary theses in *Time's Up*! can be summarized as follows (if you need a more detailed explanation then please refer to the book or its online equivalent):[4]

1) Because the ultimate purpose of all life forms, including human beings, is to continue their genetic line, and all we can ever know or care about is from the point of view of a human being, What Matters Is What Matters to Us.
2) To appreciate the level of threat that global environmental changes are posing to the continuation of humanity, and that it is the acts of a certain type of human being — Civilized Humans — that have brought about that threat, we have to Connect with ourselves, the people we depend upon, and the natural ecosystems that support our existence.
3) Myriad forces exist to protect Industrial Civilization — the ultimate killing machine — from human beings becoming Connected. These forces, which I have named the Tools of Disconnection, have to be undermined in order to allow us to Connect and thus make possible the continuation of humanity.

An enormous amount of cultural suspension is required to take all of that at face value. However, we have to start somewhere: in *Time's Up*! the assumption was that the reader accepted human emissions of greenhouse gases being the cause of accelerated climate change, alongside the many other environmental impacts related to civilized human activity. That was a big enough task; this is a veritable leap of faith for which I can make no apologies. We know where we are and we have to start accepting a few home truths.

❧

I want to spend a few moments discussing how undermining fits into the bigger picture of retaining a properly functioning global ecosystem, and thus helping to ensure the human species endures for the foreseeable future. The first thing to say is that *the continuation of the human race is incompatible with Industrial Civilization remaining on the Earth.* For sure there may be the odd civilization popping up here and there, but even the Roman Empire was little threat to the global ecosystem — whereas Industrial Civilization is taking the ecosystem down, and taking humanity with it.

Second, it's important to understand that civilization itself is not going to be hanging around for a great deal longer, regardless of how much we go about freeing people's minds so they might assist with the dismantling process. Peak oil isn't just around the corner; it is back there in the taillights, and we're driving over the cliff. As it becomes more difficult to maintain supplies of cheap and plentiful fossil energy, the engine of industry will start to sputter; before long entire chains of infrastructure will conk out. Before that even, the industrial food system will become something of an anachronism — it will no longer be possible to produce food on an epic industrial scale; and the food that is produced will price most people out of the market. Cities that rely on the importation of energy and food will feel like besieged monoliths of a burned-out age. The suburbs will have to become immobile food producers or its inhabitants will starve. The systems of global finance, mass communications, travel and even political power will operate along narrower and narrower pathways until the traffic, and the reach of that power, becomes little more than a symbolic activity.

All of that will happen, and we will go down with it, because we will still be devoted to the industrial system we so depend upon for everything we currently hold dear.

We will not let this culture go, and we will die to defend it — literally.

Alternatively, we could hollow out and allow the empty shell of Industrial Civilization to collapse under its own weight. The illustration below gives one example of how this process could work, albeit in a simplified way.

The three large boxes are only representations of different aspects of creating a viable future. As Derrick Jensen has said on countless occasions with reference to the work of activists, carers, artists, thinkers, writers, homemakers, community builders and everyone else in the milieu of a functioning society, "We need it all." But for the purposes of building some kind of guiding model for undermining, the three boxes will do.

Enabling Change

This is where things have to start. We cannot assume there is any momentum for real change, and I think that is a fair assumption based on the complete lack of genuine progress toward a deindustrialized, non-destructive future made since the beginning of the modern environmental movement. So, to highlight the obvious major task, *undermining* is the key in enabling the change to take place, and that is predominantly what this book is about. Fitting around and complementing the undermining process are three things that have to happen, regardless of any undermining that is taking place.

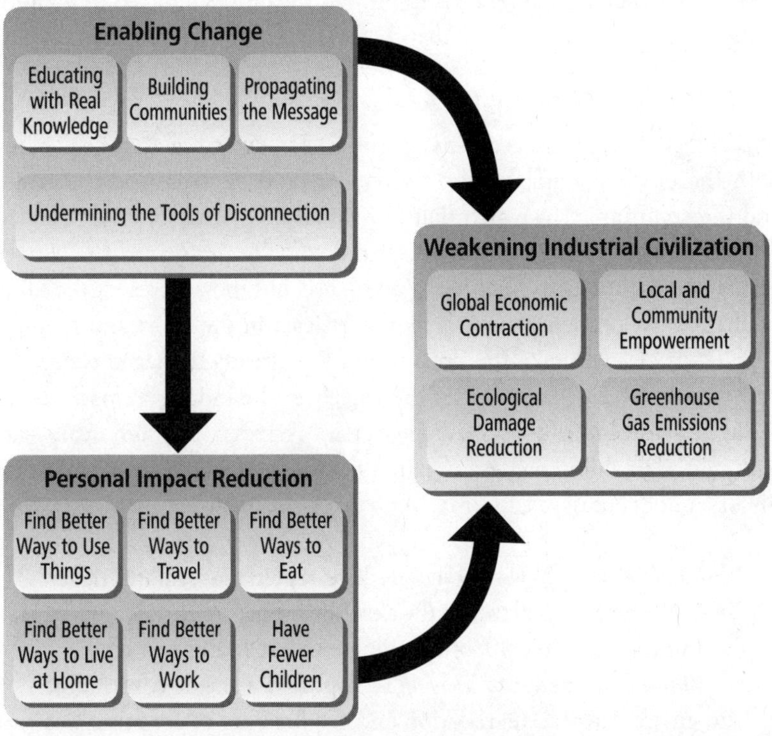

Educating with Real Knowledge is about taking charge of how knowledge is used in society and what knowledge is considered relevant moving forward. I outlined some of these key aspects, or skills, in the final chapter of *Time's Up*! The emphasis on the practical application of this knowledge cannot be made strongly enough. Authors such as Ran Prieur and Sharon Astyk take this to levels I will not attempt to duplicate here.

Building Communities is both a practical and a psychological process. There are elements of community building in many of the chapters later in this book, as strengthening community is undoubtedly one of the key ways the industrial system can be undermined, as well as reducing the physical damage to the natural environment. I strongly recommend the works of Alastair McIntosh as primers in this area.

Propagating the Message is the effective communication of the information necessary to start off and maintain momentum in effecting change. Whatever medium is used — but, as we will see, some media are less subject to interference than others — we have to remain "on message," as hackneyed and overused a phrase this may be. Change the message too much and the impact of any work carried out so far could be fatally wounded, even if these changes may seem to be well-meaning and accommodating at the time.

Personal Impact Reduction

This aspect of the model contains six things that, taken together, can change both the physical impact of an individual (and by extension the family and the community in which that individual lives) and the psychological makeup of everyone who makes a serious effort to perform such changes. The six items are not exhaustive in any sense, but they represent the kinds of changes we will all have to make — at least in the short and medium term — in order to take the pressure off the already damaged ecosystem and, as we will see later, clog up the wheels of the industrial machine. As the large arrow indicates, such change cannot happen on a significant scale without the Enabling process. Again, I have written about this at length in my first book, but here I summarize in just six sentences:[5]

> *Find better ways to Use Things:* Reduce, repair, reuse, in that order, with the emphasis being on the absolute reduction of the number, volume and complexity of the things you are looking to acquire.
>
> *Find better ways to Travel:* Transport is a major contributor to environmental degradation and the breakup of communities

so, following up on the three Rs, reduce the distance and the frequency of all journeys, along with the energy intensity of the methods used to travel.

Find better ways to Eat: Employ a combination of reducing the trophic level of what you eat (stay low on the food chain), reducing dependence on the industrial agricultural and food processing system, and using food production methods close to those in nature.

Find better ways to Live at Home: Your home is also a major cause of environmental degradation both directly (energy and land use) and indirectly (construction materials), so both of these areas need to be tackled, but without simply transferring the impact from direct to indirect (e.g., using a solar panel to produce the same amount of electricity as always).

Find better ways to Work: This will be addressed at length later on, but as a starter, consider that working in the industrial machine makes you a party to both disconnection and to perpetuation of the power of the system.

Have Fewer Children: Or, more specifically, have fewer high-consumption children; the impact of population is a combination of absolute numbers and the way those children, and subsequently adults, live. This may not be as critical a factor in the longer term.

Aside from the direct effects of carrying through these changes, there is also the small matter of preparing for what is to come later; as Carolyn Baker writes in *Sacred Demise,* "In my opinion, collapse will become psychologically intolerable for those who have no inkling of it, who are emotionally tethered to possessions, status, careers, and lifestyles that provide identity and security."

By refusing to follow the strictures of the industrial world in terms of consumption, travel, lifestyle, career, etc., you are already on your way to coping better with whatever is likely to happen in the future.

Weakening Industrial Civilization

Both of the previous areas feed into the weakening of the industrial system, and thus the creation of a longer-term positive outcome for humanity and the wider global environment. The four items in this area are fairly loose, but their positions in the box (upper and lower halves) reflect the more likely domino effects of, respectively, Enabling Change and Personal Impact Reduction. There is a *feedback loop* in effect here, although for simplicity I have not included it on the diagram. With Industrial Civilization being weakened, the impact of Enabling Change becomes more pronounced, and thus the amount of Personal Impact Reduction can be increased, both leading to a further increasingly rapid weakening of Industrial Civilization. Anyone who doubts the efficacy of undermining as a method of creating radical change should consider this carefully.

This is a powerful feedback effect; one that has the potential to kick in very rapidly indeed.

At this point you might begin to feel a little wary of taking part in the undermining process: after all, how comfortable do you feel committing to something that spells the end of the way of life you have not only become accustomed to, but dependent upon? So here's the conundrum: you can have a few decades of pretending everything is going to be fine, trying to ignore the destruction being wrought on the planet and the people that fuel the industrial system, and living in a way that feels comfortable to you; or you can accept that things are going to change anyway, but the sooner the system is dismantled, the better the chances of a long-term future for the human race. Just to add to this, the rate and impact of change is controllable to a certain extent because as the industrial system becomes weaker, and the aforementioned peak oil (and peaks in other energy sources such as natural gas, coal, uranium and — tragically — large rivers) kicks in, globalization will become a thing of the past. Industrial Civilization won't so much contract as break into discrete parts, some more self-sufficient than others, but all weakened to such an extent that reassembly cannot possibly take place. Thus, your efforts in undermining the system will resolve down to the part of the system you exist within — or, if you are smart, are just keeping a watchful eye on and a helping hand in, while edging further and further away from it.

I can't find a better person to describe this situation than Tim Bennett, writer and director of what I consider to be the most important movie ever made:

> We can wait for the train to crash on its own and hope that it doesn't kill us, and everything else. But with the children grown, perhaps we can come together and decide to dismantle, joyfully and with conscious intent, the rusty and dangerous old swing-set of a culture that no longer serves us.

This may seem an impossible task. But if the alternative is extinction, then we have nothing to lose.

We humans once knew how to live on this planet. A few still do. And that's the good news. It can be done. We can do way, way better than Empire.

I do not know if I will survive the crash of industrial civilization or the impacts of the climate change that that civilization has unleashed. I do know this: I have a choice about how I meet it. I have a choice. We have a choice.

I can meet it with a burger in my hand, a French fry in my mouth, and a cold drink spilling onto my jeans. Or I can meet it with consciousness, integrity, and the sense of purpose that is my birthright. I can meet it on the far side of initiation, a mature and related member of the community of life, standing tall, doing my best to protect and serve this Earth that I love.

This is the course I've chosen.[6]

Connection

A state of Connection is necessary to survive planet Earth. This state is not some discrete entity that can be sketched out on a mind map or project plan — though I can well imagine some people in the Sierra Club taking on "Project Connection" with gusto and proceeding to brainstorm all the great ways we can be connected to nature. It defies such crude pigeonholing, occupying instead the part of our natural selves the civilized world refuses to acknowledge: the continuum. I have described this continuum in various ways in the past, but a simple phrase that has found its niche in popular song for at least the past four decades keeps coming back to me: "It all comes round again."

Essentially, what you do will eventually come back to you. If what you do is inherently destructive, then however much you try and ignore it, cover it up, distract from it or even pretend it is a good thing, that destruction will come back at, if not you personally, someone, somewhere down the line. A Connected state allows us to see — no, that is too simple — it allows us to *know* that continuum. It may have taken climate scientists many decades to establish the true link between emissions and climate change, but it doesn't take a host of scientists to tell you that introducing a technological infrastructure to a desert, extracting brown tarry emulsion from deep below that desert, transporting it to a place several time zones away, exposing it to high temperatures in vast cylinders and extracting the individual components of that formerly homogenous mass in order for them to be used in products as diverse as aircraft, trucks and ships, plastics and fabrics, inks and road surfaces — all of this is bound to have a destructive impact in the mind of the connected individual.

You don't need to analyze it; it's obvious.[7]

It is no coincidence that Connection itself is a continuum, spanning the arc across which cling the individual, the community or clan, the wider tribal entity (but, significantly, not a single civilization), the human diaspora, the entire conscious web that links all sentient organisms together and again the individual that seems to hold this collective awareness somewhere inside.

Other connections exist that may seem trivial in comparison but are no less important in the scope of humanity's great adventure. While the corporate world is hell-bent on homogenizing every aspect of human culture and simultaneously molding the symbols of humanity into nothing but swooshes, arches, four-note jingles and spotlit edifices; that nagging part of our mind keeps asking, Who am I? For a victim of Industrial Civilization, such a question is easily answered if you wear Nike, eat at McDonalds, use Intel processors and watch Fox News. You are what you wear, eat, use and watch: how elegantly the phalanx of consumer symbols slots into the modern psyche. Then again, can such a significant and deeply personal question really be answered by a machine?

Writing on the cusp of the nineteenth century in the Scottish border county of Selkirkshire, Sir Walter Scott seems to suggest we are nothing without a connection to place:

> Breathes there the man, with soul so dead,
> Who never to himself hath said,
> This is my own, my native land![8]

We need a homeland, a native land, a place that is special to us. Whether its meaning lies in the people we share it with, the memories it holds for us or the way it feeds, waters and protects us, there is — somewhere — a place we are connected to. A connection we call "Home." No artifacts of the consumer lifestyle are an adequate substitute for such a vital, personal connection.

Whether it is ecological, cultural, spiritual or something indefinable that tugs at the soul, at whatever scale of humanity we consider, Connection is always present; and when something is so ubiquitous,[9] but without any apparent disruptive force creating these conditions, then it must be necessary for our continued existence.

Collapse and Connection

BY CAROLYN BAKER

Inherent in the paradigm of Industrial Civilization is the notion of separation. Humans, it is believed, are separate from the Earth community, from each other, and from their own bodies. Because they are "separate," they are by definition in competition for resources and anything that brings pleasure or well being. From the separation assumption issues a distorted notion of Darwin's "survival of the fittest" in the form of social Darwinism. Few of us understand how firmly the separation assumption has become embedded in our psyches.

However, in a chaotic world of endings, unravelling, catastrophe, or protracted demise, relationship will be a pivotal issue. For this reason, the survivalist mentality which purports to "go it alone" with an "every man for himself" attitude, not only will not serve those who embrace it, but will profoundly put their physical survival at risk. For our well being, we will absolutely require connection with other human beings in times of chaos and crisis. Therefore, cultivating a broader perspective of relationship in advance of the coming chaos may be exceedingly useful in learning how to navigate relationship challenges in the future — challenges on which our survival may depend.

Not only will we be compelled to relate differently to humans, but to all beings in the non-human world as well. Only as we begin to read the survival manuals that trees, stars, insects and birds have written for us will our species be spared. The very "pests" that we resent as unhygienic or annoying may, in fact, save our lives. One year ago, the honey bees used to circle around me on warm days when I ate my lunch outside under the trees, sitting on the grass. Today, I sit under the same trees on the same grass, but the honey bees are gone. No one seems to be able to tell us why. Maybe it's time to ask the bees to tell us why.

If we recall our hunter-gatherer ancestors, we realize that they held a deeply intimate relationship with nature; in fact, their lives depended on that relationship. Our indigenous ancestors have revealed unequivocally that they could not survive without a deeply personal connection with nature. The Lakota gave us the beautiful expression Mitakuye Oyasin or "all my relations" — meaning that we are all related to every member of the non-human as well as human world. Native peoples often speak of "standing people" (trees), "fish people", or "stone people"; as if trees, fish and rocks are persons to be communed with, not objects to be possessed.

Today, we live in civilized societies that dominate nature, and we have been taught that we need not bother communing with it. But, no matter how estranged we may feel from nature, something in our ancient memory recalls our intimacy with it. Therefore everything we need to restore our connection with nature is already available to us.[10]

Disconnection

So, if Connection is necessary to our existence, how then can we bring ourselves to sacrifice a pristine forest for a shopping mall?

Recently, while sailing north on the Patuxent River — her banks dark with vegetation where just a few months ago there were only naked boughs — I saw a tall plume of black smoke rising over the forest to the east against an otherwise clear blue sky. As soon as I could gain moorings and secure my boat, I drove to find the source of this disturbing sight.

In barely five miles, I came upon a scene of mechanized destruction which drew an involuntary cry of disappointment from me. A parcel of once-rolling forest was being destroyed.

The fires I witnessed from the Patuxent were still pluming skyward later in the day, as heavy grading equipment began to level the topography, taking away nature's landscape, sculpted over the last hundreds of thousands of years to turn it into an anchor supermarket with eight accessory stores totaling 100,000 square feet — plus acres of impervious tarmac paving.[11]

Civilization encourages us to shut the door, shut the windows, shut the blinds, shut our minds from the reality of the world. The connected world is still going on out there, but we would rather let the caustic rain of civilization wash it away and supplant it with "connections" that have been manufactured to keep us in our place. In our disconnected lives we are made to feel safe, even though we are on the edge of catastrophe; we are made to enjoy what we do, even though we have forgotten what joy feels like; we are made to experience self-worth, even though we have become worthless; we are made to feel in control, even though we have no control at all. The system has us where it wants us. And now it can use all of us like the metaphorical batteries and cogs that signify our labor and our spending, and our naive compliance in which we live our synthetic lives, from the plastic toys we grasp as babies to the flickering, energy-sapping screens that fix our attention on the advertisers' world, from the blacktop roads we populate in countless streams of metal caskets with wheels on the way to and from our designated places of valued employment, to the offices and factories and supermarkets and call centers where we spend a third of our lives operating in order to keep the machine spinning, in order that we can be given currency that we, in our docility, reinsert into the system so it can keep growing, and taking, and killing everything it is able to reach.

And when we feel weary, we take a packaged, predetermined vacation. And when we feel hungry, we eat a packaged, predetermined meal. And when we feel bored, we go to a packaged, predetermined slice of entertainment. And when we are of no more use to the system, we are retired — and only then do we, in the moments of reflection we never had time for during our urgent "productive" years, think about what we could have been had the system not taken us at such an early age. We have become, in effect, an entirely new subspecies — for although our genetic DNA is unchanged from pre-industrial times, our *cultural* DNA is far removed from that of any other group, tribe or society that ever walked the Earth prior to the emergence of this rapacious version of a human being. *Homo sapiens sapiens* is a connected species. *Homo sapiens civilis* has had the connections ripped away from it.

With such a massive upheaval in the way humanity behaves and, consequently, the way we (refuse to) interact with the rest of life, that cultural DNA takes on a significance far beyond, say, finding a new way to extract food from forest plant matter or being fleet of foot across the grasslands of Africa. Civilization's cultural imbalance with the rest of life has created — at least in our heads — something entirely separate from the pantheon of living things. Perhaps the term *subspecies* was far too modest; after all we were proud enough to add a second *sapiens* to our title, simply because we wanted to feel good. Wouldn't it be much simpler just to hug a tree?

Fuck the trees.

How many channels have *they* got? How many gigabytes can *they* store? How much money can you make from them?

That's more like it. You see, in the civilized mindset it was easy to value the tree: all we had to do was think about money, and everything else slotted neatly into place. How much money can civilization make from a tree? It depends how many it cuts down — and it's not just the money from the wood, for that is a pittance compared to the money civilization could make from an absence of trees. The teeth of the chain cut into the arboreal flesh one last time, leaving a glorious space for — what do you want? A new parking lot, an out-of-town retail park, a blockade of oil palms, a herd of grazing cattle, thousands of acres of soybeans, an open pit coal mine, a toxic sludge lake; a city or two ...

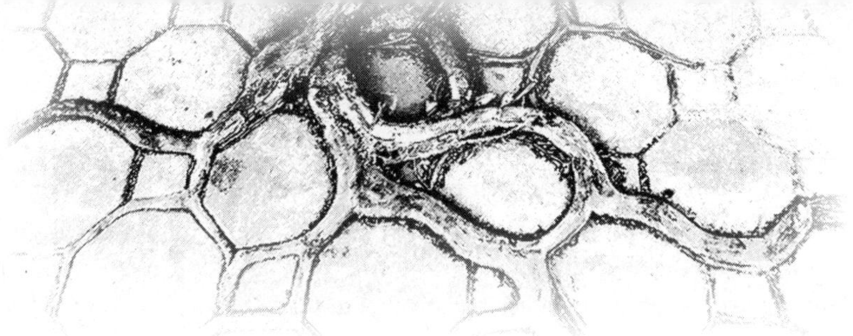

CHAPTER TWO

Undermining the Tools of Disconnection

THE TOOLS OF DISCONNECTION have been around for as long as civilizations have existed. Most likely they have their origins in the most basic functions of civilized society, such as enforcing a hierarchy of authority, ensuring the availability of a large and reliable workforce and maintaining a constant flow of resources into, and waste out of, the system. The effectiveness of these Tools in controlling every aspect of human behavior is not, as would be imagined, in their direct application, but through the remarkable side effect of disconnecting people from anything but the activities of the civilized world.

Thus, what are otherwise long-used Tools of Control are also Tools of Disconnection. The control creates the disconnection, and the disconnection reduces our ability to prevent the industrial machine from controlling us still further. Climate feedback loops, such as the darkening of Arctic seas increasing the absorption of solar radiation, are critical for understanding the environmental catastrophe ahead of us. The feedback loop of disconnection is even more critical, because *it explains why we have done nothing at all to stop this catastrophe.*

Humans are remarkable animals. What probably sets us aside from the vast majority of other creatures on Earth, as far as we know, is self-determination — our ability to ignore instinct and decide for ourselves how we behave. Whether as cause or effect, the facility that accompanies this attribute is our knack for inhibiting our "fascination" with things that are key to our immediate survival, such as the presence of running water or the movement of food prey. During those periods that we direct our attention to non-instinctive elements of the world we are able to decide our fate in a more deterministic manner: in effect, we are able to plan ahead. In a non-civilized society this has tremendous advantages for longer-term survival, such as creating secure settlements and storing food. Unfortunately, as Raymond de Young argues, our ability to pull ourselves out of instinctive behavior requires considerable mental energy. As we become fatigued we are vulnerable to a wide range of external stimuli that in the civilized world are least related to survival. Our apparent strength is thus converted into a culturally generated weakness by those who are able to exploit that defining human characteristic:

> Our ability to be fascinated can be used against us. In the wrong hands, our tendency to be involuntarily fascinated can be abused as a tool used to distract or deflect us from our own better intentions.[12]

Anyone who accepts the label of "citizen" is, to some extent, culpable for keeping us disconnected from the real world, be it through a role in marketing or advertising, the imposition of "democracy" and the rule of law, the promulgation of fear, the application of physical abuse or the offering of false hope. You may recognize your role, or at least the role of someone you know, in even this short list; the wider Tools encapsulate virtually every process and artifact that exists in civilization.

In the previous chapter I outlined a brief thesis, culminating in the statement that the Tools of Disconnection have to be undermined. The idea of undermining something that is invisible to most people is an odd one, but in the context of Industrial Civilization, this statement really makes a lot of sense because, although the Tools of Disconnection do not comprise a simple set of physical implements, the way they are imposed upon civilized people is through an enormous range of unquestionably physical things. As I guide you through these Tools it will become clear that the way the industrial system creates a disconnection between us and the real world is not through metaphorical tools, but *real things* the system has at its disposal to ensure the machine keeps turning and that we don't stop it. Understanding this is the first step toward developing a strategy that will not only be effective, but also wholly practical.

The idea of a set of Tools being used both on us and on others with our active participation is disturbing enough of itself. What is even more unsettling is that, despite our participation in their use, we have almost no knowledge of their true nature. The system carefully protects them from people who have the wherewithal to undermine them. It is therefore imperative that this Veil of Ignorance is addressed, for its existence may well explain why civilized humanity has singularly failed to act decisively in the face of the incomparable horrors right on our doorstep.

The Road to Hell, and How We Got There

BY DAVE POLLARD

Keith Farnish tells us we need to get angry before we will be moved to act to undermine the Industrial Civilization that is killing our planet.[13] Then, he says, we need to focus our attention on the "Tools of Disconnection" — the means by which the perpetrators of our disconnection from our intuition, our positive emotions, our senses, each other, and all life on Earth keep us disorganized, confused, fearful and dependent. Our undermining actions, he asserts, should be aimed at accelerating the inevitable demise of Industrial Civilization with minimal suffering, balancing the risks to ensure we don't get caught, and acting strategically to get maximum impact from our actions. The sooner we precipitate civilization's fall, he says, the sooner its damage can be minimized, the sooner nature can begin to restore balance to our world, and the sooner the survivors of collapse can begin creating a better, sustainable way to live.

So who are these "perpetrators"? They are the private and public corporations that depend on endless accelerating use of resources, production, consumption and waste, and which, as the book *The Corporation* explains, they pursue with pathological and amoral single-mindedness.

They are the politicians, judges, lawyers, police and military forces that, working hand in hand with wealthy corporations, create and enforce laws and wage wars in their own self-interest, not ours. They are the media, the shills, the advertisers and PR firms, the education system and the bought economists and junk scientists who perpetrate the propaganda that everything is fine and there is no other, better way to live than Industrial Civilization.

And they are the religions, the therapists, and the techno-salvationists ("human ingenuity and invention will solve all our problems") who are complicit in reinforcing the propaganda by telling us that it is our fault as individuals when things are bad, and that with necessary struggle, Industrial Civilization will prevail and make things better for all of us despite our personal weaknesses and sins.

The combined economic, political, media and psychological power and hegemony of these perpetrators constitute the self-reinforcing and completely uncritical and totalitarian system that Mussolini dreamed of — it was labeled Fascism but he called it Corporatism. Its task is to completely subjugate and control the populace, to brainwash it so completely that there is no opposition, no dissent, just a perpetual machine of unthinking monolithic human production and consumption.

Through its political messages, its advertising, its scare tactics, its lies, its withholding of information, its theft and violence, its indoctrination, its creation of false choices and false rewards, it keeps us in its thrall, disconnected. Each of us an obedient part of the system.

But what is this "system"? Can it really control us that effectively in this world where often-conflicting information and ideas are ubiquitous and free? And why would so many people — not just psychopaths like Mussolini — willingly become perpetrators of such a system?

The progressive-liberal worldview holds that we are all, at heart, innocent and good. Surely, then, the perpetrators of this terrible, unsustainable, teetering system had the best of intentions? They must have meant well, mustn't they?

This worldview also holds that getting angry isn't the answer, that we need to appeal to people rationally, with the facts. The truth, we believe, cannot long be suppressed, and when people learn it, they will, if this system is so bad and brutal, instinctively work to dismantle it and replace it with one in the common good, a truly democratic system.

Harvard psychologist Daniel Gilbert, author of *Stumbling on Happiness*, provides some clues as to why this doesn't happen. Our large brains, he argues, have made us too smart for our own good. Our brains can now construct their own reality, completely disconnected from "real" reality, and live happily in that illusory place, in effect mistaking it for "real" reality. And, as Eckhart Tolle has explained, an unintended consequence of the evolution of our complex brains is that we now have an ego capable of inventing and believing stories that provoke negative emotional responses, which in turn produce other stories in our heads. This vicious cycle of negative intellectual and emotional activity in our brains, disconnected from what is really happening here and now, has made us all mentally ill.

So two paradoxical consequences of our large brains are that (i) we can be fooled and emotionally manipulated by misinformation in a way no other creature can, and (ii) even if we are one of the perpetrators of this misinformation, we can fool ourselves into believing it, especially if that belief is reinforced by others who credulously accept the same beliefs.

Despite all of this, despite the fact that we are all in a sense perpetrators, all so disconnected and confounded by our egos and the imaginary realities our brains have invented that we don't "really" know what is real or what we are doing, Keith is correct about what must be done: we must act to dismantle industrial civilization. But how can we do that when we are very hobbled, very handicapped, very caught up in this vicious system of our own making?

First, we have to inform ourselves about what is really happening (by reading and studying thoroughly and by thinking critically and challenging everything) and about what our "real" options are (by studying history and reading both fiction and radical nonfiction). Second, we have to get angry enough at the system that is killing us all (it doesn't much matter who the perpetrators are, or if we are ourselves perpetrators or complicit) to shake ourselves out of our passivity and unawareness and act. Third, we need to influence and educate others. Fourth, we need to become models, finding radically alternative ways to live and modeling those behaviors. And fifth, we need to reskill ourselves to facilitate both the work we must do to dismantle industrial civilization and the capacity to live good lives during and after civilization's collapse.

This is a tall order. The first step toward well-being is to appreciate the challenge we face, and the first step to doing that is to understand the Tools of Disconnection and how they keep us cowed and dependent.

The Tools of Disconnection

There are 15 items in the following list. The significance of each one depends on how much you consider each Tool impinges on your life, which, to a certain extent, depends on where you live and what kind of life you lead. What is almost certain, though, is that these Tools are far more significant than you may at first realize; especially when you get to the final one.

Each Tool is split into four key parts: a brief description of how the Tool manifests itself and operates, a few examples of how you can recognize it in operation, how the Tool directly affects human behavior and the wider world, and which institutions and collective bodies are most commonly involved in the application of the Tool. This breakdown should help you start to formulate ways in which they can be undermined, because, as much as I can start things moving, most of the ideas are going to come from other people — people like you.

1) Reward Us for being Good Consumers

Description

It is fairly easy to make civilized people happy, or at least give people the sense they are happy; they just have to be primed in the right way. Key

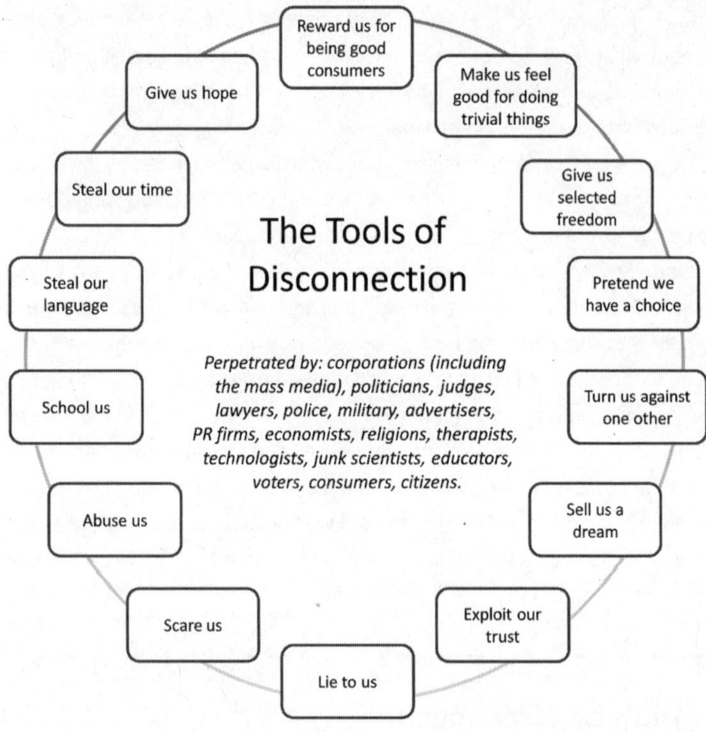

to creating this malleable state of mind is making people believe from a very early age that "happiness" is something more superficial than having a deep and genuine state of contentment. The marketing of consumer goods and services ("experiences") taps into the desire for happiness with positive images that reflect enjoyment of whatever is being marketed. This is compounded by continual messages that consumption in general is a "good thing" and the consumption of anything new and fashionable is likely to lead to improvement in our quality of life, and is easily transferred to the next generation via parents and peers who have already been primed from birth.

Identification

At a personal level, this can be recognized through being aware of anything that makes you feel better yet is clearly a product of the consumer culture. So, for instance, if you are watching or listening to an advertisement and begin to feel happy, regardless of the source of the advertisement, then that Tool is in operation. The same can be observed of other people who are showing signs of happiness where no source beyond that which has been manufactured is evident. The popularity of shopping malls, cinemas and package holidays are further evidence that the genuine need for happiness has been subsumed into industrial-scale consumption.

Consequences

The two main consequences of consumption happiness are, first, we become less inclined to seek deeper, more satisfying forms of happiness from the real world — such as the enjoyment of dipping our toes into cool water on a hot day — instead seeking out disconnected sources of "happiness" through material consumption. The second, less direct, consequence is that increased consumption through our desire to be happy leads to environmental and social degradation, particularly where the things we consume are manufactured, powered from and disposed of.

Perpetrators

A plethora of parties directly involved in commerce, including consumer journalists, advertising executives, marketing professionals, salespeople, travel agents and product developers are all ensuring we feel good about our consumer habits.

2) Make Us Feel Good for Doing Trivial Things

Description

To distract from the important it is necessary to emphasize the trivial. Nowhere is this more so than in the way "environmentalism" is imposed upon civilized people. For example, if I approach a local authority with a desire to live in a more sustainable manner, the chances of being told to go off-grid (self-sufficient in energy and other services), grow and forage my own food and stop buying consumer goods are zero. On the other hand, I will happily be exhorted to recycle and change my light bulbs. If I ask a motor company, I will not be told to stop driving, I will be advised to pump up my tires or buy a more economical (new) car. A corporate retailer would never recommend buying local produce and scrapping processed food but will have an ample supply of branded "bags for life" because we all know carrier bags are the greatest threat to life on Earth! Follow the advice of the system and you will never have to worry about the big things, for the small things are what we are told really matter.

Identification

The most obvious clue to this Tool's usage is the source of information: in conversation even an oil executive will admit we are screwed if we keep using oil; but on a much less personal level, every single instrument of Industrial Civilization has its own set of pro-forma "environmental" messages that are designed to ensure that our behavior remains just the same as always. No advice that emanates from the mouthpiece of a government, a corporation, mass-market media or even a mainstream environmental NGO (non-governmental organization)[14] is going to adversely affect the industrial system. You can also use your instincts: if it feels too easy or trivial or "against nature," then you are probably on the right track.

Consequences

Sweating the small stuff is akin to putting a Band-Aid on an amputation stump. Not only is it too little, it is almost certainly too late, because it is in the interest of vested corporate interests to keep us totally ignorant until they really have no choice but to provide some relevant information which, as shown, is of no substance anyway. By exploiting our civilized aversion to conscious effort and major change, we are made impotent — and content with it. Meanwhile, Industrial Civilization continues to destroy the global ecosystem.

Perpetrators

Almost everyone is party to this by virtue of passing on the advice given by authority — it feels good too; however, we can single out politicians at all levels, corporate public relations, mainstream environmental journalists and NGOs as some of the worst offenders.

3) Give Us Selected Freedom

Description

Freedom is relative: a tiger brought up in a cage will see the cage as its domain and feel as comfortable as any half-ton feline can in that situation; but a tiger captured and forced to live in a cage will be deeply troubled, driven insane by the limitations of the enclosure. Thus, brought up in a "democracy" where freedom equates to voting for one or other variety of entirely similar political parties, we express that "freedom" by voting — abstention is seen as an act of rebellion and a failure to use the "freedom" to vote. Similarly, we are free to protest, as long as that march or rally falls between the lines set by the police and the rules they enforce.[15] The level of freedom varies depending on where that protest is executed — and in some parts of the world being executed may well be the punishment for such illegality. But as a writer, a former protestor and a former voter, my freedoms stretch only to the point where the system perceives a threat. I may have more leeway in how I can express myself than the equivalent person in, say, China, but within the confines of the society's rules I am no nearer to creating change.

Identification

The truest test of freedom is to try to break the rules. Assuming one abides by Common Law (a simple protection of individual and collective liberty) and Natural Law (within which the natural world operates) the limits of "freedom" will quickly become apparent the moment your actions impede the ability of the industrial system to control people and upend the natural ecological balance. Brought up in the same version of civilization for life, we often find it difficult to recognize where the boundaries lie, especially when we are constantly told that people from Nation X have to be "freed from tyranny" or that rules exist to "protect us from those who would remove our freedoms." Those phrases alone should start alarm bells ringing.

Consequences

If we already feel free, then we have no desire to extend our freedoms; we remain within the legal confines of the system we occupy, and thus do not threaten the system. Disconnected from any genuine opportunity to choose the outcome of our lives, we are never likely to challenge that which, in reality, keeps us chained to the Culture of Maximum Harm.

Perpetrators

Anyone involved in the establishment or enforcement of legislation is responsible for setting the boundaries of freedom. Most civil rights groups operate within these boundaries, and exacerbate the problem by calling for incremental freedoms rather than absolute ones.

4) Pretend We Have a Choice

Description

The buzzword of politicians who subscribe to the philosophy of free-market capitalism (and very few don't) is "choice"; but that choice lies within a very narrow band of options. Thus, we have a "choice" of television channels, a "choice" of detergents, a "choice" of cars and a "choice" of oil companies from which to buy our fuel. Notice that the moment any radical (or rather, less narrow) choice is offered — such as private health care becoming optional — then the system closes ranks, ensuring that such choice is curtailed to the degree the system will tolerate. Should we, for instance, choose to educate our children in a way the system doesn't approve of, then the definition of choice becomes rapidly evident — as we will see later in this chapter.

Identification

Most people or institutions offering real choice (i.e., between things that are self-evidently different) do not use the word "choice"; fewer still harp on the amount of choice being offered. Those who pretend what they are offering *is* real choice are the ones who would gain most from our choice being strictly limited. If this sounds confusing, it is: you are meant to be confused; otherwise you might recognize that what you are being offered isn't a choice at all.

Consequences

As with faux freedom, the continual presentation of faux choice as genuine choice conditions humans to readily accept this pretence. Such conditioning breaks down our ability to resist, leaving a compliant populace that readily becomes excited by a new games console but fails to recognize a life beyond just playing games. This is a very powerful but subtle tool.

Perpetrators

Ably assisted by the usual crew of marketers and salespeople, the mindset of accepting pseudo choice derives from elite members of civilized society who want to ensure compliance with normal civilized behavior — specifically, the consumption of material goods. This is channeled through politicians of all types via the mass media ("You've never had it so good!") and corporate executives via the advertising machine ("The greenest SUV yet!")

5) Turn Us Against One Another

Description

How do you get two good friends to argue? In a disconnected world it's not that difficult: bring up which football team is better, or ask who is causing the climate to change. If you want a real scrap, then try abortion rights or religion. Bestriding all of these in the divisiveness stakes is politics, which encompasses all the above — except perhaps football. It is in the best interests of the system to divide us along lines that in sober discourse would seem absurd. Take the so-called difference between the "left" and the "right" political parties of any industrialized nation. There is barely any difference between the various political parties when it comes down to brass tacks — they all support large-scale commerce, top-down enforcement of power and the continuation of the destructive industrial system. But here's the trick: in order to ensure we don't reconnect with the real world — that which lies outside socio-political trivia — we are divided into artificial "parties," "sects," "factions" and "fan-bases" that appear to give us individuality but actually just keep us fascinated in our day-to-day squabbles.

Identification

Wherever you see division of ideas that on closer inspection appears to be just different shades of the same paradigm, then you have observed disconnection through division. The idea of Divide and Rule is ancient in civilized terms, but it is only fairly recently, in the age of information overload, that politicians have been able to squeeze differences out of common ground. A recent "consultation" on airport expansion in the UK brilliantly exploited our civilized NIMBY attitude by focusing on which place would be best for new runways, rather than whether expansion itself was a good thing. Unless you do look at the big picture, it is hard to see you are being turned against someone with whom you otherwise share common ground.

Consequences

Localism and community are, as we will see, vital components in reconnecting humanity with the real world. If we fail to see the bigger picture and recognize how much we are being divided on spurious grounds, then we will fail to see how much we have in common. We will remain disconnected from each other — wedged further apart in many cases — and thus our only common ground will be with the authoritarian figures and institutions that pretend to speak for us. They speak for no one but themselves.

Perpetrators

In the short to medium term, the leading perpetrators of Divide and Rule are the leaders and enthusiastic supporters of the various cultural divisions. Too many to list here, but as examples we could use Catholics vs. Anglicans, Republicans vs. Democrats, Sunnis vs. Shi'ites, Barcelona supporters vs. Real Madrid supporters, Windows consumers vs. Apple consumers; the list is morphing constantly as people's loyalties and beliefs shift. The real perpetrators, though, are the commercial powerhouses of the industrial world who use our natural tribal instincts for their long-term financial gain.

6) Sell Us a Dream

Description

This, along with Abuse Us, is one of the most superficial of the Tools, yet the simple mechanics of advertising continue to maintain a powerful hold over people in all walks of civilized life. More savvy Consumers (yes, I see the irony) are learning to see through mass advertising, particularly television, radio, newspaper and billboard forms, which has brought forth two interesting effects. First, in more mature industrial economies, advertising to create consumer demand is becoming more technologically advanced and individually tailored. Second, the more traditional forms of advertising are finding their niche in burgeoning industrial economies, such as India, China and the Middle East. This two-pronged attack on our natural reticence to waste money on things we don't need is working wonders, with markets continuing to grow in all parts of the industrial economy as we eagerly swallow the dream of mass consumption.

Identification

It's advertising — easy to spot, sometimes tricky to recognize as pure marketing, but ubiquitous in almost every facet of civilized life. If someone is encouraging you to buy something you would not otherwise buy, then that is the system selling you a dream.

Consequences

As with Reward Us for Being Good Consumers, the consequences are a combination of living the life the industrial system approves of, rather than the life we would live in the absence of ubiquitous and — let's be honest here — very clever advertising, and the continual degradation of the global ecology as a direct result of this consumption.

Perpetrators

Anyone who makes money out of our buying things we would otherwise not buy, or who encourages us to do the same, is a perpetrator. Thus, anyone in the advertising and marketing industry; anyone involved in corporate-funded media, including "liberal" publications that carry advertising; anyone who provides us with the means to make such unnecessary purchases, thus the entire retail banking and loans industry, along with those who enforce the recollection of the resulting debt, is culpable.

7) Exploit Our Trust

Description

This Tool is more accurately (and verbosely) described as "Exploit Our Trust in Authority Through Imposed Hierarchy," for the genuine trust one may have in a close friend or relative or a legitimate leader is something we do not want to subvert. Unfortunately that latter genuine trust is rare in the atomized, divisive societies that are part of Industrial Civilization. What we have instead are figures of "authority" we are trained, from our very first exposure to hierarchy, to trust implicitly. Thus, we trust police officers, teachers, managers, some politicians (those that have the same color buttons as we do) and the people who operate in the rarefied levels way above our daily awareness — the political and corporate elites.

Public trust in authority is well documented, for instance with the experiments of Stanley Milgram, but is not an evolved part of human behavior: we learn to trust authority through the presence of imposed hierarchy, which makes us more willing to carry out activities — such as operating highly destructive commercial machinery, aiming and firing missiles at non-combatants or "merely" taking our part in the industrial machine as an enthusiastic worker — that would otherwise be considered inhuman.

Identification

Wherever there is an imposed authority structure in place — rather than the kind of authority that has been earned by mutual understanding — then it is almost certain that trust is being exploited. It is important to always be aware of the difference between earned and imposed trust, and while it may be disingenuous to distrust someone simply because you have no personal experience of the person's particular qualities, it is thoroughly sensible to question all forms of authority. In the Culture of Maximum Harm, the vast majority of authority is unearned, and exists to maintain that culture.

Consequences

The personal consequences of trust exploitation are complex: not only are we highly likely to accept the words and deeds of a far wider range of individuals and institutions than without this Tool in place, we are less able to build close trust relationships of the sort that are essential for maintaining self-sufficient communities — our "trust radar" is off kilter. The net effect is that we willingly work as part of the most voracious entity on Earth, effectively contributing to its destructive potential. The perhaps more tragic (although possibly intentional) side effect of this is our inability to build communities that depend on genuine trust.

Perpetrators

We *all* take part in this exploitation if we are part of any hierarchical system, be that within a corporation or even just a small company that has a management structure, a political and judicial system that assumes authority through application of legislation, or a family that imposes authority simply by virtue of physical size and strength.

8) Lie to Us

Description

We could describe everything promulgated by a system that seeks to disconnect us from the real world as a lie. There are big lies and there are small lies, and it is hard to tell the difference between them unless you know the endgame. Perhaps among the smaller lies — albeit having an impact far beyond its stature — is the act of greenwashing. When something is actually more harmful to the natural environment than it is claimed to be, then greenwashing is taking place. This activity is so common as to be routine in advertising and promotion, not least because superficial acts of "greenness" are commercially beneficial. It is not just corporations that lie about their ecological credentials.

Passing through an enormous slough of state- and industry-sponsored lies, we arrive at the lie that underpins the commercial behavior of all Industrial Civilization, the lie that has driven public opinion for at least the past 100 years and has contributed to virtually every state-sponsored war not attributable to religion prior to that: *Economic Growth is a good thing.*

There is not space to unravel the detailed reasons this is a lie, except to say that almost all systematic environmental harm, along with uncountable human atrocities, has been committed in the embrace of this lie. It is seen as normal to accumulate wealth, as an individual, as a city, as a nation, as an entire species: though quite how *all* of humanity can become richer on a finite Earth is never addressed. Simply, economic growth is a fundamental part of the civilized package, and Moloch help us if we fail to appreciate that![16]

The lie of Economic Growth is personified in a raft of institutional messages: from the positive note the mass media gives to rises in corporate profits to the negative PR that emerges from business in relation to any social measure that might threaten growth. The lie of Economic Growth is justified with reference to all sorts of things that *not* having economic growth would impact, such as our Standard of Living and the level of consumer "choice" offered by modern society.

Identification

Putting aside the sheer tackiness of greenwashing — if something appears too good to be true then it is — the underlying lie of Economic Growth is clear, and its identification is equally so. Getting into the mindset from which such an integral part of our daily lives is recognized to be pure corporate propaganda, however, requires a level of deprogramming that can be achieved only by undermining the message itself. If you watch and listen out for the Big Lie in everything you do for one day, its prevalence will come as a shock.

Consequences

In contrast to the "Make Us Feel Good for Doing Trivial Things" Tool of Disconnection, institutional lies exploit our natural receptiveness to large-scale human issues such as security and good health, presented in the context of being possible *only* in a healthy economy (more irony). In doing so the real big-ticket items — the ones that are the result of the industrial economy, such as the wholesale poisoning of watercourses, the systematic removal of natural forests and the destruction of indigenous, non-civilized cultures — are perceived to be less important. As our priorities change, so does our behavior: we become slaves to a message. The outcome is that we find ourselves able to respond only to what the system tells us is important, and we neatly ignore what the system has wrought upon the wider world.

Perpetrators

The main perpetrators of institutional lies, from the smallest act of greenwashing to the monumental mind-meld required to embrace infinite economic growth, are the great institutional orifices: the political system in its entirety, the corporate PR and marketing industries, and the mass media — both state and corporate controlled (although there is little to distinguish the two). Conspiracy is essential for institutional lies, and the acceptance of such lies on such a grand scale; but the effort of maintaining the conspiracy between these bodies is well worth it. Once we have been sold the lies convincingly, then keeping everyone "on message" is relatively simple: just keep lying.

9) Scare Us

Description

Lies and fear intertwine deeply in the civilized world. The Big Lie described earlier uses a range of tactics and allies to maintain and, in newly industrialized nations, strengthen its grip on our psyche. To a great extent fear comes into this. The mere act of threatening economic collapse or even just stagnation is enough to pack us off to the shops in obedient traffic queues. In fact, most persuasive lies use fear.

It is no surprise that civilized humans have, throughout history, fallen foul of such monumental scaremongering tactics as referring to native African people as Savages who must be educated in the ways of the Civilized Man; justifying the exploitation of vast areas of land by imperial powers through a fear of other nations' "greed"; the demonization of everyone with left-leaning politics as Communists, Socialists and (yes, this strikes fear into people) Liberals; and not forgetting the mass hysteria whereby anyone who is less than sympathetic to the industrial West is labeled a Terrorist by the system.

It is through the application of scare tactics that people who might not be so vulnerable to simple persuasion are brought "on side," even through something as innocuous as not being seen as a success or being accused of abnormal behavior. We are social animals and we do like to conform to whatever is normal: it takes a brave person to step out of one's comfort zone.

Identification

By their nature, scare tactics appear as the truth, albeit wrapped around a grenade with the pin *just* hanging in place. It is important to recognize that such imposed fears have a downward trajectory. True, once an institutional lie based on fear becomes embedded in the culture, then you are far more likely to hear it from your peers than from figures or instruments of authority; but certainly at their early stages these ideas emerge from the usual institutional mouthpieces: politicians, the mass media, Business Leaders[17] and those who use fear to promulgate belief in something that is supposed to be all loving and all caring.

> However, if you do not listen to me or obey all these commands, and if you break my covenant by rejecting my decrees, treating my regulations with contempt, and refusing to obey my commands, I will punish you. I will bring sudden terrors upon you — wasting

> diseases and burning fevers that will cause your eyes to fail and your life to ebb away....
>
> If in spite of all this you still refuse to listen and still remain hostile toward me, then I will give full vent to my hostility.... I will leave your lifeless corpses piled on top of your lifeless idols, and I will despise you.[18]

Let's face it, if an idea has genuine credibility, then why would it need to be presented in such a frightening way?

Consequences

The natural response to fear is not the same as the response to aggression (see "Abuse Us"), for in the face of fear there is little to fight except our own state of mind. In the event of a genuine, tangible threat greater than ourselves, the evolved response is to escape, which is why the instigators of this Tool of Disconnection create helpful outs: we don't need to run, because they will keep us safe from whatever is the threat de jour. Consequently, we stagnate — fall into a behavioral pattern we feel will keep us safe, not realizing that all we are really keeping safe is the success of the industrial machine.

Perpetrators

Among the vast supporting cast available to the civilized elite for promulgating fear are newspaper journalists, television pundits and a host of lowly politicians on the greasy pole to power. However, a culturally embedded fear, such as the need for a "War Against Terror," is just as likely to be propagated by people like you and me.

10) Abuse Us

Description

If you aren't scared enough, then you have to be hurt. This is not just an unfortunate side effect of your failure to follow the rules of civilization; it is a key way civilization is imposed. Abuse is endemic across every social class, every political color, every institution and cultural subdivision of the world we recognize as normal. Yet, despite its intrinsic nature it truly rears its head only when we threaten to upset one of the numerous flows of money and power that keep it functioning. At that point, if you have not already been scared off, then violence follows. This is deemed acceptable. As Derrick Jensen puts it,

> Civilization is based upon a clearly defined and widely accepted yet often unarticulated hierarchy. Violence done by those higher on the hierarchy to those lower down is nearly always invisible, that is, unnoticed. When it is noticed, it is fully rationalized. Violence done by those lower on the hierarchy to those higher is unthinkable, and when it does occur it is regarded with shock, horror, and the fetishization of the victims.[19]

When a member of the public, taking part in a protest, is beaten by a police officer with a side-arm baton, that act is protected by the hierarchy in which the police officer operates: context dictates that the beating was a rational act of self-defense. When a similar, or lesser, act is carried out by a member of the public upon a police officer, then that act defies hierarchy: it is condemned loudly and continually by all who have a voice, even the majority of those involved in the protest itself.

Identification

We have become so conditioned to accept the casual application of violence — in the face of attempts to gain liberty, to connect once again with something that is not forcibly imposed — that identification of violence as a Tool of Disconnection has, perversely, become simple. An act of aggression that is not categorized as "violent" by the mass media is most likely to be an oppressive action; something designed to keep people in their place. We can thus recognize systemic abuse by the fact that it is not regarded as abusive!

Consequences

If we are able to accept abuse as part of a just society,[20] then what is clearly an ethically unsustainable act becomes normalized. Part and parcel of life in a family dominated by one or more abusive parents or partners is the normalization of abuse: it is no longer reported; it is tolerated, even welcomed in the most extreme cases. The abused become incapable of fighting back. The ripple of abuse spreads out to all parts of society: we, the abused, may become the abusers. In effect, we become disconnected from our ethical selves and no longer see people and the wider natural world as victims: abuse is just business as usual, so we stop fighting back.

Perpetrators

Primary among the institutional abusers are those that directly inflict "security" on behalf of the corporate and political elite: military personnel, police officers, private security guards and other related enforcers. However, this is not enough to create the conscious acceptance of abuse; that requires a more subtle imposition of hierarchy, particularly patriarchal hierarchy. Thus, it is those who teach the rules of civilized society — the schoolteachers, the clergy, historians, and yet again the mass media, among others — who help make all of us abusers by proxy, and willing to assist with the disconnection process.

The previous ten Tools describe a continuum of sorts, a series of institutional activities that move from the more positively glossed and hands-off to far more negative and direct methods. Reinforcing these are a variety of Tools that, at first glance, appear to be less-than-subtle methods for disconnecting people; yet their subtlety is truly striking when you realize how intrinsic these four Tools are to civilized culture, and how long they have been disconnecting us. It's almost as though they have always been there.

11) School Us

Description

School is a device to disconnect children from reality. The role of the public "education" system in the civilized world is to prepare children for their future as workers. Within (and rarely outside) the walls of schools and colleges our precious progeny are made to ingest slice after slice of appropriate information, carefully selected so eventually the graduates of these institutions will be qualified to perform a money-earning function within society. In these terms, it's fair to consider just whose side the school system is on.

> Was it possible that I had been hired [as a teacher] not to enlarge children's power, but to diminish it? That seemed crazy on the face of it, but slowly I began to realise that the bells and the confinement, the crazy sequences, the age-segregation, the lack of privacy, the constant surveillance, and all the rest of the national curriculum of schooling were designed exactly as if someone had set out to prevent children from learning how to think and act, to coax them into addiction and dependent behavior.[21]

As creatures of an umbilical tendency, we seek out connection to something all our lives, primarily with other people but also with the wider ecology of life. In the absence of any of that then we, and particularly our recently de-corded children, will embrace anything that mimics real connection. The difference between real connection and the surrogate that civilization offers is that the latter creates dependency, sometimes by accident, often deliberately. The Tool of Disconnection that manifests itself in the form of school buildings, schoolbooks, teachers, administrators and government-enforced curricula does a splendid job turning the deepest desires of the Jesuits ("Give me the child until he is seven and I'll give you the man") into a reality for the masses. Individuals who do not wish to be part of this system are labeled "rebellious," "delinquent" or "dysfunctional" and are made to conform via a series of increasingly punitive measures.

If we are to make a value judgment on the benefits of public schooling, we first have to ask a serious question: What kind of education is offered by a school system that vomits out young adults completely dependent on civilization, disconnected young adults whose only learned skills make them more effective wage slaves?

Identification

From the age of four or five, in most industrialized nations (though notably a couple of years later in those criticized as "socialist" by many) children are compelled to attend a state-approved institution for about 35 hours a week. Within the free time of all 5- to 16-year-olds (typically) are further periods of compulsory labor, known as homework. During vacation periods, those students failing to achieve an acceptable level of attainment are encouraged to attend schooling Gulags, dressed up as Summer Schools. Compulsion is the watchword. No system that is so mentally nourishing, and so beneficial to the individual as the school system's promoters claim, would need to compel, *by law*, anyone to attend on a regular basis. They would just go. But it isn't, and so they are, which makes identification of disconnection by schooling as easy as A-B-C.

Consequences

Compulsory schooling is a waste of the evolved mental and physical abilities of young people who, in the uncivilized world, would be spending that period of their lives learning how to survive on their own terms and within a functional community. In "less developed" areas of the world, children are being taught that school is a gift from the civilized world that will give them a bright future — often at the expense of the vital, connected life skills of no use to the industrial machine. (Why would you need to know how to fish when you can work in a call center and live in a city slum?) The result is a global population less able to fend for itself, and thus dependent on the industrial machine to provide for it. An extremely dangerous position to be in, on the cusp of collapse, but greatly beneficial to the system all the time it wants to achieve its rapacious aims.

Perpetrators

Presumably we should point the blame at everyone who carries out the day-to-day schooling of children, but it is not as simple as that. Schoolteachers are often highly enlightened members of society, given sufficient freedom to be so, but they are often hopelessly constricted within a system, the larger whole of which is the true perpetrator. In reality, the system is led from the top down by managers, administrators who in turn are controlled by corporations and political elites who manipulate curricula to their own ends (witness the universal presence of Citizenship courses in an increasing number of school systems, as well as subjects increasingly being focused on business skills and entrepreneurialism) and is propagated by naive organizations, charitable trusts and the like, who believe universal education actually results in a net gain in useful knowledge. It was not so long ago that the Church was the universal provider of schooling in many highly industrialized nations, and it is still widely the case that, aside from the adoration of Mammon, children are encouraged to worship whichever deity the legislature of the day considers suitable.

12) Steal Our Language

Description

Words are enormously powerful; in many ways they are a defining feature of human culture, not only because of the number of ways they can be used — in the form of poetry, debate, storytelling, song and innumerable others — but also because we have become conditioned to accept certain words as having significance beyond their physical incarnation. These words are more than just symbols; they are tools that can be, and are, used to manipulate the way we think and act. I will keep referring to the "real world" in this book, which is shorthand for everything we *need* to sustain us as human beings, physically, mentally and whatever may lie beyond our ken. That this simple expression has been turned on its head to mean the Civilized World (as in "getting back to the real world" or "yes, but in the real world...") demonstrates how determined civilization is to harness the power of words. So important is this phenomenon that even the notion that words are powerful has been subverted to prevent people from recognizing it, as shown in a speech made by (though undoubtedly written for) Ronald Reagan in 1985:

> Even if national unity cannot be achieved immediately, you, the youth of Germany, you who are Germany's future, can show the power of democratic ideals by committing yourselves to the cause of freedom here in Europe and everywhere.
>
> You know some may not like to hear it, but history is not on the side of those who manipulate the meaning of words like revolution, freedom, and peace. History is on the side of those struggling for a true revolution of peace with freedom all across the world.[22]

There is a great deal of lexical misdirection going on here. Most obvious is the claim that the manipulation of words is not a historically significant factor, in which case why has every civilization and, more pointedly, every imperial force sought to control both access to literature and the meaning of language? More subtly is the repeated use of the word "freedom," which on one hand Reagan decries the manipulation of, yet from the earliest throes of Western imperialism right to the present day has been expressly used by civilized governments to mean "our way of living."

Laying claim to the meaning of that of which we are an intrinsic part is perhaps the most insidious misuse of language, and one of the most effective ways of keeping us disconnected from the (real) real world. The idea of "nature" is rich and complex, implying that which is in its pristine and unconfined state, something that interlinks everything we depend upon. The civilized world would rather we use the capitalized term "Nature," implying something that is outside of us and thus far easier to fear, subvert and control.

Given the previous Tools of Disconnection, there can be little doubt of the industrial system's ability to control the media and style of human communication. Once you control the communication channels — be that through newspaper articles, television news broadcasts, school curricula, published reference materials such as dictionaries, or corporate advertising — then you can impose whatever language specifications you like. This can work in two ways.

First, you make the acceptable or normal become unacceptable and abnormal. For instance, the word "savage" (from the Latin *silvaticus*, meaning "woods") has been fully and possibly irreversibly redefined, initially, most likely during the European Enlightenment period, to create a mental separation between that which is "cultured" and that which is not, and progressively to make it possible to impose imperial rule upon other human beings in less-civilized parts of the world. This extract from a widely referenced Internet English dictionary makes further comment unnecessary:

sav·age [sav-ij] adjective, noun, verb, -aged, -ag·ing. —adjective

1. fierce, ferocious, or cruel; untamed: savage beasts.
2. uncivilized; barbarous: savage tribes.
3. enraged or furiously angry, as a person.
4. unpolished; rude: savage manners.
5. wild or rugged, as country or scenery: savage wilderness.
6. archaic. uncultivated; growing wild.

Similar treatment has been dealt upon the words "wild," "animal," "undeveloped," "uncivilized" and, in a particularly effective example of Newspeak, "anarchy/anarchist," which means nothing more or less than having no formal leadership structure but which makes a disapproving appearance in every news broadcast that involves people rebelling against the industrial system.

Second, you make that which is implicitly damaging and destructive into something not just acceptable but preferable. Remove the "un-" prefix from uncivilized and undeveloped and you have a couple of terms that are only ever used in a positive sense in mainstream communication: civilized and developed. Not only are these two words, and their derivatives (civilization, development) used to indicate that which is good, but they are aspirational concepts, applied to such diverse areas as international conventions, government policy, corporate greenwash and even the literature of aid organizations. A whole phalanx of other words (see previous sections for their application) such as "progress," "education," "growth" and "sustainability" have been appropriately moderated to ensure that the only meanings we now recognize are the meanings the Culture of Maximum Harm has approved.

Identification

As language is so fundamental to who we are, culturally, it can be difficult to step outside of that bubble in order to see the true meaning of words and how they have been manipulated to suit the needs of the system. It turns out that isn't strictly necessary. It is the carrier, rather than what is being carried or communicated, that makes the difference to what is perceived by the target. Thus, when you hear that an oil company's profits have fallen to less than a billion dollars, expressed in sullen tones by a news presenter on a corporate or state-owned television channel, you know you are being expected to perceive that as bad news, not as news that fewer greenhouse gases are being emitted by that particular company. When you see the words "*Arbeit Macht Frei*" wrought in iron above a factory gate, recognize that these are not simply three words giving a positive message (however twisted that message is) but rather three words that express the desires of the factory owners for you to give yourself over to the concept of work being a "good thing" and to whatever befalls you afterward. It is never too late to see the true meaning of something.

Consequences

Language is a powerful inheritable *meme*, meaning it is something that is easily passed from generation to generation within a cultural setting. If we carry in our heads a set of definitions and cultural meanings that are not to our long-term benefit as human beings, then we, and those who follow, will act in a way that is deleterious to our long-term survival. To progress as a human being is to ensure each generation inherits in turn something that is at least as abundant and sustainable as the previous generation inherited. To progress as a civilized human is to do whatever benefits a civilization in its ambitions to dominate formerly free human beings and the wider natural world. The meaning creates the outcome.

Perpetrators

Every civilized speaker helps perpetuate the disconnection that mangled and manipulated language imposes upon a culture; but in the spirit of "the medium is the message," the major culprits are those who control the means of communication: media proprietors, editors, journalists, broadcasters and reporters, publishers, political orators, public relations firms, censors.... This is a long list! Effective, targeted communication provides the momentum for all industrial economies to thrive and widen their power base; so it is not surprising that so many different parties are involved in undertaking this vital function.

13) Steal Our Time

Description

Between 1997 and 2007 I didn't grow any food. We had moved into a house with a decent sized garden, and we loved pottering around outside on the weekend, pruning here and there, mowing the lawn, keeping the weeds in check, that sort of thing; but growing food takes time, not just physically but in your head. I had a full-time job just over an hour's railway commute away, meaning I spent about 11 hours a day away from my family, my garden, my neighborhood, my community, being instead boxed away in an office carrying out a service that ensured other people could carry out a service that allowed other companies to move large amounts of raw materials around the globe, gamble with people's pensions or just generally screw humanity into the ground. My time was valuable — as a part of that system.

In 2007 I became one of the lucky ones and walked out of the machine.

Most of us can't do this yet. It's a privilege I hold dear. Then again, it's a dream few people have; there are bigger, more exciting aspirations that flood the senses from the moment we are sent to school in the civilized world. As we grow we are trained, then we get a job (and if we don't we are considered unemployed), then we might have some children whom we will send to school as soon as the system tells us to; meanwhile we continue to work even longer hours so we can buy more of the things the system wants us to buy — the "essentials" of life and the "little luxuries" like a vacation that sucks up about a month's earnings for the sake of a week away. If we are lucky we might get to see the kids long enough to read them a bedtime story. Then at some point, perhaps 65 years after we are born, we are "retired" from the system with maybe a small stipend to show for all those years of hard labor. Now we have the time: maybe 10 or 20 years of being active, a window during which many of us do grow food, meet our neighbors, play a part in our community — and look after the grandchildren that their working parents have precious little time to care for themselves.

Between starting school and retiring from the labor market a crime is committed upon the population of the industrial world: the theft of time. In our chronologically restricted existence it is the role of the industrial system to steal as much of our time as it possibly can. If it is not spent in or traveling to and from a place of work, it is spent playing catch-up, carrying out the things that have to be done — like cleaning, cooking, eating, making essential repairs ... and sleeping. That genuinely useful period of time, though, is being ever more tightly wedged alongside the civilized demands of watching television about, going on extended shopping trips to buy and socially networking via goods that have been produced by millions of other people who once had time of their own. These are people whose time you have stolen.

And here's another thing. Between 1997 and 2007 it would have taken me only 15 minutes each evening to tend a few seedlings, hoe between the rows and tie up the fruit-laden plants; just 15 minutes I could so easily have shared with my children instead of, or maybe as well as, a bedtime story. But I didn't *think* that time was available. Such was the temporally fucked-up state I had accrued over those years on the treadmill that I thought every moment not carrying out a systemically prescribed task was a moment wasted. Until that mindset could be broken, I was no threat to the system: I didn't have the time.

Identification

The theft of personal time is damn hard to identify, such is our acceptance of the daily and weekly regimen imposed on our lives. Sure, there are obvious activities that are not linked to survival or the continuation of the human species that we carry out, then wonder — in a moment of clarity — why on earth we just wasted that last hour. ("That's an hour of my life I'll never get back," we half-joke.) There are also milestones in our lives when we see that others have achieved things that we could have, had we spent our time more wisely. But time is not a simple progression of ticks on a clock — perhaps the greatest symbol of oppression in the industrial world. Time contracts and dilates as we go through the day, lose focus on the now and drift into a melancholy dream state (notwithstanding the bacon slicer about to carve off a digit or two), or enter a crisis state that pulls our senses into order and slows down time for long enough to allow our survival instincts to kick in and save lives (and our fingers).

In fact, given the relativistic nature of time, identification of Time Theft is most likely a matter of teamwork. A trusted friend or a partner, or maybe a child itching for you to get off the computer and read that bedtime story or just play for a while, is going to provide more help pulling you through that thick skin of unreality than you can do yourself. And so you too must be other people's guide to their profligate use of this most precious of gifts.

Consequences

It is impossible to overstate the negative consequences of Time Theft on society and the wider environment. Taken as a whole, the civilized population devotes over two-thirds of its collective lifetime to activities that assist the industrial hierarchy in its drive to gobble up every available natural "resource" in order to create wealth for the very few. The remainder of this time, aside from the few moments of clarity that surprise us with their eccentricity, is occupied by the bolster of sleep we need each night just to keep us functioning. Even the amount and quality of sleep we are able to obtain is shrinking as late shifts, catch-up chores and the inevitable visual entertainment encroach on our slumbersome hours.

By ensuring we have little time to think, let alone act, on our own terms, the industrial system controls us. Not only will a failure to break the clock lead to the inevitable crash in the supply of everything we depend upon for our collective survival, it will ensure we are too preoccupied to even notice this happening.

Perpetrators

Time pressure pushes from all directions, and it is all too easy to blame the people you love for occupying those periods in which you "need" to work, get jobs done and chill out in front of the TV, computer or store display window. Reality check: it is not the people you love who are stealing your time, but everyone else. Every institution, every commercial enterprise, every single artifact of Industrial Civilization is clawing away at the shreds of your remaining years. The people and activities you should be spending your time with have been pushed aside by the forces of commerce because, like it or not, time is finite, and no one knows that better than those who want to steal your time away for their own benefit.

14) Give Us Hope

Description

November 4, 2008, might not seem to be a particularly significant date in the annals of world history; yet it is perhaps the single most important day in the history of political grassroots activism. Here is part of the speech the person in question made on that date:

> To all those watching tonight from beyond our shores, from parliaments and palaces to those who are huddled around radios in the forgotten corners of our world — our stories are singular, but our destiny is shared, and a new dawn of American leadership is at hand. To those who would tear this world down — we will defeat you. To those who seek peace and security — we support you. And to all those who have wondered if America's beacon still burns as bright — tonight we proved once more that the true strength of our nation comes not from our the might of our arms or the scale of our wealth, but from the enduring power of our ideals: democracy, liberty, opportunity, and unyielding hope.[23]

In that speech Barack Obama, 44th president of the United States of America, used one particular word in such a way that there was no doubt what had swept him to power. The day Obama accepted victory was the day the Hope rhetoric fully engulfed America; the posters, still crackling freshly in the Chicago breeze, were emblazoned with the same word; button badges and sweatshirts adorned with slogans playing on this word were already for sale online.

What is actually significant is not that someone of mixed race and cultural origins completely atypical for the historical position assumed power, not even that the route to victory was paved with the shoulders of millions of genuinely passionate, normally disenfranchised people. No, what is significant is that no one seemed to understand that the victory had been won by exposing a concept for what it really was, in a way that no satirist, no author and no activist had ever been able to do. Finally the sinuous mantra of the social optimist had been beaten into a circle, and promptly swallowed its own tail.

No one who follows the course of world events can doubt the Obama presidency was, and is, just business as usual for the oil barons, warlords and media tycoons of the industrial world. The irony is that anyone who has paid attention to events that change world history would have known what was happening all along, had they not been swept away by the frenzied election coverage. Hope is anything but a world-changer: it has never been anything other than a means of sublimating the will to create change.

It is clear that few people in the world of grassroots activism understand what a hollow ring that word still has, which is a terrible shame, because there is some genuine value in hope, used in its proper sense, as a means of bringing people together at critical times. Even as a committed "hope skeptic" there is no campaign or action I do not embark upon without some small sense of hope attached but, as writer and cofounder of The Dark Mountain Project, Paul Kingsnorth, states,

> We need to get real. Climate change is teetering on the point of no return while our leaders bang the drum for more growth. The economic system we rely upon cannot be tamed without collapsing, for it relies upon that growth to function. And who wants it

> tamed anyway? Most people in the rich world won't be giving up their cars or holidays without a fight.
>
> Some ... believe that these things should not be said, even if true, because saying them will deprive people of "hope", and without hope there will be no chance of "saving the planet". But false hope is worse than no hope at all.[24]

False hope is the application of a wish, a prayer if you like, upon something that on its own is unlikely to succeed. Rather like a Green Party candidate in a British constituency that has voted Conservative for the past 60 years, the only likelihood of success is with the removal of all other potentially successful candidates. On the other hand, a Green Party candidate in a constituency that has a history of liberal voting, backed by a platoon of activists and the support of the local press, may be justified during the vote count when nothing more can be done, in hoping for victory. Unfortunately, as Caroline Lucas, the first ever Green Party Member of Parliament in the UK, has been witness to, becoming a member of a behemothic, corporate-led system, in the hope that change can be made is about as effective as throwing a coin into a fountain and hoping to water the spreading deserts.

Identification

For once, this is easy to spot. The use of the word "hope" is profligate in the speeches, essays and articles of a wide range of people who use the word, and related terms like "hopeful" and (without irony) "hopeless," in one of two ways. First, you will hear and see it as a way of appealing to the human spirit in place of constructive action, manifesting itself in the form of vigils, symbolic human chains, petition signings and all sorts of other ineffective activities — what could be called "fluffy hope." Second, it will be in the form of a call to arms, where the object of this call is made to feel duty-bound to act on behalf of the requestor — usually a politician or a corporation proxy, such as the press release of a sponsored event. It will be obvious to you by now that this is nothing but "false hope." Very rarely you will feel the warm and positive glow of genuine hope: but no one will need to tell you to act, because the work will already have been done.

Consequences

In the presence of hope, action ceases — real action, that is, not the symbolic activities mentioned above that masquerade as action. Hope is the killer of change; it is the mental glue that prevents us from deciding that maybe we haven't done quite enough yet, or realizing that we haven't really done anything at all.

Perpetrators

Hope and symbolism go hand in hand, and it is those who deal in symbols such as the flag, the rosette, the cross, the button badge and the cluster of glowing tea lights that are the guilty parties in this suppression of action. So, beware the symbols and those who distribute them: politicians with votes to collect, religious leaders on a mission, charities and NGOs with their fundraisers and, more ominously, their calls to (symbolic) action. And you too: every utterance of the H-word makes someone else a little more impotent in changing their world. Such a simple, yet dangerous Tool of Disconnection.

The Most Powerful Tool of All

Reading through this glossary of the Tools of Disconnection, what might strike you is that everything discussed here is common knowledge. You might be thinking, "So what's the big deal?" In the real world that would be inexcusable. In the civilized world that's perfectly understandable.

Writing this glossary of the Tools of Disconnection, it was hard for me to hold back my emotions: I wanted to rage, to express my fury and utter contempt for the system that has kept us in disconnected servitude for so many centuries, civilization after civilization each having its opportunity to proffer a hand of freedom to the enslaved populace but ultimately bowing to the destiny that befalls every civilization. There is no place for freedom where wealth and power are at stake. No place for freedom and certainly no place for connection.

> Connection permits us to understand our humanity.
> Connection makes us a threat to the system.

So we have to be kept in the dark. The Tools of Disconnection operate at the limits of our perception: we just about see them; we hear them but as a whisper; we can even touch their feathery tendrils. We sometimes hate them and we sometimes embrace them. But we do nothing to stop them.

Why?

Because there is something else going on we can't quite put our fingers on, a mechanism that works through light and dark to protect the system from our latent wrath. For have no doubt, if we ever become fully aware of the extent to which we are being disconnected from the real world then the system will be dust.

> The greatest trick the Devil ever pulled was convincing the world he didn't exist.
>
> (Roger "Verbal" Kint, *The Usual Suspects*)

This Veil of Ignorance that the Culture of Maximum Harm uses so brilliantly is no secret if you know where to look: the Wizard of Oz used it in the form of smoke, pyrotechnics and a curtain to distract the inhabitants of the Emerald City from his lack of might; Doctor Who used it in the form of a perception filter to divert attention from the thing his enemies were looking for; Saruman the White used it in the form of a voice that commanded total acquiescence in the face of a potential threat. Trite, maybe even laughable, examples from popular culture, yet they show that the idea of a system protecting itself from normal sensory awareness is nothing new.

One Greek man was more than aware of how this kind of thing worked. To demonstrate the mindset of the typical person compared to the mindset of the enlightened individual, Plato used a simile in the form of a cave:

> I want you to go on and picture the enlightenment or ignorance of our human condition somewhat as follows. Imagine an underground chamber like a cave, with a long entrance open to the daylight and as wide as the cave. In this chamber are men who have been prisoners there since they were children, their legs and necks being so fastened that they can only look straight ahead of them and cannot turn their heads.[25]

The situation he goes on to describe is of a puppet performance being projected as shadows onto the part of the cave the prisoners are able to see. And that is all they can see. Desmond Lee, the translator for the Penguin edition of *The Republic,* from which The Simile of the Cave comes, suggests the simile can be easily extended to cinema or television — the latter being the primary outlet of information in the civilized world, for the moment. But the simile extends further than a simple visual illusion, for the shadow theatre is not so much mimicking the events of the world beyond the Cave as actually *being* the events of the real world as far as the prisoners are concerned. What happens on the projection wall is so compelling, and the prisoners so tuned into these images, that nothing else exists: the projection of a false world is the real world, as long as the prisoners remain imprisoned, and as long as the shadow theatre continues.

Breaking the chains and moving into the light will take a former prisoner into a different dimension, not just physically, but in awareness of what is going on around her. Dazzling at first, the Real World shortly becomes the truth, with the shadow theatre a mental relic of an old world — a false world — that up to very recently *was* the real world. The newly freed person is at liberty to tell the prisoners about this real world, but will fail:

> "Then what do you think would happen," I asked, "if he went back to sit in his old seat in the cave? Wouldn't his eyes be blinded by the darkness, because he had come in suddenly out of the sunlight?"
>
> "Certainly."
>
> "And if he had to discriminate between the shadows, in competition with the other prisoners, while he was still blinded and before his eyes got used to the darkness — a process that would take some time — wouldn't he be likely to make a fool of himself? And they would say that his visit to the upper world had ruined his sight, that the ascent was not worth even attempting. And if anyone tried to release them and lead them up, they would kill him if they could lay their hands on him."[26]

There are ways to free others and to connect them with the real world, but they do not involve simple suggestion, and they cannot be imposed by force. The curtain in front of the booth protecting the controller, the mysterious force pulling attention away from the truth, the powerful voice preventing all rebellious discourse and thought — these and more operate, like the shackles and the ever-running light projections in the Cave, to keep people rooted to the spot. We see the world that civilization offers us as the truth. Before we can point out the livid details of how we are kept disconnected and help others join forces in undermining the Tools of Disconnection, *we have to undermine the things that prevent us from even believing we are disconnected.*

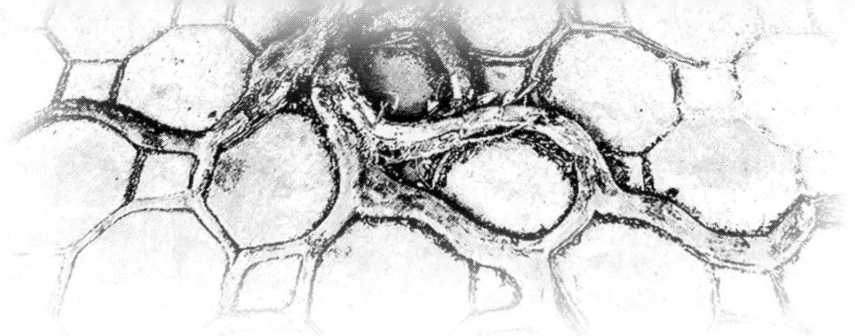

CHAPTER THREE

The Principles of Undermining

Some people take great strides in their lives, always looking forward to the challenges ahead; some people look down and discover they are treading on nothing but illusions. This is a chapter about both of these kinds of people. The first kind are those we are taught we should aspire to be: the kind who want to excel at school, eagerly take career guidance and strive to gather whatever qualifications are necessary to ease themselves into a job; the kind who take their work home, if not in their hands, in their heads, and for whom life follows a career path; the kind who retire when they are told to. The Veil of Ignorance is working overtime to keep these people from looking down.

The second kind are those we are never told to be: the kind who might stand up in a classroom then stop halfway through their prepared speech, distracted by an internal twitch; the kind who abandon a railway journey halfway to work, then stand on the rain-washed platform in shock; the kind who see the future as a gift, and the past as a series of lessons.

Which kind of person you are might not be clear even to yourself, although if you did think, "What's the big deal?" in response to reading about the Tools of Disconnection then — and I'm sorry to have to break it to you this way — you may not be ready for what is to come. But all is not lost, because inside *every single one of us* is an Underminer, a free human being fighting to return kin and community to a connected state once more.

We need a cure for cancer: it's your job to find it. What will you do?

Convention would suggest a combination of chemotherapy, radiotherapy and excision to be the best course of action, depending on the nature and progress of the disease. This costs money, so you campaign for more funding to provide medicines, machines and reduced surgical waiting lists. The treatment often works, but the cancers keep coming.

So what of the cure?

You need to ensure that money is put into research for better treatments and the possibility of a vaccine against virus-borne cancers; you also want to provide extensive information about how to avoid carcinogens and reduce the chances of developing cancer, through lifestyle changes. But the cancers keep coming. Think out of the box! You start looking beyond the comfort zone that most cancer charities confine themselves to: you find evidence that the cause of many cancers is in the air, the water and the soil — carcinogens expelled by industrial processes responsible for the production and disposal of the goods and services the same people suffering from the cancers avidly consume. You work to close down the worst of the factories, plants, incinerators and industrial farms. Victory in the courts! New rules are drawn up; the worst offenders are told to change.

But what of the cure?

What of the *cure*? Surely your job is done — others continue the fight, but you have done well to drill down to the heart of the problem, further than the mainstream campaigners ever thought of going. Did anyone consider shutting down the reason for these toxic processes existing in the first place?

Apparently not.

Civilization has rampant cancer; cases are increasing even as death rates decrease — the sense is of a battle that has no end or, as *The Onion* put it so drolly, "World Death Rate Holding Steady at 100 Percent."[27] Well, of course people will die, but in the case of cancers the solution is so blindingly obvious that only a fool would deny the cure.[28] The problem is that there are an awful lot of fools around, some of whom we call our allies, some of whom we have learned to implicitly trust, some of whom are even called "radical."

For a few years, between my personal environmental enlightenment[29] and the moment it became clear that the whole of civilization was the problem, I thoroughly enjoyed and admired the work of a huge range of writers, professional journalists and bloggers. All but a very tiny number, including some of those many consider true radicals, are no longer on my reading list. These people aren't really the "enemy" as such; they are essentially in a region of environmental thought that should be considered as *mainstream*. The vast majority are by no means malicious, and very many of them genuinely want to make a positive difference — but in hindsight it should have been obvious all along that these people were never going to create change. They were, and are, stuck in a paradigm that considers any answer lying outside of the civilized world as at best irrelevant and at worst dangerous. Some people, though, probably far more than you or I dare to imagine, are already Underminers, and it is those people whom the rest of the book is aimed at.

Survival and Undermining

BY CRIMETHINC.

Whatever medical science may profess, there is a difference between Life and survival. There is more to being alive than just having a heartbeat and brain activity. Being alive, really alive, is something much subtler and more magnificent. Their instruments measure blood pressure and temperature, but overlook joy, passion, love, all the things that make life really matter. To make our lives matter again, to really get the most out of them, we will have to redefine life itself. We have to dispense with their merely clinical definitions, in favor of ones which have more to do with what we actually feel.

As it stands, how much living do we have in our lives? How many mornings do you wake up feeling truly free, thrilled to be alive, breathlessly anticipating the experiences of a new day? How many nights do you fall asleep feeling fulfilled, going over the events of the past day with satisfaction? Most of us feel as though everything has already been decided without us, as if living is not a creative activity but rather something that happens to us. That's not being alive, that's just surviving: being undead.

We "like" fast food because we have to hurry back to work, because processed supermarket food doesn't taste much better, because the nuclear family — for those who still have even that — is too small and stressed to sustain much festivity in cooking and eating. We "have to" check our email because the dissolution of community has taken our friends and kindred far away, because our bosses would rather not have to talk to us, because "time-saving" technology has claimed the hours once used to write letters — and killed all the passenger pigeons, besides. We "want" to go to work because in this society no one looks out for those who don't, because it's hard to imagine more pleasurable ways to spend our time when everything around us is designed for commerce and consumption. Every craving we feel, every conception we form, is framed in the language of the civilization that creates us.

Does this mean we would want differently in a different world? Yes, but not because we would be free to feel our "natural" desires — no such things exist. Beyond the life you live, you have no "true" self — you are precisely what you do and think and feel. That's the real tragedy about the life of the man who spends it talking on his cell phone and attending business seminars and fidgeting with the remote control: it's not that he denies himself his dreams, necessarily, but that he makes them answer to reality rather than attempting the opposite. The accountant regarded with such pity by runaway teenage lovers may in fact be "happy" — but it is a different happiness than the one they experience on the lam.

If our desires are constructs, if we are indeed the products of our environment, then our freedom is measured by how much control of these environments we have. It's nonsense to say a woman is free to feel however she wants about her body when she grows up surrounded by diet advertisements and posters of anorexic models. It's nonsense to say a man is free when everything he needs to do to get food, shelter, success, and companionship is already established by his society, and all that remains is for him to choose between established options (bureaucrat or technician? bourgeois or bohemian? Democrat or Republican?). We must make our freedom by cutting holes in the fabric of this reality, by forging new realities which will, in turn, fashion us. Putting yourself in new situations constantly is the only way to ensure that you make your decisions unencumbered by the inertia of habit, custom, law, or prejudice — and it is up to you to create these situations. Freedom only exists in the moment of revolution.

And those moments are not as rare as you think. Change, revolutionary change, is going on constantly and everywhere — and everyone plays a part in it, consciously or not. "To be radical is simply to keep abreast of reality," in the words of the old expatriate. The question is simply whether you take responsibility for your part in the ongoing transformation of the cosmos, acting deliberately and with a sense of your own power — or frame your actions as reactions, participating in unfolding events accidentally, randomly, involuntarily, as if you were purely a victim of circumstance.

If, as idealists like us insist, we can indeed create whatever world we want, then perhaps it's true that we can adapt to any world, too. But the former is infinitely preferable. Choosing to spend your life in reaction and adaptation, hurrying to catch up to whatever is already happening, means being perpetually at the mercy of everything. That's no way to go about pursuing your desires, whichever ones you choose.

So forget about whether "the" revolution will ever happen — the best reason to be a revolutionary is simply that it is a better way to live. It offers you a chance to lead a life that matters, gives you a relationship to injustice so you don't have to deny your own grief and outrage, keeps you conscious of the give and take always going on between individual and institution, self and community, one and all. No institution can offer you freedom — but you can experience it in challenging and reinventing institutions. When school children make up their own words to the songs they are taught, when people show up by the tens of thousands to interfere with a closed-door meeting of expert economists discussing their lives, that's what they're up to: rediscovering that self-determination, like power, belongs only to the ones who exercise it. [30]

There are 14 Tools of Disconnection listed in Chapter 2, along with something that acts to protect these Tools from detection. That's not all: there are all sorts of potential variations on these Tools, as well as other discrete areas you might have already thought of and could have been put in the list, given enough time and space. To give one example, there is something we might call "Control Our Food," which is pretty much what is imposed upon anyone who lives in a city or suburb, or anywhere else where there isn't ready access to or the desire to grow or otherwise produce edibles. What about, "Take Away Our Creativity"? Art and the innate desire to create beauty are managed by industrial society as a predominantly commercial form of expression, putting the lid on more esoteric and impulsive desires.

But both of these can be considered in the context of other Tools of Disconnection, such as "Pretend We Have a Choice," "Sell Us a Dream" and "School Us." Further, there is a lot of crossover among the listed Tools themselves, making isolation for the purposes of undermining a tricky job. *That is why we have to look beyond the individual Tools and consider the whole.*

The point of listing the Tools of Disconnection was to establish the battle-lines. This is what we are up against: a sprawling, many-limbed creature that smothers and snips as we push through and connect. Swirling around all of this *is* the Veil of Ignorance: now that is something we can consider in isolation, and indeed will; but as far as the wider Tools go, they have to be looked at as this horrible creature. It has strengths as well as weaknesses. Some of us can go for particular weaknesses; others can use our expertise to attack the more resilient parts of the creature. It may morph into other things; it may multiply, grow stronger under pressure, or weaker when it doesn't feel threatened. We have to be prepared.

Time to let go of the analogy. I think it's clear what we are faced with, and now we need to do some serious thinking on the ways to deal with it. It seems sensible to break down the solution into the different aspects of civilized humanity that have become disconnected, starting with the larger scales and then moving much closer to home, in many ways just to make it clear that we matter individually and in small groups just as much as the wider human race does. That will form the basis on which the second half of this book is structured.

Now there is the matter of creating a Game Plan — something that can be used in a wide variety of situations, easily adaptable and, just as importantly, easily understandable to everyone who is going to make use of it. No plan will cover every eventuality; sometimes you have to think on your feet, be instinctive, throw the game plan out of the window. But if we can construct something good enough, then for the most part it should prove useful for the task to come.

The Toolbox

What can you do? I ask this with earnestness that approaches concern. Watching the movie (or, if you are a purist, reading the graphic novel) *V for Vendetta* provides a salient excuse not to get involved in anything too testing: lacking a brilliant tactical mind, technical expertise and a host of combat skills puts the observer very much in the category of a participant of the masked mass that marches on Parliament then stops, awaiting the explosive denouement with hope. I think that's a failing on the part of the observer, not in any lack of ability but in misreading the essence of the tale. The character "V" is an *image* of rebellion — a gestalt of the many elements required in wider society to bring down a destructive and oppressive culture. Parliament itself is a *symbol* of the system that destroys and oppresses. These two elements together imply that no one act is sufficient to do the job; no one successfully executed task will undermine the Tools of Disconnection on its own. Many people need to do many things upon many targets.

That should help put into perspective the onus that is on each Underminer. I am not "V" and neither are you; we are.

As you will see later in the book, there are actions big and small, complex and simple, high profile and low profile, long term and quick win, which are all valid parts of the itinerary of an effective Underminer. Where you fit into this will be determined by numerous factors of timing, ability, connectedness and patience, to name but a few. That said, there are certain attributes we as Underminers should consider vital constituents of our metaphorical Toolbox. Owing to personal circumstances, not everyone will be able to make the grade in every area, but we can all at least be moving toward being the best we can.

Physical Fitness

It is certainly not the case that you will be spending all your time running from safe house to safe house, pausing only briefly to scale a downpipe and traverse a pitched roof in the lashing rain, but nevertheless physical fitness is an important factor in many actions where at least a semblance of mobility is required. It is also allied closely to mental alertness and well-being. You should keep yourself in good condition, regardless of anything — you never know when you will need it.

Mental Fitness

Mental fitness is, if anything, more important than physical fitness. There are many activists who, by necessity, cannot take a physical part in certain types of activity but are valuable contributors in many other often extremely important ways. Having a fit and agile mind, a positive attitude and a range of mental capabilities that can be called on when mere physicality just won't cut it are vital to successful undermining.

Stamina

If physical and mental fitness are the nuts and bolts, stamina is the locking washer that provides continual strength without expending too much energy. Some people can walk for a day without stopping but can barely run 100 yards; others can stay focused on a complex mental task but would struggle to learn a new skill. Stamina allows you to carry on with something when others, in particular those that would seek to stop you, are unable to go on.

Empathy

It is impossible to overstate the value of empathy, yet empathy is often considered to be a sign of weakness or softness in activist circles. This is wrong. Empathy requires a level of connection with others to the extent that, when it fails, the entire venture can collapse. Consider its usefulness in building and maintaining support for something radical, assessing whether someone is genuine or a "plant," being able to convince a target you are on their side. These are wildly different applications of the same attribute, all of them relevant to undermining.

Communication

Where empathy allows true connection to another individual, communication tends to be more superficial but wider-ranging. A capacity for good communication might include being able to address groups of people, even entire nations; writing convincing copy, possibly under an alter-ego; building networks of supporters; and producing works in a variety of forms to express an important idea. It is, at its root, about transmitting something from the few to the many.

Creativity

Mental fitness may provide the womb in which ideas gestate, but without creativity being present the ideas may be unfit for purpose. There is nothing wrong *per se* with using an existing idea, or dealing with a problem in a known way, but the industrial system is — by economic necessity, as much as anything else — always finding innovative ways to control people's lives. We have to innovate in return, not merely to stay ahead of the game, but to work out how to bring down a constantly changing enemy.

Patience

Some things come only to those who wait. If you have a really good idea then you should stick with it, but the opportunity to execute that idea may be very narrow — perhaps one day in every four years, as a very obvious political example.[31] By all means work on something else while you are waiting, but don't miss that opportunity simply because you couldn't be bothered to wait (next time, whatever good idea you had may no longer be applicable), and certainly don't imperil yourself because you were too hasty.

Tenacity

While patience is enduring the passage of time in search of a moment, tenacity is enduring a constant barrage of moments that can easily knock you off course. Like the budding writer who keeps submitting her work, knowing that to stop is to fail, the tenacious Underminer will only stop when to continue would be of no possible benefit. This is particularly relevant in the early stages of the undermining process — the boring bit, if you like — where the hundred-and-first memo is the one that bears fruit or the fiftieth phone call is the one that puts you through to the right person.

Attention to Detail

Allied to tenacity is the importance of not letting details slip by. At all points in the undermining process, right up to any tidying up that is necessary, a single detail may make the difference between success and failure. This is one area, and there are many others, where teamwork can be crucial: while one person may be focused on getting the job done, another should be making sure nothing has been missed. If you can maintain an attention to detail while also seeing the bigger picture then you are truly blessed.

Instinct

We all have instinct, and most of us ignore it. The gut feeling that something is too risky, going wrong or needs a last minute adjustment is not just innate; it is born of experience and knowledge. By ignoring instinct you are ignoring a lifetime of learning. I would much rather trust the instincts of an experienced hunter in knowing that today is not going to be a good day than waste time and energy on a futile search for food. Undermining is, at times, seat-of-your-pants stuff, so pay attention to your instincts, as they might be more right than any bloody-minded determination to follow the script.

You have probably noticed that there are all sorts of things missing from this list, skills such as computer expertise, linguistics and engineering. They are not missing. The Toolbox is replete with all of the things necessary to *acquire* all of those skills and virtually anything else you might need.[32] Admittedly some of those skills may take far longer to acquire than you have time for, but most of them are within reach of anyone with the necessary attributes.

Phases

Three or four years ago I wanted to make a small cold frame to keep the frost off my seedlings. There was this old wooden door I had been saving for the occasion; it was getting a bit rotten at the base and had taken a bashing from the winter rain where it leaned on its side next to the wood pile. I also had a few other timbers, some hinges and a bucket of long screws that had been salvaged from a wooden shop display a relation had been asked to remove.

For weeks the cold frame remained unmade; just a load of churning plans in my head. I'm lucky that I can think in three dimensions, but twisting the models around in my mind seemed to make no difference to my self-imposed recalcitrance. Then one day, as the sun shone down and the patio finally dried out, I grabbed hold of (or rather wrestled with) the door, took out a saw and cut a lump off the bottom of it. Within two hours the basic structure had been made and screwed into place, and I was looking for some wood preservative in the shed. The cold frame was dry that evening.

It wasn't a masterpiece of the joiner's art, and it would later need some clear plastic over the panes to stop water pooling in the door, but the point of this vignette is to explain something about the way problems are solved. The obvious conclusion is that I just needed a reason to get on with the project and should have got off my arse a bit sooner. The reality is that without those weeks of rotating a wireframe drawing in my head, subliminally pondering points of stress and how to ensure the structure would last for longer than up to the next high wind, there is no way I could have "just" grabbed the door and got on with it. Time had to be spent getting the idea right; otherwise I might have just ended up with a cludge — a top-heavy, structurally unsound folly that jammed on the wall as it opened and fell apart the moment one of my lovely children decided to perform a dance on top of it.

When we are faced with a problem such as how to undermine the Tools of Disconnection, there are an awful lot of structures to put in place, all sorts of connections to make and tools to assemble and a hell of a lot of careful thinking to do.

It is a truism that 90 percent of a successful outcome is in the planning, but equally true to say that most of the fun is in the execution. The act of undermining may have deadly serious intentions, but it doesn't have to be a grim exercise, carried out with the weight of humanity riding on your

shoulders. It might feel like that sometimes, but it isn't really. Nevertheless if we are to do such an important thing, then we had better do it properly. With the Toolkit in place we now have to look at the different phases of any game plan. This consists of five discrete areas, not all of them essential to carry out in all cases, but nonetheless very important to be aware of, especially if you are doing this as part of a team.

The five phases are Identification, Investigation, Exposure, Execution and Housekeeping. To take a real-world example, the process of hacking a computer system is, in the vast majority of cases, not just a simple smash-and-grab. If you take that approach, then (a) you will probably fail in your task and (b) if you do "succeed" you are almost certain to get caught. In reality, hacking is a purposeful, methodical process that requires a great deal of preparation and expertise.

First, the target must be carefully identified as that which you are going to perpetrate the hack upon; not just whether it is the intended target but whether it is also a worthwhile one.

Second, the target must be "scoped" in order to ascertain exactly how you are going to carry out the attack, what skills are required, how much time you need, when is the best time to carry it out, and so on. This is also the stage during which you decide the trigger points for calling off the hack or continuing.

The third phase is not commonly used in hacking, but there may be occasions when exposing the target as, say, an easy hit is sufficient to complete your task.

Next is the actual "hack" itself: getting in and doing whatever you intended to do. This is perhaps the "fun" bit, although the risk of getting caught at work is not fun for everyone.

Finally, and often overlooked, is the housekeeping phase, where any evidence of your activities needs to be appropriately dealt with. You may wish to leave a stain on the system of your target, but it's unlikely you will want the target to know who left that stain or how the hack was actually carried out — after all, you may want to do it again.

Notice, I have not taken any moral stance on whether hacking is the right thing to do or not. Morals are different from legal matters. As we will discuss in the next chapter, certain actions transcend mere legislation, which, after all, is in place only to satisfy the will of the industrial system.

Identification

> If you know the enemy and know yourself, you need not fear the result of a hundred battles. If you know yourself but not the

> enemy, for every victory gained you will also suffer a defeat. If you know neither the enemy nor yourself, you will succumb in every battle.[33]

Knowing our enemy isn't the only reason to list the Tools of Disconnection in such detail; there is also the matter of being able to identify when one of these Tools is being applied to us as individuals, a community, a society — the entire human race. If you have a moment, go back to Chapter 2 and scan through the Tools one more time, paying particular attention to the means of identification. What is immediately obvious is they can be boiled down to just a few key things. Actually they can all be boiled down to just one thing — Industrial Civilization — but that's not particularly helpful. We need to be able to specifically identify when a Tool is being used in a particular situation so as to judge the relevance and importance of any action against the target. As you will see in the next chapter, this is critical given the vast number of symbolic targets often existing for the sole purpose of keeping people from acting against targets that really matter.

For the sake of completion, and before a little bit of creative thinking, here are the most common ways the Tools of Disconnection identify themselves:[34]

- Structures and systems, such as governments or compulsory schooling, seem to exist for no good reason other than to perpetuate the industrial machine.
- Concepts, such as the need for economic growth, that would not come about naturally are being enforced by these structures and systems.
- Ideas such as "freedom," "choice" and "hope" are being applied to those same structures and systems.
- Useful activities, such as strengthening communities or growing food, are replaced with trivial ones such as "leisure shopping" and watching television.
- Activities that go against human nature, primarily those that cause personal disconnection from the real world, are justified on extremely spurious grounds.
- The meanings of common words and concepts are changed to suit the needs of the Dominant Culture.
- Here is a situation you are likely to come across at least a few times in your life.

An election is taking place in your country. There are two main parties, along with a scattering of other parties and independent candidates. The two main parties divide along their normal lines, one seeming to appeal to people in blue-collar (manual) work, the other to those in white-collar (office-based) jobs. Other divisions exist on various ethical and ideological grounds, further dividing the electorate. A third party emerges that appears to provide a more radical alternative, giving less power to corporations by promising more environmental regulation and workers rights, while also handing many of the powers of central government to regions/states. The third party has a huge advertising budget and looks to be splitting the popular vote in many areas, making way for an alternative. The third party is also driven by a rapidly growing grassroots movement, based on blogging and viral promotion. Some independent candidates claim that this is just another mainstream party promising things they cannot deliver and only independents can truly represent the will of the people, who are quite frankly fed up with mainstream politics completely. There is a deep recession taking place, and the independents say only their types of ideas can pull the nation back into recovery from the messes the mainstream parties always seem to leave behind.

What do you do?

The previous description is a fair reflection of the political situation in most industrialized countries. Within that statement are a number of yawning issues and questions, some explicit, some implicit. I managed to pick out 11 "clues" to guide the identification process, and you will have undoubtedly spotted some yourself, maybe more than I did. Here are my 11, embedded into the text:

An election

1. Elections are a form of symbolic empowerment that rarely cause fundamental change except, possibly, where a formal dictatorship has been in operation.

is taking place in your country.

2. Countries, regions and states, as opposed to non-geographic nations or tribal lands, are created by the imposition of artificial boundaries, usually along with a synthetic national identity.

There are two main parties,

3. Political parties in large-scale elections can never be representative of the needs of a people; they will always be a vague approximation.

along with a scattering of other parties and independent candidates. The two main parties divide along their normal lines, one seeming to appeal to people in blue-collar (manual) work, the other to those in white-collar (office-based) jobs.

4. "Representation" is framed in terms of everyone identifying themselves as a particular type of worker in a paid job. This even applies to so-called Communist (Marxist) systems.

Other divisions exist on various ethical and ideological grounds, further dividing the electorate.

5. Most of these divisions exist not for any practical purpose, but to give the impression of choice.

A third party emerges that appears to provide a more radical alternative, giving less power to corporations by promising more environmental regulation and workers rights,

6. Terms such as "environmental" and "rights" are rarely defined. Also, what does the small print say?

while also handing many of the powers of central government to regions/ states.

7. This may be genuine, but it may also be "divide and rule" in operation.

The third party has a huge advertising budget

8. This raises the question of where the money has come from.

and looks to be splitting the popular vote in many areas, making way for an alternative. The third party is also driven by a rapidly growing grassroots movement, based on blogging and viral promotion.

9. Is this genuine grassroots support or is it an "Astroturf" operated by the party's real beneficiary?

Some independent candidates claim this is just another mainstream party promising things they cannot deliver and that only independents can truly represent the will of the people

10. How can they be independent if they are determined to be part of a hierarchical political system?

who are quite frankly fed up with mainstream politics completely. There is a deep recession taking place, and the independents say only their types

of ideas can pull the nation back into recovery from the messes the mainstream parties always seem to leave behind.

11. Economic growth is a given in the case of all parties and all candidates.

The first thing to point out is that this is not a textual analysis, but a situational analysis: it is making you question every situation you are faced with, regardless of its form. Obviously the analysis raises a lot more questions than it answers, and that's the point. By identifying where the Tools of Disconnection are being applied in any situation, what you are doing is focusing on the real issues at hand rather than the distractions that are likely to lead you into a dead end and an awful lot of wasted time and effort. By analyzing the situation in some detail, the simple question What do you do? has been transformed from a puzzle into a set of undermining opportunities.

Investigation

Without investigation you have little or nothing to back up any claims you make; nor will you be sure of the accuracy of the information you might be using later on. Furthermore, you may be in danger of going too deep into a situation you have no control over. To take the earlier example of the computer hack, many systems contain what are known as "honeypots" that positively encourage hackers to try out their skills, and which are diligently recording the details of everything that is taking place. Honeypots sometimes also contain false information, leading the hacker to believe they have struck gold when they have in fact just struck a brick wall. Good investigation will help avoid the situation where time and effort are expended spooning the contents from a honeypot or, in more general terms, taking on a target in a way that is going to become more trouble than it is worth.

On a more positive note, good investigation can often unearth leads and information more important than were originally expected, such as a "naughty" company being found to be using the same computer systems as a "very bad" company (obviously these are relative, and quite silly, terms). In non-computer parlance, spending a little bit of time — actually a lot of time — observing the comings-and-goings of an activity or organization you are keen to undermine will save you an awful lot of trouble later on. *Ozymandius' Sabotage and Direct Action Handbook*[35] states, "Reconnaissance is essential. It is what enables you to get into, move around, and get out of a site without getting lost, hurt or caught. It also enables you to assess the needs of the hit in terms of equipment."

With specific reference to physical direct actions, which can take a huge variety of forms, it goes on, "If anything goes wrong — if security guards or the police turn up, if you set off all the alarm systems, or if you hurt yourself and need the quickest route out — it is planning the hit that will save you from ultimate imprisonment and the curtailing of your sabbing career." As I stated earlier, I take no moral stance with regard to whether an activity should be carried out on legal grounds or not. Ultimately that is up to the perpetrator.

Prior to embarking on the investigation proper, you should get some understanding of the nature of your target's operations: if it is a company, public body, charity, religion or other organization, you need to know how it operates both within its "marketplace" and internally; if it is an individual, then you need to know a bit about the person's history and personal life.[36] Having prior experience in the area in which the target operates is extremely valuable and will always give you a head start. In addition, as investigative journalist Nicky Hager writes, it's not always obvious where the information you need is going to come from; you sometimes need to be brave:

> The key to getting information from people is just being brave enough to ask. I find that most people are willing to help. This should be our assumption. Two or three phone calls are often all it takes to locate someone who can help you on the way to the information you are looking for. Once I start asking around, information usually pours in and often does in unexpected ways. During the *Secrets and Lies* research, for instance, I phoned a woman in a small town who, I had heard, knew about an arson threat against environmentalists. After talking helpfully for a little while she said, "it's really my husband you should be talking to, he's in Coast Action Network". I waited apprehensively for him to come to the phone, as Coast Action Network was the pro-logging group that had been set up as part of the PR strategies. He turned out to be one of the real local people who had joined the group. He was soon telling me how he had left in disgust when he realised that all the group activities were being planned at the Timberlands' headquarters. He became one of my best sources.
>
> Another time, I phoned an environmentalist who had been a victim of anti-environmental violence. He suggested I talk to a

> woman he went to university with, who had told a curious story about the Timberlands issue. This woman, it turned out, was being courted by a young man who had confided in her about an exciting job he had had: infiltrating an environmental group for $50 an hour. When I checked the story I found that had he had indeed joined the group and asked lots of questions during organising meetings, that he had had no involvement in environmental politics before or since that time and that he was son of a senior staff member of the PR company Shandwick New Zealand.[37]

Investigation with a view to undermining is akin to carrying out a crime, in that you are trying to do something that runs counter to the desires of the target. Anyone with experience of carrying out nefarious activities (whether strictly legal or not) will already have a fair grounding in the activity known as "scoping" (i.e., the research process), but if you have experience in preventing such activities (e.g., as a PR professional or a security expert) this can be equally valuable, and in some cases more so. Even if you don't have personal experience, it doesn't rule out less complex, and far more common, types of undermining: someone with a sufficient Toolbox will be able to get along fine, and with practice become highly adept.

The dictum "know your enemy" provides an excellent guiding principle here and underlines the primary rule of investigation, namely that you should never go into the role unprepared. Although it can be a long and highly drawn-out process, the level of research you carry out will vary tremendously depending on a number of factors, including

- how risky the investigation is likely to be to you
- how much prior experience you have
- what level of damage you wish to inflict on the target
- how difficult the target is likely to be to penetrate/expose
- how much time you have

I cannot tell you how much research to do and precisely what to look for — remember, it's your investigation, or that of the group you are part of — but the more you do, the better your chances of success. However, if you need to get something out into the open very quickly, then you may be restricted in how much you can do, in which case always try and minimize the risk to yourself.

Exposure

Exposure is the nexus between public ignorance and public awareness. Essentially it is when something not previously known becomes known. It is a rather esoteric beast as the nature of that "something" could range from technical information or cultural knowledge right through to the physical manifestation of an undermining action. In most cases, though, exposure tends toward the earlier part of this spectrum, involving data and documentation rather than tactical openness, and as such it could be considered a form of Execution in itself (see later). Regardless of the nature of that "something," the exposure process is unlikely to be creating anything completely new: much more likely it is simply increasing awareness of that "something," from perhaps just a few executives within a corporation to every member of staff, or from a few politicians to the entire electorate.

In very few cases will exposure ever involve the fine details of the undermining process itself and certainly not the details of the people involved. Egotists do not make good Underminers. As demonstrated below there may be a case for describing how something is going to be done, but without jeopardizing the Execution phase. Situations where details of what is going to be carried out are made public or (it makes my stomach ball up to write this) passed to the relevant "authorities" have almost always been in advance of symbolic activities such as legal marches and protests, where the outcome is certain not to undermine anything except the moral superiority of the people responsible for these activities.

Exposure may not always be present as a discrete phase in the undermining process, but some exposure is almost inevitable with the vast majority of activities. Where it is a material component of the undermining process there is often a fine balance between taking the deliberate exposure route and working the undermining process through as far as possible before exposure becomes desirable. Three fairly generic types of undermining will help demonstrate how relevant exposure is in various cases:

1) In the case of information that has been purposefully withheld from the public eye in order to allow a destructive activity to take place, exposure through the leaking of such information is *highly desirable*. There may be decisions to make regarding the detail of the information leaked, how the leak is timed and who is involved, but ultimately the aim is to expose as widely as possible through the most effective channels before the information can be successfully refuted or covered up, the subject matter is no longer topical or the public simply loses interest.

2) An activity that requires a lot of individuals to take part in many locations may intuitively be something that should be kept secret in order to reduce the effectiveness of any countermeasures, but, in order to encourage as many people as possible to carry out the activity, exposure may become an important factor in gathering support. The decision may be difficult to make, but in some cases advance exposure *can be useful.* The level of exposure must be carefully managed so as not to make undermining any more difficult than it may already be. It is a fine line and may be a case of trusting your instincts.
3) More risky undermining activities tend to rely on early exposure being avoided, and in some cases the perpetrators will want to *avoid any exposure at all.* This could be to allow for repeated undermining of the same or similar targets using similar methods; or it could simply be to reduce the likelihood of the Underminer(s) being identified via indiscreet use of communications. In these cases, reduced exposure leads to reduced risk. Sometimes exposure is just not part of the game plan at all and may be an unnecessary distraction from the activity itself, such as when impeding the flow of disconnecting media such as political propaganda or corporate advertising.

The fourth case implicit in this is when exposure is inevitable. To rule out the possibility of exposure in the planning process would be foolish, as no undermining activity is ever going to be completely airtight, however well you prepare. The rule of thumb is that if exposure is not at all desirable, then make sure you are prepared for the repercussions if it does happen. The next chapter will provide useful ground rules to help with this.

Execution

In most cases this phase is the culmination of the undermining process. As suggested in the previous point, exposure can be a form of execution, but simply putting a document in the public eye is usually not enough in itself — something has to be done with that document for the undermining process to be effective. Thus the execution phase is, more than anything else, the "action" part of undermining. This will be covered in great detail in Part Two. At this juncture, though, it is important to understand the place execution takes in the whole undermining process, as it is often overstated or even considered to be the only thing that matters. In a very few cases it may be the *only* thing that matters; at least that's how it will seem at the time.

Let's take the case of something that happened to me a couple of years ago, not initially intended as a piece of undermining but turning out to be so. The story, which was reported extensively in the local press, was that I was on my way back from dropping off my children at school (yes, I know, but we've equipped them with everything they need to counter the institutional messages thrown at them) when I saw some hedge-cutting taking place and stood in front of the machines long enough to halt the entire process.

In reality I heard the sound of chainsaws, thought about what might be happening, then carried on walking until it hit me that the chainsaws shouldn't be there at all — it was June and birds were still nesting. I ran back to where I had heard the sound, saw a hedge-lopping machine that had already ripped the top third off 20 yards of hedge, and stood in front of it, all the time shouting to the operator to stop. After a few discussions with the workers and their manager over the phone, the contract company agreed to stop the process until the local council could come to a decision. The contractors left, and I called the local paper. What followed was a rash of photo ops and interviews, a front-page article, a reversal of the council's decision, a slew of letters to the local paper and those that reprinted the article, a follow-up article saying the council was going to establish a "Friends of the Park" group, the cancelation of the entire project for two months and the cutting contract being rescheduled for all subsequent years, more birdsong that summer than I have ever heard in all my years living around that park and more people using that small patch of green than I could ever remember. From an apparently spontaneous protest, something had fundamentally shifted for an awful lot of people in the local area. Connections had been made.

The undermining was not spontaneous.

Some situations don't allow for conscious thought, but they are not undermining situations. Pushing a child from the path of a car about to take her life, punching an assailant about to take your consciousness, fighting a security guard about to take your liberty — these are things born out of necessity, and they come from deep within. Thought takes time, so you react and have to deal with any consequences later.

Thinking back on that odd day, it became clear that without having spent a long period of time in the company of road protestors I would never have considered running back and standing in front of a cutting machine; it would have seemed far too risky, whereas in reality I was never in any real danger, unlike the second-generation fledglings due to have their nests ripped apart. The undermining came even later: insisting I was not going to move until the project had been canceled and then calling up the press to publicize the actions of the council contractors and the necessary moves I had taken; those steps were even more deliberate, but both came from observing and taking part in other activities. Remember the story of the cold frame at the beginning of the chapter? This was essentially the same. A plan that had been ready for who knows how many years had found its target and been executed with surprising success.

The point is, there is no such thing as the successful execution of an undermining activity without thought or planning. It may be your "gut instinct" that causes you to initially protect, halt, disrupt, remove or destroy something, but as an Underminer it is what came before that turns that instinctive action into something with far wider repercussions. Execution is just one part of the process.

Housekeeping

The following four operations are all the same, except for one thing — see if you can spot it:

- An office intruder carries a soft, lint-free cloth with him. Some things can't be avoided, so even with latex gloves there is the possibility of a small tear exposing a fingerprint. The thicker the gloves the less detailed the work possible and at some point it might be necessary to remove them, if only to pick up a dropped screw from between two carpet tiles. The cloth is to be wiped across any surface that may have been touched.
- A logging saboteur never takes her tools home with her. The chain link fence has to be breached with a suitable cutting tool, and the spikes that will end up causing no end of trouble for the sawmill aren't going to sink in deeply without a lump hammer. The fence is retied as best as possible. As for the tools, burial is the only option; burial far away from where the operation took place, and far away from the home of the saboteur.
- The administrator account has been compromised. The next move is not to access the data but to switch off security auditing; then the data can be siphoned from the system and onto a server umpteen hops and even more spoofed IP addresses away. With that done, the log files are cleansed of any incriminating data; file access times are reverted and auditing is once again switched on.
- An in-depth discussion between a courier and the mailroom supervisor reveals more than just the loading bay opening times. There is enough

information gleaned to convince any suspicious staff member that the toilet renovations have, indeed, been carried out for health reasons, while the person remains unaware of the hidden microphones just above the urinals. The press of a button and a blue light signifies the mailroom supervisor will remember nothing.

So the last trick was blatantly stolen from the *Men In Black* movies and cannot — as far as we know — be executed quite so neatly outside of Hollywood;[38] but apart from that, all of these operations are essentially of the same nature. Some type of intrusive activity is covered up to reduce the likelihood of the perpetrators and, ideally, the nature of the intrusion being discovered.

Housekeeping, as I mentioned earlier, is a vital stage in any undermining operation and must form part of the overall plan. Even the most hastily executed operations should include an element of housekeeping even if it's just ensuring as few people as possible know the details, or making sure the mud on your shoes has been well removed before returning home. But housekeeping isn't just a case of cleaning up after yourself. At all stages of any undermining operation you must be aware of your overall game plan. The adrenalin rush as you ascend in the elevator toward your quarry should not distract from the tactic of donning a fluorescent yellow vest and using the back staircase on your way down to avoid being associated with whatever was carried out far above. Even such simple things as using the identification mask prefix when making a telephone call qualify as housekeeping. They are the details that get missed in the execution phase — the "fun" bit that, in all your excitement, can drown out the reason you are doing something in the first place.

Did you remember to call Simone from the phone booth on the corner and let it ring three times?

You need to sit down together in the little alcove at that bar where there is always music and the locals spend more time falling off the stools than actually staying on them. Stage one may be complete, but there is a whole lot more to do. For the moment, though, have a drink and celebrate your little victory against the system.

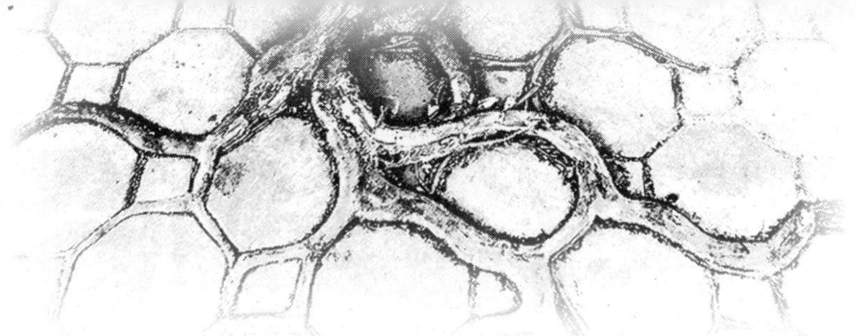

CHAPTER FOUR

Ground Rules

I'M LOOKING AT THE BACK OF A PACKET OF SALTED ROASTED PEANUTS. The ingredient list is refreshingly simple: peanuts, vegetable oil, salt. What is below the ingredients is more interesting. There is a line that says, "CONTAINS PEANUTS," and below this is a further affront to basic intelligence: "MAY CONTAIN NUTS." The cultural reach of this now infamous phrase is such that it has become a parody of itself. The warning is ludicrous on one level (of course a pack of peanuts contains nuts), overly paranoid on another (facing up to the constant threat of litigation) and yet completely sensible at the level where a peanut allergy could cause anaphylaxis and possibly death.

When *Time's Up!* was published, one of the most common reactions was that the section on undermining was reckless: it didn't give nearly enough warning as to the possible repercussions of carrying out countercultural actions. In particular, where the concept of relative risk was discussed, I was accused of not giving sufficient space to the possible human impacts of such outcomes as the power grid being switched off or even, and I write this with slight incredulity, people losing their Podjobs[39] due to economic contraction. Responding to this at the first "peanut level" I should write, "Warning: This book contains information about Undermining." At the second peanut level I would have to rewrite the text to ensure there could not possibly be any inference that I would be encouraging people to do anything that could possibly be considered illegal or even hurtful, regardless of the target.

This chapter is about the third level.

I have no intention of putting a bright orange sticker on the front of this book stating the bleeding obvious, but I don't think many people will have a problem with that. On the other hand I also don't care whether something is illegal or not. That might make a lot of people uncomfortable, but please let me explain. The word "illegal" does not mean something that goes against any of the fundamental moral tenets of humanity. When I use the words "legal" and "illegal" it refers to those rules that have been put in place for the benefit of the industrial system: in some countries and states they may be referred to as laws, statutes, regulations, acts or decrees, but they are all nothing more than temporary measures to impose a cultural viewpoint.

On the other hand, I do care whether something is *lawful* or not. Humanity has, whether formally or not, passed down something called Common Law, which constitutes the basic rules that should be observed in a just society under all but the most extreme conditions. For instance, under Common Law it is wrong to intentionally kill or harm someone without their consent; it is wrong to take something that rightfully belongs to someone else; it is wrong to impinge upon someone's basic human rights of clean air, fresh water, food, warmth, shelter, companionship, liberty and other things related to human dignity. Actually, there are surprisingly few things that could be considered to constitute Common Law, which is significant, because anything more specific would imply a particular culture being imposed upon an individual or collection of people.

This distinction between legal and lawful is important, not only from a practical standpoint but also a moral one. An undermining activity may be illegal in a certain part of the world but it is *not likely to be unlawful*. In all likelihood an undermining activity will run counter to the legal system in place yet lead to a greater availability of the basic rights enshrined under Common Law. Try telling a community that their action against an industry polluting the well from which they take their water is illegal and they will tell *you* in no uncertain terms where to stick that industry's statutory permission to pollute!

Level Three on the Undermining Warning Scale is about protecting basic human rights — your own as well as the rights of others — that may be affected by any actions you carry out. That is why this chapter exists, and why you must read it before going onto the good stuff in Part Two. I cannot absolve myself of all responsibility for the outcomes of undermining simply by writing some words, but I can try to help the Underminer grasp the difference between when it is right to do something and when it is not.

Focus

Ask me how change will happen and you will always get the same answer. You know the answer but it still needs to be said because most people, even those in the brightest, most radical threads of environmental activism, have forgotten the point of what they are supposed to be doing. Ask me what to undermine and you will always get the same answer. You know the answer but it still needs to be said because most people, even those who are determined to remove the system and all it stands for, have lost their sense of perspective. Go back to the discussion about cancer, about finding a cure.

Did anyone ever consider shutting down the reason for these toxic processes ever existing in the first place?

What is the reason for the systematic destruction of our life support system? Disconnection. We see Industrial Civilization as an acceptable way of living, even as it destroys everything we need to survive. The machine works to mask the destruction and works even harder to ensure we embrace the machine, that we become part of the machine. Connected human beings see the destruction and see the disconnection happening. Connected human beings are a rare species and are becoming rarer with each new television channel, each new road, each new city and each newly disconnected culture.

Focus on the reason.

Undermining is removing the bricks from the walls of disconnection, cutting the lines of communication between each part of the ecocidal machine, tearing up the script of civilization's freakish performance. The time for symbolic gestures ended long ago, yet we still as a "movement" believe they can create change. It seems that this cloudy organism that even the most disenchanted campaigners still call the Environmental Movement is being held together by the sheer power of hope, and that somehow if a critical mass of people banging on the machine's unyielding carapace bang hard enough it will shatter, a burning light of reason will shine out and the great institutions of power will turn into petals that drift on the breeze of our desires. Hope is dead. Symbolism is dead. Get used to it.

The windows of shopping malls crash down as another carefully aimed Black Bloc boot finds its mark against capitalist greed; an airport's expansion is halted as a portion of land is broken into a mosaic of tiny holdings each claimed by a different person; a new road is rerouted and scaled down because a group of tree-sitters and tunnelers made it too expensive to justify the original plan. The time for public, direct action may still be with us, but it is gradually becoming as symbolic as the marches and the rallies that our Leaders so enjoy watching us waste our time and energy organizing and participating in. Direct action, as we currently understand it, may eschew banging on a great symbolic shell, but in turn it barely scratches the surface as the machine moves to dominate another million people every week in its hunger to swallow up the last vestiges of uncivilized, industry-free humanity.[40] Traditional direct action is perhaps no more than a distraction — it has its place, particularly in local, rapidly changing situations where a cessation of something deeply immoral may buy sufficient time for something more permanent to be undertaken. As a means to an end, though, it is not the answer.

Time and energy are great levelers when it comes to deciding the priorities of your actions. As we spend more time, and personal energy, striving to earn money to support a lifestyle far removed from our indigenous lives, we find we have less of it to spend on the things that *really* matter. The simplicity of a connected life is an oxymoron to those who take all their cues from the industrial system: wake up, get dressed, eat, go to work, work, eat, work, go home, eat, watch television, go to bed. That's the stuff of a simple life, isn't it? Simple in form, but immensely complex if you take a second to look at what makes that daily routine possible. Take apart an old computer and trace the origins of each component from raw material to usable item; consider the infrastructure required to research, manufacture, transport, sell, power and dispose of that computer; take in the immensity of everything else you use in your "simple" daily life.

Don't relax — keep those images at the front of your mind.

We are taught not to consider the whole but merely to fulfill our places within that whole; cut off the rest and be content with our lot. The Connected life is a simple life in comparison to the absurd complexities required to present the evening viewers with their soap opera or bring even the most basic foodstuff to the tables of city dwellers. The connected life is a straight line to the tangled web of our daily school, work or "leisure" lives. That last comparison is vital — leisure in its proper sense is what you experience outside of the necessary tasks required to survive. Outside periods of food stress — something that is becoming more common in the industrial world with each passing season — non-civilized cultures have (or had) abundant leisure time in which to commune with each other and the environment that provides for them. Leisure in civilized terms is a manufactured experience, almost always involving the transfer of money and frequently requiring compromise among those being foisted into whichever activity they have been allocated to.

The problem is, when it comes to trying to change things for the better, our priorities have been screwed up by the system we have been brought up in. Back in Chapter 2 we considered the amount of time, to which we have to add energy, we have lost to the civilized way of being, and this reflects heavily on what we think we are capable of getting done. It's quick and easy to sign a petition to save the rhino or light a candle in the name of peace; and that's often all we think we have the time and energy to do. When you consider how incredibly trivial most of the things we carry out during our daily lives are, then it has to bring us up short. Otherwise what chance do we have of getting out of this mess?

External Risk

A major sticking point for many people in promoting and undergoing tasks designed to undermine the industrial system, something that could fairly be described as "sabotage," is whether these tasks could be harmful to others. A conversation I had with a broadcaster from the USA highlighted this. "One other thing I disagree with is the 'Sabotage' part, which seems to risk the possibility of needlessly hurting people: '[W]ill anyone die or be seriously harmed as a direct result of what you do, and are you prepared to take on the responsibility for the harm you may cause?' I advocate non-violence."

As do I.

We need to get this out into the open, now. "Violence" is a heavily loaded term, often used by the mass media and frequently used by politicians in order to turn people away from any positive actions people may be using that "violence" in support of. Of course I don't support acts that intentionally seek to harm people or other living things in their undertaking.[41] Nor do I support acts that even indirectly cause harm to others. The only situations in which such acts would be acceptable in my, and I would imagine your, eyes is in the defense of yourself and others, or survival. On the other hand, the "violence" that is condemned by the mouthpieces of the industrial system is rarely violence at all. This is a shining example of our language being stolen from us for the benefit of Industrial Civilization, and especially those who control the Dominant Culture. Smashing a window is not violence unless someone gets harmed in the process; cutting a cable is not violence unless someone gets harmed in the process; barricading the entrance to a factory is not violence unless someone gets harmed in the process.

- Hitting someone in the face with a riot shield is violence.
- Keeping someone incarcerated in solitary confinement is violence.
- Forcing pigs into farrowing cages to give birth is violence.
- Clear-cutting a swathe of forest is violence.
- Pouring sewage sludge into a living river is violence.

I do not advocate violence; nor do I need to because undermining rarely, if ever, leads to the harming of living things or, for that matter, anything that is genuinely representative of real humanity. Undermining targets the Tools of Disconnection. Undermining brings down the causes of violence and oppression. Undermining is not only a necessity in these horrific times but a *moral good.*

But there are always going to be objections. One of the most intractable objections is to the eventual aim of the undermining process: the dismantling of Industrial Civilization. Back in Chapter 3, I gave two clear reasons why this is not contradictory to, but in fact entirely compatible with, the perfectly reasonable desire to continue the human race. Of course there will be those who scoff over the claims of apocalyptic thinkers, suggesting instead that we have nothing to fear from climate change, the continued pollution and despoilment of the global ecosystem, the spread of endemic disease, the collapse of the global food supply, and the twin specters of peak oil and peak water.

Even if we do have something to fear from these things, the application of technology will save the day, apparently. And if you believe that technology will save the day, then of course it *will* save the day in your eyes rather than fail to do anything except make us believe everything is going to be all right. (Interestingly this is almost exactly the argument for the existence of God and why nothing that goes wrong is ever God's fault.) Furthermore, if you believe that technology is a universal good, which logically follows from believing technology will save the day, then you will be more than happy with the subversion of human beings into industrial slaves, an irradiated Earth outside of the survival domes we have created for the lucky few future city dwellers, and a meal consisting of genetically modified everything.

But for the rest of us, those who are taking notice of what's going on in the outside world, what I have said time and time again continues to apply — the system will collapse under the weight of its own abuses, and when it does collapse it will be a human tragedy of unimaginable proportions.

Undermining the industrial system may seem extreme, but it is *simply hastening the inevitable* while also reducing the time the machine has to carry out its ecocide *and also giving us an element of control over the form of the collapse.* And let's be honest, do we really have anything to fear from the switching off of the corporate-controlled television system or the complete loss of faith in so-called "democratic" systems of government? Do we really have anything to fear from the industrial grain giants being unable to build a brave new energy future around biofuels or for the advertising industry becoming incapable of selling us new versions of things we never needed in the first place? Do we really have anything to fear from the recreation of genuine human communities and the collapse of the profit-motivated global banking industry?

The movers and shakers in the industrial system have everything to fear from these things. We the people have everything to gain. *Undermining is not about initiating mass murder; it is about saving lives on a grand scale.*

A second objection is that the individual acts of undermining may have repercussions that are not within your control to prevent once the act has begun. To give one hypothetical example, a group of people may think it is a reasonable act of undermining to shut down a nuclear power station and thus prevent the many Tools of Disconnection dependent on the power grid from functioning. Putting aside for the moment the possible harm that may result from suddenly shutting off the power (admittedly hugely overstated by politicians in particular; after all how many hospitals don't have back-up power? And how likely are road deaths really in the event of a mass traffic-light failure?), there is the huge issue of how to control a nuclear reactor from overheating as a result of the loss of cooling systems. We might like to crow about the folly of having a source of electricity that is a cause of death and illness if not shut down properly and then kept under constant expert supervision, but that does not absolve those responsible for the uncontrolled shutdown from the potential harm this may cause.

As far as I can see, the uncontrolled shutting down of a nuclear power station is not justifiable, given the risk to others. Furthermore it could be considered as much a symbolic act as sitting on an airport runway. Symbolic or not, *the risk to others far outweighs the possible end benefits.*

But there are occasions when some kind of harm may be justifiable, albeit posing a moral question that no one but the Underminer can answer. Let's say a chemical plant, representative of thousands of other chemical plants around the world, springs a leak, causing damage to the surrounding local environment, and only the quick-thinking actions of a passerby prevent the damage from becoming worse. The small amount of damage turns out to be reminiscent of Agent Orange on the jungles of North Vietnam in microcosm, yet the chemical company has said the production process is safe. The domino effect is a downturn in the public's confidence in the industrial chemical production system: people don't want these things near their homes, yet the plants cannot operate without being within reach of a source of workers and the expensive infrastructure associated with populated areas. Everything starts to be questioned from the bottom up, and somewhere in infospace the question Why do we need this? is posed. The question becomes a meme. The meme becomes a turning point.

No matter that the "passerby" happens to be in league with the person who caused the leak in the first place; a genuine feat of undermining has been achieved. But what is the damage? Are the initial defoliation and associated toxic effects justified by the outcome; and what if the outcome was not so successful?

The fact is no one can accurately predict the outcome of any action, which means that a different way of moral thinking is required for undermining. Even if the intention is to do good, and even if the likely outcome is a net positive, and even if the actual outcome is greatly positive, does that justify the harm that may have been caused by the undermining? No amount of quantitative analysis can deal with such a question — in some ways it is morally repugnant to try and make a judgment of harm vs. harm that echoes the executors of carpet bombings in World War Two or the missile strikes of recent Middle Eastern imperial aggression in trying to justify "acceptable losses." Morality is not mathematics.

The ultimate judgment should actually be a question of Karma. In other words, Are you, the Underminer, prepared to take full responsibility for the outcome of your actions?

If you are not prepared to do so, then you have no right to carry through any such action. This does not, of course, remove the very serious need to carry out some form of risk analysis in advance of an undermining action, but here's the kicker: the nature of undermining is such that it is most likely not going to cause any actual harm to another person or to the wider environment in which it is carried out. This has to be a battle in which the only real victim is the system itself.

Personal Risk

That said, there is potentially one other type of victim in undermining, and that is the Underminer. Going back to the discussion I had with my broadcaster friend, the other main question raised was, "If Industrial Civilization is murderously protective of itself, as you suggest, which I don't necessarily deny, how do you remain alive and free when you imply that if anyone dies as a result of taking your suggestions, that's *okay*, as long as the risk has been calculated? In other words, how do you get away with writing this stuff?"

A good question, though one that does not necessarily follow from what I have written in the past. In my writing, there are two things I have been very keen to emphasize in relation to personal risk:

1) Concentrate on the Tools of Disconnection.
2) Don't get caught.

The first point has already been covered in some detail, but the focus here is that by concentrating on the Tools of Disconnection you are not doing anything the system recognizes as a clear and present threat; therefore you are considerably less likely to be a victim of violence or oppression if you steer clear of the kinds of direct action tactics I mentioned earlier in this chapter. Less likely *for now*, that is.

That last proviso is critical, because at some point the industrial system will recognize that undermining is a threat to its very existence and begin to resist in all the ways we have become used to. Look at the range of punishments meted out to people the system claims are terrorists and you get an idea of what can happen when the Culture of Maximum Harm decides to defend itself. Common sense thus dictates that you follow all of the normal steps any Enemy of the State would take to ensure their continued safety — and here is where "Don't get caught" comes into play. I outlined a few of these steps in the previous chapter when discussing Housekeeping in particular, and I will go into some detail about the mechanics of specific types of undermining — including some of the ways personal risk can be reduced — in Part Two. But it is important to say that you must always be aware of how much risk you are exposing yourself to at each phase in the undermining process and try and minimize that level of risk. In particular you should make sure you really know what you are doing and rehearse each discrete task in as realistic a setting as possible. Knowledge and practice are vital factors in reducing personal risk.

In addition, where specific risk areas can be identified, list each one and compare it to how much you are really prepared to sacrifice in the pursuit of your goal. Some risks, such as being physically injured, will be less of a problem to some people, whereas attaining permanent psychological harm — admittedly far more likely when worrying about our precarious state rather than the positive effects of actually doing something about it — is likely to be a risk too far for most of us.[42] Incarceration for some people may just be part of the game, whereas for others a loss of liberty, for however short a time, may be something you are not prepared to bear. There is a great deal of personal preference involved in calculating acceptable levels of risk. In short, if it *feels* too risky then you are probably not ready (or perhaps not keen enough) to undertake the particular task you have in mind.

But here it takes an interesting turn, because when it comes to the question of *reducing* the level of personal risk in an action, it turns out there are two entirely different paradigms, one of which seems inherently reckless, but neither of which is necessarily wrong.

Anonymity

Undermining in secret is often the only way to achieve the desired outcome, especially at the early stages in the process; but true secrecy — as opposed to simply not letting on what you, or your group, are doing — is impossible without anonymity. You may think you can get away without your activities being tracked and your communications being traced, but as an individual you have an identity, something that is intrinsically tied to what you do. What your identity does can be connected to what you do, potentially exposing your person to danger.[43] If you can protect your identity, then you have a far better chance of being able to conduct your activities without exposure — at least until you decide to expose the undermining yourself.

But there is a proviso, and that lies in the complex and usually poorly understood nature of anonymity itself. The concept of anonymity is much like randomness: easy in theory but in reality it can only approximate. Thus, when attempting to create change while at the same time remaining protected from detection, the blanket of "anonymity" is often no more than gauze or, at best, a threadbare coverlet.

The wide distribution of like-minded people across the Internet means that centralized facilities, such as chat rooms and forums, can be useful rallying points for the general discussion of ideas and the planning of activities. However, the need to be available to a global audience also makes one vulnerable to interlopers who may appear genuine (they are trained, after all, and may even have been activists themselves) but are not as they seem, even to the experienced user. True, the complexity and segregation of the global Internet — if that is the primary means of your undermining —

makes it difficult for any one authority to track activity it considers to be threatening; add to this the ability to apply powerful encryption algorithms and route data across multiple pathways, and it becomes possible for any two parties to communicate in relative secrecy. On a superficial level at least, any eavesdropper or data interrogator will struggle to attain useful information on either party due to their lack of identity. Combined with traffic encryption and distributed routing, the Anonymous moniker provides something akin to the dead letter box of Cold War street corners. It is not foolproof, but it helps. However, if you are careless with personal information of any sort, no amount of technological privacy will prevent your electronic self being linked to your real self.

Even if you are not explicitly using the Internet for organizing or carrying out undermining, that doesn't mean your activities are not being broadcast in such a way — mobile phone messages, physical visits to places, financial transactions and so many other things are all recorded and potentially available to whichever authorities are granted this privilege. It pays to understand Internet anonymity because it reflects a lot more than just the technology involved.

Anonymity is not just a protective mechanism, though. In 2008 a concerted campaign, which continues as I write in 2011, began to target the pseudo-religious Scientology organization. Known as "Project Chanology" — a name deriving from the 4chan website on which much of the planning took place — this campaign managed to expose the activities, materials and the people involved in Scientology to a remarkable degree, especially considering the influence that Scientology purported to have over everything it touched.[44] The people responsible cast themselves as Anonymous, producing videos and written statements that emphasized the nature of this many-headed yet headless entity. The sign-off evolved into something of a catch phrase that at once was sinister yet comforting to those who shared their views both in opposition to Scientology and in favor of power given to the ordinary person by virtue of collective anonymity:

- We are Anonymous.
- We are Legion.
- We do not forgive.
- We do not forget.
- Expect us.

More recently, Anonymous has acted as a trigger point for — and sometimes the main instigators of — actions relating to freedom of information ("Operation Payback" is one example) and rebellion against totalitarian regimes, not just those in the Middle East and North Africa but regimes that manifest themselves as corporate power against ordinary people. Some aspects of the Anonymous "brand" have been purposely manipulated for personal gain, such is the cultural aura that attaches itself to anything that the system does not understand, but within Anonymous itself ego and self-gratification are left at the gate: there is no authority, there are no leaders.

Why Anonymous Works

BY THE HIVEMIND

If you were to start answering the question, "Why Anonymous Works?" You need to ask a psychologist how a person's mind works and then a sociologist how a counter-culture works, and then think about how the Internet changes some things we think about in terms of both how a person's mind works and how the Internet is a society by itself. The Internet creates this awesome veil of anonymity. Anonymity plus a big group of people equals invincibility.

The Internet existed long before Anonymous, and no super-consciousness has sprung from any Usenet group, Yahoo! mailing list or Internet forum before now. Something was added in the case of Anonymous that took it beyond whatever limitations lie in other online communities. Personally, I believe it to be the anonymity. If you don't know who someone is, you have no preconceptions as to how they will perform; you don't know of or have any negative impressions of them that would lead you to believe that they may not meet your standards. Additionally, with no identity there is no credit, no glory, no ego. All that matters is accomplishing the goal, and the payoff that comes with that accomplishment. When who came up with an idea no longer matters, the idea itself is much more easily considered, scrutinized, improved upon, acted upon or discarded, and it's this mechanic that allows Anonymous to react so quickly to change. It works because we have the ability to communicate in real time, from the street, or online in fora addressing our interests. It works because my interest isn't necessarily your interest, but our interests may intersect somewhere and when that happens, we can play nice with each other. It works because we're all the same. There is no "Elite Anonymous" except in the imaginations of Scientology and the few deluded who think they speak for the hive. It works because our decentralized nature offers few targets.

Anonymous is comprised of a vast spectrum of interdisciplinary skills and talents. This is the Legion part and it is multi-disciplinary. For example, there are Anons currently re-composing shredded documents from the Egyptian Secret Police archives. Some Anons may be older than a number that will be younger. There are other Anons designing and printing posters, fliers and handouts for the latest protests and demonstrations outside $cientology Org$; outside Capital Buildings; in the streets of Paris, Tripoli, San Francisco, Cairo, Toronto, Vancouver and Tehran. These are Legion too, and the same demographic applies.

And there are the Legion of Photoshop, Illustrator, Photography & Graphics artisans, and dynamic media artisans — animators, videographers and editors; sound engineers, music composers and performers; actresses and actors; makeup artists and costume designers. It goes on and on and on and the demographic scales are wide. There are many different types and kinds of digital technology talents. These too are Legion and also have a very wide demographic scale. Hardware experts, programmers, application designers, electronic engineers, audio engineers, video engineers — many of these individuals have digested all the massive.tomes on Internet Protocols to a degree where many of them can quote chapter and verse from any of them, any time. I know and have known many such specialists; they have memorized a stack of books taller than you, and taller than me. Their knowledge is deep, intimate and always expanding.

In the early 1990s, it was projected that online usage would expand exponentially, and so it has, to the point that kids with only recent experience of the Internet think they can lecture us about it. I think understanding their language demonstrates the depth of their perspective.

For example, the term "butthurt." See, it used to be that discussing politics and religion was taboo in social situations. Why? Because some asshole would become butthurt when you suggest a view they disagree with, and they'd threaten you with a beating. So back when most socializing was done in bars, nobody talked politics or religion. But with the Internet, the butthurt have lost all power. Now they can be mocked mercilessly and in anonymity. Now ideas must stand on merit, not fists. Now you're free to say God's a myth, or that Bush is an idiot, or that Tom Cruise is the greatest actor of all time. And as a result, this entire culture has come to realize that being butthurt is a BAD thing. That if you have to threaten others or storm out, you probably have the weak position. A "lulzcow" is someone that's butthurt, fails to realize how powerless a position that is, and just keeps ranting and allowing themselves to be teased. The Internet — and the trolls[45] in particular — have led this revolution whereby the butthurt have lost power. This is very, very significant in terms of human civilization, and few realize it yet. There are entire governments built on butthurt that are now at risk of collapsing. Bush's fear-mongering was butthurt. Iran's leadership is butthurt. Scientology's leadership is butthurt. You get the idea.

Or the idea of "'ulz." To goons,[46], "lulz" is just a bastardization of "lol." But it has a much richer meaning than this. From the perspective of existential philosophy, life has no meaning and no purpose. This fills people with "existential angst." That's the fear people have of living pointless lives. It drives people to adopt false beliefs — just so long as the beliefs provide us with (fictional, objective) purpose or meaning. And in a meaningless, pointless life, we are radically free to do anything — even to kill ourselves. But we're also free NOT to kill ourselves. We're free to enjoy ourselves. So "lulz" is the opposite of "angst." It's the subjective joy we find in our meaningless and purposeless lives. And a community that embraces lulz is a truly existential culture. Pursuing lulz involves working to create the world we wish to live in.

"Not your personal army" is an important phrase, and emphasizes the independence of channers. Each is responsible for their own actions. Nobody else's actions reflect upon you, and yours reflect only upon yourself. Nonetheless, complex, organized, leaderless action can be implemented and achieve great things. This illustrates that Anonymous is aware of the "obedience to authority" effect explored in Milgram's work, as well as Ashe's work in conformity. We are all independent.

Obviously, real-time or very close to it communication just didn't exist before Anonymous because if it had then certainly with such a simple formula of common ground plus Internet access one of the thousands and thousands of communities would have spawned such an entity as Anon outside the chans.

The term "hivemind" is used when multiple people make the same response at the same time, not because of some prior agreement on any issue, or because of some super-fast communicative powers of the Internet, but because they think the same way. Anonymous works when enough people who think the same way all work on one project at the same time. Not because one person proposes an idea and they agree or are swayed, but because it would be what they would all be doing anyways as individuals. It's not the real-time communication that gives such a group incredible speed and efficiency, it's the lack of communication required to accomplish whatever goal is set. This also explains how the hivemind can function without any central leadership or hierarchy: with no need for constant communication to check with the others in the group if something is acceptable, you don't need any form of administration to settle disputes. Should any dispute rise in a hivemind, the two (or more) opposing sides split off from each other, as variations in thought processes become more evident. I'm not saying that these splits are peaceful, easy or simple, the birth of 7chan, the purge of the channers from Chanology, the endless arguments over loli that used to be rampant, all are examples of the hivemind fracturing and variations becoming clear enough to cause a split. However, no amount of splits ever really impacts the efficiency of the process, and because there are usually clear definitions as to what sides exist in the split, it's able to be processed by the community as a whole at a much more rapid pace. There's no attempt at reconciliation or compromise, there's a declaration of where you stand on the topic, assessment of how many may agree with you, and then action.

In my experience, the ideas that move forward in Anonymous always spring forth from a small subsection of minds (some in communication before the idea is released, some not) and then spread. It is impossible to tell, however, which ideas in your own mind are ones that will take off. We all have lots of ideas: passionate beliefs, jokes, artistic endeavors, wild fetishes, directed and undirected rage. Many times an Anon will share these ideas with the rest of the hive in some fashion, be it [via] a message board, IRC channel, or forum. Most of these will fall flat, never to be heard from again, but a select few rise to the top. When a thought of an individual does fail, it is not a failure of Anonymous; [it] was never an idea Anonymous had. When something an individual Anon puts forward is embraced by the hive and catapulted to success, it is not the success of the initial thinker. That was an idea Anonymous had, it just happened to start in that one person's corner. The idea of "taking credit" for the success of an Anonymous initiative is as nonsensical as one neuron in your brain taking credit for a correct answer on a test.

Which brings us to another strength of Anonymous: Anonymous does not fail. Individual Anons fail, all the goddamn time. Individual Anons lose their jobs, lose their girlfriends, go to jail, have chronic health conditions, commit suicide, and quit. Anonymous does none of these things. Individual Anons do not win when they take part in Anonymous. If Anonymous did not succeed at an action, it's not because Anonymous somehow failed. The action clearly was not the will of the hivemind, and the people who undertook it were just confused, pretending to be something that they weren't. Even if they worked with Anonymous before that action, even if they worked with Anonymous after that action. The only things that count are the things that succeed.

When deciding to join the ranks of Anonymous, you make a conscious and firm decision that it is not about who you are, what you want, it's about what Anonymous is. And, in removing that, you consider things as a unit. When there is a discussion going on, I'm not thinking about how I personally feel, I'm thinking, "Does this represent Anonymous?" and "Would Anonymous do this?" Anonymous really is the first global iteration of "We the people." And the people is getting fed up.

Hive mind bees do it because it's all they know. No free thought or expression, just instinctively following scents and responding with behaviours. Anons are not like bees. If one Anon doesn't like the way the "hive" is going, they'll drift off and do their own thing.

Also, bees don't do it for teh lulz.[47]

Openness

I am lucky, in the place where I live, to have certain freedoms that are not granted to people in other places, such as the right to author books and articles that in some countries would be punishable by imprisonment at the very least. But if I'm being honest I am surprised not to have been "spoken to" by now. Articles that have appeared on The Unsuitablog have, I know, been considered a threat by corporations and political institutions alike, but one tactic I have turned to has been that of publishing any correspondence between me and my less-than-ethical target. The fact that I make a point of publishing emails has probably worked in my favor, given that I have never once received even a solicitor's letter demanding I take down or alter an article.

John Young, architect and author of the website Cryptome, has received a number of complaints and personal visits from the FBI during his long years of making public the kind of information many members of the industrial system would rather remain private. He documented one such visit in November 2003 on the pages of Cryptome:

> Cryptome received a visit today from FBI Special Agents Todd Renner and Christopher Kelly from the FBI Counterterrorism Office in New York, 26 Federal Plaza, telephone (212) 384-1000. Both agents presented official ID and business cards.
>
> SA Renner said that a person had reported Cryptome as a source of information that could be used to harm the United States. He said [the] Cryptome website had been examined and nothing on the site was illegal but information there might be used for harmful purposes.
>
> SA Renner said there is no investigation of Cryptome, that the purpose of the visit was to ask Cryptome to report to the FBI any information which Cryptome "had a gut feeling" could be a threat to the nation.
>
> There was a discussion of the purpose of Cryptome, freedom of information, the need for more public information on threats to the nation and what citizens can do to protect themselves, the need for more public information about how the FBI functions in the field and the intention of visits like the one today.
>
> SA Kelly said such visits are increasingly common as the FBI works to improve the reporting of information about threats to the US.

> Asked what will happen as a result of the visit. SA Renner said he will write a report of the visit.
>
> Cryptome said it will publish a report of the visit, including naming the agents. Both agents expressed concern about their names being published for that might lead to a threat against them and/or their families — one saying that due to copious personal databases any name can be traced.
>
> Cryptome said the reason for publishing names of agents is so that anyone can verify that a contact has been made, and that more public information is needed on how FBI agents function and who they are.
>
> Cryptome noted that on a previous occasion FBI agents had protested publication of their names by Cryptome.
>
> Cryptome did not agree to report anything to the FBI that is not available on the website.[48]

Notice the unremitting, almost blasé level of openness in the report: the address and telephone number of the FBI office, the names of the FBI officers, the words used — undoubtedly recorded openly during the visit — including the reservations that the officers had of their names being published, despite them visiting a private residence without a warrant. This level of openness yields no quarter. If a person is completely dedicated to the practice and dissemination of open information, whether that of the system in general or of themselves, then they must not start making deals or promises of "just some privacy." Everyone involved has to be clear that this is how it works, and by moving into a space marked "Openness" all of their activities will be scrutinized in public.

The success of the Cryptome approach — John is still very active in the field of freedom of information — is partly made possible by the popularity of the website. With upwards of 100,000 unique visitors a day it is not going to fall out of the public domain without considerable noise. It follows that anything placed on the Cryptome site will have been rapidly read (and reposted) by enough people to make any attempt at removal or corruption appear to be an attempt to suppress information. Such openness isn't restricted to very popular websites. The average mainstream journalist might not last long in his job once he starts getting visits from the security services, but widely read and respected people such as John Pilger and Johann Hari are high profile enough to get away with authoring stories that would be edited to oblivion were they the work of lesser journalistic hands. But even high-profile journalists have to seek out sympathetic publications such as *The Independent* and *The Nation* due to the incestuous nature of the mass media and its umbilical ties to the industrial system; and tragic endings have befallen the most respected writers, such as Lasantha Wickrematunge (killed in Sri Lanka in 2009) and Uğur Mumcu (killed in Turkey in 1993), who crossed the line too many times in the eyes of the institutions they were considered a threat to.

Nevertheless, as I have made clear, the indirect and non-confrontational nature of undermining provides a level of protection not afforded to traditional direct action, and openness can be a useful additional protection if you have effective safeguards in place. Even a blog that has just a few loyal readers may be sufficient protection for the author to promote her activities and, possibly more important, record her state of mind and body, such that efforts to suppress the activities would be exposed — perhaps in the absence of posts, perhaps in the use of "safe words" that only certain readers know of. This safety device can be extended to sending regular text messages, emails, letters, even making chalk marks on walls or drawing blinds at certain times of the day. This might sound dramatic, but for some people these little extra measures can be just enough to give an Underminer peace of mind.

The Air Gap

Anonymity and Openness are often personal choices in conducting your operations, but for some people, particularly those operating in conditions where exposure could be a matter of life or death (think free-speech advocates in current-day Burma or anti-corporate activists in Pinochet-era Chile, for example) then the decision whether to remain open or anonymous may be a case of doing it one way or not at all. As I have said, the practice of undermining may well become something that occupies a similar space in the so-called "Free West" and other industrialized regimes that give the impression of being free, so long as you continue being a good consumer, worker, student, citizen….

This means that your own liberty may well depend upon other people, and in particular the way that they interact with you. It would do no good at all if you were undertaking a complex team operation under the protection of anonymity, only to find your anonymity exposed by the very people you entrusted to keep schtum about your actions.

We are not talking about trustworthiness — although that is a critical factor in working as part of a team, and worth researching in some depth[49] —

but rather a lack of operational integrity. In the finance industry the activities of two potentially contradictory operations (such as a company working for rival clients) are kept separate by a protocol known as Chinese Walls. In computer terms the separation is best understood in the context of a firewall or, more precisely, an air gap. They are not quite the same thing: a standard firewall will let some traffic move between networks, whereas an air gap provides a complete break between two discrete networks, much as Chinese Walls are meant to provide, though sometimes don't due to carelessness or corruption. In the case of undermining, the air gap must be maintained between the Underminers and everyone else.

As a relatively high-profile activist, I don't believe it is possible for me to carry out more than a few low-key undermining activities under the mask of anonymity, so openness is likely to be my "protection" of choice; writing this book is akin to spraying myself gold and shouting "Arrest the shiny man!" but that's the way I do things. Yet just because I choose this modus operandi doesn't mean I have any right to force it on others. From time to time people contact me about activism and offer to tell me things I would rather not know. It may be just a suggestion as to what they are planning to do, but it's far too easy to match text from emails to personal names and personal names to locations and so on, to the extent that I have to politely ask them not to tell me anything and, very rarely, not to contact me again for their own safety. It goes without saying that I also securely delete anything they have sent me. Others may not be so careful.

It is very tempting when armed with a bit of privileged information to tell someone else about it; human nature provides the hearth on which the fire of self-aggrandizement burns. Surely just telling my best friend or the nice lady in the shop I've spoken to every day for the past three years can't do any harm — just to get it off my chest and, if we're being honest, to appear a bit more important and interesting for a while.

Resist the urge.

That information may have come to you second or third hand, but it is not yours to pass on. We have to start getting the idea that certain things should be kept separate, and if undermining grows as quickly as it needs to in these desperate times, then we have to get the idea pretty damn quick!

Leaving the Cave

A few years ago I operated in the same bubble that was filled with the people I looked up to — those authors, journalists and bloggers who seemed at the time to hold the answers to questions I hadn't even asked yet. They had the answers, so I thought they must also be asking all the right questions. But no one asked the question, How can we rid the world of Industrial Civilization? Had I seen that question in print all that time ago, I might have thought of Timothy McVeigh, al-Qaeda or Shining Path: perpetrators of the seemingly unthinkable, and nothing I would dare associate myself with.

Now that question seems perfectly rational.

On sunny days in the last few months before we moved to southern Scotland, I would walk the suburban streets of Essex and imagine how it felt for people inside the walls of the houses in the culs-de-sac, blissfully unaware of the loss to come, certain that happiness was a night in front of the television, a trip to the shopping mall or a week on a package holiday. In a peculiar way I envy them; really envy them.

"I wish I didn't know about any of this. I wish I was like everybody else in the world, and tomorrow it would just be over; there wouldn't be any time to be sorry ..." (David Lightman, *War Games*)

But as an Underminer loss is something that has to be accepted — losses of the superficial, the mainstream Culture of Maximum Harm and also a heap of things most of us would rather we could hang onto. It's a bit like one of those moral conundrums that doesn't have a right answer: do you push the fat guy off a bridge to save a group of Boy Scouts, or whoever was foolish enough to wander onto the railway line without looking out for the approaching express train, or do you let the Scouts get squished?

Go back a few pages and you can start to spot a pattern here. We can argue until we are blue in the face as to whether it is morally right to push the fat guy off the bridge and onto the handle that operates the railway switch, in a particularly gruesome rerun of a Lemony Snicket puzzle, so the directionally deficient Scout troop doesn't get turned into bouillon with woggle croutons; but in the end the answer lies much lower down the decision tree. Feel free to set up a fence or to signpost the rail network into mercy; that's the Health and Safety response, and it's also the response of a world where no one learns any lessons except which lines not to cross and which orders to obey.

Shout to them! They might hear you in time, they might not.

Jump off the bridge yourself.

Everything's so last minute isn't it? In a way it has to be: the chaos isn't coming any slower; the oil isn't being put on hold until the next big idea; the methane bubbles from the melting permafrost aren't taking a short holiday while we all think of a way of refreezing the tundra.

The psychology of the Underminer is something different from the way the "experts" tell us human beings should behave in the face of dire circumstances. The fact is, different human cultures deal with challenges and happenings in all sorts of different ways, but the conventional models of human response are based on the civilized world alone.

To be an Underminer is to take back our innate humanity and stop grieving for the loss of what we have to lose as if we are inert bystanders. To be an Underminer is to celebrate what we can do, and what we have to gain from our actions.

> Wildness springs from the freeing of our instincts and desires, from the spontaneous expression of our passions. Each of us has experienced the process of domestication, and this experience can give us the knowledge we need to undermine civilization and transform our lives. Our distrust of our own experience is probably what keeps us from rebelling as freely and actively as we'd like. We're afraid of fucking up, we're afraid of our own ignorance.
>
> In a very general way, we know what we want. We want to live as wild, free beings in a world of wild, free beings. The humiliation of having to follow rules, of having to sell our lives away to buy survival, of seeing our usurped desires transformed into abstractions and images in order to sell us commodities fills us with rage. How long will we put up with this misery?[50]

You cast off the chains, look into the light, walk to the mouth of the cave and RIP THE HEADS OFF THE PUPPETS!

We all need a release every so often.

It's time to move on for, as Goethe so keenly observed, "All theory, dear friend, is gray, but the golden tree of real life springs ever green." Part Two is the guidebook itself, the directions and maps to the legend of Part One. Some of the undermining tasks are risky; some are not. Some of them will take years to achieve; some can be carried out with barely a second thought. It is not an exhaustive guide to everything you can possibly do to undermine the Tools of Disconnection, partly because there is no way that a single piece of work could contain everything of relevance or even be able to keep up with every new and valid idea that would be of use in the undermining effort. More importantly it is not for me or anyone else to tell *you* what you should be doing. What I can offer is a good idea of the kinds of tasks that can make a difference at a level of detail that is enough to get you started as an Underminer, but not so great that it can only be applied to that particular task. It is nice to think we are individuals who have our own favored ways of doing things.

As we go on you will understand the context of these undermining tasks, and start to see how you can develop your own — you may even have your own ideas already. The future needs to be made by imaginative, strong and inquisitive minds. More than that it needs to be made by free minds, and so that is where we will start.

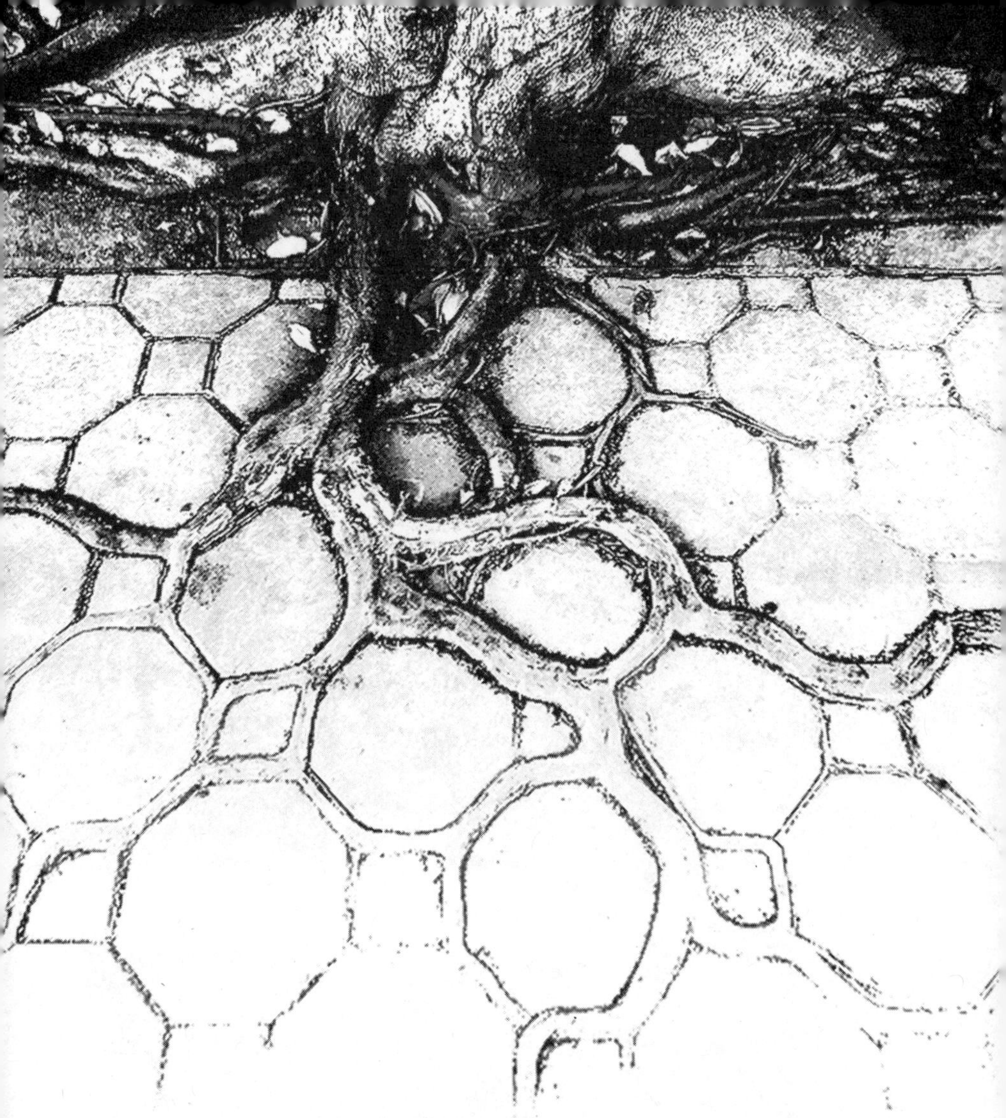

PART TWO

Undermining

And outside, the silent wilderness surrounding this cleared speck on the earth struck me as something great and invincible, like evil or truth, waiting patiently for the passing away of this fantastic invasion.

— Joseph Conrad, Heart of Darkness

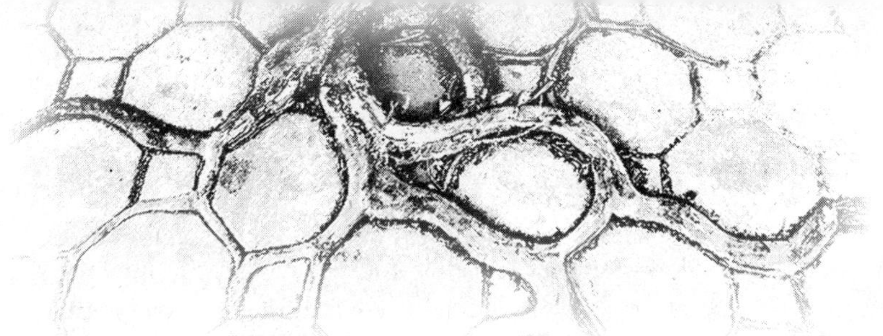

CHAPTER FIVE

Removing the Veil

AT BIRTH WE ARE CONNECTED TO THE REAL WORLD and then, subtly, without our nascent consciousness even being aware of it happening, a veil is slipped over our minds. As we proceed through our lives, layer after layer is wrapped around us to suppress any inquisitiveness we may have. We are enmeshed in lives that leave little room for inquiry and are so set in our ways by the constant forces that have governed our thoughts that we do not seek out truth — we seek out only what the system has taught us are worthy goals: money, material possessions, career progression, synthetic happiness and whatever "dream" our adoptive country is driven to aspire to.

This chapter is about undermining the Veil of Ignorance in its many forms, so that we are able to at least recognize what is going on around us and, even with no further help, allow us and those we care about to make our own decisions. In order to undermine this, the most powerful tool of all, we must first learn what makes it tick.

Back to the Shadows

You have to imagine being at the back of the cave again: sitting shackled upon the bedrock, able only to peer into the gloom at the flickering lights and oh-so-familiar shapes that describe your every external experience and thus create your internal perception of what is real and what is fake. The whisper in your ear says, "This is just a puppet show; the real world is just over your shoulder." The shout in your mind says, "What you see is all that is!" And the shout drowns out the whisper.

There lie the difficulties: it is not enough simply to stop the puppet show that projects the world that the puppeteers need us all to think is the real world. The audience, rapt in their attention-deficit, can continue the show in their minds until it starts up once again, just as the tiger pacing cagewise in a new, larger enclosure still perceives her previous constrictions as all the space there is. This is how the Veil of Ignorance operates: it is both without us and within us. Just as we are the System, we also become the Veil.

You have to be honest here, for although you may feel — possibly in a smug way — that you are not part of that charade, you are still very much living within the confines of a system designed to create wealth for the few, give power to the unworthy and enslave everyone who benefits that system in any way at all. To be fair, it is nearly impossible not to be a slave of the system in some way, even if you just use money from time to time, have a part-time paid job or listen to a mainstream radio station for an hour a day (and wear a watch to signify when that hour has passed). Nevertheless, you are still — to all intents and purposes — shackled in some way at the back of the cave looking, if not straight on, slantwise at the images; if not enraptured by the sounds of the machine, taking some pleasure from their presence; if not completely addicted to, feeling the tug of the smells, tastes and other pleasures that entwine your senses.

Now go back to the exercise and stop feeling superior. This is serious, for this is the most difficult undermining task there is — if you fail here then you won't be helping anyone but the few people who don't even need your help. Sorry to be so harsh: I hate this as much as you do.

There are a few pointers here, but don't mistake me for a guru or a fully fledged escapee. Ignore the next few paragraphs if you already have ideas

Exercise: Your Cave

Put yourself at the back of the cave. You have been shackled there your entire life. Don't just picture yourself, but occupy that body — unable to move except to follow the shadows on the cave wall; unable to feel the physical discomfort of your situation; unable to sense anything other than what you are meant to sense. What would it take for you to realize that the world being presented to you in the form of a puppet show to which there is no alternative reality is not reality at all? What would it take for you to feel confident enough to walk away from the only thing you have ever thought was real?

forming in your head, for they are just my own musings that might interrupt your far more potent thoughts.

> *Refuse to sign up to or pledge allegiance to systems of authority, even when compulsory. Encourage others to do the same and make the most of your refusal in public, thus helping undermine the accepted top-down power relationship in civilized society.*

I am shackled, but how shackled am I? If I really try to move in the physical world then maybe I can turn around, stand up, walk away. The chains that bind my arms, legs and body, the collar around my neck, the head brace that limits where I can see are maybe no more than mental confines I have built for myself, partly as a protection against the painful position I have been in all my life, partly as a result of being conditioned to what is "normal." I think I was shackled at first as a baby and then a toddler I was told where to go, pulled back, corrected, kept within walls of brick and steel, because that's what parents are taught to do — conditioned to do. But the real conditioning came from the institutions my peers and I learned to embrace so early on: television, shops, school, the police, politicians and other authority figures (my superiors). I had freedoms. I could cycle away, climb trees and swim in the sea, and take risks beyond the awareness of my observers, but I always learned to be safe, to return on time, to spend most of my life in the thrall of the institutions that eventually controlled how I thought. As I sat still and correct in the classroom I gained comfort from what I excelled in, and so learned to associate school with reward, not forced compliance. But I always was an oddity, seeing the accepted world as something to challenge — within the confines of my narrow moral sphere. (A police visit was enough to ensure compliance with the legal system very early on.) Eventually we all slipped into a sort of trance, always carried on the shoulders of future promises and necessities: a career, a nice house, a marriage, some children, holidays when work allowed, television at the end of the day, shopping for nice things and guilty treats at the weekend, and maybe a happy retirement and a trip round the world if we were really ambitious. I was bound to stay in the cave; bound by the limits of my experience, and bound by the expectations of the rest of the civilized world. I could walk away if I wanted to, but I didn't want to.

What would it take for me to see the world I occupy for what it is? What would it take for me to lose confidence in the made-up world and embrace the reality denied to me? Many things: first the removal, from birth, of the confines and rules that were there solely to ensure I learned the "right way" to live. Second, shutting off the streamed information that kept me turned away from and unaware of the real world. Third, the idea that compliance is normal and non-compliance is abnormal. Finally, for now, deprogramming my mind in order to shut off the internal dialog of compliance — the virtual cage that I would continue to pace even if I were set free.

This is hard, damn hard! Beyond anything I have tried to scale up to now. And for goodness sake — I have to be time traveler to achieve some of it.

If you skipped that bit to work on your own ideas, then the undermining tasks immediately ahead may not tally your own ideas. I am in no position to judge them; I trust they are worthy of you and an honest reflection of where you feel you are at present. There is the chance, though, that some of the following *will* tally with the problems you have set yourself, so at least play along for a bit. To the four challenges above: freeing up of developmental limitations, shutting off information streams, changing attitudes to compliance and removing the internal cage, we need to add a fifth challenge, that of creating an environment in which important information is freely available, for without information we operate in a vacuum.

When I refer to "task" in the text, I am usually referring to something that is multi-faceted, requiring all sorts of individual undermining actions that will appeal to different people at different times, across a range of risk levels and with varying degrees of difficulty. That's especially the case in this chapter, given the number and range of institutions that need to be undermined in their effectiveness. As with all the actions described, *you should take them only as examples.* I am aware of more that I could include in here, and there are far more that you are bound to think of or come across in your undermining travels. For all of the tasks ahead you must remember the rules in Chapter 4 — they are there for a reason, but I won't reiterate them for time is short and space is shrinking with each word I write.

A Curriculum for Disruption

What we are trying to achieve here is the ability for individual humans to pass through their developmental years without having the Veil of Ignorance placed upon them and within them; more specifically without being subject to the draconian set of rules and ideals that civilized society imposes through the efforts of the various institutions that are "responsible" for childhood development. In non-civilized societies no such institutions exist: the functions of practical and moral education, the setting down of rules (or norms of society to be more accurate) and less serious things such as how free time is spent are just part of the normal process of bringing a child up to become a fully fledged member of that tribe or community. In civilized society there are schools and education offices, religious institutions, all sorts of establishments related to the application of law and statute, and the whole apparatus of retail and entertainment to ensure citizens learn the correct way to enjoy themselves.

At the outset of the undermining process, simply sweeping away these formal institutions is not going to happen; instead they need to be directly countered in some way to, at least initially, soften the blow. This is enormously difficult to achieve at any scale without first having a vast legion of Underminers in place — but in order to have a legion there need to be vast numbers of people who haven't been subjected to the Veil of Ignorance. You see the problem. This problem doesn't seem so difficult when you approach it from two different sides.

Task 1: Challenge the Engines of Compliance

Schools: that's where we need to start, I think. Remember me saying that teachers are some of the most enlightened people in society but the environment and context in which they operate is what causes them to "school" people rather than "educate" them? The distinction is critical if we are to develop a way of undermining this problem. So we need to change the language. It's a subtle thing but potentially has tremendous impact. Think of every place you see or hear the root word "education" (as in "educate," "educational," "educating," etc.) and write down every example you can think of. The vast majority will be found in relation to institutions like schools and colleges, with a sizeable other relating to industry and religion. Very rarely is the word "education" used when referring to what I call Real Education: what has to be done to prepare a person for a specific and vital activity such as gathering, growing or catching food, or caring for another human being.

In the lead up to school assessments (such as SATs), if you or your child goes to school, refuse to take part in coaching lessons or test practices — they are nothing to do with education. Tell parents and students what you are doing: start a rebellion!

Now, I want you to use the correct word(s) in relation to the misuse. For instance

- Department of Education = Department for Schooling
- Physical Education = Forced Exercise
- Religious Education = Religious Indoctrination
- Educator (a.k.a. teacher in a school) = Teacher of Approved Information

Fill a page with similar examples; get it clear in your head what is being challenged here. Try to do the same with two other key root words: "work" and "do" (meaning your job — paid labor in a formal setting a.k.a. wage slavery), substituting all examples where it does not imply some genuinely useful or important task being done. Now we need to put those changes into the public realm, which gives the opportunity to cover all sorts of bases here that will be relevant elsewhere.

One simple but highly effective undermining action is *expressing yourself appropriately in conversation and writing.* The way you talk and write will affect how others think because humans, as we have discovered, are very keen to follow others' leads. Talking in a way contrary to how others talk feels wrong, even offensive: like pronouncing someone's name incorrectly or saying their baby is ugly! But you are not being rude; you are just using words in an uncivilized way (bearing in mind what civilization actually stands for). You will feel the need to follow how others speak, which you must resist — this is about changing your own attitudes as much as those of others. Instead just use what you feel are correct terms in place of the terms that have been imposed upon people. Here's an example:

Friend A: What does your Jack do now?

You: He has ups and downs like everyone but generally has a good life.

Friend A (confused): I don't understand, does he have a job?

You: Yeah, all sorts of jobs: fixing things around the house, cooking occasionally, tidying up, looking after the kids, gardening ...

Friend B: I think she meant "What does he do for money?"

You: Oh, you mean "wage slavery"? (laugh)

Friend A: If you want to call it that, then yes.

You: He's still at the building depot. Nice bunch of people, boring job. He'd love to do something else.

Friend B: There are all sorts of adult education courses out there if he wants to learn something new.

You: He doesn't want to go back to school; we're trying to cut our expenses, so maybe he won't need to do it for long.

Friend B: What about the kids? Is Aaron still in junior school?

You: Yes, but we're making sure he gets a good education as well.

It's a bit stilted, I know, but it illustrates a few points, not least the need to be polite and subtle most of the time. You can always slip in the odd challenging phrase like "wage slavery" or "indoctrination," but be careful — you are trying to encourage people to think about the terms they use, not alienate them. Have a go next time you are involved in a conversation. Try it on a phone-in radio show: be subtle but get your changes across quickly; if you get the host to change her language then you get a bonus point!

In writing it's a lot easier to be deliberately contrary, but in most cases people are writing to make a point rather than just conversing, so the opportunities for influencing how others use words related to indoctrinating institutions are limited. Nevertheless there are various channels through which your words can be read by those who would otherwise accept the popular usage of terms. (Forget blogs or Internet forums, the people who read those are likely to be the people who agree with you already or who are too opinionated to be influenced in such a subtle way.) For example, you can use community newsletters or websites (always on the lookout for contributors); letters, emails and text messages to local newspapers or radio and television shows (text messages especially, are rarely edited so you don't have to be so subtle); and, if you are any position to do so, official documentation such as press releases, brochures, newsletters and promotional materials from "educational" establishments and businesses. Although this is initially just about changing wording to prevent the indoctrination of young people and future and current wage slaves, it will be obvious what potential lies in these and other outlets.

Change the press releases of the company you work for to tell the truth about the product or service it is offering. If releases are sent out by mail, it is a lot easier to be anonymous.

Use radio and television blocking devices to disrupt broadcasts during advertising breaks, public "service" announcements and multi-part TV series (to discourage further watching).

Relabel museum exhibits to reflect the true history of Empire, Colonialism and Exploitation. Also, add "Still to Come" labels to natural history exhibits, with the names of threatened species.

Remove commercial promotional and sponsored materials (such as posters, banners and flyers) from schools.

Another way to correct meaning is through what you might call *Signage Realignment*. We will go into the details of this both practically and legally, in relation to Subvertising, later on, but suppose every instance of the word "School" (the term has lost most of its negative connotations — we tend to treat it in the sense of a protective school of fish rather than a place of enforced learning) on signs, painted on roadways or attached to buildings was replaced with the words "Mind Prison" or simply "Prison." It might just be confusing — albeit funny — if there were a prison nearby, but excepting this, can you imagine a big yellow School Bus instead relabeled "Prison Bus" and every signpost indicating the direction of a school instead indicating the location of the "Mind Prison"?

Now, this might all seem like an attack on the people who I have lent considerable (and some might say unwarranted) support to, but remember it is not the teachers we are attacking so much as the institutions themselves. In fact *teachers are potentially some of the most powerful Underminers of all,* being in a position of influence right near the beginning of the human indoctrination process. It would be tempting to implore all teachers who aspire to be genuine educators to leave their place of indoctrination, but remember: this chapter is just the start of the undermining process. The Students of State-Approved Learning are not going to be leaving in droves (yet), and neither is there going to be a dearth of willing indoctrinators. In fact the leaders of the school system will be delighted to see the backs of those most likely to rebel, to be replaced by inspiration-free Teacherbots. No, at this stage it's the teachers themselves who need to take matters into their own hands.

Hello, teachers! Essentially, you are going to impart as little of the system-approved information as you can possibly get away with while getting across a great wad of real-life factual information, at the same time inspiring your new students of undermining to become their own people, rather than subjects of an oppressive system. That's a lot to ask, I know. Then again, who better to ask than those people who have a unique gift — within civilized society — for imparting knowledge? Your training may have included a large slice of state-sponsored brainwashing as to the merits of the school system in creating well-rounded individuals, but it also included all sorts of techniques for ensuring you are able to keep the attention of a room full of young people, ideally absorbing everything you convey.[51] Add to this that, as a teacher, you are likely to be something of a role model, and you have a ready-made undermining opportunity. Obviously you need to be careful: at this point, if you are not well versed in the Rules of Undermining, I recommend you go over the relevant sections again. Risk levels vary tremendously depending on the amount by which you deviate from the official curriculum, the subjects you are teaching, the actual information you are aiming to get across and your position both professionally and legally — it's probably not a good idea to be sharing *The Anarchist Cookbook* with third grade children, or anyone else for that matter. That said, there is a hell of a lot you can subtly and not so subtly slip into your lessons (for goodness sake, don't write anything in your lesson plans) to create the first inklings of undermining that will echo in the minds of receptive students.

This is beginning to sound like religious indoctrination, but as the trickster Derren Brown takes every opportunity to point out, I am completely open in my motivations here, and the intention is not to brainwash but to *prevent* brainwashing. As an example, suppose you are a teacher of history in one of many nations whose governments (and increasingly corporations) are keen to ensure that the activities of various groups of people are seen as acceptable, indeed the necessary course to perpetuate the Veil of Ignorance. This has been encapsulated perfectly in Australia with reference to the Stolen Generations — Aboriginal children taken away from their homelands and families, especially during the first half of the 20th century. There are many critical points you could make in the teaching of Australian history[52] that could undermine the civilized view still existing that such actions were justified. For instance, the real nature and motivations behind colonialism (predominantly economic), the religious fear and doctrinal opposition to non-Christian beliefs, a conscious lack of understanding of any culture that isn't the Dominant Culture, a complete disregard for the feelings of those who do not conform to the norms of civilized society, and so on. These are serious points that would have fundamentally challenged the status quo so much that, prior to formal government apologies this century, to teach such concepts could have been a breach of contract, resulting in formal action. All the more reason to do it.

Every subject has its equivalents: science teachers could challenge the idea that technology is neutral or that it is ever acceptable for a school to receive funding from a corporation; food technology/domestic science teachers could challenge the whole concept of processed food, agriculture, food monopolies by supermarkets, and instead extol the virtues of going back to basics; language and mathematics teachers could use all sorts of "inappropriate" scenarios as a basis for learning; geography and social studies teachers could challenge the whole basis of civilization, capitalist ideology and the free market, with particular reference to environmental and cultural destruction; citizenship teachers should probably not teach the subject at all, or at least encourage students to challenge every single aspect being taught — Citizenship is an aberration and one that is in danger of creating a whole generation of disconnected individuals.

Task 2: Commit Small Acts of Rebellion

Young people are natural rebels, and quite a few manage to slip through the net of enforced compliance. Labels are placed on them: delinquent, oppositional, behaviorally challenged — anything to try and put them back into little boxes so they fulfill their civilized potential. Acts of rebellion born of free ideas and liberated thinking should be celebrated, but we punish them.

Take a school uniform. It has two purposes: one of them is to imbue a sense of belonging or, to put it another way, to show that the wearer belongs to the school; the other is to remove any opportunity for unwanted expression. A simple way of subverting this is simply by *refusing to wear the uniform*, thus removing the sense of being owned, and providing an opportunity for self-expression. Of course, schools being what they are, this is an offense punishable by detention, suspension and possibly even expulsion. And for what? Refusing to conform to a sartorial ideal that exists only to oppress young people into a standardized way of thinking and behaving.

This has gone to court on numerous occasions, one such case in the US concluding that "*parents' rights to control their children's upbringing, including their education, cannot override school rules* that are considered 'reasonable' to maintain an appropriate educational [sic] environment."[53] In other words, the school system is more powerful than any parent or student. This on its own is a reason to rebel. But, if you're not feeling so brave, or you are comfortable in uniform but rebelling in other ways (sometimes it's smart to stay undercover), then as a student why not see how far you can push the policy without breaking it, and encourage your friends to do the same in the name of creative and personal freedom. It's a very liberating thing, breaking rules.

Playground chants are as old as playgrounds, and they have a long and fascinating history of subversion. Here's one I remember from my mind prison: "We break up. We break up. We don't care if the school blows up. No more English, no more French, no more sitting on the old school bench."

I haven't recited that for 30 years, probably, but it came back to me as easily as breathing, such is the power of a good chant. Roger Waters of Pink Floyd knew all about that when he slipped an ironic double negative into "Another Brick in The Wall." Can you think of any good chants? A friend of mine told me of one that I hadn't heard before that's a bit gross, but all the better for being something children will love reciting: "Yum yum bubble gum. Stick it up a policeman's bum. When it's brown pull it down. Yum yum bubble gum."

Whatever age you are, you can start a chant and see how far it gets. It works especially well when sung to the tune of whatever is popular at the time — more memorable, you see. And if you do find your little darling coming home with a letter complaining that they have been saying "bad" things in the classroom/playground/corridor, etc. then you can feel a glow of pride that they, and possibly their friends, have moved a little closer to freedom.

Task 3: Create Resilient Individuals

Even a concerted undermining effort by every teacher who currently feels the need for change isn't going to create a rapid sea change in attitudes. These things take time, time that we haven't really got if we want to ensure that another generation isn't lost to the Machine. If you remember, the power of undermining lies in the feedback effects that can be generated by its application in the right places at the right times; in the case of trying to cast off the Veil of Ignorance, if young people aren't equipped with the ability to counter brainwashing, then any rebellion is likely to fizzle out before it starts. Therefore, the second element needed alongside direct challenges to brainwashing has to be resilience.

If you have ever been caught in a terrific downpour, you will understand the power of natural forces to change the way you feel. For a few people, being drenched by a sudden shower is an uplifting experience, but for most it is pretty miserable: you feel cold, soggy, drained of energy and desperate to get under cover. A good raincoat and a wide-brimmed hat can do wonders for your outlook on the weather conditions, as can being regularly soaked. Just ask someone who works outdoors in all weathers. Anyone who delivers mail will tell you that after a while the combination of suitable clothing and constant exposure to the elements makes that sudden downpour just a routine thing. In order to face up to the storms of being exposed to the school system and, for good measure, any number of other commercial, political, religious and otherwise doctrinal mind traps, we need to be equipped with the correct protection.

Good parenting is absolutely key to this. You wouldn't send your children walking the streets without the ability to safely cross roads and look out for other hazards, so why would you send your children to school[54] without the ability to process, in an objective and suitably critical manner, the information they are given? One big problem is that as a society we tend to bring children up not to question the words of adults. This is formalized in the legal system, where the evidence of a "minor" is not considered as reliable as that of someone who has passed some arbitrary measure of longevity, and something we tacitly support every time we accuse a child of lying simply for the reason of being a child. The first hurdle to get across therefore, is to *listen* to young people — not just give the impression that you are listening, but actually give them your time and your attention. This will be rewarded many fold, for not only will they listen to you in return, they will also start to feel that they matter. Self-esteem is often bandied about as a pseudo-therapeutic term, but it really is important: people with self-esteem can take things on the chin, and then some. People with self-esteem will challenge what they have been told, especially if they suspect the motives of the person doing the telling. This is the first, and probably most useful part of a person's armory against a system that wants to break down any resistance a person might offer during her formative years.

Another form of mental resilience is to provide *genuinely useful knowledge.* The assumption that schools equip students with all the knowledge they will need for the outside world may be true if that "outside world" is just the world that encompasses offices, factories, supermarkets, home entertainment systems and sports bars; but in the real world we understand with some horror that that is exactly what is lined up for them if we do not do something about it. As John Taylor Gatto writes,

> The products of schooling are ... irrelevant. They can sell film and razor blades, push paper and talk on telephones, or sit mindlessly before a flickering computer terminal, but as human beings they are useless. Useless to others and useless to themselves.[55]

The skills required for real life, the kind of life that can be experienced only when the synthetic trappings of civilization are stripped away, are not the kinds of skills that are taught in schools for the most part. My children adore cooking both at school and at home, this being one of the three critical practical skills that I reckon all people should acquire immediately (the other two are food gathering and growing, and the ability to build simple structures). It is no surprise that the few really useful things taught in schools, such as cookery, needlework and woodwork, are under constant threat from the "need" to teach the kinds of things that will prepare young people for the world of economic slavery. Essentially we need to make sure all children have the really important skills and knowledge from as early an age as possible. If you know how to knit, then teach them how to knit; if you are a dab hand in the kitchen, then show them what you (and they) can do; if you grow vegetables, then get them to help you — give them a patch themselves; if you have long forgotten how to craft a dovetail joint, then have fun making mistakes together. Whatever you do that's of genuine use in the real world, share it. And if you can't do it, then learn how to do it together.

This may not seem like undermining, but with each genuine skill you learn, the other things that the system would like you to prioritize somehow become less important. What's the big deal about knowing a list of US presidents or how to maximize profit? I can build a shed from scrap wood! Being able to put knowledge into perspective is a fantastic thing, especially when someone tells you that you have to do something "because you'll need to know it in later life." As a parent or carer, you can easily become an inspirational Underminer.

For every genuinely useful piece of knowledge that may be imparted at school, or any other outlet that may provide useful information (magazines, documentaries, news broadcasts, information booklets, etc.), there are likely to be dozens, maybe hundreds, of pieces of crap that are either irrelevant or serve to promote the industrial agenda. Finding out what is useful and what is not is vital, not so much as a learning tool but as a way of insulating yourself from rubbish. You may not be an expert in physics or history, but there is no reason why you (as a parent with a child or as a student) can't work to build up certain skills that will be sufficient to identify when bullshitting or brainwashing is taking place. Some schoolteachers are actually encouraging the set of skills known as *Critical Thinking*, possibly to the dismay of the school authorities, and this should be encouraged. In fact children should be taught to think critically as soon as they are able to think. There are lots of guides around as to what critical thinking entails, but in a nutshell it is the *process of taking a piece of supplied information and gleaning the real meaning from it.* So, for instance, if there is an article in a newspaper today (I bet there is) about the state of the economy, you are superficially likely to glean the following information from it:

1) Economic growth is a good thing.
2) Recession or "stagnation" is a bad thing.
3) We need to spend more money to keep the economy growing.
4) It is very important that people have jobs.

And so on.

But there is so much more to take from the report. Look at who wrote the article, what newspaper the article was published in, who was quoted in the article as saying the kinds of things above, who owns the newspaper that contained the article, what logical fallacies the writers and the interviewees used in the article, what assumptions were made about what is "good" and what is "bad," what economic and political motivation might be behind the article being written.

And so on.

Critical thinking, or in this case critical reading, is not an intuitive skill for anyone brought up in the Culture of Maximum Harm. Sitting in the back of the Cave we have all learned not to question what is presented to us. But what if you start to notice inconsistencies creeping into the movement and speech of the shadow puppets? Maybe they take different points of view for no obvious reason, or maybe they treat you like an idiot today when yesterday you were being told how important you are. The basic skills of critical thinking really are fundamental to being able to undermine the information that is meant for our unquestioning consumption. The sooner both you and the people you really care about are able to see through the noise — in effect see through the Veil of Ignorance — the sooner they will be in a position to question, and undermine, what they are being told.

Nature versus nurture is an argument that will rage for as long as civilization reigns, people keep having babies and child psychologists keep feeling the need to justify their privileged position. I honestly have no idea whether there is such a thing as a Born Rebel; I suppose people can be genetically predisposed as more or less susceptible to external influences, but I wouldn't like to place any bets on how this affects their future. We have to assume that everyone can have their worldview changed and, particularly in the case of young people, built up from scratch through whatever nurturing process they are subject to. It's no accident that the vast, vast majority of people brought up in the civilized world are fervent supporters of the civilized way of life. School, however early it is foisted upon children, is not the earliest powerful influence on the way we think.

Call me a hopeless optimist, but I think there is a way around this situation without even having to dismantle the industrial mind-control system. (We will get around to that later). I still have in my possession a book by the Enid Blyton, creator of Noddy, The Famous Five, The Secret Seven and the apocryphal lashings of ginger beer. Along with Roald Dahl's beautifully subversive *Danny, The Champion of the World,* Blyton's book *The Children of Cherry Tree Farm* has pride of place among my childhood influences. This warm tale of privileged children moving to a halcyon rural setting and encountering the countercultural teachings of a "wild man" known as Tammylan, strikes me as curiously out of place for an author so otherwise enamored by an image of middle-class colonial Britain, but there you are. The "wild man" may have been a metaphor for the need for urban-dwellers to learn more about the countryside, but Tammylan is also a model for anyone wishing to indulge in a bit of subversive *Knowledge Sharing.*

Here is how it might work. Let's say you have a group of friends who, as these things tend to happen, are popping children out at more or less the same time (excuse the imagery but that's how it felt to me just over a decade ago). The parents regularly gather to talk to each other about such things as toilet training, walking exploits, language development and the price of shoes, while the little so-and-sos bash each other over the head with plastic bricks and get themselves filthy digging around in whatever form of matter is closest. From the very earliest times, these gatherings could easily be spent sharing all sorts of skills not only among the parents but also with the children. What about a seed-planting afternoon, where each child can be equipped with a pot of seeds and a watering can alongside a patch of earth?

Demonstrate the basic principles, and let them do their worst — or rather best, because they *will* do their best to copy something when it's couched in an unapologetically positive manner. If it's autumn rather than spring or summer, go seed-gathering; encourage them to strip grass stems and flower heads, as well as making the most of any nuts and fruits that are available. In early winter you can look for signs of decomposition and hibernation, enjoying the shapes and colors of leaves and branches, and the last remnants of the beauteous fungi season. In late winter the first signs of rebirth emerge in the form of bulbs and buds that you can identify and use to talk about the cycles of life.

And that's just one tiny aspect of knowledge sharing. Depending on the skills that abound and the age of the people involved (believe me, you can start far earlier than the "education" system would have us believe it's possible to), the horizons are pretty much limitless. At any time of year you can build a shelter; share the joys of playing and making melodic and percussion instruments; learn about local history from those who have actually experienced it; express yourself through drawing, painting, song, poetry and so on; and, very pertinent to this section, start on things like critical analysis of the news. We all have things we can share, yet we are often either too modest or too in awe of the school system to do so, thinking that someone else, someone who has been approved, can do it better than we can. It's nonsense, of course. I'm no expert at joinery, as I think I've demonstrated, but give me a pile of timber and a few tools and I'll have a bloody good go at showing a group of kids how to make a raised bed to plant vegetables in; they will probably end up doing it better than I could.

There's no process behind this idea of knowledge sharing, as such, but there are a few pointers that will help ensure it fulfills the vital purpose of protecting people from an imposed ignorance of the real world. Most important, I think, is to get the commitment of a core group of people, whether they be "teachers" or "learners" (the quotation marks imply that they are interchangeable depending on what is being shared), for without commitment there isn't likely to be the enthusiasm, or the willingness to persist, that is necessary in developing important skills and building knowledge. Don't be afraid of asking people you might not know very well, especially if they also have children; most of us don't know who we will get along with until we spend some time with them. Be generous with your ideas but also your attention — the quietest, most introverted people can also be the most talented. Don't balk at things that might seem too difficult or "advanced" or even potentially dangerous. It's all relative when you think about it: handling a saw or picking irritating plants is usually safer than crossing a road — though you might also want to learn how to spot poison ivy or giant hogweed, always a valuable lesson. As with the potential things that can be shared, the ways they can be shared are also wide and varied; see what works for your group, and if enthusiasm starts to flag, remember why you are doing it. You are giving someone something of immense value: the ability to remain free.

Everything Is Abnormal

A few years ago I found myself walking up and down Oxford Street in London. I was looking for a pub where I was supposed to meet a few people prior to a music gig at the 100 Club. I found the pub but then had an hour or so to kill, so took it upon myself to free a few people.

The first liberation was outside a shop — I can't remember exactly what it was, but there was a flat-screen television in the window showing rolling advertisements, and on this side of the window was a woman in her forties staring. Just staring. From my pocket I brought out what looks like a car immobilizer: black with a button on top and a small infra-red LED bulb at the front. I clicked and immediately the television in the shop window went off. (It was a Sony; they are always quick.) The woman seemed to wake up, then turned and walked away without a second glance. In HMV, a music and movie store, I got a little more brazen, turning off the screens above the checkouts — the ones that screen music videos interspersed with adverts — and then came across a row of four screens all showing the same commercial for a movie boxed set. I stood behind the adjacent row of DVD shelves and switched off the first screen (a Panasonic; it took a little longer). The young man who had been raptly watching the commercial moved to the next screen. I switched off this one and he moved on. I switched off the next two, unavoidable due to the acute angle between me and the screens, and he moved away entirely.

No one has ever caught me doing this. No one expects someone to be doing this, so it doesn't happen — it's a technical problem.

At a John Lewis department store a few weeks ago, armed with a home-soldered high-power version of the key fob,[56] I walked around the audio-visual section switching off row after row of televisions that had been showing adverts, wasting electricity and encouraging people to succumb to the dream of entertainment Nirvana. (As I write this, some English cities are experiencing looting and near-riots that the mainstream media are refusing to acknowledge as the direct consequence of the consumer culture. It is no coincidence that the targets of non-state-approved looters are the very same things that corporate marketing has transformed into Objects of Desire: flat-screen televisions, designer trainers, iPads, smart phones and so on. The looting is simply the logical extension of rampant consumerism.) The staff were in a technical frenzy! Something *must* have gone wrong because there was no way all these screens could have been switched off on purpose. Why would anyone want to do that?

Here's one reason.

At the beginning of the decade, these self-styled in-school broadcasters approached North American school boards with a proposition. They asked them to open their classrooms to two minutes of television advertising a day, sandwiched between twelve minutes of teenybopper current affairs programming. Many schools consented, and the broadcasts soon aired. Turning off the cheerful ad patter is not an option. Not only is the programming mandatory viewing for students, but teachers are unable to adjust the volume of the broadcast, especially during commercials. In exchange, the schools do not receive direct revenue from the stations but they can use the much coveted audiovisual equipment for other lessons and, in some cases, receive "free" computers.[57]

If you work for a school board or educational body, insert anti-civilization messages into materials, curricula and advisory notes. Remove references to things that encourage children to take part in civilized society/commercial activities.

Remove advertisements from public transport, and maybe insert/overpaste your own. Cover up advertising screens.

Sound familiar? There is very little difference between advertising and force-fed "informational" programs in schools, and the same kind of thing in railway stations, along streets, in bars and restaurants and anywhere else you might want to or need to be. The only difference, I suppose, is that children are legally coerced to go to school and thus are a captive market for whichever authority or commercial enterprise wishes to push their message home. But when you are standing in a railway station with the giant screen blaring and glowing Murdoch's finest televisual spew across the concourse, do you really have a choice whether to watch it or not? It will creep into your subconscious — I guarantee it.

We have to be careful at this juncture. The part of my mind that barely contains a tempest of pure anger grabs an axe and takes a swing at the power cable stretching from the ground to the largest flat-screen advertising hoarding I can find. Shortly after, a pair of cuffs embraces my wrists and, rightly or wrongly, I am charged with criminal damage. We have to get a sense of perspective. Switching off television sets remotely is worth doing because, although the undermining effect is small, it takes little effort and is very low risk. On the other hand, a very large screen, although symbolically a "great catch" is no more of a Tool of Disconnection than a bank of televisions that could be switched off at the push of a button. This is important.

We also have to take note of what we are trying to achieve in this chapter, the very start of the process. The information flows we need to deal with first — television and radio bulletins, print media headlines, Internet news sites, billboards and signs, direct human communication and other more subtle means — are those that keep us turned away from the real world. Specifically those that keep pushing the message "Everything is normal" or, to quote a famous wartime saying, "Keep Calm and Carry On." Remember the Biggest Lie of All, the idea that economic growth is essential? That is just one example of a totally abnormal, counterintuitive idea dressed up as "normal." Another is that we, as ordinary people, should have strong, stable governments. Another is that Our Leaders know what is best for us. Yet another is that civilization is the One Right Way to Live.

All of these patently absurd things and more are normalized in the regular communications that reach us via the various forms I listed above. The messages are everywhere and unless we can find a way of dealing with them directly, then no amount of mental insulation is going to be enough to counter their inexorable leakage into our brains. I can only provide a launch pad for doing this because the system keeps adapting and changing the ways it promulgates these lies: as we become savvy to its methods then it has to find new ways to keep us believing — new words, new media, new tricks. There is a whole industry, a supra-industry, at work to ensure we remain good citizens.

What becomes clear is that we need to strike at the core.

Task 4: Attack the Communication Core

In the excitement of getting things done we mustn't lose sight of the undermining process. This is particularly relevant when faced with difficult questions such as, How do we attack the core of the "normalization" machine? The Identification phase comes first — in other words, identifying what qualifies as a relevant target. Time for another mental exercise: take a piece of paper and something to write with and *for one day,* with an open and connected mind, jot down in some detail everything you suspect is trying to make abnormal ideas and behavior seem completely normal. Here are a few suggestions to start you off:

- A politician being addressed on the radio as though she truly represents the needs of large groups of people.

- A company promoting extreme consumption during a particular seasonal period as normal human behavior.
- A major sporting event or the activities of a celebrity drowning out the reporting of more important items in a newspaper.
- A community event or project being sponsored by a multinational corporation.
- The drop in a corporation's profits reported on TV news as though it is a loss.

If you are calling a radio station about something, rather than tell them you want to give an anti-system message, start talking about something conventional, then change without warning to saying what you really want to say. Don't swear, you will be cut off.

Okay, now that you have done that, look through your list and decide which item you would like to deal with first. There are all sorts of factors that will determine that, including, very importantly, how strongly you feel about something. Motivation is such an important factor in undermining success that personal interest in something is a perfectly valid reason to act on it. Other factors could include how much time you have at the moment, how energetic and creative you are feeling, what is directly affecting you and the people you care about most and what risks you are prepared to take. That last point should drive home the importance of proper investigation, the second phase in the undermining process.

Until the undermining process becomes second nature, you should refer to Chapter 3 on a regular basis; even I can't remember everything in it, and I wrote it. Work through your chosen target, bearing in mind that it

a) has to be something that acts as a Tool of Disconnection
b) must contribute to our acceptance of things being the way they are

When it comes to Exposure, it depends on what your undermining actually comprises as to whether this phase is relevant. Go all the way through to the Housekeeping phase as though you are actually carrying out the process, identifying all the potential pitfalls and how you might overcome them. Always keep in mind what you are trying to achieve — if at some point the undermining looks like it won't achieve your aims, even after changing your game plan, then maybe it's best to bail out and start again. I'm going to work through an example at a high level here, which might be of use. It is related to something I addressed briefly on The Unsuitablog in 2010, and it manages to anger me intensely even though I don't live in the country in which it takes place.

> *If you are web browsing, use a browser that has advert blocking software such as Adblock Plus. This effectively breaks the advertisers' business model and ability to brainwash, so is one good piece of software to recommend to others.*

Black Friday is an event of pure commercialism that occurs in the USA once a year. Although not originally named for this reason, it now signifies the time of year when retailers typically move from being "in the red" to being "in the black" due to the increase in material consumption. In practical terms it is the start of the pre-Christmas shopping season and used as a trigger to get shoppers buying goods they would not otherwise consider buying, ringing up huge debts on their credit cards and adopting a pattern of frenzied consumer activity that sometimes culminates in violence in order to obtain those precious Black Friday Bargains.[58] The extent to which this normalizes otherwise absurd behavior — making the purchase of superfluous things appear routine — is quite extraordinary. If we consider civilized humans in the USA as *de facto* Consumers, then Black Friday takes this up another level, to the point at which "normal" consumer behavior appears conservative.

Undermining Black Friday can seem in one sense to be a point solution, attacking something that is exceptional rather than a normal facet of civilized society, but if it is possible to deal with something so discrete, then it may provide some very useful ammunition for dealing with the general problem of the Human as Consumer.

Black Friday is predicated on good communications. The "bargains" offered are generally not particularly good, and are always limited in number — partly to maintain the sense of urgency, but also because retailers are not stupid and have no intention of making a loss on any day of the year. Here's a typical run down, in this case from an NYDailyNews advertorial:

> **MACY'S**
> Deals from 4 a.m., with closing times varying by store.
> Doorbuster deals for the earliest customers and free shipping at Macys.com for orders of at least $99. Men's Timberland puffer

jacket, $34.99; women's puffer jacket from Style & Co., $24.99. Girls' boots from Steve Madden and Madden Girl, $39.99.

FOREVER 21
Deals from 8 a.m. to 2 a.m. (Times Square location).
Customers who spend $40 and over will receive a special gift with purchase — a locket with lip gloss inside (limited quantities, while supplies last.) Select items $3–$12. Buy one get one free all apparel markdowns.

KMART
Deals from 6 a.m. to 9 p.m. Thanksgiving Day; 5 a.m. to 11 p.m. Friday.
Doorbusters (like a woman's peacoat, $19.99), last for only six hours. Select board games will go for $5. A Craftsman C3 drill/drive is $49.99 and a 42-inch Zenith flat-screen is $399.99.

See? It's crap. Which is why the communication of Black Friday as something that is apparently exceptional is so important; and it has really worked such that retailers no longer have to advertise their deals — they just wait for the queues to appear at the allotted time and hand out flyers as people rush the store doors to get whatever might be reduced. This is indeed a masterful piece of cultural manipulation.

Dealing with this can take many forms, and such is the importance of undermining communications that I've provided a list of the different approaches that you might want to consider as an Underminer, and briefly how this might be applied to Black Friday:

1) *Stop the message:* Make sure it isn't originated at all, or at least stopped at source before it can be propagated in any way (e.g., jamming the printing presses that produce the flyers; socially engineering employees to prevent a retailer's Black Friday strategy from being written).
2) *Block the message:* Prevent communications from being completed in some way (e.g., intercepting the delivery of flyers to stores; taking down hoardings near to stores).
3) *Reverse the message:* Communicate something that is the reverse of what the originator intended (e.g., creating a Black Friday Facebook page that suddenly cancels the event; press releases to radio stations from retailers saying how damaging Black Friday is to the planet).

4) *Subvert or parody the message:* Communicate something that alters the sense of the message, often in a humorous way (e.g., creating a "Black Friday" event for the Amazon Rainforest in which all trees are free to the first 1,000 loggers; "subvertising" hoardings to show the true impact of consumption on child workers).
5) *Amplify the message:* Change the message to such an extent that it becomes unbelievable (a form of subversion) or, at best, causes problems for the retailer (e.g. creating a Black Friday website that advertises items as free; acting as a company spokesperson saying on radio that Black Friday deals are to be extended indefinitely).

Set up a press briefing, posing as your target of choice and then brief the press in a way that entirely undermines your alter-ego's normal stance. Alternatively, make statements that are even more unethical than those of your alter-ego, but still credible.

Notice that none of these actually prevent the target of the message from getting to the stores. The idea here is to undermine the *means* by which human behavior is altered to fit the industrial model. By impeding access to the stores you are doing something quite different, which is relevant to the fourth section in this chapter.

None of these ideas on its own is going to be singularly effective — for instance, stopping only one batch of flyers among a blizzard of paper — but this is a team effort even if in isolation. That sounds strange, but remember the feedback loop: if only a few people start undermining in a methodological and effective manner, then it clears the way for more undermining to take place via the people who have been reconnected through the efforts of you and the loose band of individuals who happen to be doing similar things at the same time. So it's worth doing, providing it is the right thing.

Walking through a specific action should be useful at this point.[59] I'm going to take the example of the annual round of company profits or (more rarely) losses that are announced. When profits — we are talking about money earned on top of all expenses, indicating overall growth, which is then taken largely by shareholders — are announced, any rise is treated in the mass media as Good News:

> Energy giant Shell has released its full year results, showing a profit of just over \$18.6bn (£11.5bn), a rise of 90% on last year.
>
> Yet these good numbers are hardly surprising as a barrel of oil is now over \$100 — only the second time in history that has

> ever happened. Prices have risen quickly at 15% compared with the same period last year. As the volatile situation in Egypt continues, worries over the rest of the Middle East has pushed prices even higher.
>
> Holly Pattenden is head of oil and gas analysis at Business Monitor International. She told the BBC Shell's results were good news for those with pensions linked to the company.[60]

When *profits* fall this is treated as Bad News:

> Profits at private healthcare group Bupa tumbled 72% to £118m in 2010 in a year of cost cutting, write-downs, and redundancies.
>
> Bupa blamed difficult economic conditions in the key UK and US markets, where unemployment and health care reforms have affected operations.
>
> Profits were hit after the company made a £249.2m write-down on the value of properties and acquisitions.[61]

The aim here is to counter this absurd attitude.

You are going to pretend to be a representative of a major corporate institution in whatever politically defined country you live, and help people to understand that they are being kept in the dark as to the destructive nature of economic growth. Spend a while considering how you would most effectively do this, based on your own personal toolkit, what kind of experience you have, who you know and trust, what might have the greatest impact in a particular time and place, and so on.

Okay? Now here is just *one way* this could be done; it isn't necessarily the way I would do it, and probably not the way you would do it either, but let's be open-minded. Sarah is a woman of mixed race (Afro-Caribbean/Caucasian), who was born in Britain and has lived there all her life. She does not have a particularly distinctive regional accent but could be recognized as being of mixed race by her voice alone. She has some experience making presentations through her job, and has undergone basic in-house media training although she has never had to use it. It is approaching the end of the financial year, and companies are starting to announce their annual profit figures. Few major companies are showing a loss, except one large oil company that has written off the cost of a major buyout failure. The usual "big growth is good, less growth is bad" reports are coming through the media. Something that could undermine this mindset is a statement by the British Chambers of Commerce (BCC) that clarifies the reality of this. Sarah concocts the following:

- Financially, all profit is good for that particular company, because it means money for the shareholders, and the shareholders own the company.
- More profit means more money for the shareholders, and bigger bonuses for senior management and investors. (*Remember this is all being stated in a matter-of-fact way.*)
- Less profit means less money for the shareholders, executives and investors, who will not be able to afford as expensive cars, holidays and houses.
- If a company loses money, then the shareholders, executives and investors will be upset, and will lose money, and possibly their jobs.
- We can tell a healthy economy by the amount of energy it is consuming, the amount of consumer goods the public buy and the volume of greenhouse gases being emitted by that economy. If the economy does not grow, then these things will also not grow. (*Again, this is stated in a matter-of-fact, not at all getting the real point, kind of way.*)

So that's the message. It will obviously need to be bulked out a bit and overlaid with a bit of corporate-speak, but Sarah has experience of this, working for a corporation herself. Now, how will Sarah be able to get it across most effectively to the largest number of people? Typically, Chambers of Commerce are led by middle-aged white males, but middle-aged white males are not seen as particularly media friendly, which is one reason young women are often put in PR positions. Sarah fits the bill, and being of mixed race might (ironically, considering the history of white power and influence) make it easier for her to get a slot on network public radio, for this is where she is going to be executing her undermining.

She rents a cheap room in an office block near to the real Chamber of Commerce, with a direct telephone line that has a number with the same area code as that institution. Financial radio shows are not listened to by very many members of the general public, so she chooses a mainstream breakfast slot on the same day as a couple of major profit announcements are due. (These are listed well in advance in the financial press.) Early that morning she listens to the target radio station, making sure no one from the real BCC has been interviewed or been quoted on the news — this is important as her details will be checked if there is duplication.

A few minutes before the show starts she calls up the radio station, via its news desk number, using an alias. She claims to be the newly appointed

PR representative for the relevant industrial sector(s) at the aforementioned Chamber of Commerce, and has an important statement related to today's profit announcements — the expectation of revealing news makes the show's producers particularly interested. She is given a five-minute interview slot. At the allotted time she is contacted through the office number she has provided and manages to get her points across, in order, in a sober tone that does not suggest anything underhand is taking place. She does not engage in further discussion with the presenter except to clarify the points made. She ends the call and leaves the office, having paid the rent in cash. That day is not a good one for the economic belief system.

Task 5: Fray the Edges

Attacking the Communication Core is enough work to keep a team or many individual Underminers working in every country, region and state busy for years. If you find this or any of the other tasks to your liking and you are finding success in what you do, then stick with it. Even if a key foundation stone of the thing you are undermining becomes dislodged, it may still remain functional. We need people working in all areas, and that is especially important in this chapter.

When Charlie Veitch heckled Sky News presenter Kay Burley through a megaphone, live on British television, he was exploiting one of the few genuinely open channels remaining to the casual Underminer. The result was a wonderful piece of undermining, and there was nothing Sky News could do about it.

"Kay, this is the Love Police, my name is Detective Charlie, we have a warrant out for your arrest. You have been convicted of being a propaganda-pushing Murdoch shill. You are feeding lies, you are perpetuating the circus of mainstream media — corporate-controlled mainstream media. You're only doing it for money; you know what we call people who only do things for money. What you're doing is very dangerous, Kay."[62]

Planning something like this isn't easy: you have to know when news is breaking, know where the reporters and the presenters along with their interviewees will be putting across their mainstream propaganda and also make sure your message is perfectly misaligned with what is being spouted at the time. Having a battery-operated loud speaker in your bag is certainly a good start, along with some suitable comments. Being in the right place at the right time isn't so easy, but if you are prone to hanging around government buildings and political headquarters, then a little breach of the peace may be in the offing. Who knows, the TV might just carry your words rather than those of your Beloved Leaders.

Often in the life of even a mainstream activist there arise opportunities that are too good to pass up. The exposed transmission cable, the open door, the unlocked gate, the unattended uniform closet — these are real examples of the interesting paths activism can take. Remember me mentioning conventional direct action as being a potential distraction activity, such as a march being a "front" for something subversive taking place in the absence of police presence? This has an analogy in the world of politics:

> A Labour aide who advised the Government to use the attack on the World Trade Center to distract attention from "bad" news stories was fighting for her job last night.
>
> Jo Moore, who works for Stephen Byers, the Secretary of State for Transport, Local Government and the Regions, was widely condemned for showing spin at its worst when her news management memo was leaked.
>
> Miss Moore's memo, written at 2.55 pm on September 11, when millions of people were transfixed by the terrible television images of the terrorist attack, said: "It is now a very good day to get out anything we want to bury. Councillors expenses?"[63]

Create a dodgy corporate video that was only intended for internal use, and post it on YouTube (and WikiLeaks) as a "leak." Include information that is close enough to the truth to be credible but edgy enough to cause a stir. Steal the introduction and ending from an existing corporate video, using video capture software.

Jo Moore's cynical transgression was not to be the last time attempts were made to "bury" unsavory news beneath something that had more front-page potential; nor was it the first, because the best ideas tend to be those that have been hanging around in some form seemingly forever. So, there is the aforementioned march that allows for actions the marchers themselves — and certainly not the organizers — would not have intended to be carried out. In the specific case of the Veil of Ignorance, making a concerted attack on the means by which we are disconnected from any awareness of being exploited is also *an excellent opportunity to carry out undermining actions that potentially have even greater impact and longevity.*

A lot has been made in recent years of attacks that use multiple computers to flood the networks of targets, usually corporate websites or those of other oppressive regimes. Denial of Service describes a way of making computer systems inaccessible to the outside world. Due to the resilience and, more importantly, the network bandwidth available to even the smallest operations, simple Denial of Service is usually impractical and, without first-class security measures, is almost certain to be tracked back to the originator. Distributed Denial of Service (DDoS) largely avoids this problem by using not one very large data stream, but a large number of relatively small data streams. Strictly speaking, there is nothing illegal about DDoS if it is not being carried out in a wholly malicious manner: all companies want lots of Internet traffic, and DDoS is usually just a very large amount of Internet traffic, albeit not the type that they were hoping for.

Anonymous has frequently been accused of instigating DDoS attacks, such as during the aforementioned "Operation Payback," but such is the nature of Distributed Denial of Service that anyone with an agenda and a target can orchestrate a successful attack, at least for a short while. Anonymous do not publicly condone DDoS, but other loose-knit groups such as 4Channers and LulzSec openly promote(d) their use of DDoS, although often the motivation is less about attacking the system than about having a laugh at someone else's expense. There also is little doubt that national governments have instigated DDoS and simple Denial of Service attacks for political reasons, and there is considerable evidence that corporations have at least been party to similar tactics for commercial reasons. It is certainly a popular technique.

This is not the place to go into the mechanics of such a technique — there is plenty of information online, but remember to browse discreetly. Suffice it to say such attacks have been instrumental in moving particular agendas along in the intended direction, whether that be taking revenge on an institution for involvement in a specific act or making a concerted effort to undermine the raison d'être of an organization. The imposition of the Veil of Ignorance is especially pertinent here, given the importance such organizations (corporations, political and lobbying groups, media outlets, etc.) attach to continuous communications. But DDoS is not just a frontline attack mechanism; it can be also be used as a smokescreen for more subtle interventions.

Let's suppose the Chinese arm of a Western media conglomerate is assisting Chinese government propaganda in creating more and more industrial workers from a vast, and formerly largely self-sufficient, population. The content of the conglomerate's Chinese website is controlled by the parent company that is getting the benefits of Chinese market loyalty for their media products (and their advertisers' goods) in exchange for allowing the government to vet the content of their website. As a result of this cozy arrangement, the company website is fully accessible from Chinese Internet cafes and via state-controlled Internet providers. The arrangement is sound: the media company does what it is told and rakes in profits from the growing Chinese consumer market. There is a major DDoS attack, bringing down a significant part of its Internet presence and requiring the full attention of its technical staff. Can you see where we're going here?

While the staff are occupied combating the attack, including trying to trace the myriad different attack vectors and protect their infrastructure from the risk of an open front door, a back door of an entirely different type swings open. A telephone rings on the help desk. At the other end of the line is, apparently, a person from a company contracted to provide security services to the one that is under attack; the caller asks for a range of information, including passwords to edge servers and routers, in order to — as requested — increase the bandwidth of the victim's Internet presence, thus permitting their US-based website to get back online.

The well-meaning help desk staffer, currently fielding numerous calls from stressed internal staff and worried clients, provides the information, is thanked by the caller, and gets on with answering the next query. What actually happened is that the caller had been party to the DDoS via news on a hacking forum. The caller then searched the name of the company along with the terms "client" and "security" to find out which, if any, other companies provided them with technical services. With this information and a basic knowledge of what might be useful in the future, all the person had to do was phone an overworked member of the help desk, via a number-masked line[64] and try to glean the kind of knowledge that would never be given out on a less frenetic occasion.

What the caller does with this information is another story.

Melt the Guns?

A question bugging me while planning and writing this lengthy piece of work is whether there are ways of speeding up the undermining process that don't rely on feedback loops. Can we, for instance, stop the violence committed upon the members of civilized society through one mass act of undermining? This idea has its roots in the various Peace Movements that reached pre-eminence in the 1960s — the concept that without weapons of mass murder being "in the system" then there can be no mass murder, and thus a peaceful and just society can become a reality. On a superficial level this would seem to be the case.

Relentless acts of physical violence committed upon the populace by those who wish to gain power are a clear expression of perhaps the most direct Tool of Disconnection: "Abuse Us." It seems that the earlier along the civilized road a society is, the more likely the use of more direct forms of control and disconnection — "crude" methods, for want of a better term. Forced labor, forced incarceration, forced religion and other direct manifestations of physical abuse and coercion have historically been in the gift of those who have the most effective arsenal of weaponry, be that in terms of quantity, quality, ability — whatever it takes to be pre-eminent in the power stakes. Later on in the civilized story the means of controlling a population tend toward the more subtle, initially using the *fear* of violence as a natural reaction to prior actual violence, then moving toward a much more overarching system of control using all the Tools of Disconnection required for the purpose of long-term cultural management. For all this latter subtlety, the potential for systemic violence remains, and is used whenever anyone threatens the running of the industrial machine.

Ultimately though, is it the weapons *per se* that act as those initial and reserved control mechanisms? In a world where the AK-47 and M16 have superseded the machete and the firebrand as the killing tool of choice for young, oppressive regimes, it would seem that to stop the manufacture and supply of weapons would also reduce the level of oppression. To a certain extent this is true; but what of the machete? This multi-purpose, ostensibly peaceful tool is used under a variety of different names (panga, cutlass, etc.) for clearing brush across the world. During the Rwandan Genocide of 1994 the machete was responsible for at least half of all of the recorded 800,000 murders.[65] Stopping the flow of machetes from Europe and China might have reduced the scale of the massacre, but who is to say that other potential weapons, such as clubs, axes and rifles, would not have been used instead? And anyhow, 84 percent of households already had a machete 10 years before the massacre took place — it was and still is predominantly an agricultural tool. As a friend of mine pointed out, "A knife in a bushcraft setting is an invaluable tool; in an inner city a threat of violence." He went on to add an important proviso: "Weapons can be used as much for self-defense against aggression as for committing aggression for dominance."

It seems that the problem of weaponry as a tool of mass control is not so much with the nature of the arsenal as with the nature of the people controlling that arsenal. We know that people can be persuaded to kill with sufficient authoritative systems in place, and thus a far more effective means of undermining the use of weaponry in any society is to remove the authority that controls the level of abuse on a mass scale. Later on, in Chapter 6, the industrial machine, which includes the systems of weapon manufacture, will be challenged head on, but first and foremost, it is authority we need to look at for all sorts of reasons, not just how people are ordered to kill others.

Not at Home to Mr. Smith

Once or twice a week I go into people's houses and fix their computers. Usually they will pay me a bit of cash; on a good day they will have something to barter for my work, but more of that later. Sometimes I need to call up Internet service providers or telephone companies, and without fail the person on the other end of the phone refers to me either as "Sir" or "Mr. Farnish." It makes me squirm. Not on my behalf, but on behalf of whoever I am speaking to. If I get the chance, I will ask to be called "Keith," which the person will do at first, and then revert to type, partly because the empodded souls in these positions are having their calls carefully monitored for any etiquette aberrations, partly because they have been conditioned to be subservient to the customer.

The point of titles and the various forms of address inherent in civilized society is to impose order upon its members. Debrett's, the "modern authority on all matters etiquette, taste and achievement," lists literally

Exercise: Hierarchy

The civilized world rests on layers of hierarchy, from those it considers to be at the very top — the elite financiers, politicians, media moguls and landowners — right down to those it considers to be irrelevant. There are others who exist on the edges whom it would consider to be a threat to its existence should they appear on the radar of that multi-layered entity. You are on the edges. You need to help dissolve the hierarchy.

The problem is that no single event not of the system's own making can force that hierarchy to collapse. Force is not necessary, though. Like our faith in the goodness of the industrial economy, the existence of this great stacking monster depends on belief: if people stop believing that a hierarchy is necessary, then it will collapse under its own weight, the glue of belief having magically dissolved away. How do you undermine this belief?

hundreds of forms of address appropriate to the form of communication being used and the relative "positions" of the various people engaged in that communication. With reference to meeting the Queen of the United Kingdom, etc.,[66] Debrett's suggests,

> Upon being introduced to The Queen, and on leaving, a bow or curtsy is made. The bow is an inclination of the head, not from the waist. The curtsy should be a discreet but dignified bob.
>
> In conversation, address The Queen as "Your Majesty", and subsequently "Ma'am" (to rhyme with Pam). When conversing with The Queen, substitute "Your Majesty" for "you".[67]

Given the opportunity, I would love to speak to a member of royalty, ideally a monarch, and speak on a first-name basis. In the UK and other sovereign states of Europe there are no punishments for this simple act of rebellion, but in some parts of the world you would be advised to tread carefully. Tempting as this would be, whether you keep your head or not is not really an issue, because the true undermining that needs to take place is about addressing *attitudes* to compliance — challenging, as I wrote above, the idea that compliance is normal and non-compliance is abnormal.

Task 6: Grant No Authority by Proxy

Whenever we look up to someone in a social sense, we are accepting their authority over us in whatever context this "looking up to" is set. For example, when I was about four years old I had somewhere acquired a very large pencil that I was gently throwing up in the air and catching while walking home with my mother. Across the road walked a policeman and a policewoman, coming in the opposite direction. Apropos of nothing, I dropped the pencil, which would under normal circumstances have meant just picking it up and carrying on my way. But something odd happened: I felt ashamed, and so I carefully picked the pencil up and glanced across almost as though I were seeking permission for this act of recovery. No one had explicitly told me that this was the way to behave in the presence of the police, but this shy deference to public figures of authority seemed nonetheless embedded in me. Many years later I would find myself on Tower Bridge in London asking a police constable exactly which law stopped me approaching the entrance to an airline industry party in one of the two engine towers and personally addressing each attendee in turn as to what exactly they were celebrating.

Let's be clear, politeness is a good thing in most circumstances, as is diplomacy in the general sense. I was both polite and diplomatic in addressing this constable; I was not, on the other hand, deferential. He was telling me not to do something; I was asking him under what authority and section of public law he could demand this of me. Somewhere along the line I had changed from being a person who blindly accepts authority to someone who questions it on every occasion I come across it. My father put it best: "After the age of 13, I never called anyone 'Sir' again." And why should he have?

And why should you — or anyone else for that matter?

The title of this section is "No Authority by Proxy." The word "proxy" is important; I am not saying there should be no authority at all. Anyone can earn authority, at least for a specific instance, such as a crisis in which one person may take on a role that needs leadership. "Authority" in the civilized world, though, is almost always Authority by Proxy — in other words, that which is given over because we have been taught that hierarchy is the natural state of things. Thus, the police officers[68] I deferred to when I dropped that oversized pencil were actually given their authority *through my act of deference.*

To some readers this might come as a bit of a surprise. Surely authority is something that is imposed by force. Well, yes, but only until force no longer has to be used because the subjects of that force now accept that authority. What I am effectively saying is that *without acceptance of authority, that authority cannot exist.* We are talking about a change in mindset here, a mental rerouting that by its mere happening effectively undermines the system of Authority by Proxy that civilization depends on to control the behavior of its subjects. So, how can we remove this acceptance?

If you were thinking along the same lines as I was a couple of pages ago, then you may already have a few ideas in mind. First, I would say, we return to language. Earlier in the chapter I gave an example of changes in language that can be made in attitudes to education and work. The same approach can be taken for attitudes to authority: your job is to find a situation where you are either in the presence of an "authority" figure or discussing matters that relate to "authority" and undermine the pretence that authority can be enforced simply by virtue of someone's position in a fixed hierarchy.

Go on, have some fun — just watch the reactions.

The ideal here is for these language changes to "go viral," such that the change is passed on from person to person, eventually becoming embedded in the language of the people you are able to verbally influence. Going back to the Toolbox, we find that Communication (obvious) and Tenacity

A Cultural Side Note: Japanese Social Hierarchy

Writing with what one would have to call a Western perspective, it comes as no surprise that the focus of this book is predominantly European and North American, with various English-speaking southern hemisphere nations making an appearance. I take no great pride in this, though, as I have made clear, identity is critical to personal freedom, and thus I cannot ever identify with anything other than the place where I live and the people I relate to. Unfortunately this makes it impossible for me to address some of the more problematic areas that need to be undermined if the industrial system is to become a thing of the past.

One of these is Japanese social hierarchy.

Briefly, the relationship among different members of Japanese society is complex, but significantly derived from Confucian principles. Thus, "in order to seek harmonious relationships with others, which are the precondition of social integration and stability, individuals should respect and follow tradition and social hierarchy."[69] Such principles are common in other nearby nations, including the birthplace of Confucius, China, but in Japan the totality of hierarchy — particularly in the workplace — makes undermining far more significant than in less hierarchical societies. The seemingly easy act of being less deferential to your "boss" or a politician challenges centuries of hardwired order that only the most liberated Japanese individual could begin to shift.

I can only provide general assistance with this. More specific, culturally targeted undermining is something that this book is not able to do. The growing legion of Underminers needs to include a host of cultural emissaries, perhaps like you, who can take the struggle back home and into the heart of their own form of Industrial Civilization.

(not so obvious) are key skills that will need to be applied in equal measure. The words themselves depend on what you normally use in conversation and, probably more important, the way you use them. So I may talk about a certain politician in scathing terms — don't we all? — but there is more to it than that. We may think Politician X is an idiot, but he is still given deference owing to his position in society. Expressing that in a non-deferential way is harder than simply saying "Politician X is an idiot." The same goes for the concept of hierarchy itself. Make a point of breaking down the layers of "authority" in your mind: remember that social strata can exist only while you accept it.

When you have taken the mental bulldozer to the upper classes, the ruling elites, the company executives, the people who seem to have a certain standing simply because of who they are rather than what they have done, then you are in a position to talk to your friends about everyday things, but with a slightly different edge. And after that take any chance you get to address the mass media in your normal workday communications — assuming you still work for the system — face to face.

There will come a time when you will have a chance to level the hierarchy in a physical sense, just like my constable on Tower Bridge who shamefacedly deferred to his sergeant in finding out exactly which law I was breaking. As I said, politeness and diplomacy are fine; but *if you can make the other person, the "authority" figure, feel that you are equal to them, then you have just collapsed a layer* — if temporarily. If you can do it in public, then that collapse may last.

Diana Gould [on monitor in studio]: Why, when the *Belgrano*, the Argentinian battleship, was outside the Exclusion Zone and actually sailing away from the Falklands — why did you give the orders to sink it?

Margaret Thatcher [in studio]: It was not sailing away from the Falklands, it was in an area which was a danger to our ships and to our people on them…

DG: … outside the Exclusion Zone …

MT: … but it was in an area which we had warned [turns to presenter] — at the end of April we had given warnings that all ships in those areas, if they represented a danger to our ships, were vulnerable. When it was sunk, that ship which we had found was a danger to our ships. My duty was to look after our troops, our ships, our navy. And my goodness me, I live with many, many anxious days and nights …

DG [interrupts]: But, Mrs. Thatcher, you started your answer by saying it was not sailing away from the Falklands; it was on a bearing of 280 and it was already west of the Falklands so, I'm sorry, I cannot see how you can say it was not sailing away from the Falklands …

MT [interrupts]: When it was, when it was sunk …

DG: … when it was sunk

MT: … it was a danger to our ships …

DG [interrupts]: No, but you had just said at the beginning of your answer that it was not sailing away from the Falklands, and [shifts confidently in chair] I'm asking you to correct that statement.

MT: Yes, but it's within an area outside the Exclusion Zone, which I think what you were saying is sailing away …

DG [interrupts]: No, I am not …

Presenter [interjects]: I think we are arguing about which way it was facing at the time.

MT: It was a danger to our ships.

DG: Mrs. Thatcher, I am saying that it was on a bearing 280, which is a bearing just north of west. It was already west of the Falklands, and therefore nobody with any imagination can put it sailing other than away from the Falklands.

MT: Mrs. … I'm sorry, I forgot your name [Presenter: Mrs. Gould] … Mrs. Gould …

DG: Erm, you know …

MT: When the orders were given to sink it, and when it was sunk, it was in an area which was a danger to our ships. Now, you accept that, do you?

DG: No, I don't.

MT: Well, I'm sorry, it was …

DG: Erm, no Mrs. Thatcher.

MT: … you must accept that when we gave the order, when we changed the Ex … the rules, which enabled them to sink *Belgrano* …[70]

There is probably no better example of leveling, of undermining, the hierarchy than when Diane Gould faced up to the then British Prime Minister, Margaret Thatcher on an afternoon television magazine program. Through this simple act she not only made Thatcher look vulnerable, she wrung out an admission that the rules had been changed and the Exclusion Zone was just a parody of fairness. Too bad there were not more people like Diane around at the time to repeat and build upon her exceptional attack.

A little jolt. It's easy to get high on the act of undermining, and that's no bad thing, but at the back of your mind must remain some idea of why you're doing this at all. Civilization is unsustainable at any scale, and the more resource intensive the civilization, the shorter the time it can last. However, we have to bear in mind that the construct called Industrial Civilization is actually a composite of a great number of different — albeit not very different — civilizations that have collided and merged into one enormously destructive entity. It is only because of the huge scale of Industrial Civilization, being able to take what it needs from anywhere on Earth with our tacit approval, that it has lasted as long as it has.

In the absence of civilizations, there is no reason that any self-contained indigenous tribe cannot last for as long as the environment it lives within remains stable. Give or take an ice age or two, there is no reason formerly civilized human beings can't do the same. However, it would take a complete change in psychology to make this possible, such as removing the perceived "need" for societies to have hierarchies with certain people being more powerful simply because they have felt the desire to grab power from others. I make this point because the next example of undermining derives from the ancient, egalitarian[71] traditions of the most durable societies on Earth.

The foam-pie-in-the-face (other glutinous substances are also available) method of getting one over on people who clearly need to be brought down to size, intentionally or not, can be traced back to certain means by which many tribes maintain a flat societal structure. An enlightening case recorded by Richard Borshay Lee in the presence of the !Kung Bushmen of the African Kalahari describes how he wished to show gratitude to the group of !Kung he had been studying for a year by slaughtering the largest ox he could find and sharing it out. However, Lee, because of his research method of not sharing the food he had brought with him in order to maintain a controlled study environment (ironic, given his presence would have affected the outcome anyway), was already open to "accusations of stinginess and half-heartedness." When he came to mention his "Christmas gift" to the Bushmen, he was continually told that the magnificent ox was skinny and only good for soup from its bones. Despite — though, in hindsight, he eventually realized because of — his constant claims of the beast's high quality, the accusations continued right until the slaughter, upon which the true quality of the animal was revealed.

> /gaugo had been one of the most enthusiastic in making me feel bad about the merit of the Christmas ox. I sought him out first.
>
> "Why did you tell me the black ox was worthless, when you could see that it was loaded with fat and meat?"
>
> "It is our way," he said smiling. "We always like to fool people about that. Say there is a Bushman who has been hunting. He must not come home and announce like a braggard, 'I have killed a big one in the bush!' He must first sit down in silence until I or someone else comes up to his fire and asks, 'What did you see today?' He replies quietly, 'Ah, I'm no good for hunting. I saw nothing at all [pause] just a little tiny one.' Then I smile to

myself," /gaugo continued, "because I know he has killed something big."

"In the morning we make up a party of four or five people to cut up and carry the meat back to the camp. When we arrive at the kill we examine it and cry out, 'You mean to say you have dragged us all the way out here in order to make us cart home your pile of bones? Oh, if I had known it was this thin I wouldn't have come.' Another one pipes up, 'People, to think I gave up a nice day in the shade for this. At home we may be hungry but at least we have nice cool water to drink.' If the horns are big, someone says, 'Did you think that somehow you were going to boil down the horns for soup?'

"To all this you must respond in kind. 'I agree,' you say, 'this one is not worth the effort; let's just cook the liver for strength and leave the rest for the hyenas. It is not too late to hunt today and even a duiker or a steenbok would be better than this mess.'

"Then you set to work nevertheless; butcher the animal, carry the meat back to the camp and everyone eats," /gaugo concluded.

Things were beginning to make sense. Next, I went to Tomazo. He corroborated /gaugo's story of the obligatory insults over a kill and added a few details of his own.

"But," I asked, "why insult a man after he has gone to all that trouble to track and kill an animal and when he is going to share the meat with you so that your children will have something to eat?"

"Arrogance," was his cryptic answer.

"Arrogance?"

"Yes, when a young man kills much meat he comes to think of himself as a chief or a big man, and he thinks of the rest of us as his servants or inferiors. We can't accept this. We refuse one who boasts, for someday his pride will make him kill somebody. So we always speak of his meat as worthless. This way we cool his heart and make him gentle."[72]

In the modern form of pie throwing, comedic parody and highbrow satire, such Leveling Mechanisms do appear to work, at least on a temporary basis. Certainly politicians have been brought low by vicious satire, as demonstrated during the popular heights of the British magazine *Punch* in the mid 19th century, and the later television show *Spitting Image*, but whether such an approach can alter the attitudes of an entire society definitely needs more work — after all, both *Punch* and *Spitting Image* were the products of the same culture that they mocked, and they could easily have been stopped had they truly overstepped the mark. *Pure ridicule,* as opposed to the more highbrow satire, on the other hand is certainly something that could, as with the tribal example above, be very effective in the right hands.

If you ever find yourself near to where an outside broadcast is taking place — especially those involving greasy politicians, corporate executives or broadcasters who like to put a negative spin on "bad" protests that break the law — "accidentally" trip over their cables or into their equipment, thus disrupting the broadcast. You can claim it was a trip hazard.

Taking the leveling further, Peter Gray took the following from the studies of Christopher Boehm in explaining how indigenous tribes maintain their flat social structures:

> Hunter-gatherers are continuously vigilant to transgressions against the egalitarian ethos. Someone who boasts, or fails to share, or in any way seems to think that he (or she, but usually it's a he) is better than others is put in his place through teasing, which stops once the person stops the offensive behavior. If teasing doesn't work, the next step is shunning. The band acts as if the offending person doesn't exist. That almost always works. Imagine what it is like to be completely ignored by the very people on whom your life depends. No human being can live for long alone. The person either comes around, or he moves away and joins another band, where he'd better shape up or the same thing will happen again.[73]

In a community it is a significant step to take from just ridiculing a person's attempts at self-aggrandizement or ignoring them entirely, to the point that the person is sent away. In undermining terms, the difference is nowhere near as great because the objects of the undermining are unlikely to be within your community, and there is little chance of "sending them away" except in a virtual sense. Thus it would make sense to apply whatever approach suits your own talents. Just concentrate for now on finding ways of leveling hierarchy through humor, parody, ridicule and especially the ways in which people can be encouraged to collectively turn their backs —

but not turning a blind eye — to the systems of power that keep us looking upward. There will be plenty more opportunities for using these in a later chapter, when we explore the joys of subvertising and related activities.

Task 7: Recognize We Are Worthy

There is a common, if slightly icky, phrase that is used in certain areas of political and corporate activism and reflects the nature of hierarchy perfectly: The shit always rises to the top. "No," you say, "it's the cream that rises to the top, isn't it?" In the minds of those already at the top that may be the case, but we only have to look at who is running nations, corporations and other more ethereal entities and it becomes clear that those at the top most definitely share more characteristics with lavatory excrement than lactate emulsion. People sometimes ask a question that really bugs me. It goes something like, What would you do if you ruled the world? It's a great question if you have any aspirations toward ruling the world, but given what was in the previous section, it's clear that "ruling the world" is hardly something that anyone with any morals would want to do. Sharing the world, now that's another thing entirely.

That makes the response to another, related but even more common, question pretty simple too. What if women ruled the world? Gut reaction? A nicer place, I suspect most will think. Social activist and academic Riane Eisler puts this into perspective in her book *The Real Wealth of Nations* in a passage concerning the configuration of top-down systems of domination. Among the four "core" components she sets out (three of them being authoritarian structure, high levels of abuse and violence, and justification through cultural beliefs and stories) is the "rigid ranking of one half of humanity over the other half" exemplified across a wide range of cultures and belief systems, not least the economies of the industrial West and more recently emerged East. She writes:

> This superior/inferior view of our species is a central component of inequitable, despotic and violent cultures. It provides a mental map that children learn for equating all differences — whether based on race, religion or ethnicity — with superiority and inferiority.[74]

Eisler goes on to describe the high cultural value given to "masculine" qualities and behaviors, such as "manly" conquest and "heroic" violence, over "feminine" caring and nonviolence, perhaps implying that the opposite would be preferable. But given that the idea of any population group being predominant implies power and hierarchy, it is highly questionable whether any such change would be a change for the better. What we need to avoid in our undermining, therefore, is elevating people through any kind of hierarchy because — as I have said — in civilized society, the shit always rises to the top and who wants to be considered a piece of shit?[75]

Now obviously that creates a bit of a conundrum. If we are keen to collapse hierarchy, and thus create a situation where people are not under the jackboot of unearned authority, then we will need to carry out a very important task, in addition to bringing down the layers above, that does not simply substitute one group for another — in other words, *ensuring there are neither layers at the top nor layers at the bottom.* The key to this lies in the methodology, which is essentially helping people who feel they are at the bottom of the civilized pyramid to feel wanted and worthwhile. That includes you.

How do you feel today?

Pretty crappy, I would guess if you are an employee of a large organization that exploits its staff and anyone else that it needs to, so it can create money for itself. Not too good, either, if you are someone who is a victim of a society that insists that to be "someone" you have to have money, material possessions, good looks, ambition, drive, and be born the right gender, color and with a silver spoon in your mouth. Sorry to remind you of this — maybe you were feeling okay until that point. Well, here's the alternative view: you are a human being, just like everyone else. The fact that you are reading this means that you probably give a stuff — which is more than most people who are further up the hierarchy can say — and you want to make things better. That makes you a decent person. And consider the civilized world in general: do you really want to "excel" in the way that this toxic system defines excellence? If not, then you don't need to feel bad about not being or having the things society says you should be or have. The people at the top are never content: it is their lack of contentment that has driven them to the top, and kept them there. Imagine always having to be richer, more influential and more erudite than everyone below you just to stay there. Imagine having to maintain a vast network of flunkies and always being ruthless in your activities in order to get just one rung further up.

How do you feel now?

This is the kind of feeling that needs to be passed on. Remember the analogy far, far back in the book that described removing bricks from the bottom of the building in order to destabilize it. That's what *creating real self-esteem* is about. Building self-esteem in the civilized sense is merely about elevating someone within the existing social structures and rules that define what it means to be a worthwhile person. *Real self-esteem* is about ignoring these existing structures and rules and raising someone's opinion of himself or herself in an objective sense — that is, regardless of what other people might think.

Some forms of therapy do this, but to pick your way through the minefield of pop psychology that masquerades as "making people better" is no easy task. Real self-esteem is the domain of the good friend, someone who is really trusted. And it's self-reinforcing: by giving people the help they need to collapse the mental layers above, you will also become trusted by others who know the person you are helping; it's also a very lovely accelerant, for those who have been helped are almost certain to pass on that help to others who trust them. Before you know it there is a rapidly spreading fan of people who *feel better in themselves*, regardless of anything imposed by a system that seeks to put people in "their place" in order to create the kind of desperate needs that drive economies.

I'm leaving this task open, as personal relationships of the sort that are required for this to work are as different as individual people. What works for one relationship might not work for another. But the basic message is clear: as individual human beings, we do not have to subscribe to whatever social structure has been imposed on us; nor do we have to aspire to those goals that have been put in place simply to create an appetite that can never be sated. We are better than that.

Deprogramming

The previous section leads neatly into the fourth major aspect of removing the Veil of Ignorance: that of, to use the imagery at the beginning of the chapter, removing the tiger's need to keep pacing the invisible cage. To be clear, we are addicted to industrial civilization. Not just the material trappings, the dream we are sold, but the meaning of civilization as the only one right way to live.

The distinction is important because we actually have two discrete problems to deal with, only the first of which has been addressed at all. That addiction to the material dream, the consumer paradise, will be further taken up at length in later chapters as it is difficult to avoid in any day-to-day dealings with institutions in the civilized world.

The *meaning* of civilization; now that's a more subtle problem.

Task 8: Loosen Civilization's Mental Grip

We return to words again, and to a piece I wrote some time ago called "The Problem With ... Civilization." At the time, I was working through the process of getting a book published and I realized, with some disappointment, that I had not pinned down with any kind of accuracy, not so much why civilization is a bad thing but why it is not a particularly good or special thing. To put it another way: civilization — meh!

The expectoration "meh" is an indicator of being able to take it or leave it, coupled with polite boredom. For such a tiny word, if we can call it that, it is remarkably disarming. Take the following exchange:

> "Have you seen ______'s[76] latest outfit? It's amazing! The hat! The SHOES! I can't stop talking about it!"
> "Meh."

With just three letters the previous explosion of sartorial lust has lost all its importance. The same approach needs to be applied to Industrial Civilization and the complete acceptance we have that this is the One Right Way to Live; acceptance that is so complete that we don't know, as a culture, what civilization even means. It has become so fundamental to our belief system that we treat its existence much as we do our heartbeat: it just happens. For sure we have to keep it healthy, by learning how to become good citizens and then plugging ourselves into the job market and the consumer culture, but apart from the occasional dire warning that the economy might be in trouble, we have little awareness of what this thing actually is on a day-to-day basis. And that's how the system would like it to remain.

It's such a grand term: Civilization. But it is really just a word, like "leaf," "stone" or "baby," that has defined itself in the highest sense possible — "civilization" speaks to us with such importance because it demands to be heard, and hear we do, by defining ourselves in its image....

> Civilized
> Civility
> Civil
> Citizen

They all mean the same thing, in truth: City Dweller. The most obvious physical manifestation of civilization is the city, something totally alien to any uncivilized culture. Cities are one manifestation; there are others that are less physical, but no less integral for all that. According to the influential but now sadly defunct Anthropik Network there are five key features that are common to all civilizations:

1. Settlement of cities of 5,000 or more people.
2. Full-time labor specialization.
3. Concentration of surplus.
4. Class structure.
5. State-level political organization.

Set up a food-sharing scheme in your local area to help undermine the large-scale distribution networks. Have meetings and discuss self-sufficiency in general.

The four other features all require structures and systems in order to operate as effectively as possible so, for instance, in order to concentrate surplus food (so it can be given out, or rather sold, on demand) you must, as a civilization, have storage and distribution systems, the means to generate that surplus in the first place (i.e. mass agriculture), accounting processes and, of course, a means of asserting authority over that surplus. All of the five features listed, point to the primary function of civilization: a tool through which power and wealth can be accumulated by a select few.[77]

You see that? It's just a "tool," but a very significant one because it is the sum total of *all* of the Tools of Disconnection. Civilization is disconnection. In those terms it is obvious that we cannot possibly tackle it head on, which is why the whole process of undermining is discrete, based around different elements of this culture. But as a symbol of everything we experience, everything that doesn't connect us to the real world, the meaning of civilization is something that can and must be tackled. So first, we understand what it is so that the nature of civilization is revealed in its true, and to be frank, rather mundane colors. Then we take the essence of that understanding and try to unpick it, in the most public ways possible.

It's quite an odd thing, when you think about it, that we do not usually hear the word "civilization" in normal discourse. It tends to be reserved for discussions about history or documentaries that revel in the Great Civilizations of the past. Yes, we hear the word "civilized" a lot, but the meaning of that is false: good, moral behavior is not civilized; it is just good, moral behavior. We also hear the word "citizen," again in purely positive terms as someone who abides by the rules of society and is generally a well-rounded person: but someone who abides by the rules of society and is generally a well-rounded person is not necessarily a citizen; if such a person is a citizen, it is because she or he just happens to be a subject of civilization. But we don't hear the word "civilization" much.

We also don't hear the word "white" much. For as long as Industrial Civilization has existed, white people have been the rulers, and only under exceptional circumstances are people of any other race permitted to be in positions of relative power, in which case this is noted. Barack Obama is a Black president. George W. Bush and Bill Clinton were not White presidents. By not identifying a person in power as white, the default, we are effectively made to ignore the fact that white people run civilization. By not identifying the society we live in as civilization, we are effectively made to ignore the fact that we are subjects of the Culture of Maximum Harm.

There are special categories of Underminer, and this task requires one of them: professional communicators. The effectiveness of this task is heavily dependent on the reach of the message. The term "reach" indicates not necessarily the raw number of people communicated to, although that is important, but also the proportion of the most malleable groups of people. I know that referring to people as malleable sounds rather sinister, but let's be honest: there are plenty of people who are such deeply controlled civilization victims that it will take a special effort to change their minds, and in many cases it may be just too late.

On the other hand, children at school and people who are already distrustful of the system, such as the long-term "unemployed" or those who feel they have been generally shat on by society, are much more likely to be influenced by a *message that goes against the grain*. This ties in with the Diffusion of Innovations concept I wrote about at length in *Time's Up!* — the idea that you have to start change with a very small group of receptive people (Innovators) who then influence a larger group of less receptive people (Early Adopters) and so on. Of course, if you can send a message out to a huge number of people in one go, then you are likely to capture a similar sector of people without having to work so hard targeting your audience. Both approaches are useful.

Regardless of approach, the message has to be consistent. Consider the following examples.

- Unless we are talking or writing about all humans as a species, then we refer to human beings as "civilized humans" or "civilized people." So it is civilized people who are causing climate change; it is civilized people who are sucking the oceans empty of fish and filling the waterways with pollutants; it is civilized people who are consuming global energy supplies at an expanding rate. The scientifically accepted phrase Anthropogenic Global Warming (AGW) is wrong — hell, I have used it over and over again without realizing I was tarring an entire species with the same brush. The correct phrase is *Civilized Global Warming* (CGW).

- The same applies to societies. Unless we are purposely referring to indigenous and/or non-civilized societies, then we must refer to large groups of people as "civilization" and more specifically "Industrial Civilization." So, it is Industrial Civilization that is melting the polar ice-caps; it is Industrial Civilization that is paving over and clear-cutting natural habitats; it is Industrial Civilization that is causing mass economic slavery across the globe.
- People in their daily lives are not "citizens"; they are people. When you are referring to those who willingly submit to the rules and norms of civilized society, including turning a blind eye to the behavior of governments and their corporate masters, then you can talk about citizens. Otherwise, you talk about "people" or, for more impact, "human beings" or perhaps "non-citizens."

The form of the message is up to you, as long as you are completely consistent in your approach. Tempting as it might feel, you must resist all urges to refer to ordinary people as citizens (to my horror I hear even some of the most radical environmental and human rights groups doing this), and you must differentiate between civilization and the rest of human existence to the point that it becomes first nature.

These word substitutions need to be inserted across the mainstream media: newspapers and magazines, widely read blogs, television, radio and such. If you are a writer for a mainstream outlet, there is no reason you should not do this immediately, for the sake of accuracy if nothing else. An editor may question the changes — though if you are an editor then you should be questioning people who don't make these changes — to which you say, "Anything else would be inaccurate." If you have complete control over your output, then just go for it. In television and radio there are all sorts of opportunities to push something out that will have even more immediate impact. You might not be a presenter or newsreader — if you are then that's wonderful — but as an "expert" in something you might be called upon to speak on a topic, during which there should be ample opportunity to substitute words. As a teacher, musician, actor or other person who engages an audience over a long period of time you can make that word substitution pretty much permanent.

The goal of this is to distinguish between civilized living and all other types of living, a distinction that, as I have said, most people have absolutely no awareness of. The idea that civilization is just one particular way of living needs to be repeated, and repeated. As your undermining efforts develop then you can *make this distinction between real, connected living and civilized life in ever more strident terms.* Over time, and with sufficient effort from many quarters, people will inevitably become deprogrammed from a passive acceptance of the culture.

Once deprogrammed, they can stop pacing and start walking away.

The Information Clearing House

I have a computer file called *insurance.aes256*. I am not the only one. Nor am I the only one to be helping other people to obtain this file and store it on their computers to be shared out to others. I don't know if this file contains anything important, it could be empty, but there are people who desperately, urgently want to know its contents. Some of those people are petrified that it contains information that they want to keep secret and that somehow it may have slipped, unnoticed, out of the back door. These people will do all they can to ensure that information is never revealed — but what can you do about a file that is so deeply encrypted that the most powerful computers in the world would take until beyond the end of the Earth's existence to crack the cipher? Remove every copy of it? Some chance — the genie is well out of the bottle. And if you do decide to pursue this crazy dream, then what if it *is* empty?

The idea of a widely shared, heavily encrypted file that *might* contain valuable, confidential information is a tremendously simple form of undermining. Freedom of Information is complex and far too large a subject to be covered here in any detail: if you want to get some decent background information, I recommend you plunder the archives of both the Electronic Frontier Foundation and the general freedom advocacy group Article 19.[78] From an undermining point of view though, as we have seen, the apparently benign act of Exposure can be the endgame in certain undermining acts. Take the example of Daniel Ellsberg, who in

> *If you are party to confidential information that, if released, could damage the reputation of a company or public body, send it anonymously by mail to one or more newspaper editors.*

1971 was finally — after years of research and lobbying — able to see his wishes of a full release of the infamous Pentagon Papers come to fruition.

The Pentagon Papers detailed the many lies and cover-ups made by a succession of US government administrations during the course of the Vietnam War, acts that helped ensure the public remained largely on side during a campaign that killed untold thousands of innocent people in the pursuit of a political ideology. It is common knowledge today that the Vietnam War had almost nothing to do with protecting people; instead it was about ensuring that America continued having political and economic influence in Southeast Asia. Ellsberg would have preferred to have remained an anonymous source, but this was never likely given the number of parties he offered the Papers to, and he was to have an uncomfortable few years in exchange for his whistle-blowing efforts. Nevertheless, as former Senator Birch Bayh stated,

> The existence of these documents, and the fact that they said one thing and the people were led to believe something else, is a reason we have a credibility gap today, the reason people don't believe the government. This is the same thing that's been going on over the last two-and-a-half years of this administration. There is a difference between what the President says and what the government actually does, and I have confidence that they are going to make the right decision, if they have all the facts.[79]

If Bayh is right, then the release of the Pentagon Papers was one of the most significant acts of undermining ever carried out; for it turned a public that was otherwise slavishly observant of everything civilized governments say into a public that would always be distrustful of anything said by representatives of those same governments. That Ellsberg did not lose his life, as some less fortunate whistle-blowers have, is testament to the value of keeping the story and the main protagonist in the public eye once it became obvious who that protagonist was. The same applies to the modern, if conceited, version of Ellsberg — WikiLeaks cofounder Julian Assange, who has been outspoken in his aims and remained in the public eye in order, most likely, to keep himself alive.

We must be careful about highlighting certain cases that have become globally known. Whistle-blowing and associated acts, such as the leaking of documents, are taking place all the time. Undermining in terms of making available information that should be available is not just random whistle-blowing or leaking, though; it has two very specific purposes.

First, we have to bear in mind that without useful information, most types of undermining will stall at the Investigation stage. A corporation, media outlet or government provides only the information it wants you to see, which is not likely to be the information you want to see. The information you want to see could be anywhere, and could come from anywhere; thus, there needs to be some way of reducing this information entropy so that Underminers can get what they need. Centralization is not necessarily a desirable aim, as a centralized system is easy to shut down compared to a distributed system,[80] but something is required that suits the needs of the Underminer. Whatever that is, it has to *make the release and propagation of useful information easy, efficient and relatively risk-free.* The risk-free element is important because those who have privileged information are unlikely to even want to risk their jobs, let alone their safety.

Second, we want to make it impossible for those who would keep information from the people whose world is being destroyed as a result of our failure to know what is going on, to keep information in a privileged manner at all. In other words, *there needs to be no point in keeping things secret* because the information is bound to come out anyway. This is perhaps a less realistic purpose, given the nature of commerce and politics, but it is truly within the spirit of undermining that the foundations upon which something is built are made so weak that further building becomes a hazardous task.

Both of these purposes are closely entwined in such a way that they can be addressed under one task heading, albeit a huge task that is already engaging millions of people across the world and has already caused untold fallout both good and bad.

Task 9: Make Information Free

Imagine a perfect system of information exchange.

Maybe you have a better imagination than I have, but I can't come up with anything that would qualify as "perfect." Even saying something to the person standing next to you, in a clear voice, in a quiet, otherwise unoccupied room is subject to misinterpretation. So you say everything twice, and ask the other person to repeat back to you what you said and what it means; and then she gets hit by a car on her way out.

So let's not try and imagine something perfect; instead build — at least in theory — something that fulfills the information needs of the Underminer, while also making the lives of those who withhold privileged and damaging information very difficult indeed.

The first observation is that any system of information exchange has to be media neutral. Useful information can come in the form of the spoken word, symbols and signs, written text or illustrations, printed matter, recorded materials in a dizzying array of formats, electronic data either in physical storage or in transit, and everything in between. Clearly the vast majority of *available* useful information comes in electronic form at present, but so does a tsunami of useless, and potentially off-putting, data, meaning that it is actually very difficult in the age of electronic communications to sort out what is useful and what is not. Other forms of information may be far more useful, but more difficult to deliver — such as printed confidential documents or physical recordings made covertly. We potentially need it all.

Second, the system has to observe the maxim that any information may be potentially useful, and thus the provision of information is a matter for the provider, and the use of that information is a matter for the user. It is not down to any intermediary (i.e., whatever might be transporting the information from the source to the destination) to decide whether something is worth transporting. Obviously whoever provides the transportation means has the right to opt out of fulfilling that role based on potential risk, but ideally the transportation process will be one that negates the need to make that decision.

Third, there has to be provision to put at least some protection in place for any party that requires protection from detection; although it is preferable that protection should exist regardless of whether special efforts are made by the various parties involved. This includes allowing for information to be "scrubbed" of any handling evidence, be it electronic headers, fingerprints, background noise that might identify who recorded the information or any other incriminating artifacts. (As a side note, nothing can be completely "idiot proof," and as I have pointed out repeatedly, Underminers must always be aware of the risks to themselves and others and take appropriate steps to reduce those risks.)

Finally, any system must make it technically easy for information to be deposited and retrieved to ensure that no one, within reason, is excluded from the process. As described in Part One, it is often the people who are in the most lowly (but also critical) positions in society who have access to some of the most useful information. If any obstacles are placed in the way, such as requiring knowledge of data authentication keys or having to travel vast distances, then the information may be lost at the first hurdle.

This is sounding like a horribly complex task, but it doesn't have to be. Let's say, for instance, that the information an Underminer needs is held in a particular building or on a particular computer server. The system put in place only has to account for the needs of those who are in contact with that resource. The above list is idealistic to a certain extent, but as long as the general principles are observed *within the context of the information required* then a viable system can be put in place with only a little effort.[81]

As long as anything put in place observes the general principles, it can be as small and simple or as large and complex as you want. If you want to provide a way for others to leak information about nothing but pesticides, then as long as that is stated, you are providing a valuable service for those who can provide and use information about pesticides. Furthermore, you may be — and most likely only ever want to be — a *contributor* to the general purpose of information openness; so if you are able to host a few files, or act as a node for information to pass through, or perhaps help with sifting information into relevant areas, then that is still vital work. I won't go into the technical details of doing this, but rest assured there are plenty of opportunities for carrying out this kind of work, some of which I have already hinted at, and this leads to how it is possible to fulfill the second purpose of this undermining task: making information secrecy obsolete.

Sheer volume and ubiquity of normally privileged information is the key. Prior to September 2011, the information-freedom group WikiLeaks had been releasing only a small portion at a time of the now historically significant Cablegate data. Yes, it is tedious work verifying the integrity of such information and removing personal details where innocent parties would be put at risk, but in many ways the Cablegate release was a PR effort made to continue the promotion of WikiLeaks. More significant is the unknowable quantity of useful information sloshing around the edges of the Internet; in unsecure office filing cabinets and unlocked drawers; in the hands of "lowly" administrative, delivery, processing and disposal workers; in the heads of the same people, and far more who just happen to have been entrusted with the information because they are willing workers who would never betray the trust of their masters. All of this and so much more is waiting to be made available at the touch of a button and the passing of a memo. Such a huge volume of information requires a huge range and number of outlets and methods of transmission, any of which you may be able to create or be a part of.

Pretend you work for a company, and phone radio and TV stations to speak on the company's behalf. Expose the truth behind the company.

The tipping point comes when the amount of useful information that is freed exceeds the amount of information that is kept out of view. If a company or a government cannot plug the leaks through normal means, then it has three choices:

1) Fire and/or have everyone arrested as a possible suspect, thus making continued operation impossible without a complete restaffing of new people, who will, incidentally, already be exposed to the possibility of leaking information.
2) Make conditions so draconian that anyone who operates within their orbit will truly feel like a slave and will be unwilling to continue.
3) Make all information openly available.

If you know where I am coming from, you will already have realized that by *making secrecy an unattainable goal* you are actually making industrial civilization completely untenable. Civilization thrives on people's ignorance, which is what this entire chapter has been about redressing. Hierarchy and edifices of power can exist only where people are unaware of their true aims and methods of attaining these aims. Do you really think that corporate slavery would be accepted in human society if people were not led to believe it was for their own good rather than the good of those who sit at the very top?

I am not saying that through the vital tasks in this chapter the whole of civilization will be able to look at and around itself, and understand with startling clarity what the truth is. For one, we, the Underminers, are but few at the moment. But I do know that with ingenuity, courage and effort we will start to remove the Veil of Ignorance from the minds of those who continue to believe that Industrial Civilization is the one right way to live.

This will make what is to follow a whole lot easier.

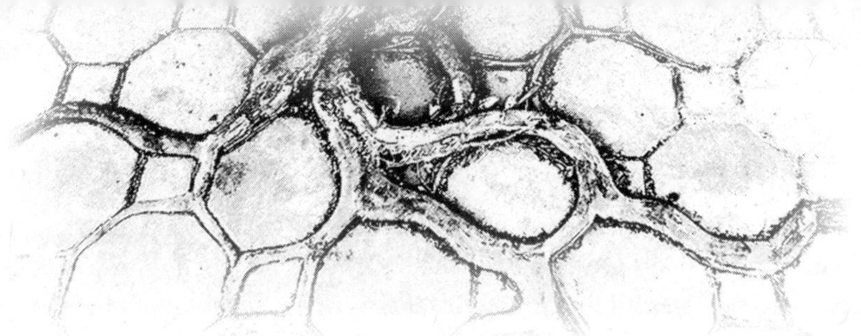

CHAPTER SIX

Undermining the Machine

THE DEATH OF RACHEL CORRIE on March 16, 2003 was tragic but inevitable. Rachel was crushed by a bulldozer operated by a member of the Israeli Defense Forces while attempting to prevent the demolition of a pharmacist's house in the Palestinian town of Rafah. I realize that discussing many aspects of Rachel's death is contentious; but discussion is important because among the political and ideological toing and froing is little mention that it was bound to happen. Amidst the intense and often dangerous work of the International Solidarity Movement (ISM), Rachel Corrie's presence in the Gaza Strip was a genuine expression of empathy with the plight of ordinary Palestinian people caught up in a horrific situation. That the work of the ISM also involved "embracing Palestinian militants, even suicide bombers, as freedom fighters, [adopting] a risky policy of 'direct action' [including] entering military zones to interfere with the operations of Israeli soldiers"[82] was part of the inevitability of Rachel's death. But it was not the underlying reason.

The driver of the Caterpillar D9 bulldozer, a Russian with considerable operational experience, claims not to have seen the activist standing in front of the machine's armor-plated blade. This is entirely possible. The fact that the targets of the bulldozers were the homes of Palestinian people, whose presence was illegal only by virtue of a politician's decree, makes the claim of anyone not seeing a person blocking the progress of the machine irrelevant. Lives were intended to be crushed. Another life, taken accidentally or not, would hardly register as far as the political decisions that led to the razing of Rafah were concerned.

On the other side of the machine's steel blade stood the activism that Rachel Corrie both carried out and represented in all its tragic folly. As she stated, "I feel like I'm witnessing the systematic destruction of a people's ability to survive. It's horrifying. It takes a while to get what's happening here. People here are trying to maintain their lives, trying to be happy. Sometimes I sit down to dinner with people and I realize there is a massive military machine surrounding us, trying to kill the people I'm having dinner with." Yet, for whatever reason, she felt that by standing in front of a machine built entirely for destructive purposes, operated by a driver employed not to question his role, ordered by a political regime that felt entirely justified in taking lives at the stroke of pen, the destruction would be stopped.

War is a symptom. You do not stop anything by dealing with the symptoms. You stop things by dealing with the causes. The causes of the ongoing Israeli-Palestinian conflict may appear to be complex, yet it is only the ongoing story that is truly complex and fraught with contention. The causes are simple: the leaders of a nation desire something they don't have; the leaders of another nation do not want to give that something away. Substitute "nation" for "religion," "corporation," "military establishment" or any other institution and you have the cause of every war fought in modern times.

And even then you aren't addressing the root of the problem: why does anyone or anything want what the other has?

Stopping the Shopping

Why do people want to buy things they do not have? This isn't an easy question to answer because there are all sorts of forces operating on individuals, their families, their peer groups and their other spheres of influence. How these individuals, families, etc. respond to the various forces depends on other factors, among them the intensity of and time spent under the influence of the commercial selling machine, and whether other influential people have already been suitably "primed" to be fully fledged Shoppers.

In order to undermine the forces that make people want to buy things they would not need if they weren't being persuaded to buy them, you need to understand how those forces manifest themselves. Why we would want to focus on shopping *per se* is that the forces involved in making people buy things are the same forces that make people behave in all sorts of other highly destructive (both externally and internally) ways that serve to keep the industrial machine functioning. So, off the top of my head, here are what I consider to be some of the most powerful ways Industrial

Civilization makes us want to shop, and keeps us shopping even when we don't want to. You can probably think of a few more:

- Advertising appeals to the emotions — in particular the contrast between negative emotions (dressed up as "you don't have this") and positive emotions ("you do have this"). The nature of advertising is such that it can, as with movies and live music, be carefully tuned to make us feel whatever the advertiser and their client wants us to feel.
- The consumer culture has created a general sense of the "need" to shop for everything, using whatever currency the state deems acceptable. Almost by default when we need something (let alone just wanting it) our first response is to consider buying it, new, from a major retailer; in addition, we will buy from whichever place is uppermost in our mind as a result of advertising and physical presence.
- Obsolescence is designed into everything we purchase, by dint of its limited "shelf life," its lack of durability, its no longer being "in fashion" or even there simply not being enough of whatever it is.
- The mass media, in particular, imbue us with a sense of duty by making us afraid of economic failure on a larger scale than we can normally appreciate. Thus, we are urged to "spend our way" out of a recession or "prop up the economy" with our spending. Meanwhile further investments (grants, tax breaks and rule changes) are made to assist the things that make us buy more.
- Special events such as sales excite our more primal instincts by making things available for a limited period, or at a certain price if you buy a certain amount, or by creating a sense of competition with other Consumers through limited (as least in theory) numbers or locations where something can be obtained.

If you break down each item into a number of components, taking special note of the "nuts and bolts" that hold them together, potential undermining targets start to become clear. If you know how to stop people shopping, then you are well on your way to undermining the entire infrastructure of the industrial system.

Task 1: Subvertising

Defacing an advertisement is as easy as taking a leak, at least if you are a man. Take a black marker and write or draw something of your choice on the advert assaulting your personal space while you pee, taking care not to lose your aim. Having not been in a ladies' washroom since my glorious summer performing hygiene tasks at a beachfront McDonald's, I can't vouch for what happens there now — though until fairly recently adverts in washrooms were a rarity. As for the black marker, it can easily be slipped in and out of the pocket for whatever subtle purposes you require. If you are feeling a little angrier, you can take the advert off entirely. Posters and billboards still play a vital part in the system of selling us things we otherwise would not want; but there is a powerful ally for Underminers in the form of the Billboard Liberation Front, whose *Art and Science of Billboard Improvement* is perhaps the *de facto* guide for practical subvertisers everywhere. It begins,

> Billboards have become as ubiquitous as human suffering, as difficult to ignore as a beggar's outstretched fist. Every time you leave your couch or cubicle, momentarily severing the electronic umbilicus, you enter the realm of their impressions. Larger than life, subtle as war, they assault your senses with a complex coda of commercial instructions, the messenger RNA of capitalism. Every time you get in a car, or ride a bus, or witness a sporting event, you receive their instructions. You can't run and you can't hide, because your getaway route is lined to the horizon with signs, and your hidey-hole has a panoramic view of an 8-sheet poster panel.[83]

Print out your own newspaper headlines for insertion in headline boards outside news stands (they are rarely locked), or even create your own board you can place in prominent locations. Different kinds of headlines can have different effects: you can create scares; you can undermine public figures or organizations; you can parody the media itself....

Subvertising as a concept obviously goes beyond the physical billboard, stretching across the realms of electronic communications and digital media and beyond. Its purpose is to change the meaning of a message into whatever the perpetrator desires, ensuring it is *always different from the original intended message.* Thus the Nike Swoosh becomes an evil grin overseeing row-upon-row of sweatshop workers; Ronald McDonald transforms into a murderous clown intent on corrupting children; General Motors is revealed to read "Global Murder"; the British Conservative party is exposed as performing one big CON, and so on.

In the context of this task, it is the emotive aspect of advertising that needs to be reversed, neutralized or parodied, depending on what is most appropriate. If an advertisement suggests that buying a certain smartphone will make your life better, the obvious retort would be that it makes the lives of the people making the smartphone components immeasurably worse, ripping them out of their former communities, despoiling the local environment and bringing a culture of greed and monetary want to places where previously there was something far more important. Not easy to put on a billboard — but a simple image of someone hanging themselves from a factory roof could do the trick.

Despite the obvious criticism that a small group of Underminers can never match the reach and numeric superiority of the corporate advertising giants, subvertising — first given prominence by the group Adbusters — is a *very good introduction to practical undermining.* First, it is fairly low risk, and generally you aren't doing anything illegal — though it's a good way to practice being covert in a relatively safe environment. Second, with success it can lead to bigger things. As I mentioned earlier, doing something quick and easy can still give you a buzz; it's contagious, not just to others who might like doing the same thing, but for your own sense of adventure. Once

an easy task is wrapped up, then more challenging tasks won't seem so distant. Third, subvertising is a great outlet for creativity. Who but a creative person could have thought up the subvertising below?

Where, what and how you subvertise is down to your imagination, always following the rules, of course. In Chapter 3 the point about who can potentially be an Underminer is that there is no obvious place to look; and this applies in the case of subvertising — you don't know who could be influenced by a piece of emotion-reversal subvertising. If it is a lonely bus stop with a 3x6 advert on the side, then it's as good a place to start as any. You stand a hell of a better chance getting your job done unnoticed in a quiet spot than climbing to the top of a gigantic freeway billboard. Although, for anyone planning to do the latter — hats off to you!

Task 2: Building Barterland

Get something you have grown, baked, produced or made yourself — something you think most people would be happy to pay money for. I can understand if this seems like a tall order, but I also know that we all have the potential for creating beautiful and delicious things if only we have a bit more faith in our abilities. If you're feeling a bit humble or embarrassed, get something provided by a member of your family or a close friend. Now take it to a supermarket, and when you get to the checkout with whatever you have decided to buy, ask the cashier (the clue to your potential success is in the title) how much she will knock off your bill in exchange for your own goods.

I can almost guarantee that, even if the cashier is friendly and sympathetic, the transaction will fail, because the supermarket could never accept anything but cash or a cash equivalent, such as a credit card. If you try the same at a small local store or a market stall, your chances of success are greatly enhanced; but let's stick with the supermarket for the moment, because now I want you to call a supervisor, in a polite way, and ask why bartering — for that is what you are trying to do — is not acceptable. Don't accept excuses like "It's company policy" as an answer: you want to know why that particular type of transaction is not permitted. A reasonable argument might be that it's just too complicated to process something that has no agreed, tangible value, and cannot be further exchanged easily.

And that's the point. A supermarket, and anything else that operates on capitalist principles, will exchange goods or services only for something that can be further exchanged, either for other goods and services or other forms of finance, such as bonds or shares. Bartering operates outside the capitalist system, more or less,[84] and it makes "authorities" very nervous. Take this quotation from the IRS:

> If you engage in barter transactions you may have tax responsibilities. You may be subject to liabilities for income tax, self-employment tax, employment tax, or excise tax. Your barter activities may result in ordinary business income, capital gains or capital losses, or you may have a nondeductible personal loss.
>
> Barter dollars or trade dollars are identical to real dollars for tax reporting. If you conduct any direct barter — barter for another's products or services — you will have to report the fair market value of the products or services you received on your tax return.[85]

But hang on! How can you report a "fair market value" of something that, by its very nature, operates outside the capitalist system? When I carry out computer repairs at people's houses in my local area, I am placing an arbitrary value on my time, based on what I think people can afford as well as making the trip worth my while. In all cases I offer customers a barter option, which some — an increasing number, to my joy — take up. It also gives an opportunity to discuss the reason I prefer to barter rather than take cash. How can all of that be encompassed in something as crude as "fair market value"?

The power of bartering, and its cousins gifting, lending/borrowing and timesharing, lies in its simplicity. The IRS note refers to Barter Exchanges; in fact it goes to great pains to emphasize the function of such exchanges rather than getting into a public tizzy over informal bartering. The obvious reason for this is that barter exchanges, like other market economies, formalize the process of exchange, making it far more complex than it needs to be, and thus they play easily into the hands of the financial system. Informal bartering, on the other hand, just is. Two parties mutually decide on the value of something against something else and make the exchange, perhaps right away, perhaps later on, as in the form of a service that may be carried out whenever it is required. I built a website for a local farm that was branching out its business, and in exchange I got all the materials to build a raised bed, along with a load of soil and a few bags of manure. In addition, I'm giving ongoing support that will be paid for in the form of corn for our chickens.

This is nothing unusual. People barter, gift, lend and share all the time — but on being asked how they pay for things, they will invariably respond by stating various types of formal payment — credit card, personal check, bank transfer, cash, and so on. The mindset in the Dominant Culture is that we have to pay for everything, and be paid for everything, using a formally agreed method approved by the system.

Even when we don't.

This is the fault of the corporations that have controlled the way we trade from their very first appearance in the civilized world. We have to not only physically abide by the rules they have set up but we have to *think* that we have to abide by these rules and there is no other way to do it. So, go to that supermarket and expose the corporate control of our thoughts for what it is. And when you have become suitably frustrated, start thinking in a different way, and doing things in a different way. For a start, use your local stores and businesses, which will undoubtedly be more amenable to alternatives, and encourage them to accept — and publicize — non-capitalist methods of payment. If this becomes a reality, then help publicize what they do. *Get local people to use local services, and discourage them from feeding the corporations* that are keeping the illusion of capitalist infallibility

Exercise: Not-not Bartering

Argument: We don't trust or know each other well enough to barter.
Counter argument/opposition:

Argument: We don't know the intrinsic value of things without a cash equivalent.
Counter argument/opposition:

Argument: There is no way of profiting from bartering without obvious fraud.
Counter argument/opposition:

Argument: We cannot easily store everything we desire for later use.
Counter argument/opposition:

Argument: Bartering gives no opportunity to gain status through material wealth.
Counter argument/opposition:

Argument: Bartering is socially unacceptable in a capital society.
Counter argument/opposition:

Argument: Bartering requires preparation and, usually, pre-agreement.
Counter argument/opposition:

alive. Not only are you taking money away from the corporate machine, you are undermining the dangerous message that the way we used to do things between each other — the simple way that everyone could understand and embrace — is no longer acceptable.

To be fair, it's an easy message to propagate. I made up a list of the reasons we, as civilized people, no longer barter or carry out any of the other informal things mentioned earlier. As an exercise, go through these points and think of a counter argument or some reason why each is not relevant.

Most of these "reasons" are complete red herrings, because they are framed in the mindset of Industrial Civilization. For instance, why would you want to profit from bartering at all? The point of the exercise is to force you to think in an uncivilized manner — face down the arguments head on, and think from the point of view of an Underminer. Now go and start bartering, and don't carry on reading until you have done it at least once.

Task 3: Fixing Things

We all need practical skills. At the end of *Time's Up!* I outlined some of the key attributes for living in a post-collapse society. This was not just some crude list of bushcraft skills that will mean you can kill, collect, heal and shelter as necessary — though all of that is incredibly useful — but a collection of ideas that contributes to the development of a longer-term strategy for building a future, such as learning how to work together as a team. The contribution of practical ability to this list was purposely understated, but for some types of undermining it is practical skills that come to the fore.

While I willingly submit to others with more ability than I, when time is of the essence or something has to be done just right, there is really no substitute for getting down and dirty with your hands, particularly when it involves those jobs that all too easily get skipped because buying something new is so easy. Let's take the example of a toilet. Last week the toilet wasn't working. I had never, probably to my shame, stripped down a toilet cistern. (I really would love to install a composting toilet, but at the moment our garden is above a steep slope down to a river, so anything that gets into the soil will likely end up somewhere in the burn below; using a large plastic trap in a very big hole will have to wait a bit longer while I get this book finished.) Anyway, to deal with the toilet, I vaguely knew how to get to the sump connector and had bought a flap valve (a tiny sheet of shaped plastic) for £1 from a local hardware store.[86] This would be no big deal to a plumber, but to me the moment I fixed the cistern back on the wall, having effected a repair, and flushed the loo, was a moment of joy. I had learned a useful skill, and saved the cost of a plumber and an entirely new sump — for that is what a plumber would have fitted — in the process.

And a few weeks ago I learned to carve spoons from pieces of wood.

There is no smugness at all in any of this, just pleasure, and a great deal of disappointment because each time you learn a new skill it becomes clear how many other skills we have lost and are just starting to claw back again. For most people, sadly, those skills will never be regained — instead, as society collapses, the repeated pressing of remote control buttons and sending of multimedia messages will be used as a pathetic surrogate for learning how to survive in the new world. This is tragic, when it could be so positive.

I'm in no hurry to undermine the plumbing profession — hell, when the shit hits the fan, we'll really need to be able to deal with it — but as a way of undermining corporations such as The Home Depot, OBI, B&Q and Lowe's, *being able to fix things yourself and for others at little or no cost* is very handy. There is a key question to raise here that adds to the effectiveness of repairing as undermining: is buying something new really that easy? On the face of it, especially if you live in a city, that would seem to be the case; but assuming that the place you are buying from won't accept barter — so we are talking corporate retailers here — you have to use cash. Where does that cash come from?

A small part of it might come from welfare benefits, but for the vast amount of money any of us have, we have to go out and work for it, using up a considerable chunk of our lives in the process. This is something I'm going to address later. In addition, think about the people who make the things you are buying or who carry out the services you are using: again, that is time they do not have for themselves, their families, their community. And, of course, there is the incalculable ecological cost of the processes involved in producing goods and making commercial services viable.

Convenience might be one word for this. There are others.

Obsolescence is the word we use to describe the limited lifespan of something, such as a hinge being able to open and close only so many times before it shears off or a bearing eventually wearing out through friction. Built-in or Planned Obsolescence are terms used to describe a deliberately limited lifespan. By design. On purpose.

Almost all "consumer" goods have Planned Obsolescence, for if they didn't, then you wouldn't need to replace them at the rate required to keep a business profitable. Durability is one way of controlling the rate at which things are replaced or need repairing, and there is little doubt that as goods become cheaper, their durability is reduced — this is the market economy operating as it should do (i.e., you get what you pay for). Simple lack of durability in cheap goods has little to attach a conspiracy to; basically we have been stimulated as a society to want a great deal beyond what we actually need, so as demand rises, the things we want are produced in increasing numbers for as little money as possible, and inevitably quality suffers. Of course our expectations have to be managed too, so we have been very cleverly manipulated into not expecting goods to be durable. This is achieved through a combination of managing Consumers' priorities away from quality and need toward functionality and desire; and by purposely making older goods undesirable, so when they do break we aren't really that bothered about it. Fashion plays a major part in that, and I shall attack that in the next section.

Beyond this manipulation of expectations and desires is something more sinister, probably first expounded by Bernard London in 1932, and revealed by Adbusters to be a source of a far more subtle modern application of Planned Obsolescence:

> In a word, people generally, in a frightened and hysterical mood, are using everything that they own longer than was their custom before the depression. In the earlier period of prosperity, the American people did not wait until the last possible bit of use had been extracted from every commodity. They replaced old articles with new for reasons of fashion and up-to-dateness. They gave up old homes and old automobiles long before they were worn out, merely because they were obsolete. All business, transportation, and labor had adjusted themselves to the prevailing habits of the American people. Perhaps, prior to the panic, people were too extravagant; if so, they have now gone to the other extreme and have become retrenchment-mad.
>
> People everywhere are today disobeying the law of obsolescence. They are using their old cars, their old tires, their old radios and their old clothing much longer than statisticians had expected on the basis of earlier experience.
>
> I would have the Government assign a lease of life to shoes and homes and machines, to all products of manufacture, mining and agriculture, when they are first created, and they would be sold and used within the term of their existence definitely known by the consumer. After the allotted time had expired,

> these things would be legally "dead" and would be controlled by the duly appointed governmental agency and destroyed if there is widespread unemployment. New products would constantly be pouring forth from the factories and marketplaces, to take the place of the obsolete, and the wheels of industry would be kept going and employment regularized and assured for the masses.[87]

To all intents and purposes, London's policy idea has been implemented wholesale, though instead of the "duly appointed governmental agency" controlling obsolescence, ordinary people entranced by the consumer culture do it themselves via their trash, recycling bins and domestic landfill; insurance companies and their property development partners do it by demolishing old buildings and constructing new ones in their place; vehicle manufacturers do it by offering trade-ins for old cars and trucks, to be replaced by shiny new models. The corporate-controlled governments of the modern civilized world can just sit back and enjoy the fruits of the Planned Obsolescence machine they put in operation, occasionally making the odd tweak to keep us replacing things at the correct rate. So what can we do about this that isn't already obvious?

This product is designed to rapidly become obsolete so that you have to buy another one.
The economy depends on your stupidity.
Support your economy: support obsolescence.

Adbusters' Micah White, in his riposte to London's pamphlet, says we are locked in "a vicious cycle with two exits: the consumer's debt ridden grave or the freedom of the culture jammer who refuses to replace the junk that breaks — the junk we never needed anyways." Refusal is certainly one course of action — coupled with the determination to repair that which does break and the awareness that we don't need most of the things we have. What about something a bit more underhand and proactive?

A few labels placed in strategic positions on product boxes, shelves, shop windows, advertisements and brochures can do wonders for people's perception of the consumer culture. It's also a lot more fun than dumbly traipsing round shopping malls with eyes dulled by the constant promise of all-new everything.

Task 4: Enjoying Recessions

It's time to get positive. As I write this, the global economy is still struggling to recover from the kind of nosedive not seen since the 1930s. Only today the main share trading platforms lost between 3.5 and 5 percent of their total value. That's not to say that the fall continues day after day — if it did then by the time you read this the economy would be ruined and the global ecology would be singing a many-voiced song of jubilation in all the languages of life. Somehow I doubt that's the case, for now.

Of course, this runs entirely counter to the mass-media and political messages we are supposed to obey. In Chapter 5 we saw how our friend Sarah posed as a representative of the economic glitterati and gave out a message that most right-minded people would see as completely counter-intuitive — that economic growth has to continue in order to make rich people even richer, or words to that effect. But that is essentially what we are being fed all the time, except with the top layer — the fat cats — neatly ignored so we don't stop to wonder why we get so concerned about things like recessions.

Like all effective military maneuvers, there should be a second front, just in case the thing that is being undermined manages to recover and take a different route. So let's all put on a big smile and share the joy of economic failure.

Did you feel the joy? It's a difficult one to pull off first time because, as you would have heard and seen countless times during that day of "bad" news, the brainwashing is relentless. Nothing, I repeat, *nothing is more important to Industrial Civilization than keeping the economy buoyant and healthy.* If you could undermine only one thing in your life, I would

Exercise: Smile, the Economy Is Crashing

This is a great little exercise for making your day brighter. Keep the news on the radio or television for a while, and listen to the economic pundits. You might want to check at the beginning of the day to make sure it's "bad" news, because no one wants to feel grumpy without good cause. As the pundits and "experts" drone on about Company X losing money, Stock Market Y dropping a few hundred points and the GDP of Nation Z stagnating, smile. In fact, laugh. Don't be mocking or sarcastic — take real pleasure in the situation by lighting up your face with a grin, celebrating the news that the killing machine of Industrial Civilization is falling, bleeding, writhing in pain as the Dollars, Euros and Yuan gush into a great lake of institutional debt. This is not your problem, it is your release. Today is a good day because the economy is having a bad day.

recommend you undermine this belief, for without belief there is no reality — something that politicians know only too well. *If civilized society can be made to believe that a failing market economy is good news, then the market economy will fail.*

Set up or help promote a Freecycle network or other household item giveaway scheme.

Disrupt "legitimate" commercial activities by acting as a Rogue Trader, for instance by bidding on resources or land set aside for exploitation when you have no intention of buying. (Make sure there is a "cooling off" period). Use the resulting furor to publicize your reasons.

A quick point of clarification: I use terms like "industrial economy" and "market economy" deliberately, to distinguish the trading, buying and lending systems of the civilized world from anything that is real and connected. The word "economics" derives from the ancient Greek words οἶκος (oikos), meaning "house," and νόμος (*nomos*), meaning "law" or "custom." It is quite true that there isn't necessarily any purity in the form of economics from which the Greek term is derived; however, there are types of economies, such as the general management of food and essential items within the household, and the informal trades and exchanges that take place in close-knit communities, that should be nurtured. These types of economies are the kinds that matter, for if you do not know where your next meal is coming from, or do not have enough fuel to keep warm, and have no means to borrow or trade to satisfy that need, then it is bad news. You are allowed to frown.

But move outside the realm of domestic and community economies and we enter a type of system that thrives on exploitation; it encourages greed and hierarchy; it values profit and growth above stability. The industrial machine needs us to believe that kind of economy is good, and so we must be distressed when it is wounded. Which is why we have to learn to smile at its downfall.

Then we can teach others. On November 12, 2008, the Yes Men, along with a team of designers and writers, released a fake version of *The New York Times*. The aim was to tell the news that people might want to hear, rather than the news they are made to hear:

> The papers, dated July 4th of next year, were headlined with long-awaited news: "IRAQ WAR ENDS". The edition, which bears the same look and feel as the real deal, includes stories describing

> what the future could hold, if we forced Obama to be the president we'd elected him to be: national health care, the abolition of corporate lobbying, a maximum wage for CEOs, etc. Less momentous, but poignant, was columnist Tom Friedman's letter of resignation, full of remorse for his consistently idiotic and fact free predictions about the Iraq war.[88]

I'm not going to copy the front page here, because what is important is not the message produced on that day — it supported a healthy economy, for one thing — but how it was broadcast. There is no question that an enterprise such as producing a high-quality handout, however thin, to thousands of people is time-intensive and potentially expensive; but it is worth it if the message is powerful enough. The entire paper, along with a number of other articles was replicated on a website bearing a striking resemblance to *The New York Times'* own site. We have to be careful not to get too excited about websites, for although they are considerably easier to replicate and alter than print media, the real work is getting people to stumble upon the fake site and continue to believe that the fake is the real one for as long as possible. I will come back to this point later in the chapter. The tangible piece of media, placed in the hand and having the kind of appearance to encourage a person to read and take it at face value is, in my opinion, a far more powerful thing than the ephemeral byte-exchange taking place on a computer screen. One advantage is that it can be kept (*The New York Times* reckoned the fake would become a collector's item) and re-read at the recipient's leisure. The tactile nature of the paper makes it something that imbues a sense of ownership, especially if it has been given with a smile and the impression that this is something the recipient really wants. The communication and empathy skills from your Underminers Toolbox are essential here, as are artistic and writing talents. Oh, and a way of getting the things printed without too much expense.

Try to avoid the clichéd glossy leaflets and advertising flyers, and don't bother slipping something inside something else unless you are trying to undermine the thing you are infiltrating, like a bicycle advert in Big Trucks Monthly. Chances are that anything that takes the form of a piece of junk mail will be treated as such. The same with pop-ups and dodgy redirects on websites as opposed to proper pages — they will likely be blocked or ignored or worse, get your host blacklisted.

Now back to the message. For this exercise I want you to take a genuine article about an economic subject from a mainstream newspaper. As with the listening task, concentrate on "bad" news. What you now need to do is reverse the message entirely, putting an unremittingly positive spin on something that really should be positive. You might want to take out references to individuals who have been hurt through little fault of their own, for they are victims of the system after all. Once you have corrected any typos or grammatical errors, send or give the happy news item to a friend or colleague as though you have cut and pasted it from a genuine news source — well, you have — and ask them (as if it is genuine) what they think of it. If they are left with the feeling that it's a spoof, then you have a bit more work to do. If they get some kind of positive feeling from it, then find out why, and note the parts that particularly worked. If they start questioning whether the entire economic system is bullshit designed to make us slaves of the machine, then you, my friend, are a genius and could have a very bright future bringing down the economy.

Task 5: Locking the Mall

If shopping mall or supermarket car parks are locked up overnight, add your own padlocks and chains. Do the same for storefronts/roller blinds if they are already locked.

If you thought "Stopping the Shopping" meant preventing people from getting to their chosen place of retail therapy, then this is the task for you. You will remember the discussion in Chapter 5 about Black Friday: there I suggested all sorts of different ways of preventing the consumption message from getting through but not how to prevent the targets of the message from getting to the place they were being influenced to go to. The latter task was excluded because it falls outside the Veil of Ignorance — the Shopper or Consumer is already keen to shop or consume, hence the titles so willingly donned by victims of the consumer culture. At this stage drastic action is needed to undermine the act of consumption — but not just any old action, because *it is undermining only if it reconnects people to the real world.*

So, choose a lovely day, a day on which people could be doing something so much better than warming their credit cards. A weekend is good, say a Saturday in the summer with the forecast set to suit days of adventure and exploration — walks in the woods or on the beach, time spent together tending the garden, playing football, idling by a river or building a den. Things people used to do before shopping became the most popular leisure activity in the civilized world. That means you start on a Friday night, at closing time.

Many parking lots have locking barriers to prevent drive-ins or stop anyone using that precious Tarmac for anything other than parking cars. (And on that point, why is it I have never met a skateboarder I didn't like yet have had more arguments with people driving cars than in any other situation?) Have a look next time you pass such a barrier. Is there a way of locking it shut manually? Is it already locked shut when the store or mall is closed? Take a photo of the barrier, or find a photo of something very similar and estimate the size of the locking points — the two places that, when connected, mean the barrier cannot be opened. Now get the best-quality toughened lock you can: a decent second-hand motorcycle chain will do the job very well. Are you starting to feel like a criminal? That's the mindset you need, because laxity will mean you get caught. You could have be seen by security cameras or caught in the act; you might have left fingerprints; the lock purchase could be traced back to you. Don't be complacent.

The strange thing, though, is you may not even be breaking the "law." Tampering with private property is perhaps the worst thing that could be pinned on you, but you are not breaking and entering — quite the opposite — and you are not trespassing, because you never went beyond the barrier. Odd, isn't it? Undermining is like that.

The next day, that sunny Saturday, the cars queue up at the locked barrier — and some of them drive away to do better things. On the radio, news of traffic queues at the Giganti Mall dissuades others from even bothering to set out. The day is enjoyed in a different way. Some people even question why the act of "sabotage" was carried out.

It's a lot more serious to block a public road than a private one — any misdemeanor taking place on private land has to be privately prosecuted, and if there is no one in sight then that "no one" can hardly be convicted of trespassing. Shopping malls, retail parks, leisure parks and other behemoths of the consumer culture have private roads. Vans are relatively cheap to rent, and there is no law against covering vehicle identification plates on private land. I think that's enough information to be going on with.

Use hazard warning tape (available from lots of suppliers) to mark off car parks, entrances and any other commercial or government access routes. It's amazing how accepting people are of simple "security" measures.

Moving into less risky territory, have you noticed how radio shows are increasingly relying on traffic reports from members of the public? They like to be right on the ball and will snap up any news of road closures and delays being offered, as long as the report sounds authoritative enough. Now suppose your nearest Giganti Mall had an electrical failure or a damaged roof that was leaking water into the shops; or perhaps there are emergency repair works on the approach road, meaning it's not even worth trying to get to the mall today! You don't even have to arrange that. You can just make it up; not too often because after a while the radio station will stop trusting callers, but once in a while a little road closure or blackout could do wonders for the lives of those planning to immerse themselves in retail hell. Team up with a couple of other people to make the story more convincing and likely to be broadcast; this applies to a variety of other undermining tasks for which more is, indeed, more. If you feel like a bit of acting, then it shouldn't take too much effort to transform yourself into the communications director of one of the malls or leisure complexes affected by the "incident" — it certainly reduces the chance of the radio station calling the place up to verify the story.

Getting Too Clever

Just out of interest, would you have put any other messages on the billboard banner, something that makes people think rather than be informed of a closure? This is a common mistake made by creative activists who (and I don't want to make enemies here, just state the truth) are sometimes so full of their own cleverness that they completely miss the point of what they are trying to get across. I have been guilty of this, writing too-subtle fake press releases with the intention of making the recipient think, rather than simply getting the necessary "information" across and producing spoof logos that are more creative than they are effective.

We forget that civilized people are essentially trained to read only headlines and accept things at face value, which is why television uses sound bites by politicians rather than complex analysis. It's not so much a time thing, far more a way of conditioning the public to see everything in terms of discrete, disconnected packages. Most people won't get the clever allegory or the subtle metaphor contained in an artistic countercultural performance — they just see a smug student dressed up as a prison guard shouting random words. So, when it comes to the Undermining message, unless you know the audience will really get something, keep it simple.

On a smaller scale, there are countless billboards that advertise sales, grand openings and other commercial fakery that draws in people who might otherwise have stayed at home with their friends and family. And before anyone says, "Shopping is a social event," may I just remind you of the communities that have been ripped apart by those out-of-town retail celebrations, and the lives torn asunder by overspending in the desire to keep accumulating material goods? These billboards don't need custom treatment such as a nice piece of subvertising entails; instead, an all-purpose paste-on banner proclaiming, "Closed until further notice!" or "Canceled!" can be used on almost anything related to retail. Alternatively, if you're feeling more destructive, or simply need an outlet, then tear the billboard off, or — as I discovered a couple of years ago — tear a corner, leaving enough loose paper for someone else to finish the job. Encouraging latent Underminers to do something useful is all part of the mix.

Fashion Makes You Ugly

Yesterday,[89] the cofounder and former CEO of Apple Computer died. I do not mourn the passing of Steve Jobs as so many people are doing while I type these words. The media sources vomited out pre-written tributes, and countless members of the culture of celebrity have made their thoughts known, without exception glowing and full of admiration for a life spent filling homes and offices with technology. He was a giant in the world of computers, a poster boy for the hi-tech generation. It would be apt if, after a short while, he was forgotten, replaced in the minds of the many by another, more up-to-date model.

Callous doesn't come close to it, but then callousness is normal in the world of fashion. Steve Jobs, along with a host of designers, financiers, marketing people and the inevitable shareholding string-pullers, created a new paradigm for the fashion industry, whereby something formerly cutting edge and luxurious became an affordable commodity, then used goods on eBay and finally detritus in the garbage stream at astonishing speed. Breathless consumerism, accompanied by lung-bursting screams as the first in line for Version Next of Product Latest gets his hands on the electronic equivalent of fool's gold.

Fashion exists to keep humans in a state of psychological flux: malcontents always looking for the next thing to desire. What is especially evident in the destructive monster called Industrial Civilization is that the idea of fashion is increasingly becoming the driving force behind economic growth. Where once it was enough for industry to ensure that everyone had what most people in the industrial world now consider basic goods, such as a pair of shoes, a warm coat, a radio and a refrigerator, now the saturation of the Western economies with such "basic" goods, along with ever-shrinking profit, means that baseline consumption has to be augmented by a constant desire for different versions of the same thing.

Make up stickers saying things like "Product of Industrial Agriculture," "Energy Waster" or "Made in Sweatshops," and stick them on relevant items in supermarkets and large stores.

Mention "fashion" and we think of clothing. Haut couture and the catwalk freak show. It is that, but it is much more, and it goes beyond the physical to symbolize a cultural mindset that embraces manufactured rapid turnover and the rejection of anything that isn't defined as "current" by those who tell us what we should desire. The net effect of this contrived aesthetic obsolescence is a trail of environmental destruction, factories full of slave labor, entire cultures forced into frenzied consumerism, and the scarred minds — such young, embattled minds — that take the brunt of fashion's brutal marketing army.

Nature doesn't do fashion. Trees don't compete in the bark color or leaf shape stakes; rivers don't meander deeper into the bank to impress their peers; birds don't all change the length of their plumage or the sound of their calls because some bird in the next meadow told them it was the latest thing. Neither would we without the presence of an industry driven entirely by money. The fashion industry takes us from the cradle and teaches us that acceptance is determined by the cost of your shoes, the color of your nails, the functionality of your phone — the way we express every aspect of our outward appearance to the world. This is not just clever marketing; it is — as writer and teacher Ana Salote[90] says — mind control.

Fashion Is Scary Medicine

BY ANA SALOTE

Only powerful mind control could fill the streets with so many black leggings. Where did all those tons of cotton Lycra and dyes come from? In two years' time where will they be and why?

Why are we still promoting and celebrating an industry driven by disposability and waste, one that sucks in a ridiculous proportion of our hard-earned (for women particularly) cash? Part of the answer lies in the way language shapes perception.

Mexican Toltec wisdom discusses this power of language to create and destroy. According to the Toltec, words are not just sounds or symbols; they are a force that shapes our perceived reality. As we use them we assent to their culturally assigned meanings. Words cast spells.

It begins simply with the act of naming. Attention is the ability to discriminate and to focus only on that which we want to perceive. During infancy adults showed us where to direct our attention and reinforced it by repetition so we learned our reality. Language was the first step in the process. To name something is the beginning of attention. By the involuntary process of learning our mother tongue we imbibe the values enshrined within it. This is part of a process by which humans are domesticated in the same way as other animals. It occurs before more intentional methods of manipulation that may be easier to detect and resist.

To see beyond this inherited reality it is important to consider our words and the conceptualization that surrounds them, to consider the unconscious agreements we make with our own language and, if needs be, to reframe those agreements in our own terms. To be free is to choose our own meanings and use words with impeccable attention to their import.

Every time the word "fashion" is used it is mentally tagged with youth, glamour, excitement, air-brushed perfection, the Dream. We need a new language to give an alternative account of fashion — to add counter tags like waste, exploitation and mind control. Fashion: let's encourage a new verb to grow from the noun revealing its true nature. How about fashing (brain-fashing), an ugly word for an ugly thing.

> Fashing: the exploitative or damaging creation of an artificial need.
> British Fashing Week.

Dispensing with fashion needn't mean People's Party blue overalls. I have never seen an Indian woman of whatever size, shape, age or income look anything but elegant in a sari (unless teamed with clunky shoes and an acrylic cardigan — but saris weren't meant for temperate climates). Ditto any people who dress timelessly to suit their environment, from Lakeland sheep farmers to the Inuit. No, it's fashion that encourages clonewear; you just have to change the uniform four times a year, blind to the fact that it is often ugly, impractical, tacky and unflattering — we've all got a damning photo to prove it. It's part of fashion's essential paradox that newness and innovation lead to conformity, so any satisfaction must be shallow and fleeting.

Classics can give service and pleasure for lifetimes, as can genuinely unique pieces. We need a new word to describe this anti-fashion, one that means crafted, enduring and beautiful. The art of adornment needn't die, but it does need to shift its focus away from volume to quality, its values from novel to beautiful, and its time scales from months to decades.

Here's one for the fash-pack's T-shirts. "Fashion eats Earth and shits landfill." It may be more accurate to say that fashion shits mattress filling, and bra tops for remote tribes. But accuracy doesn't always make the best sound bites.

Task 6: Embracing Unfashion

As well as the reclamation and clever use of words, there are many other ways to undermine the fashion industry and its resulting mindset — we just need to understand how fashion controls *us* to work out how to undermine *it.*

A very powerful — possibly the most powerful — method by which fashion is imposed upon people is *social peer pressure.* The idea that someone important, and possibly influential, to you has something you do not have is more than enough to create personal "need." This factor is heavily exploited by industry, most obviously in the form of *advertising* that suggests collective desire (notice the number of adverts that use happy crowd or friend scenes) but increasingly through virtual social networks such as Facebook and Twitter and by direct viral networking. In all commercial sectors, creating (fake) peer pressure is common practice. Within larger groups, such as office staff and school students, individuals are often handpicked for their ability to spread the message, armed with materials to make their job easier:

> *When friends and family start talking about what they have recently bought, especially non-essential goods, talk about what you didn't buy, thereby reversing the normal civilized assumption that it is a good thing to buy consumer goods.*

> The Dubit Insider Programme allows young people aged 13–24 years old to get involved in campaigns that impact our lives every day. These campaigns include many that can improve the lives of those taking part and of those around them — these are known as social marketing campaigns. We also offer those of you aged 16 and over the opportunity to work with some of the UK's top brands and commercial companies.
>
> What are the expectations once you become a Brand Ambassador?
>
> Once you have been approved and placed onto a team, you will be asked to complete weekly tasks. These will be uploaded

onto Insider each week. Tasks can vary from team to team and can involve anything from:

- Flyering
- Posting on message boards and social networks
- Emails
- Instant messenger conversations
- Organising small events
- Hosting small parties

You will be asked to provide evidence of each piece of work you carry out, i.e. photos, screenshots, etc.[91]

It's very easy to sign up to such groups; in fact while researching this section I did so myself, using a false identity. (Damn! I breached their Terms and Conditions.) Could it be coincidence that the day after signing up, using an Earth Blog email address, the Dubit Insider website disappeared, with the domain redirected to the research arm? Possibly, though if not, then it could be evidence that it *only takes a hint of exposure* to put the frighteners on unethical operations.

Peer group dynamics are complex, but in general terms there tends to be a hierarchy of sorts, even within the most egalitarian groups. In very large groups, such as an entire school, it is very unlikely that any one person can have sufficient influence to spread a message to everyone else — networks are necessary so that the various "leaders" of the groups can interact, and in many cases such interaction rarely happens. That is why marketing campaigns, whether overt or covert, attempt to achieve a critical mass so that at the very least the most influential people are influenced. In the case of fashion, there are commonly "fashion leaders" — you know the sort, the person who walks into a bar with a new pair of shoes and is immediately surrounded by a cluster of adoring disciples. The problem is that if you are one of those fashion leaders, then you are most definitely not going to be interested in undermining the fashion world.

The key therefore has to be getting the undermining message into the system so that *the hierarchy can do its work for you.* The "message" could take the form of altered marketing materials — if you are somewhere in the distribution chain, then you have an important part to play in this — and many other related undermining actions. But I think more subtlety is needed here. At schools around the world, for that is where the cult of fashion seems to really take hold, at least outside the constraints of uniform, different brands can take on a life of their own once they have been accepted as the coat/hat/shoe/belt/undergarment/bag of choice. One such brand is Superdry, which exploded in UK schools from 2010 onward:

> The Superdry brand has grown by word of mouth. There is no advertising or sponsorship and no cash spent on celebrity endorsement deals, although the company hit the jackpot when it mailed one of its trademark leather jackets to David Beckham. The soccer star was repeatedly photographed in it, generating a stream of publicity.[92]

Now, what would it take to undermine Superdry? Perhaps an *endorsement by a very unfashionable, unpopular person,* at least in the eyes of young people: can you imagine the effect of a dull politician or a fading pop star being seen wearing a currently fashionable product in public? Mocking up something like that wouldn't work — it might be seen as ironic once the fakery was uncovered — so it needs to be real. We are talking about fashion here, so it's time to get creative.

More subtly, but on a larger scale, another way that fashion promotes itself is through the use of *targeted media,* such as technology and clothing magazines (who will readily promote product X in exchange for advertising revenue) along with newspaper supplements, that show new products as being "essential" or at least highly desirable. Far cheaper, as far as industry is concerned, is the blanket press release to *kneejerk bloggers,* desperate to be the first to report the latest big thing and extremely willing to publish these press releases verbatim. Straightaway we see an opportunity. If such blogs, and there are many that will print the most outrageous things if it gets readers, are desperate to get the latest news, then their fact-checking is likely to be a bit sloppy. If a press release were to emerge from a top fashion house or major retailer claiming it was cutting down the rate of change of their ranges to, say, once a year because of the absurd nature of fashion and the impact it was having on both the personal finances and the mental state of the public, then who knows what would happen? And what about a fake leaked memo containing breakdowns of the various social groups, identifying *which were most stupid and gullible* — and thus how easily they could be convinced to keep changing their electronic goods for the latest model? Something like that might even get past the checking processes of a major television news channel or website, if the "source" was convincing enough.

Such techniques could work very well in the sphere of fashion, but I also think there is a lot to be said for simply *making people feel good* in other areas. We would not seek to be seen as the person with the latest thing, always ahead of the pack, if we knew we had nothing to prove. We would not desire to look "better" if we had a healthy body image already. We would not have to conform to what everyone else was wearing, seeing, hearing or using if we saw no need to be one of the pack. Self-confidence creates magnificent defenses against the cult of fashion, so go and make someone feel better now and turn them from a fashion victim into a happy human being.

Melting the Big Guns

This is the bit that most publishers would want taken out. The reason will become clear very quickly. I don't expect many people reading this will feel especially comfortable about what is to follow, but it has to be written and you need to at least know why these actions are so vitally important for the future of humanity.

There is a close and incestuous relationship that keeps the industrial world functioning at a global scale. The three main players in this relationship are *governments, corporations and the economic system.* Two of those things are most definitely tangible (i.e., they can be described in physical terms); these two are the corporations, of which there are many, though only a relative few that wield genuine power, and the governments. The governments do not actually comprise the majority of politicians; it is the superstructure of government we are talking about: presidents, prime ministers, cabinet members, high-level advisors and spin-doctors, the judiciary, the military and the senior civil service make up the bulk of this. The economic system, while having tangible elements, such as trading floors and banks, is more ethereal. It is best described as a *paradigm*. It brings within its realm things such as policies and rules of operation; it forms part of our culture; it embraces belief systems, faith, the hearts and minds of society itself. Never underestimate the importance of the economy in civilized society.

The relationship among these three things is complex and multi-layered but in summary:

- Corporations have many of the same rights as human beings, while not having the responsibilities of humans — they are rarely held legally accountable for anything because to do so would lower their exalted status.
- These rights, along with other rules that protect the finances of the rich and a string of clauses that permit the systematic abuse of human beings

and the wider natural environment by those in power, are created by governments.

- Corporations exist to make money for either shareholders or private owners,[93] and as such they are entirely dependent on a healthy market economy for their existence. Should the economy as a whole contract, then shareholders and private owners would make less money.
- Governments, being institutions run for the purpose of maintaining the status quo (i.e., Industrial Civilization existing), also depend upon a healthy economy partly so their operations (such as wars and the obligatory public/private services) are paid for, but mainly because the corporations insist upon it.

I still think that's a bit wordy, so for ease of understanding (and a lovely piece of graffiti) think of the recycling triangle and you pretty much have it:

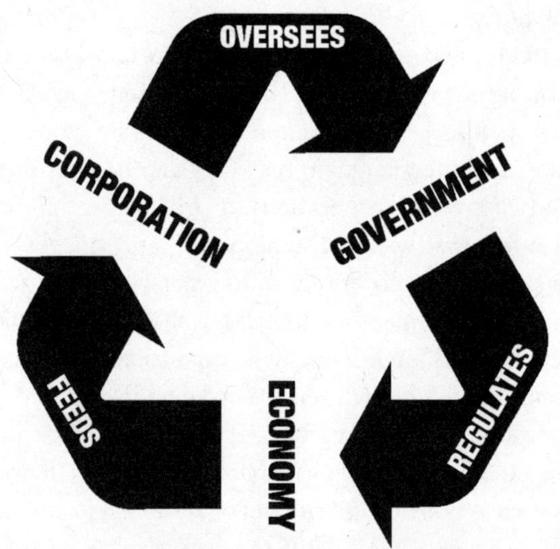

It stands to reason that *if you take away any one part of the triangle, you destroy it entirely.* To all intents and purposes, the engine-room of civilization will come to an immense grinding, crunching halt. So, assuming you are up for the challenge, how can we achieve removing one or more parts of the interdependent triangle?

If you have ever been a mainstream activist, you might see your targets right away, because it has almost always been governments and corporations that are targeted by actions, albeit usually in a polite and diplomatic way (governments) or a guiding and understanding way (corporations). A more radical activist will likely see the same two targets, with one eye on the economy — but the economy is surely not anything that can be attacked, or undermined, with any success. By all means attack governments and corporations as best you can; undermine their craven lies and greenwashing bullshit, because they need to be undermined big time. For this section, though, we are going to take on the global economic system — in a way it has never been taken on before.

Empathy is a wonderful gift, and here we need to use that gift; we need to have empathy with the mindset of ordinary civilized people. It doesn't take a great imagination to predict the reaction of someone having the economic safety net further pulled from under them. Forget that this "safety net" is made of false promises that stand for nothing when times are really tough; people genuinely believe that they need to keep the economic system propped up with their spending, and in turn that when they really need it the economic system will cushion their fall.

Times are hard, and with this current paradigm things will only get worse. The central banks can keep pumping pretend money into a pretend system but it won't make a blind bit of difference in the end. Look down: there is nothing there, you are on your own, and the bastards that kept you believing in the goodness of the industrial economy are sailing their yachts into the sunset. As a wise punk once said, "Ever get the feeling you've been had?"

Economic growth hurts the global ecology; it fills the atmosphere with warming gases; it creates slaves by the million; it fuels the machine of destruction. Economic recessions, slumps, crashes — call them what you will — give the global ecology welcome breathing space, but in turn hurt ordinary people who have complete faith in the system and depend on having a job, ready cash and all the accoutrements of civilized life to sustain them. Economic failure hurts. We must understand that, even as we smile.

Scrapping the industrial economy is the Big Deal: it has to be done; otherwise humanity is finished and just about the rest of life with it. There is no "Plan B" for the economy; no clever financial sleight of hand; no "sustainable growth" or "steady state economics" — all lies designed to keep you part of the system, compliant and consuming. We can undermine the economic system wholesale if we have the courage, but we can also stop the hurt even before the undermining does its work. First, by taking away the

Exercise: Don't Expect, Don't Register, Don't Vote

I just put on the fire another letter inviting me onto the Electoral Register. It caught quickly and helped warm the house. That's just about the best thing you can do with such a letter; perish the thought that anyone would actually fill it in and send it back, thus putting your details on record as a Voter and thus a fully fledged Citizen. Even if, through some fluke of bureaucracy, anyone in my home did end up registered, you wouldn't find us anywhere near a polling station on Election Day; what's the point?

George Carlin put it better than anyone else, I think:

> *I have solved this political dilemma in a very direct way: I don't vote. On Election Day, I stay home. I firmly believe that if you vote, you have no right to complain. Now, some people like to twist that around. They say, "If you don't vote, you have no right to complain," but where's the logic in that? If you vote, and you elect dishonest, incompetent politicians, and they get into office and screw everything up, you are responsible for what they have done. You voted them in. You caused the problem. You have no right to complain. I, on the other hand, who did not vote — who did not even leave the house on Election Day — am in no way responsible for what these politicians have done and have every right to complain about the mess that you created.*[94]

We don't expect politicians to speak for us. At best, they are ordinary people; at worst, they want to take away your freedom and control your life. We expect even less of governments: they speak for no one but the system they are an intrinsic part of. Therefore we don't register and we don't vote.

"Don't Expect, Don't Register, Don't Vote" is a series of personal, positive and constructive acts that anyone can do without doing anything! It is also a meme that can spread very easily through word of mouth, blog, graffiti —whatever floats your boat. By refusing the mandate to be "represented," you take the mandate away from politicians to represent you. They become powerless to claim they are anything but a bunch of toadying, corporate-loving elitists. And the best thing of all is you don't even have to do anything to achieve this. What a perfect piece of undermining.

Don't Expect
Don't Register
Don't Vote

POLITICAL FREEDOM IS EASY

reason we have to work so much: the consumption and debt trap that plies its trade through the application of fear and dreams; second, by stealing back our time from the offices, factories, call centers, supermarkets and every other example of unnecessary toil we no longer need to undertake because we have far less need to earn; finally, we take away the faith the economy needs us to have in it in order to keep going. Sorry, Tinker Bell, you have to go out.

We don't need the industrial economy, it needs us. But when the industrial economy goes, we need to be in a position of safety for ourselves, those who depend upon us and those we care about. This is not selfishness, it is common sense. The three undermining tasks that follow are also common sense: like a row of dominoes, one can set off the other if enough of a jolt is given. Furthermore, any one of them could be enough to undermine the economy on its own. Before we take the plunge, though, why not show your lack of commitment for the system by pulling out one of the hooks that binds you to it?

Task 7: Throwing Off the Chains of Debt

Civilized people carry debt throughout their lives, from a simple credit card transaction to a rent-to-own deal on a new piece of furniture; from a loan that gets you through the next set of bills to a mortgage on a property you could never afford were it not for debt. Some things we often don't see as debts but rather necessary parts of life, such as mortgages or credit cards, are no better than the loan from the man with the cheap suit in the shop with gadget-filled windows. The difference between that and the mortgage is little more than the price of the suit and what's in the shop window.

Before we can change our personal and, by extension, our collective circumstances, we have to be liberated; we need to be free of things that keep us dependent on the civilized world. Debt makes people powerless — it *creates* dependency. This is the point where economic control has to begin. We have to learn that all forms of money borrowing, even from friends and family, are debts, and we have to learn from the earliest possible moment that all forms of debt are bad.

Very significantly, the creation of debt (invariably with interest, also known as usury[95]) allows the global economy to exceed natural limits, ensuring that damage will continue beyond the point that non-debtors would have stopped. An individual is able to exceed his or her normal ability to buy goods and services by getting in debt; therefore by *not being in debt an individual is only able to spend what she or he can genuinely afford.*

Now we are getting somewhere. It is astonishing to realize that all governments and corporations have to run structural deficits just to remain in business. In slack or recessional periods this can be simply to "keep the lights on," but primarily it is so they can invest in whatever infrastructure is necessary to grow their relevant economic sectors. Such investments include IT and telecommunications, roads, buildings, tax breaks, "educating" the population and waging wars. This nicely parallels the personal debt trap: we are taught to accept debt on a personal level as institutions convince themselves en masse that structural debt is essential. Not only this, but such institutions also have to accept such debts in other institutions (governments, banks, manufacturers, etc.) — in effect a double bind of immensely high risk.

So, if it becomes impossible to run a deficit for whatever reason, then it will be impossible to create this infrastructure of growth. As I have said, take away one part of the triangle and the triangle will collapse. In the case of personal debt, the simple refusal of people to take out cash loans, mortgages, rent-to-own deals and so on, on a large enough scale will reduce their ability and, just as important, their *willingness* to buy what they once thought they could afford. Take away the comfort that debt provides and you take away the incentive to spend: the consumer economy starts to break apart.

This is not speculation: when the global economy crashed in the summer of 2008, there was a similar crash in consumer spending. Not only did people find it more difficult to take out loans but they also felt less willing, given the state of the potential (and actual) job situation among other things. A McKinsey report from 2009 spells this out dramatically:

> Until recently, households could use credit to smooth out consumption through the ups and downs of the job market. Not anymore. Banks, battered by mounting credit losses and plunging equity prices, have tightened lending standards for consumers and businesses. New borrowing by households has fallen sharply from its peak in the second quarter of 2006 and turned negative in the fourth quarter of 2008. In other words, for the first time since World War II, total household debt outstanding fell rather than rose. It is unclear how much of this debt reduction is voluntary and how much is involuntary. Part reflects lower demand for credit (as fewer people are buying cars and houses) [note, the issue of confidence is neatly avoided in this mainstream report],

> while part is the result of the tighter supply. Either way, consumers are reducing their debt burdens — deleveraging.
>
> With the confluence of plummeting wealth, jobs, and credit, consumer confidence is at a 41-year low. Even those with jobs fear for their future. Many households are using their cash to pay down credit cards rather than buy new goods. Others are putting money away for a rainy day. As a result, US consumer spending is plunging. Spending fell at a 3.8 percent annual rate in the third quarter of 2008 and at a 4.3 percent rate in the fourth quarter, a primary reason the economy contracted.[96]

It came as no surprise then, that in October 2011, British Prime Minister David Cameron was forced to rewrite a conference speech because it appeared to recommend the public pay off their debts. The original text, released to the press the day before, to the approbation of the financial and business lobby read,

> The only way out of a debt crisis is to deal with your debts. That means households — all of us — paying off the credit card and store card bills.[97]

The version used for the actual speech was subtly, but materially changed to read,

> The only way out of a debt crisis is to deal with your debts. That is why households are paying down the credit card and store card bills.[98]

Sound advice in the original version was perhaps too sound for the people whose careers and wealth depend on us remaining in hock to the system. Had we followed Cameron's original advice to the letter, the worst fears of the British Retail Consortium, among others, may have been realized — the economy would shrink rather than grow.[99] Fear is, as we saw in Chapter 2, a very powerful Tool of Disconnection, and you don't actually need to have a tangible threat to create fear: not if you are a government and not if you are an Underminer, according to *Rules for Radicals:*

> Rule 9: The threat is more terrifying than the thing itself. When [Saul] Alinsky leaked word that large numbers of poor people

> were going to tie up the washrooms of O'Hare Airport, Chicago city authorities quickly agreed to act on a longstanding commitment to a ghetto organization. They imagined the mayhem as thousands of passengers poured off airplanes to discover every washroom occupied. Then they imagined the international embarrassment and the damage to the city's reputation.[100]

So, that explains why the mass refusal to spend and the paying back of debt, and even the threat of such an action, is such a potent undermining force; now we need to create that situation.

Much undermining is about leading by example, and this applies particularly to personal debt, which is an extremely powerful psychological burden, and a crutch. Leading by example, you should first *refuse to take out a loan for anything.* If you really need something — and probably you don't — then save your money and buy it, barter for it or borrow it.[101] Now, encourage others to join you: start by sharing what you have — your car, your garden, your tools, even your clothes. Pass stuff on; give stuff away. You don't need that loan and neither do the people you care about. If you already have loans, and most recent students do, then seek deferral under economic hardship. Odds are pretty high you're actually experiencing economic hardship, so this is no big deal. And even if you're not, there's no sense feeding the beast if the beast defaults down the road. None of this entails risk to anyone but the industrial economy.

At a higher level of risk is *defaulting.* Many people are now living in homes with mortgages that are greater than the value of their property. Why would anyone continue to pay a debt that is higher than the asset it secures? After all, big corporations view pulling the plug on unsuccessful ventures and sticking the debt holders and shareholders as a key business strategy! Yet for some reason homeowners feel some moral obligation to throw good money endlessly after bad. This, of course, is exactly what the corporations, who have no such moral compunction, are counting on, what economists call moral asymmetry. If everyone with a mortgage greater than the value of their home — and the lender really should have predicted this situation in the first place — either walked away from it, or was legally empowered to require the excess to be written off as the bad debt it is, then of course there would be many bank failures and plunging profits. Walking away from your mortgage or any other bad loan you may have will damage your credit rating. Obviously, this doesn't matter in the long term, but it still causes concern for many people. The bailiffs knocking on your door — wherever it may be — will also cause concern (which is why not getting into debt in the first place is such a good strategy). If this is a possibility, then publicizing your actions widely could protect you from unwanted intrusion.

Taking a step beyond abandoning your underwater mortgage, don't pay off your mortgage even if you're not underwater. Simply default but continue to occupy your house. The lenders cannot afford to tell their stockholders about it, so the borrower gets the loan for no payments while the lender gets stuck. This is not such an unusual step, and it became something of a trend in the USA from 2009 onward when people realized it was a viable way of getting out of crippling mortgage debt. And it doesn't have to just be mortgages or, indeed, just as a way of dealing with a personal problem — Enric Duran took out loans and donated the proceeds to a variety of causes for three years, with *no intention of ever paying them back.* His story is taken up by the Institute for Anarchist Studies in an article and interview, some of which is reprinted here:

> On September 17th, 2008, Barcelona-based anti-capitalist Enric Duran announced that he had expropriated 492,000 Euros. For several years, Duran took out loans that he never intended to pay back and donated all of the money to social movements constructing alternatives to capitalism. This announcement came with the publication of 200,000 free newspapers called *Crisi* (Catalan for "Crisis"), with an article explaining Duran's action, and other pieces offering a systemic critique of the current financial and ecological crises. The action got the attention of tens of thousands of everyday people as well as major media outlets, who soon dubbed Duran the "Robin Hood of the Banks." Duran left the country to avoid prosecution. The group that published the newspapers formed Podem Viure Sense Capitalisme (We Can Live With Out Capitalism) and began region-wide organizing through their website, http://podem.cat, bringing together debtors, squatters, alternative economy networks, environmentalists, and everyday people to build a large-scale alternative to capitalism.
>
> Duran returned to Spain six months after the announcement ... and was soon after arrested by the Mossos d'Esquadra, the Catalan regional police on charges of "ongoing fraud" that were

brought against Duran by 6 of the 39 financial entities he took money from. He spent two months in jail. He is currently free on bail, having had his passport seized and required to present himself before a judge once a week. None of the charges have been formally brought to trial.

Q: Do you see a weakness in the financial system? Do you think that increasing the number of delinquent debtors is a viable strategy for weakening, or even taking down, capitalism?

A: The weakness of the credit-based financial system is that it depends on people wanting to go into debt and — more importantly — being committed to paying those debts back, which is what keeps the system in control. *If we're able to create an alternative that extends beyond capitalism, people will see that they have the option of a life that doesn't involve paying their debts back.* This mechanism, this defect, could amplify our capacity to construct alternatives. A lot of people could use loans to set up alternatives and then quit paying them back, because it would be possible to live in a way that is "insolvent" for the system, but "solvent" for the people in these alternative ways of living.

Q: Have people been explicitly inspired by your action, taking out loans without the intention of paying them back in order to promote alternatives?

A: I think so, because people have asked me how, and I've told them.... I'm pretty sure it's being done, but it's most likely that no one is doing it publicly because that's safer, with less personal risk. And it's not only people doing it like that; I think what's even more common is people who at some point took out loans because they wanted to consume, because they wanted to have a mortgage, whatever — and now they see the utility in doing this to change their lives.[102]

A related, but more complex strategy is *voluntary bankruptcy.* Like defaulting, this may not strictly be considered undermining because in most cases it is the result of circumstance rather than a desire to create change; nevertheless, in a situation where the only option is to continue paying off loans at impossible rates and sacrificing more and more of your time and mental faculties to pay them off, bankruptcy can not only free you from the obligations of debt, but also stick it to the companies that profit from others' misery.

Moving outward into more deliberate and less personal undermining, you could start with a bit of subvertising, focusing on loan companies and banks, changing the messages to emphasize the theft aspect of loans. Alternatively, just remove loan adverts entirely.

In a variation on pure exposure as a means of undermining corporations, send out *false press releases* from loan companies and banks to media outlets such as local radio stations, local press and even the nationals if you are brave enough. These press releases should discourage people from taking out loans because, after all, people don't really need all the toys they buy on credit. If you make the "press release" as complete as possible, and word it so that responses are not required, then there is a good chance it will be run without questions being asked. The following letter was sent to about 50 newspapers and radio stations from a mailbox 100 miles from the sender's home. It is reproduced, with the bank's name removed, to give an example of style and how to make a spoof just believable enough.

Sending letters via the postal service is the safest way from the point of view of the Underminer, but it is a one-way mechanism and, unless the recipient accepts such information at face value, it will not be as effective as you might wish it to be. This makes it especially important to make the

PRESS RELEASE — FIRST UK BANK TO STOP SELLING PERSONAL LOANS

The credit crunch has hit everyone involved in the global economy hard; and none more so than the millions of individuals who are struggling to make ends meet. Job losses, increases in energy prices and an unpredictable situation in the global financial industry are making it ever more difficult for people to plan for the future. There is a need for urgent and innovative ideas to help ease the burden on banking customers both in the UK and across the world.

That is why, starting in the Spring of 2010, First UK Bank will no longer be offering loans to its personal customers: instead it will provide a range of sound, sensible advice designed to help them free themselves from financial hardship — advice that they can carry with them in whatever they do. ☞

This may seem a perverse move from a bank that has historically been one of the world's largest lenders of money to individuals, but we believe it is time to give people back what we now realize has unethically been taken from them in the form of interest. Obviously we cannot pay back all that interest, but we can help our customers ensure they have far less need to borrow money in the future. We feel that in a financial climate that is sure to persist for some years to come, it is no longer acceptable to sell the idea that, somehow, borrowing money is the way out of financial hardship.

How will we make a profit?

In the short term we will continue to provide lending services to businesses, and also invest our savers' money wisely. In addition, card credit facilities will remain, with a medium-term plan to also phase out this service in favor of debit cards only. In the longer term we are aiming to become less profit motivated, in keeping with our ethical mindset, choosing instead to run "at cost" as far as is practicable. In a world where environmental issues are being increasingly linked with the consumption of goods and energy, there is a very strong case for economic growth to be curtailed, or even reversed, in order to reduce environmental damage.

This longer-term aspiration dovetails neatly with the decision to no longer offer personal loans, for it is undoubtedly true that the ready availability of money in the form of cash loans, credit cards and other debt instruments encourages individuals to spend more money: money that would not be available without such inducements.

Won't this cause hardship?

On the contrary, this move is designed to ease financial hardship through a combination of withdrawing inducements to borrow and spend, and also providing sound, long-term advice to customers.

First UK will be teaming up with a number of charities, well known for their work in dealing with the causes and effects of financial hardship; and also working closely with government agencies to provide the very best advice in terms of common sense use of money, reducing energy and other forms of consumption, and the availability of benefits for those most in need.

What about our competitors?

We have no doubt that other lenders will, at least in the short term, continue to offer unnecessary loans to personal customers, and benefit from the interest they charge. Someone has to make the first move and, as a leader in the financial industry, we have decided to be that "someone." In time we hope our competitors will become our partners in this brave Debt Free Revolution.

— Alan Davenport on behalf of First UK Bank PLC. First UK Bank PLC. Registered in England. Registered No: 10010010. Registered Office: 1 Station Place, London, E10 1AA.

letter as convincing as you possibly can on repeated readings, discouraging the recipient to check the veracity of the contents.

For more immediate effect, and potentially the ability to update information on the fly, it may be better to use a pre-registered and configured mailbox along with a fake website. This is a staple of groups such as The Yes Men, who have used it to surprising effect on repeated occasions. *Website spoofing* is technically complex to get right, but the "spoofing guide" included here should help get you started. This is relevant for all undermining tasks that use fake websites and electronic communications.

Despite Underminers' antipathy to symbolic action, some apparently symbolic things could be quite effective. One example is the *Default-In*. Run along the lines of the love-ins and sit-ins of the 1960s, this is a more collective, and thus socially powerful, form of individual debt rejection. It could include the public tearing up of "contracts" (not legal tender in reality) or mass calling up of banks and other loan sharks to cancel accounts. Emphasize the positive nature of debt rejection and more people will be encouraged to set up their own. We could end up with a bizarre combination of community tea party that everyone is invited to, and active rejection of a very dangerous and essential part of the industrial economy. The next logical step is to take that new-found freedom from debt and use it to liberate another part of our lives.

A Guide to Spoofing Websites and Other Internet Fun

1) Purchase a domain name easily mistaken for that of the target, ensuring you use an anonymous registrar because the first thing any decent journalist will look for is the name of the person who registered it. Also check that any services you may need, such as mailbox hosting, are available via the registrar. If you are not able to buy an appropriate domain, then your spoof will have to be of the phishing variety. (See 3b.)

2a) Create your website. Make it as close to the look and feel of those of your target as works with the type of spoof you are carrying out. Ideally you should use as much of the source code of the original website as you can, as well as (for everything that you are not changing) using the original links. Test your pages thoroughly in every common browser.

2b) If you are doing a complete hoax (i.e., presenting something completely different to the original), then the code is up to you; though be aware that anything more than a fake "holding" page will quickly be spotted by those familiar with the target. ☞

3a) Carry out your domain assignment/redirection. For a convincing spoof you will change both the domain of the hosting server and the DNS record for the domain, which is carried out via your domain registrar. This ensures that the address structure of the website is based on your own domain name. Less convincing, but fine for a one-off spoof, you can set up a Framed Redirection via your domain provider, which will mask the URL of your spoofed website.

3b) For a straight phishing attack you will be using what appears to be the official URL to go to the spoof site. Most anti-virus software will detect phishing in emails, but you could always use this technique in forums and blogs where you can edit the HTML.

4) If you are not sending out a press release or invitation to view and are just relying on the spoof, then that's all you need to do; but you won't get much traffic unless you have a really convincing URL or one that will be typed in accidentally; so, you will at least need to publicize your efforts. If you are sending out a press release, you will need to set up at least one mailbox under your fake domain name, otherwise your information will lack credibility. If you can use a third party email client, then that will protect your personal details (and the security of your own computer); most domain providers have that facility for a small additional fee. Be aware, though, that this is a form of abuse, so you may lose your account if you are found out.

5) Send out your press releases: make them as similar to the official press releases as you can, including embedded logos (proper ones) and contact details as appropriate. It is up to you whether you respond, but if you do, then keep all responses in the official form of the original. Telephone numbers are not recommended unless you have a dedicated number with enough hands to deal with the call volume.

6) Follow up. A good follow-up will add extra mileage to your undermining efforts. It can take a number of forms. A simple follow-up similar to the original but providing more detail will give the story legs; maybe include a few choice "quotations" from staff, and perhaps a video (you will need to sort out a convincing video hosting account for this). Alternatively, especially if you suspect your spoof has been found out and countered by your target, you could send a denial claiming that the target itself has been spoofed and yours is, in fact, the correct story.

7) Cover your tracks. Observe the housekeeping protocols in Chapter 3, especially if you want to do the same kind of thing again. There is no harm in leaving the original website running in case people stumble upon it by accident or via reblogging; whatever you do, don't sell the domain name to your target — why should the bastards benefit from your hard work?

Task 8: Ending Wage Slavery

What do you think is the most dangerous word in the English language? There are plenty of potentially dangerous words, such as Civilized and Development, but it may be that the word "jobs" is the most dangerous word of all. I will try to explain why with the help of two small news reports:

> Australian coal producers reacted fiercely to a carbon tax that passed the country's lower house of Parliament Wednesday, but said it was too soon to know how much the climate change regime would influence prices for thermal or coking coal.
>
> Trade groups representing mining companies said the policy would deal an unfair blow to the industry.
>
> Mitch Hooke, CEO of the Minerals Council of Australia, whose members produce 90% of the country's exports, said in a statement that the tax would undermine the competitiveness of Australian coal and slash domestic jobs, without cutting greenhouse gas emissions.[103]

This first extract is from Platts, an energy and minerals information service, so it's no surprise that it is skewed in favor of coal mining operations and the jobs that these mines provide. It's the jobs side we are interested in: apparently if mining companies have to pay more tax, then jobs will be cut — but not the amount of coal mined. That's essentially how capitalism works; but notice how the word "slash" is used with reference to jobs.

> BAE Systems intends to cut 3,000 of its 40,000 UK jobs. Apparently this is necessary for BAE to "ensure its long-term future" while the futures of the estimated 5,700 directly and indirectly affected workers look bleak.
>
> The decision to make 900 out of 1,300 workers redundant at BAE Brough is a body blow to workers in Hull and the Humberside region.
>
> As we campaign to save BAE jobs, we need to realise that such a campaign has to challenge the capitalist system itself. If the economy was democratically planned by the workers in industry together with democratically elected local and national representatives as part of a national plan, we could eradicate unemployment and the uncertainty we face today.[104]

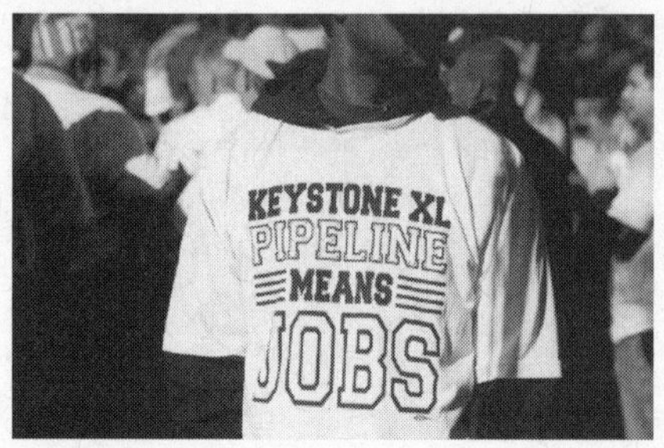

The second extract comes from an apparently opposite viewpoint, that of the Socialist Party, who appear to be anti-capitalist and anti-corporate but are also banging on about jobs. They want jobs for everyone — not useful work, but jobs.

It seems that one of the worst things anyone can do is threaten jobs. Politicians talk about the danger of job losses — as does the mainstream media, as does the radical media, in many cases, as do ordinary people. In fact, there are few things more likely to get you on the wrong side of a community than suggesting something that could take away jobs. But look at the subject of the articles: one is implying that reducing the amount of coal burned is bad — because it would cut jobs; the other is even more clearly saying that reducing the amount of money going to a weapons manufacturer is bad — because it would cut jobs. Look at the second one again: this is the Socialist Party, a left-wing group, so blinkered in their attitude that every job is a good job that even exported death is acceptable if it means a paycheck.

Can you now see why "jobs" may be the most dangerous word in the English language?

So why do we crave jobs so much? And how have we become so brainwashed that we will fight, risking the loss of everything, including our own freedom, to ensure they are not threatened? An obvious reason is money: within an industrial economy money is necessary for almost everything, and as has been shown throughout this book, we are brainwashed from birth into thinking that we have to keep the economy healthy in any way we can. If we do not actively participate in the economy, then it suffers; and, because we buy almost everything we eat, wear, sit on, sleep in, keep ourselves warm with, shelter ourselves with and have fun with, we suffer too. Or so we are led to believe.

But it's not just money. As we know, schools prepare us not for useful work, but for doing a job, a.k.a. having a career. We are never taught that a nine-to-five job in an office is anything but useful work; nor are we ever shown the concept of Wage Slavery, for that would put negative connotations upon something we have to believe in as the absolute truth: *it is good to have a job, no matter what that job is.* If you don't have a job, then you are less than human, you are unemployed, a slacker, a waster, a loser. Get a job, hippy! Yes, that's about the size of it.

Confused? You should be.

> We have to see that the economy is not "in" crisis, the economy itself is the crisis. It's not that there's not enough work, it's that there is *too much of it.* In France, we get down on all fours to climb the ladders of hierarchy, but privately flatter ourselves that we don't really give a shit. We stay at work until ten o'clock in the evening when we're swamped, but we've never had any scruples about stealing office supplies here and there, or carting off the inventory in order to resell it later. We hate bosses, but we want to be employed at any cost. To have a job is an honor, yet working is a sign of servility. In short: the perfect clinical illustration of hysteria.... The horror of work is less in the work itself than in the methodical ravaging, for centuries, of all that isn't work: the familiarities of one's neighborhood and trade, of one's village, of struggle, of kinship, our attachment to places, to beings, to the seasons, to ways of doing and speaking.[105]

Make it difficult or impossible for people to do their jobs, and you free people from slavery. This might not seem entirely fair from a personal point of view; after all, most of us need money to even survive, let alone thrive in the industrial world; but lose the debt and the incentive to spend beyond your means, and you are part of the way there. Lose the mindset that having a job is a good thing, whatever kind of job that is, and you are well along the right path. *Redefine what "useful work" means* in the real world, and acceptance by the majority starts to become a possibility.

But before acceptance becomes a likelihood there is the prickly problem of tax to contend with. Let's take a typical, albeit nameless, industrial civilized nation. A revolution of sorts has taken place, perhaps as a result of a lack of available money-earning jobs and an increasing number of people walking away from their wage slavery; perhaps because people have realized that cash and, particularly, debt are shackles that bind us rather than free us. About 50 percent less money is circulating within the personal tax system due to a plethora of part-time and lower-paid jobs, a huge number of people working for themselves and incorporating alternative methods of payment into their lives, and almost everyone being less profligate in their spending and borrowing. What would once have been hard financial times have been transformed into times of sharing, trust and low material need; and as a result, the burden on the global ecosystem, the "resource" reservoir and the lives of people who normally serve the corporate system is relieved by a significant measure.

As a further result, the burden on the public purse becomes unbearable. Only half the money previously available is entering the system, and social collapse is imminent — or so we are being told.

But that's simply not true. With such a dramatic shift in the way people live and think — a necessity to achieve such a sea change in spending and work — there is no such gulf between tax income and services. I wrote about this in some detail on The Earth Blog,[106] but in essence it would be no great shakes to achieve a 50-percent reduction in the amount of money required by the state to run services — even more as time goes on, until the concept of "public services" is simply absorbed into the communities we have created for ourselves. That's a taste of things to come, if we can do this right, and it is something we will concern ourselves a lot more in a later chapter.

A lot of undermining is needed here because of the number of discrete ways the "jobs" paradigm pervades our lives so, rather than specify different actions for every aspect of this, I will give some ideas for undermining the job culture that can be applied more generally across the board. First, it is important to outline some of the key areas that can be targeted by undermining so you can select and create actions of your own appropriate to your situation and what you are motivated most to undermine:

- the idea that having a job is a good thing in itself, irrespective of anything else, including the stigma attached to not having a job
- a lack of awareness of what "useful work" really entails and how little useful work a typical job actually achieves
- the extent to which employers own employees' lives, including their time, moral attitudes, sense of worth, social life and personal well-being
- the financial dependency employees have on their employers

I think these are the main areas. There may be more, but it's surprising how few points you can distil the jobs paradigm down to despite, or maybe because of, its impact on our lives. It may be its simplicity that gives it so much power — it is simple enough for us to clearly understand the apparent importance of us having a job, and jobs being readily available, but the Veil of Ignorance allows things to be turned against us very effectively.

"People who purposely abuse their paid working time are stealing from their employers, just as they would be if they stole money or products," says Robert Half, the employment expert who first identified — and named — time theft. "And time is a commodity that can never be replaced, replenished or restored."[107]

There is something remarkably sinister about this statement, but as far as employers are concerned "time theft" is a deeply undesirable fact of working life. The especially sinister aspect of this you already know; "time theft" as named by Robert Half, is quite the reverse of the Tool of Disconnection called "Steal Our Time" — taking back our time from the masters we serve in our place of work is undermining, and it is the first step toward employment liberty. Read the next passage and you will see immediately how many ways you can quickly and easily start liberating yourself from the job culture.

> According to the personnel directors and top management executives who were interviewed, the major types of time theft [sic] are, in order:
>
> 1. Constant socializing with other employees and excessive personal phone calls. [This was in 1988, so very little email and Internet access.] The largest form of time theft by far.
> 2. Faking illness and claiming unwarranted "sick days".
> 3. Inordinately long lunch breaks and coffee breaks.
> 4. Habitual late arrival and/or early departure.
> 5. Using the company's time and premises to operate another business [or, presumably other non-job activities].[108]

Taken in isolation and with a level of secrecy, then you are just undermining the effect of a job upon yourself, perhaps easing yourself out of the job trap slowly; making a few mental snips and crossing the odd line as to what is ethical. With less secrecy, shared within a group of trusted colleagues perhaps, this becomes a combination of collective personal undermining and making whatever employer you work for operate less efficiently — as the man said above.

Moving further outward, a concerted effort to encourage dissent among multiple people in multiple places of wage slavery could be carried out under the blanket of "anonymity" (be careful, employers love sneaking around on social networks) maybe in the form of a blog: "The Rebellious Wage Slave" to pluck a title out of the air. In many parts of the world "Work to Rule," however well intended, carries with it the political stigma of extended trade disputes, so maybe a change in terminology is needed to make these ideas more attractive to a wider range of people: I can't imagine there are many people who don't want to take their lives back from their job, however dependent they feel upon it. The possibilities are numerous and have great potential to disrupt the industrial economy, either by themselves or in combination with other activities. Undermining in this context may be more appealing as a "package" of actions. One example of this was proposed by the Global Strike 2011 movement, an unfortunately abortive attempt to take time and wealth from under the feet of the corporate elites:

> There *is* a way we can collectively fight back against environmentally destructive multinational corporations. A coordinated global general strike and boycott, combined with personal preparedness, in sufficient numbers, can cause a great deal of economic disruption. The best tactic? Non-participation. A multi pronged strategy will be most effective:
>
> 1. BOYCOTT: All corporate products, beginning with Coke, McDonalds, ADM, and Monsanto. Reduce to eliminate your consumption of gasoline. You can start this now. Lawsuits: The more of their resources are devoted to circular legal action, which is expensive, the more is taken out of their budget without producing anything. File lawsuits of every kind (class action, environmental damage, labor rights).
> 2. STRIKE: The first week of July 2011. Take your vacation time, sick leave, organize your union to strike at this time. Spend time with family at home! The main thing is: DON'T BUY ANYTHING FOR ONE WEEK. Continue as long as possible, buy the gasoline you will need for a week at least.
> 3. PREPARE: Learn what wild foods are available to you, identify them, and eat them. Start a garden, organize within your community to become as food self sufficient as possible. Store durable food a little at a time so you have a large supply by July. Plan many crops that will begin to bear by the first week of July.[109]

It's a good concept, but there is some muddled thinking here; suggesting not buying anything for a week (an excellent idea) in the same point as taking time off dilutes the "Global Strike" concept. Buying enough gasoline for a week, while at the same time trying to eliminate its use, is contradictory. In undermining, you must be clear about what you want to achieve and how you are going to achieve it, even if you may not get there all at once. You have an audience, so speak to them in way they understand and will appreciate the sense of.

> *Host a wild food dinner. Forage for food and ask guests to bring something wild of their own, or homegrown if that's not possible — it will really make them think and if you can cook well then also maybe change their diets.*

The obvious limit to how far you can take this is when your employer fires you. That is why it is so important to have already rid yourself of the worst financial burdens, taking you to *a point where you are prepared to risk losing your job.* It is no longer enough to rely on a union to protect someone working to rule or striking; workers are as disposable as they are essential, and the Western economy's employment situation heading into virtually unknown territory as I write this is only likely to tip companies even more toward the "disposable" end as increasing numbers of jobs are exported to even cheaper, newly brainwashed lands.

As we approach the possibility of any rebellion in the workplace leading to termination, one has to ask, Why should I put up with this? There is a point at which exploitation becomes unbearable and the temptation to simply walk away from work becomes far more appealing than staying on to face another day working for The Man.

As activist Ben DeVries wrote, "If you stop participating in your slavery, you will stop being a slave."[110]

A Reminder: Why We Are Doing This

There is no need to feel guilty; you are doing a wonderful thing. The Undermining of the industrial system must have seemed daunting at the beginning, but now it is becoming a reality. You might feel a little tug in the gut, as though you're dangling a hated enemy over the edge of a cliff as they cry out for one more chance. They lie; they all lie, because lies are how they allowed this to happen, lies are what made you a willing partner in all this. Do you need another reason?

> If any [spoon-billed sandpiper] chicks do survive, they must undertake one of the most perilous journeys of any migratory bird: 8,000 km (5,000 miles) to their wintering grounds in Myanmar

> and Bangladesh. On the way they pass through the world's industrial powerhouses — Japan, China and South Korea — where the reclamation of coastal wetlands for economic development is proceeding at a terrifying rate. To make matters worse, if the sandpipers do reach their wintering grounds, poor local communities trap them for food. It's hardly surprising the spoon-billed sandpiper is heading for extinction.[111]

The destruction of those wetlands is because of the industrial world's hunger for cheap and plentiful consumer goods and a lifestyle that mimics that which the West has sold to the rest of the world in order to make even more money.

> A researcher with Survival International, the London-based human-rights organisation, returned to the UK last month with transcripts of interviews with the Penan conducted deep in the jungle. According to one headman, called Matu, hunters were increasingly returning empty-handed. "When the logging started in the Nineties, we thought we had a big problem," he complained. "But when oil palm arrived [in 2005], logging was relegated to problem No 2. Our land and our forests have been taken by force.
>
> "Our fruit trees are gone, our hunting grounds are very limited, and the rivers are polluted, so the fish are dying. Before, there were lots of wild boar around here. Now, we only find one every two or three months. In the documents, all of our land has been given to the company."
>
> "There were no discussions," said another Penan. "The company just put up signs saying the government had given them permission to plant oil palm on our land."[112]

Palm oil monoculture is the next attempt by the industrial system to suck every last "resource" out of what was once a genuinely rich and important resource for the ecosystems of Southeast Asia and the indigenous people who directly depend upon them.

> We reached the edge of the oil spill near the Nigerian village of Otuegwe after a long hike through cassava plantations. We could smell the oil long before we saw it — the stench of garage forecourts and rotting vegetation hanging thickly in the air. The

> farther we travelled, the more nauseous it became. Soon we were swimming in pools of light Nigerian crude, the best-quality oil in the world. One of the many hundreds of 40-year-old pipelines that crisscross the Niger delta had corroded and spewed oil for several months.
>
> Forest and farmland were now covered in a sheen of greasy oil. Drinking wells were polluted and people were distraught. No one knew how much oil had leaked. "We lost our nets, huts and fishing pots," said Chief Promise, village leader of Otuegwe and our guide. "This is where we fished and farmed. We have lost our forest. We told Shell of the spill within days, but they did nothing for six months."
>
> More oil is spilled from the delta's network of terminals, pipes, pumping stations and oil platforms every year than has been lost in the Gulf of Mexico, the site of a major ecological catastrophe caused by oil that has poured from a leak triggered by the explosion that wrecked BP's Deepwater Horizon rig.[113]

So distant, yet 40 percent of all oil imported by the USA comes from the Niger delta, neatly tucked away from media scrutiny and our minds, disconnected in a way only the "need" for unlimited oil can make us.

So, do you want to give the system another chance?

Task 9: Consuming Confidence

Is damaging Consumer Confidence an act of terrorism?

Given the determination of the Canadian government to publicly cast aside any concept of environmental protection in favor of promoting polluting industries, it seems appropriate to use their definition of what constitutes terrorism. The Anti-terrorism Act of 2008 defines "Terrorist Activity" in two separate ways:[114] first a restatement of various international definitions based on treaties that Canada is a signatory to, such as the International Convention against the Taking of Hostages and the International Convention for the Suppression of Terrorist Bombings; second, a much more localized view of what the government in power at the time considered to be Terrorist Activity. The

Post articles or make comments on websites, suggesting that "Company X" is in financial trouble. There are all sorts of variations on this to create a lack of public/investor confidence.

first aspect is contentious in that certain aspects of treaties, such as the "financing of terrorist groups" and "unlawful acts against," are open to interpretation, particularly in the heat of battle, as it were. More pertinent, though, are the localized definitions, some of the more interesting of which I have highlighted:

Paragraph 83.01(1)(b) of the Code provides that a *"terrorist activity" consists of:*

> (b) an act or omission, in or outside Canada,
> (i) that is committed
> (A) in whole or in part for a political, religious or ideological purpose, objective or cause, and
> (B) in whole or in part with the intention of intimidating the public, or a segment of the public, with regard to its security, including its economic security, or compelling a person, a government or a domestic or an international organization to do or to refrain from doing any act, whether the public or the person, government or organization is inside or outside Canada, and
> (ii) that intentionally
> (A) causes death or serious bodily harm to a person by the use of violence,
> (B) endangers a person's life,
> (C) causes a serious risk to the health or safety of the public or any segment of the public,
> (D) causes substantial property damage, whether to public or private property, if causing such damage is likely to result in the conduct or harm referred to in any of clauses (A) to (C), or
> (E) *causes serious interference with or serious disruption of an essential service, facility or system, whether public or private,* other than as a result of advocacy, protest, dissent or stoppage of work that is not intended to result in the conduct or harm referred to in any of clauses (A) to (C), *and includes a conspiracy, attempt or threat to commit any such act or omission,* or being an accessory after the fact or counselling

> in relation to any such act or omission, but, for greater certainty, does not include an act or omission that is committed during an armed conflict and that, at the time and in the place of its commission, is in accordance with customary international law or conventional international law applicable to the conflict, or the activities undertaken by military forces of a state in the exercise of their official duties, to the extent that those activities are governed by other rules of international law.

It is no surprise at all that the Act does not define any military activity as terrorism; more surprising is the exemption of more symbolic activities such as protests and strikes from the definition, suggesting that such activities are not considered a great threat to the successful running of the industrial machine. What is worth noting, in full, is the section below, now concatenated for clarity:

> A "terrorist activity" consists of an act or omission, in or outside Canada that is committed in whole or in part for a political or ideological purpose, objective or cause, and in whole or in part with the intention of intimidating the public, or a segment of the public, with regard to its economic security, or compelling a person to do or refrain from doing any act, that intentionally causes serious interference with or serious disruption of an essential service, facility or system, whether public or private and includes a conspiracy, attempt or threat to commit any such act or omission, or being an accessory after the fact or counselling in relation to any such act or omission.

Undermining economic security is deemed to be a Terrorist Act. I'm not surprised. But look again: there are all sorts of related activities, including encouraging people to actively carry out such acts, and even discouraging them from preventing economic harm, that fit into this definition. The definition of "essential service, facility or system" is broad to the point of absurdity, and I know from experience that in the UK, for instance, all large financial institutions are considered to be "essential services" as are the data centers they depend on and the programs that run on the computer systems hosted in those data centers on behalf of those exchanges, banks and clearing houses. Stop a computer program in a stock exchange and you are a terrorist.

Shit.

Now take a breath. We have very quickly uncovered a potentially huge problem; however, back in 2003, when a work colleague inadvertently shut down an entire data center by stepping on a broom and hitting the Emergency Power Off button, he wasn't carted off to court; we just apologized formally, made it less easy to trigger the button and gave the room a good tidy up (without the broom). It seems that the key here is *intent:* do you intend to cause an Act of Terrorism, or are you simply doing what is moral and good. What is moral and good for some will be considered an Act of Terrorism by others.

Shit.

Okay, think back to when we discussed shutting off the polluting factory on the river's edge in order to protect the people who depend on that river for food. On one hand we have the "essential facility" carrying out its legal right to pollute, and shutting that down would constitute an Act of Terrorism; on the other hand we have the people having their lives endangered — in many cases intentionally — (see clause ii(B) above) by the polluting factory, which if it continued would constitute an Act of Terrorism. This has simply never been properly tested; and likely never will be because such an event would publicly expose the contradiction between state- and corporate-sponsored terrorism, and that which is considered terrorism by the corporate-controlled state.

And relax.

So, what is the relevance of Consumer Confidence here? In 1985 the US Conference Board, a highly influential industry body, started formally recording public confidence in the economy using the Consumer Confidence Index (CCI).[115] At the point of inception it was given a baseline value of 100, in the same way as major trading indices such as FTSE and Dow Jones are. At the time of writing the CCI stands at a lowly 39.8, down from a high of nearly 145 early in 2000. Other indices of confidence show a very similar pattern, and across the industrial world these indices are taken very seriously indeed.

> Manufacturers, retailers, banks and the government monitor changes in the CCI in order to factor in the data in their decision-making processes. While index changes of less than 5% are often dismissed as inconsequential, moves of 5% or more often indicate a change in the direction of the economy. A

> month-on-month decreasing trend suggests consumers have a negative outlook on their ability to secure and retain good jobs. Thus, manufacturers may expect consumers to avoid retail purchases, particularly large ticket items that require financing. Manufacturers may pare down inventories to reduce overhead and/or delay investing in new projects and facilities. Likewise, banks can anticipate a decrease in lending activity, mortgage applications and credit card use.[116]

Formal measures of Consumer Confidence affect government and business policies to such an extent that a false reading could be catastrophic for particular sectors of the economy, such as futures and options markets and those that rely on people incurring debt. The first thing to explore must be whether it is possible to do something as blatant as manipulating the various indices of confidence in order to hold back, or even cause to contract, vulnerable sectors.

For instance, we can safely say the automobile industry is heavily dependent on consumer confidence. It is also one of the worst greenwashing offenders, and has a vast, destructive infrastructure dependent upon and depended upon by this industry (e.g., road construction, metals, oil production and distribution, vehicle parts and servicing, tourism, publications and so on). This makes the automobile industry — a major contributor to the economies of many countries — an ideal undermining target both from an ethical and an effectiveness point of view. So, let's suppose it was possible to *manipulate confidence indices* so that that the auto industry had to dramatically rein in its activities in order to remain solvent. The effects would be immediate and dramatic, for not only would production and consumption be reduced, we would also see government income forecasts affected; the share prices of the impacted companies falling, leading to further downstream impacts; a reduction of investment in related industrial infrastructure; and other effects that would cause a net contraction of the auto industry. All of this simply from a faked-up confidence forecast.

Such a grand effect is likely only if the source data, or at least the source documents, are sufficiently changed, but because the global industrial system is *so* interconnected and delicately balanced, with barely a buffer in place, even manipulating the forecasts to a single industrial sector or a major corporation could be significant. Even misreporting is potentially damaging: a suggestion of a corporate buyout in one major news outlet can affect share prices, and a *nicely orchestrated rumor* that the confidence indices have been manipulated to give overly *good* news (you might call this Reverse Undermining) would have the same effect as a reputable forecaster giving "bad" news. If targeted cleverly, perhaps to a few ambitious politicians or trigger-happy financial pundits, this could be the straw that breaks the camel's back.

Just as a rumor of food shortages and potential war can cause panic buying, resulting in huge profits for some, rumors of other types can cause the reverse. In 2003 an outbreak of the SARS virus in Canada, which caused the deaths of 44 people (compare this to seasonal influenza which causes 700 to 2,500 deaths per year in Canada[117]) had a significant effect on the Canadian economy:

> The Canadian Tourism Commission [CTC] ... estimated SARS will cost the Canadian economy $519 million in 2003 alone and $722 million between 2003 and 2006. It says Canada lost 662,000 occupied room nights in the month of April 2003 — translating into an estimated $92-million loss of revenue. The CTC estimates the bleak picture is the same for the tourism job sector, where losses are estimated at 5,300 for 2003, with 7,350 jobs lost between 2003 and 2006.
>
> "We are seeing a slower rate of growth than we had forecast at the time of the budget," [federal Finance Minister John] Manley told reporters on April 23. "We're seeing continuing softness in the US economy and one is hopeful as some of the uncertainty declines we'll see a pickup in growth later in the year."
>
> But J.P. Morgan economist Ted Carmichael put a number on it. He dropped his economic forecast for the second quarter by between one and 1.5 percentage points (which puts his growth projection for the quarter at one per cent). He said hospitality and tourism would be the hardest-hit sectors.[118]

I am certainly not advocating causing a major public health scare (although tabloid newspapers seem to get away with this on an almost daily basis), but it is interesting to recall how fear alone can cause a change in behavior. Thus, if it were rumored that a very popular mass-produced toy was an immediate threat to children's health — which in so many ways is already true — then the sales of that toy would inevitably fall, to the chagrin of the manufacturers, retailers and perhaps the entire toy industry. If that rumor can be worded in such a way that local makers of traditional toys are unaffected, or even benefitted, then we have achieved two undermining tasks in one. The potential of rumors and speculation on economic confidence is unlimited.

To take this a stage further, we can take advantage of an obvious feedback loop: low public confidence causes a drop in consumer confidence indices, which is reported back to the public, which in turn causes a further decrease in confidence. Governments, in particular, normally try to intervene by pumping out "good news" about job creation, their own forecasts ("green shoots are appearing"), the possibility of tax cuts and so on; but the media invariably follow the Grim Reaper line, which further exacerbates the situation. By undermining the *credibility of politicians,* it is probable that such government intervention will fall on deaf ears. As was seen in the British Members of Parliament Expenses Scandal of 2009, it takes only a few second homes and rogue duck houses to dent the reputation of a whole institution.[119]

Finally, we need to consider large-scale market interactions and the potential for using *credit ratings* as an undermining tool, simply because to ignore the big picture would be to ignore a potentially huge target. From an Underminer's point of view there are two major impediments to directly undermining anything on as large a scale as a major corporation or a national economy. First, the places to intervene, to use Donella Meadows's terminology, are limited — if you aren't "in the system" then your actions are unlikely to be taken seriously. Second, the potential for undermining is limited to those institutions that are already hurting, which may be a perfectly acceptable outcome but at potentially great personal risk. Institutional Credit Ratings are used by bond traders, in particular, to assess the credit-worthiness of the institutions they wish to purchase debt from (a bond is simply a purchase of debt in exchange for a regular interest payment). The largest ratings agencies, Standard & Poor's and Moody's, are taken very seriously by investors so, in theory, a change in the rating of a corporation such as a bank or even an entire national treasury is big news, affecting how likely investors are to lend to them. In practice it is only "downgrades" (which, incidentally are what we would be interested in) that are significant in altering investor behavior, and really only downgrades at the lower end of the spectrum (the "Speculative Grade" ratings) cause a reduction in lending anything close to the 3–5 percent needed to make an institution flounder.[120] An investor is likely to receive information about these changes only directly from the agencies, so a high level of infiltration would be required, and it would be relevant only if the institution in question was already in a precipitous state. Still, if the opportunity should ever arise, then it would be possible, in theory, to damage an entire nation's economy with just one rogue report.

As I write, the European Union is facing a financial crisis far beyond anything it has ever had to deal with before: entire economies are already on the verge of collapse. By following the suicidal model of trying to create profit off the back of debt, the system has backed itself to the edge of a cliff; one false move and it falls. In such a wonderful moment of economic liberation we have to seize the moment with both hands and not let anyone take the initiative from our grasp.

Undermining the Media Machine

Good journalism comes at a price — usually the career and possibly the life of the good journalist. In 2006, Anna Politkovskaya, a Russian journalist and human rights activist was shot four times while in her apartment. There is no doubt it was murder, but murder by whom? The case has never been solved; nor is it ever likely to be because the apartment was in central Moscow, and the investigation team was employed by the main suspect: the Russian government. Politkovskaya predicted her own death in a 2004 *Guardian* article:

> The media promote official views. They call it "taking a state-friendly position", meaning a position of approval of Vladimir Putin's actions. The media don't have a critical word to say about him. The same applies to the president's personal friends, who happen to be the heads of FSB [Federal Security Service of the Russian Federation], the defence ministry and the interior ministry.
>
> [Russia is] an information vacuum that spells death from our own ignorance. All we have left is the internet, where information is still freely available. For the rest, if you want to go on working as a journalist, it's total servility to Putin. Otherwise, it can be death, the bullet, poison, or trial — whatever our special services, Putin's guard dogs, see fit.[121]

Such extreme measures are rarely necessary where commercial pressures and draconian editorial regimes dictate the output of virtually every "news" outlet; and so it has always been, albeit with a variety of different pressures operating depending on the particular situation the journalist finds herself in. When a journalist breaks ranks it *is* news, and that news is rapidly suppressed by whatever means possible. This could take the form of forcing a retraction from the journalist, the outlet making a retraction and dealing with the journalist itself or the outlet simply distancing itself from the story, blaming "rogue" elements.

Often the story will never get near enough to publication or broadcast to necessitate this, and it is rare that legal means or political suppression are brought to bear: the media outlet is so intrinsically linked to the functioning of the system that anything that runs counter to the desires of the Dominant Culture is unlikely to get a public airing. This is why individual blogging and other decentralized channels have become such an important outlet for electronic publication, and why the political pamphlet and the underground press are such powerful symbols of freedom from oppression. I will come back to this shortly.

Task 10: Creating Trust

In the previous chapter I spent some time looking at methods of undermining the various doctrinal messages the media propagates on behalf of the industrial system. In some ways we were using the system itself to get across alternative messages, such as taking a different "official" viewpoint on economic growth; indeed the media in its current incarnation can be a potential force for good if it is exploited cleverly. But beware! As a commercial entity, the mainstream media serves itself as much as anyone else, so before you think of using a "friendly" publication to expose some great institutional wrongdoing (I have lost count of the number of movies that end with the Great Exposé in *The New York Times* or such) remember how powerful it is. *You cannot mold the media machine to suit your own ends; you can only take advantage of its weaknesses.* There is a huge difference.

Run for election as an "Anti Civilization" candidate. Talk to potential voters about how meaningless elections are.

One such weakness is the flighty nature of *public trust.* While the vast majority of civilized people have an almost religious faith in the goodness of the industrial economy and the need to maintain systems of power that protect the various tenets of civilization, fewer people have faith in the credibility of the mass media. For a while, certainly for the majority of the 20th century, newspapers maintained a *reputation* for generally telling the truth. For instance, the British tabloids, so loved of political parties to garner support at election time, managed to survive no end of scandals and legal cases and remain a staple daily purchase of bus drivers, construction workers and bar staff. Despite many readers vocalizing their concerns about the newsworthiness of the tabloids' contents ("I know it's all crap, but …") they remained in their millions, dubious but hanging on almost every word so long as it reflected their own thoughts and prejudices.

It wasn't a deliberate piece of undermining that dealt a (perhaps) fatal blow to the "credibility" of the tabloid media in the UK; it was murder victim Millie Dowler, an overzealous detective and a political party trying to appease an angry public. The fall guy, for want of a better term, was the *News of the World*; but at the time of writing, the News Corporation "hacking scandal" that reverberated across the globe in the summer of 2011 was still making waves that threaten to flood a few more institutions. Where the undermining comes in is *making the most of the opportunity.*

Not one to hold her tongue at the best of times, author and former Member of Parliament, Louise Mensch used her position as a member of the House of Commons Culture, Media and Sport Select Committee to not only sharply question the actions and motives of various Murdochs, but also to publicly accuse the former editor of the *Daily Mirror,* Piers Morgan, of using similar techniques as News Corporation in order to gather dirt on the subjects of the *Mirror's* stories. Though she was later forced to apologize, there is little doubt that (a) this helped broaden the scope of the public's distrust of the tabloid media and (b) the *Daily Mirror* had been up to the same tricks as the *News of the World* and *The Sun.*[122]

Louise Mensch had no intention of undermining the media system, as far as I know, but the same cannot be said of comedian and actor Steve Coogan who, under the guise of his brilliant comedy creation Alan Partridge had the following to say about the editor of the similarly sordid *Daily Mail,* Paul Dacre, on BBC Radio 5Live:

> One thing that really bugs me is when people try to drag Paul Dacre from the *Daily Mail* into this.... He has nothing to do with this. And yet people keep trying to drag him into it, saying, "The *Daily Mail* must know about this," kind of thing, and it's rotten as heck, because I'm sure — I know Paul, he's a lovely man — I'm sure he'd be more than happy to stand before a public inquiry and say under oath that his newspaper had no knowledge of these things; because he's that kind of man. And I'm sure, equally responsibly, I know, I'm almost certain, and I'll bet good money on it, that he's told all his staff to preserve all the emails that [were] exchanged over the last few years so that, should they become

subject to any kind of scrutiny they'll have all the information ready for the police. That's the kind of guy he is.[123]

Irony at its best — and a beautifully crafted piece of media undermining that went out on prime time national radio, unedited because *it didn't actually accuse anyone of anything.* We can all learn a hell of a lot from the mock innocence of Alan Partridge, thinly veiling the biting satire of Steve Coogan. I mentioned not being too clever in undermining, but there is being too clever and there is simply being clever. This may not have triggered an immediate inquiry, but it certainly made the most of the *prevailing public distrust* of the tabloid media to imply that the media houses are all as bad as one another.

Alter promotional and advertising materials to show the environmental and social impact of the company sending them out. If you work in a printing or distribution role, this will be far safer.

Whichever part of civilization you are in, there is a manipulative media waiting to be undermined. An Internet forum I occasionally visit had a discussion about the absurd way Anonymous are often portrayed, which led to the following idea: "But, you know, if you want to fuck with them by feeding them obviously fake celebrity stories that they'll probably run without checking, which you can then expose, or have a lulz contest to see who can get them to run the most stupid story about Anonymous or some shit like that, go for it." This relates to the earlier ideas that exploit poor background research, but it extends into the public realm whereby a very open, very obvious competition to spoof celebrity, technology, political, sports or any other type of writer would create a flood of *fake stories,* leaving the recipient in a complete mess. A well orchestrated campaign would ensure no more than a steady stream of fakes from a wide range of sources — carefully spoofed to look like the real thing. The outcomes of something like this are numerous: libel cases, discredited writers, discredited outlets, confused readers/watchers/listeners, and so on.

A related option could be the *fake PR company* that feeds marketing materials to unsuspecting tabloids and special-interest programs. Marketing PR is big business, relied upon for essentially free advertising by a huge number of corporations. A "reputable" (if there is such a thing) PR company can feed a promotional story about a company and see it in a newspaper the very next day, or on the web a matter of minutes later. The following is not a fake press release, although you would be forgiven for thinking that. This absurd "story" found its way into three national newspapers, with combined sales of 3.2 million and approximately 7.8 million readers:

> **Too busy to eat puddings**
>
> Eight in ten Brits are too busy to eat puddings a new survey revealed yesterday. After long days at work, a stressful commute home and then endless domestic duties 1 in 6 reckon they NEVER eat puddings after a meal because they are too tight for time. And 40 per cent of adults rarely eat desserts during the week because they are too hectic to prepare anything.
>
> The findings emerged in a poll by family pub restaurant operator Fayre & Square to coincide with National Pudding Week which runs from 29 October to 4 November and is being supported by TV family favourite Lynda Bellingham.
>
> Lynda Bellingham said: "It's a shame that people consider themselves so short for time that they can't enjoy a pudding every now and then. But Britons work the longest hours in Europe and by the time we finish a stressful day at work, battle through traffic, deal with children and homework and domestic duties it's hardly surprising that desserts fall by the wayside."
>
> Fayre & Square's head of food Paul Farr added: "It's comforting to know that traditional puddings, such as Apple Crumble, are regarded as Brits favourite. To celebrate we are offering puddings for £1 during National Pudding Week, so that time stressed families can enjoy a sweet treat. Let's face it with the days becoming shorter and colder we need something to make us smile and I personally can't think of anything better than a warm pud."[124]

This is a perfect example of a press release that pushes all the buttons. I've never heard of Fayre & Square (apparently it's yet another chain of cheap pub/restaurants), but then that was probably the point of the press release. A tabloid newspaper or commercial radio station would be happy to relay at least part of this to their audience, giving the company great free advertising, because

- it has celebrity interest (Lynda Bellingham was the "Oxo Mum")
- it is topical (winter approaching)
- it has the air of authority (research findings)

- there is an event attached to it ("National Pudding Week," albeit created specifically by the company in question)

How easy would it be to create something equally "absurd" and get it in the hands of a lazy food reporter desperate for something to fill an empty column? Obtaining lists of contacts in the media is child's play: just search for "newspaper contact lists" or "radio contact lists," for instance. One too many mistakes on the part of the media outlet and you have a double-whammy: one industry (media) undermined by continual dodgy reporting, and any number of other industries (the subjects of the press releases) *unable to submit their own material* because *they* are no longer trusted by the media.

All of that is easy to do from the comfort of a desk, occasionally popping out to the mailbox to send the results of your non-electronic deeds and to get a bit of well-earned fresh air. Other forms of undermining are less static, and require a great deal of guile. What I am about to describe is not exactly dangerous, but is probably suitable only for a very small number of people. It concerns carrying out a media sting, or more accurately a sting of a sting.

A number of cases have emerged in recent years of sports stars and their agents being lured into agreeing to fix matches for money, arrangements that have been recorded and then reported, sometimes leading to criminal proceedings. In civilization we are all swung to a greater or lesser extent by the lure of money, even if we would like to think otherwise; if I got a call from a friend saying the local shop was giving away large denomination notes to the first 100 customers, I would almost certainly stop typing and nip round there, just in case. The same goes for journalists wishing to entrap someone in the hope of a well-paying story (one example of why hope is dangerous).

So how about a bit of *counter entrapment?*

As a concerned political staffer, one of a team of Underminers starts to send out whispers that a certain politician (pick one with a particularly odious record of environmental and/or human rights abuse) is accepting money in order to push bills through government to pay off some whopping, and undisclosed, personal debts. As a concerned employee of a destructive corporation, another team member suggests to certain "whispered" reporters (choose only those who have a record of supporting destructive activities in their

Undermine the reputation of politicians and corporate executives by posting mash-ups of their speeches on YouTube. The funnier they are, the more people will want to see them.

writing) that some executives are in the habit of meeting said politician in a particular place to talk through mutually beneficial deals, and here are the details of the person who can arrange the meetings. As the intern secretary of said politician (a few business cards, a convincing email address and some headed paper should do the trick), another team member will receive the contacts from the reporters and also turn up to the meetings with a handwritten apology from the politician and the willingness to act on her or his behalf. A recording device is, of course, always switched on. Should the meeting come to fruition and a story appears then, once again, there are several outcomes, all of which are damaging to one or more major pillars of civilization: political damage, though probably short-lived; damage to the reputation of the industry-cheering journalist and the media outlet; damage to the industry for which the reporter was pretending to lobby, as such things do happen all the time.

A good Underminer will be far more creative than I am. One person who does not deal in fiction, and qualifies in anyone's books as an Underminer, is the British journalist David Edwards, cofounder of the Media Lens website and author of *Newspeak in the 21st Century.* In this exclusive essay, David presents a very practical take on why we should, and how we can, undermine the corporate media system.

The Corporate Media — Undermining the Silence

BY DAVID EDWARDS

Even the word "media" is deceptive. It suggests a neutral, disinterested carrier of information. Journalists never define their employers as "corporate media," which is, by and large, what they are. This matters, of course, because the world is dominated by giant corporations — the "neutral" carrier actually involves one part of a greed-driven corporate system reporting on itself. If this sets alarm bells ringing, the process of undermining has begun.

Three-time US presidential candidate Ralph Nader got it right when he said of the US political system,

> We have a two-party dictatorship in this country. Let's face it. And it is a dictatorship in thraldom to these giant corporations who control every department agency in the federal government.[125]

And the corporate media reporting on this system are not just controlled by profit-seeking corporations, as is sometimes claimed; they are made up of corporations. These media are in turn owned by giant parent corporations or wealthy individuals; they are dependent on corporate advertisers and on state-corporate sources for subsidized news; and they are highly vulnerable to state-corporate criticism and punishment or "flak."

The idea that the right-wing press is counter-balanced by a rational, compassionate, peace-loving "left-wing" press is a key deception maintaining a system of highly restrictive thought control. Corporate media across the "spectrum" help facilitate permanent war against Serbia, Afghanistan, Iraq, Libya, Syria and Iran. They sell corporate tyranny as "democracy," endless economic growth in an age of climate crisis as "progress" and the corporate but "free press" as genuinely free.

In the same way that New Labour masqueraded as an invigorated left option for voters while in fact destroying any vestige of serious choice between the two major parties (in Britain), so the BBC, *The Guardian* and *The Independent* feign dissent while restricting choice to a fundamentally corporatized, elite view of the world.

The Independent, in fact, is not independent of Russian oligarch owner Alexander Lebedev. Like *The Guardian, The Observer* and other "quality" titles, *The Independent* is also not independent of the advertisers on which it depends for 75 percent of its revenues.[126] Even BBC stalwart and former political editor Andrew Marr, no radical, recognizes the truth:

> But the biggest question is whether advertising limits and reshapes the news agenda. It does, of course. It's hard to make the sums add up when you are kicking the people who write the cheques.[127]

The Guardian is also an elite operation, managed by editor-in-chief Alan Rusbridger, who earned £455,000 in the last financial year, while chief executive Andrew Miller took home £572,000.[128]

In 2005, even after the West's invasion of Iraq — one of history's premier war crimes — *The Guardian* urged voters to back Blair:

> While 2005 will be remembered as Tony Blair's Iraq election, May 5 is not a referendum on that one decision, however fateful, or on the person who led it, however controversial.[129]

The Guardian editors concluded,

> We believe that Mr. Blair should be re-elected to lead Labour into a third term this week.[130]

Corporate Dissent — the Fig Leaves

In a bitterly critical article that focused on *The Guardian's* warmongering, John Pilger concluded,

> The role of respectable journalism in western state crimes — from Iraq to Iran, Afghanistan to Libya — remains taboo. It is currently deflected by the media theatre of the Leveson enquiry into phone hacking.... Blame Rupert Murdoch and the tabloids for everything and business can continue as usual.[131]

Pilger has described his own role at the *New Statesman* as a "fig leaf." The same is true of Robert Fisk of *The Independent*, and George Monbiot and Seumas Milne of *The Guardian.* Really, it should be obvious that corporate interests are the dominant influence determining US and UK foreign policy in attacking countries like Iraq and Libya. As economist Alan Greenspan — former Chair of the US Board of Governors of the Federal Reserve — commented in his memoir, "I am saddened that it is politically inconvenient to acknowledge what everyone knows: the Iraq war is largely about oil."[132]

Clearly, we cannot sensibly discuss the contents of the media without reference to the nature, bias and goals of the media themselves.

John Pilger and rare exceptions aside, the above-mentioned corporate dissidents have nothing serious to say about the deeply compromised nature of the corporate media by which they are employed. They focus on issues like Libya, Syria, climate change and the economy, often with considerable honesty. But if the media is mentioned at all, it is in general terms and in passing. There may be a swipe at Murdoch, at the tabloids, or the BBC — but not much more.

This is important for Underminers because it means that even commentators viewed as the nation's most honest analysts of current affairs are silent on the fact that the corporations by which they themselves are employed are structurally corrupt. The corruption lies in the fact that, with the best will in the world, it is simply not possible for profit-maximizing corporate media owned by giant corporations and wealthy moguls, to tell the truth about a world dominated by exploitative corporate power. It is obviously a problem. And yet for the best corporate journalists it is not even an issue.

This matters because the media are the key machine that labels corporate tyranny as "popular democracy," war crimes as "humanitarian intervention" and the US and UK governments as "fundamentally benevolent." The corporate media are the ultimate "Tools of Disconnection" separating people from the truth beneath the labels — their bias and hidden priorities are therefore strictly taboo subjects. *Undermining the media means* undermining this silence. It means undermining the claims to honesty made by the best corporate media and the best corporate journalists working within them.

Demanding the Impossible

An Achilles' heel of the corporate media system is that it is made up of often well-intentioned journalists who have been recruited because they think the right thoughts and hold the right values. In other words, their vulnerability lies precisely in the fact that they are not cynical liars — they sincerely believe they are doing good, honest work.

By emailing journalists well-sourced, credible arguments, activists can quickly and easily challenge their bias, nudging them toward greater honesty. The core message behind almost everything we at Media Lens send can be summed up as "You claim to be unbiased and honest, so why have you not discussed X, Y and Z?"

In response, some journalists appear to experience considerable internal conflict — they realize that, for whatever reason, they have not been as honest as they had imagined. But they may also have a keen sense that to be more honest, to write about the excluded facts and sources we mention, might threaten their job security and career prospects — they may become "radioactive," "one of them." What to do? If they are to maintain their concept of themselves as basically honest and sincere, they must respond rationally to the criticism — they must incorporate it in some way. This is one way of undermining the silence of the media.

The Guardian's George Monbiot is a classic example of a journalist who is not quite as much of an "unreconstructed idealist" as he would like to believe. In a June 2007, *Guardian* online debate, we asked him about *The Guardian's* hosting of fossil-fuel advertising:

> Doesn't this make a mockery of the *Guardian's* claims to be responding to climate change? Is it really credible to expect a newspaper dependent on corporate advertising for 75 per cent of its revenue to seriously challenge the corporate system of which it's a part and on which it depends? Why don't you discuss this inherent contradiction in your journalism?[133]

Because Monbiot perceives himself as a truth-teller, and because he does have considerable integrity, he (partially) answered our questions:

> Yes, it does.

This was much to Monbiot's credit — criticizing the host media in this way is something journalists are not supposed to do. He later emailed us:

> I am taking your request seriously and looking into the implications of the newspapers not carrying ads for cars, air travel and oil companies. Like

> you, I believe this is necessary if we are to have a chance of preventing runaway climate change.[134]

Monbiot clearly gave the issues some thought. A subsequent column challenged the press, including *The Guardian,* to cut fossil-fuel advertising. He wrote:

> Newspaper editors make decisions every day about which stories to run and which angles to take. Why can they not also make decisions about the ads they carry? While it is true that readers can make up their own minds, advertising helps to generate behavioural norms. These advertisements make the destruction of the biosphere seem socially acceptable.
>
> Why could the newspapers not ban ads for cars which produce more than 150g of CO_2 per kilometre? Why could they not drop all direct advertisements for flights?[135]

Three months later, *The Guardian* also published an article by the readers' editor, Siobhain Butterworth, discussing "the contradiction between what *The Guardian* has to say about environmental issues and what it advertises." Butterworth wrote:

> This summer the editors of MediaLens website began an exchange with George Monbiot, which led to him writing a column in which he advocated boycotting some advertising.[136]

Butterworth then reported *Guardian* editor Alan Rusbridger's response:

> It is always useful to ask your critics what economic model they would choose for running an independent organisation that can cover the world as widely and fully with the kind of journalism we offer.... As long as the journalism is free and we allow George Monbiot to criticise us and we feel free to criticise people who advertise, that is more important than the advertising. [137]

In reality, Monbiot's challenge was a gesture — there has been minimal follow-up to the discussion, and no action. But our challenge did bring the issue to the attention of readers, and it was an example of how even the most taboo issue for the media can be challenged by polite, rational activism.

In the past ten years, we have seen innumerable other examples where journalists have improved their coverage in response to rational challenges in similar ways. These are small gains, but they are gains — they do help expand public awareness on key issues.

Critics quite often challenge us, asking, But aren't you in fact being unreasonable? If the better journalists do as you ask — if they criticize their own media, their own newspaper, their own advertisers — they will be kicked out. Is that what you want?

We are well aware that we are sometimes demanding the impossible. In fact, that is the point we are making — that it is impossible when it should not be. A truly free and independent journalist should be free to criticize the system and organization hosting his or her work. It is clearly disastrous for any media system to be unable to engage in rational, honest introspection and self-analysis. Our hope is that, to the extent that our readers perceive a collision between what we are asking and what journalists are able to deliver, they become sensitive to the need to challenge and transcend the corporate media.

While it is important to achieve incremental improvements in media performance — articles on the problem of fossil-fuel advertising do matter — the deeper goal is to undermine public faith in the corporate media so that the public chooses to demand and support more honest, non-corporate media instead.

The End of the Internet

Local Hero is one of my favorite movies — a beautiful piece of film making and a morality tale that trumps anything that has been made since that masterpiece of Bill Forsyth's was released. A subtle but deeply meaningful scene centers on a discussion between "Mac" and Danny as they walk across the low-tide sand of Ferness Bay, backlit by the evening sky:

Danny: Aye, it's some business.
Mac: It's the only business. Could you imagine a world without oil? No automobiles, no paint...
Danny: And polish...
Mac: No ink...
Danny: And nylon.
Mac: No detergents.
Danny: And Perspex, you wouldn't get any Perspex.
Mac: No polythene.
Danny: Dry cleaning fluid.
Mac: Uh-huh. And waterproof coat s... they make dry cleaning fluid out of oil?
Danny: Ah yes, d'you not know that?
Mac: No, I didn't know that.[138]

Can *you* imagine a world without oil? It's a tough one; almost doesn't bear thinking about, until you think of all the destruction that has been wrought because we *do* have access to relatively cheap oil. As well as all the things mentioned above, can you imagine a world without the Internet? Without oil there would be no Internet — no plastic cases, no durable cable coatings, no transportation of components or running of those same cables — actually, no components at all. Write a short list of all the things you do via the Internet as well as all of the things that you would not easily be able to do if the Internet were not around.

Now look at that list and cross off anything you do just because you are passing the time and/or could be doing something better. Then cross off anything that doesn't have a genuinely practical use, including providing resources for undermining. Finally cross off anything that isn't essential to your short- or medium-term survival. If my calculations are correct, then your final list will consist of *absolutely nothing*. That doesn't mean the Internet doesn't have a useful purpose at the moment, but there is little evidence to suggest that it is of vital importance to anyone's even short-term survival.

You have just taken part in an exercise that can be applied to almost every piece of civilized infrastructure: have a go with school, the legal system, global food distribution, in fact anything you think you couldn't do without — it's tremendously therapeutic.

Two things worth raising here are whether the Internet does have a genuinely useful purpose and to what extent it would be a cause for celebration or sorrow were it to disappear. For the first instance we return to the words of Derrick Jensen. In his finest work, *Endgame,* he discussed at length the concept of "not using the Master's Tools to dismantle the Master's House" and why it's a stupid concept that has about as much relevance to resistance against the industrial system as waving a flag in a hurricane. Essentially, and I have had this thrown at me many times, activists are accused of being hypocritical if they use, as tools for activism, any of the things they are opposed to. As someone who wishes to see the end of the industrial age, should I even be wearing mass-produced clothes to keep warm while I write, let alone writing this screed on a computer, let alone hosting it on the Internet for others to read and possibly use to create a huge amount of positive change? Well, yes, actually — for the time being, and as long as those things are relevant to how we live and how we can fight back.

Jensen makes the following observations:

> And who is it that says we should not use the master's tools? Often it is Christians, Buddhists or other adherents of civilized

> religions. It is routinely people who wish us to vote our way to justice or shop our way to sustainability. But civilized religions are tools used by the master as surely as is violence [and other forms of resistance]. So is voting. So is shopping. If we cannot use tools used by the master, what tools, precisely, can we use?[139]

It's an excellent point and one that cannot be answered satisfactorily because of the absurdity of the original accusation. Come at me with fists flying, and if I can't run, I will turn and fight. Come at me with a weapon, and if I can't escape, I will find something equally potent to fight back with, which, of course is what any ordinary person would do.

There are major questions to be answered about the North African uprisings that took place in 2011, such as whether the "Arab Spring" was truly a wave of popular unrest, or whether it was planned by forces way above those who took to the streets in agonized protest. Another question is whether the Internet played an important part in allowing this to happen; for whether the uprisings were planned by Western powers or not, they could also provide a useful model for future mass rebellion. Navid Hassanpour, a Yale scholar, argues that the role of the Internet in the Egyptian uprising was considerably overstated, and may have even been a negative factor:

> In a widely circulated American Political Science Association conference paper, he argues that shutting down the internet did make things difficult for sustaining a centralised revolutionary movement in Egypt.
>
> But, he adds, the shutdown actually encouraged the development of smaller revolutionary uprisings at local levels where the face-to-face interaction between activists was more intense and the mobilisation of inactive lukewarm dissidents was easier.
>
> In other words, closing down the internet made the revolution more diffuse and more difficult for the authorities to contain.[140]

Not all societies worthy of an undermining revolution are "wired up" (North Korea and Burma are two good examples), but all societies that are victims of Industrial Civilization are, by definition, industrialized. To wit, a great deal of undermining is going to be aimed at and based around high levels of technology. As discussed earlier, some commentators will claim, and have claimed, that using technology against technology is simply playing into the hands of the system. I call that bullshit. This is appropriate action. The point is that undermining is most effective when it reflects the nature of what is being undermined. A society controlled by smart phones and iPads may be vulnerable to more basic forms of attack; but without knowing how smart phones and iPads work, then any targeted effort is doomed to failure. The same can be said of a society that is dominated by digital and cable television and radio, analogue television and radio, letter-drops and billboards, soap boxes and public assembly, word of mouth. The forces of domination choose whatever level of complexity and sophistication is necessary to propagate the message best. Thus, Underminers must choose the levels of complexity and sophistication in their toolkits that best serve to undermine those forces.

So, assuming that the Internet has at least some potential to provide useful resources and tools for undermining, I have no problem with anyone continuing to use it, as long as the person using it understands that there are many, many other means of creating change — and as long as the same person is also prepared for it to one day stop working.

This brings us to the question of the impact of a failed Internet. Dave Pollard addressed this in an essay called "Living Disconnected," [141] which I quote from here, and which is also relevant to the later chapter on community. Rather than directly say whether the loss of the Internet — which, incidentally, he feels is inevitable as cheap energy becomes less available — is a good or a bad thing, he looks at the things we would have once done using the Internet and what we can do instead:

- Instead of downloading music and film, create our own music and theatre, in live performance;
- Instead of taking photos, draw, paint, sculpt;
- Instead of blogging, write a journal, and meet in our community and share stories and ideas, cook together, rant, organize, build something together;
- Instead of playing online games, organize a real-space scavenger hunt, eco-walk, or bicycle rally, or play board games;
- Instead of taking online courses, unschool ourselves in our own communities, and learn about our place … or show/teach others what we know (including, most importantly, teaching children how to think and learn for themselves);

- Instead of organizing online petitions and complaining online about the state of the world, go visit our local politicians, get involved in community activities that make a difference (disrupt, show our outrage, satirize, or create something better);
- Instead of looking for health information online, set up a local self-help health co-op, offering preventive care, self-diagnostic and holistic self-treatment information;
- Instead of porn … well, use your imagination.

As a connected person looking to help others connect to the real world while at the same time undermining the forces keeping us attached to the Culture of Maximum Harm, the question of whether the loss of the Internet is a bad thing neatly answers itself. Of course there are things we would miss, just like we would miss going to the cinema or being able to pick up a bar of chocolate after midnight in a convenience store, but none of them are critical to life, and clearly the things we would be losing are more than made up for by the things we would be gaining. There is no need to feel guilty about your aunt no longer being able to Skype her sister on the other side of the world; what did she do before, and how many people felt guilty about moving thousands of miles away because they would so easily be able to stay in touch? A friend wrote the following on the same subject:

> After an individual on my "friends" list chose to thank the internet for making their life easier, I feel the need to thank the Internet as well. So thank you Internet for further degrading all aspects of human community and face to face interaction that we have with each other. Thank you for further alienating us from each other and the land to which we should be a part of and allowing the production of ever more products that put ever more toxic products into the earth and exploit ever increasing numbers of third world peoples. I appreciate it. I truly wish for your collapse, the sooner you do, the sooner more people can get to seeing how truly beautiful the world outside of you is, and get back to living their lives.[142]

I think that is deeply moving and, in itself, a good case for undermining the Internet at the earliest possible opportunity. We have to keep in mind the history of the Internet (and why it has a capital "I") as first a military tool, then a military/academic tool, then a commercial tool and then a commercial tool with a great deal of personal intervention. Web 2.0, as it has so quaintly been called, does not herald a great revolution in individual online liberty; Web 2.0 is just a way of keeping the commercial Internet fresh and dynamic, while still being primarily a way of making money at all levels. In effect, by undermining the Internet you are undermining a very large and brilliantly executed trade network.

As the Internet goes, we still might be able to use it for good, but the opportunity for global activism will wane. No longer will a hacker in Sweden be able to bring down a corporation in the USA; but then why would it matter? Without the Internet, the corporation in the USA will, at this point in the global economic lifecycle, have little or no influence over the Swedish people.

Task 11: Undermining the Internet

By undermining the Internet you undermine a key element of global commerce: I cannot state this strongly enough. You do not need the Internet; the Internet needs you. Nevertheless, and this applies to all major components of the industrial machine, a single dramatic removal could be a first step too far. What would be more beneficial, allowing for a less traumatic readjustment in people's personal circumstances and means of relating to each other, is a stepped approach: first concentrating on the major trunks that keep the globalization machine running and the commercial hubs that allow corporations to remain in profit at the expense of all else. Trunks, such as transnational cables and satellite communication systems, and hubs, such as major network nodes and corporate data centers — that's where the most damage can be done in the shortest possible time.

Below is a section of a global telecommunications network map.[143] I have removed any trade names and other commercial labels, not because I could be accused of commercial terrorism (well, okay, that was partly it)

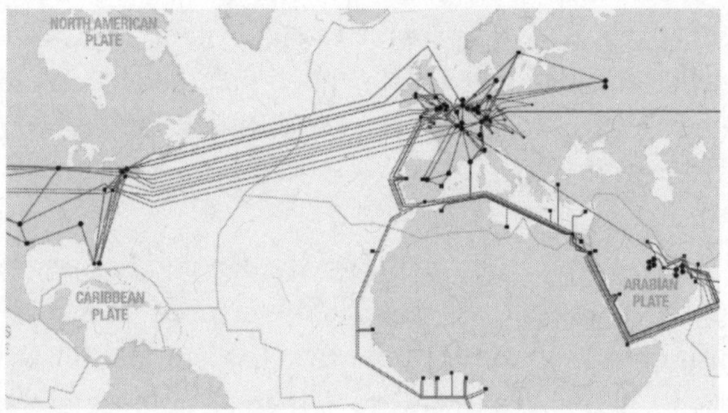

but because it demonstrates a number of weak points that are common to all major telecoms networks.

The weak points will immediately be evident to anyone who knows something about physical geography, network topology and political dynamics, but for those still in the dark, first have a look at the way the network gravitates toward certain hubs. These hubs are major Points of Presence (POPs) which on the ground tend to be large buildings studded with air conditioning outlets and full of network equipment. There are also a number of deep sea Landing Points, and the multitude of cables across the Atlantic suggests this is a fairly resilient network between North America (primarily New England) and Europe (northeast France and southwest England).

Now see where the network passes through places that have, or have the potential for, great political unrest; in this case mainly the Middle East. Finally, notice the single trunk routes that join together geographically distant locations that may be difficult and expensive to reinstate. Sometimes undermining is the same as direct action, though you don't need to necessarily cut anything to stop something from working. Power failures, routing issues, accidental shut downs and a host of other technical difficulties can at least provide temporary respite from the Great Disconnecting Network.

> BlackBerry users in Europe, the Middle East and Africa have been cut off from their online services because of a major fault at Research in Motion (RIM) in Canada. Irate owners haven't been able to get into their emails, browse the web or use the service that is most precious to them — instant messenger BBM.
>
> The users took to Twitter to vent their frustrations at the outage. A Black-Berry owner named carrryn said he or she was "HYPERVENTILATING RIGHT NOW" over the problem, while mild-mannered ex-government spin-meister Alastair Campell tweeted: "'my BlackBerry' trending ought to be good news for BlackBerry in these techie days. But it's not. My BlackBerry in blackout mode. Sort pls."
>
> [BlackBerry makers] RIM's co-CEOs Jim Balsillie and Mike Lazaridis, as well as David Yach, the CTO of RIM, went before the media to explain the series of outages. Lazaridis expanded slightly on the cause of the problem in the briefing, describing it as a hardware failure. He said a high capacity core switch designed to protect the infrastructure had failed, causing cascading

> problems as a data backlog took down service centres across Europe, the Middle East and Africa.[144]

Two points of interest here: (1) The users were furious that their precious networking tool had been taken away from them, thus revealing the hold such communications have over a large number of people. (This was front-page news for days!) (2) An apparently resilient network had failed, as it turned out, multiple times. Every network and every computer system has its points of weakness; you just need to know where to look.

Personal use of the Internet is addictive. You are probably addicted to some aspect of the Internet, whether it be social networking, gaming, chat rooms and forums, video calling, email, watching videos, sharing photos — the list just keeps getting longer. Addiction is a strange beast, for you often don't realize you are addicted to something until it is taken away from you: like a cigarette, a bottle of brandy or a shot of heroin. The Internet may not provide the external chemical stimulus of narcotics, but it certainly generates a whole lot of internal stimuli that make us want to keep coming back.

There are two ways to deal with addiction. The first is *enforced withdrawal,* taking away the source of the addiction, something I have alluded to above but which has many other variants. Many parents will come under a barrage of verbal abuse for switching off the wireless router and locking it away for a while, but it will be worth it in the end — not forgetting the parents who are probably also addicted. This "cold turkey" approach isn't as dramatic as it sounds. How many times in the past five years have you just left every means of communication at home and gone someplace else? Try it. If you have the people you really care about with you, or they are with people you trust, then why do you need to contact them anyway? The urge to check emails or update your status falls away rapidly because you are away from temptation: it really is that simple. Anti-smoking guru Allen Carr was determined that smokers (or non-smokers, as he called anyone really wanting to stop) get rid of everything to do with smoking on the day they give up; no half measures, no substitutes, nothing that might provide a slippery slope back to an addiction state. If enforced withdrawal is to work, then it will necessarily take this form because there are so many other things the unwilling (at first) withdrawee could substitute for the addiction of choice.

The second method is *personal liberation.* Undermining has to start with yourself, but, especially in the case of the Internet, weaning yourself off it will bring other people with you. It may be that half measures, like switching off social networking accounts one by one, and spending progressively more time away from the computer can work for some; and this does not necessarily contradict Allen Carr's philosophy. The Internet is not one single addiction, it is a range of addictive activities, rather like a cabinet full of prescription drugs: all perfectly legal but each one of them potentially harmful.

> "Can I chat to you on Facebook?"
> "Do you want to Skype me?"
> "What's your email address?"

A reply in the negative might get an incredulous response in a peer group dominated by technology, but how else are you going to let people know you would prefer to be contacted in other ways: by telephone (it's a start); by letter (better, and slower — good things come to those who wait); visiting in person (best of all). This stepped approach mirrors how an overall removal of technological communications could manifest itself, and also suggests *a drawing in* of peer groups and family. You may have to just say goodbye to some people forever, leaving them with an address they might find you at if they happen to be passing.

Cathartic.

We are moving into the realms of the community and the individual — just a peek into the future: chapters and lives. We will come back to this later on because we must. For now let's assume that, with our collective efforts, progress can be made in weaning ourselves and others off things that we really don't need: shopping, fashion, debt, jobs, a global economy, a global Internet. While they are still around to tempt us back (are you still salivating over that pair of shoes?) we need a few distractions. No, not distractions; we need some reality, wherever we happen to be, and for most of us it's in cities and towns.

Creating Urban Connections

The city is a symbol of our industrial past and our — according to the powers that be — bright, urban future. But there is no future in cities as they exist now; they are ravenous consumers, blind to the source of their energies — a macrocosm of the typical city dweller. Reclaiming cities will not make them "sustainable," for they cannot ever be so in their externally dependent state. But creating ecological partnerships with the rest of nature could blow apart the city mindset. The concrete-shrouded, light-drenched,

24-hour-wakened world that represents everything nature is not needs a dose of connected reality.

The approach of groups that talk about "greening" or "transitioning" urban areas into something more sustainable is blinkered at best and dangerous at worst. Such groups are almost never trying to undermine the urban mindset, and they are in many ways making us feel good about living in these hubs of civilization. Cities as we know them *are not, and can never be, sustainable.* As the global population slips and slides past seven billion, it is no surprise that the vast majority of growth in the past 20 years has been in urban areas. Part of that can be attributed to immigration from rural lands in search of jobs, although in that sense the urban areas have not just taken up any excess; they have encouraged in-migration as part of a cultural paradigm shift. Remember the etymological link between civilization and cities? Industrial Civilization is an urban phenomenon; every formerly non-civilized person who moves to a city becomes civilized by default. In the cities themselves there is little perceived need for population limits as the connections are broken between scarcity and destruction outside the Urbanosphere, and the city dweller's consciousness. Corporations and their government puppets need willing workers close to core production and service areas, so cities must keep growing at a rate that matches whatever economic growth is desired. Only in the worst slums and ghettos is the reality of city living truly revealed; there are no walls to hide behind or curtains to close. There really isn't anything that would dignify human existence.

The global population is passing seven billion because of cities. Without cities it would be impossible for so many people to exist and to remain ignorant of the destruction being wrought on the world outside. I don't want to suggest that cities need to undergo some enforced collapse and the populations within somehow deal with the consequences. I need to say that cities are *going* to collapse because there just isn't the energy, food and infrastructure to support their continued existence.

Urban populations need to prepare for the consequences before they occur. The short-term realities may have to include stocking up on food, medical supplies and the means to remain comfortable into the near future. For some there may be the immediate opportunity to move into areas with far less population density; for others that will be a distant dream, but at least those who move out will provide breathing space for those who have to stay. Urban communities have to be created and strengthened, providing necessary connections with others, giving both physical and psychological support. Mental preparation for loss and change will make a huge difference to how people deal with urban collapse. Families may be a great comfort in such times, but if you are living in an urban area and are likely to be there for some time, then you should think very carefully about whether having children is the right thing to do — it's as much for the newborns themselves as for you and the population as a whole. These are just rough pointers for dealing with the inevitable consequences of living in a city at a time of collapse.

We can prepare, but we can also challenge the brutality of living in cities while they remain centers of population for vast numbers of people. There is no place for undermining the infrastructure of urban areas at times of extreme population and resource stress; that would be as unethical as suddenly shutting down a nuclear power station. But we can use undermining to do a great deal of good: using tough times to reveal connections within and beyond the cities, connections that in the chaos of city living have been absent for too long.

Task 12: Planting Seeds of Change

The apple pie I made in the middle of October was the best I have ever made. I can cook a bit, although it's taken a while to get to the stage where I can make good food by seeming to throw together whatever happens to be available. My sister's family were walking with us through a small Scottish town in search of the last remaining orchard, a remnant of the very many orchards that existed before the town was built. A veritable harvest of windfall Cox's Orange Pippins lay on the island of grass encircled by roads; the joy of being able to fill bags with fresh fruit that would so tragically have otherwise lain unclaimed was tangible. I smiled all the way back to my parents' house and then proceeded to make that splendid pie. Someday that orchard will be gone the way of the others, though I would like to think that someday that orchard will once again be one of many others, accompanied by groves of hazel and sweet chestnut, tangles of blackberries and tayberries, gooseberry bushes alongside raspberries, all being enjoyed by families like ours. Every piece of wild food picked is a connection made; a small discovery that can light up dormant enthusiasm for the real world.

Richard Reynolds has taken the idea of green spaces on a canvas of gray and created a vibrant, barely legal movement that in turns creates unexpected joy for the city dweller and threatens the institutional idea of cities as places to merely live, work and shop.

Guerrilla Gardening

BY RICHARD REYNOLDS

Spotting potential for growing stuff on land that's not yours is the instinct of an enthusiastic gardener. Whether it's a neighbor's unloved patch or an unremarkable corner of grubby public space, if you like growing things, then it can be hard not to resist doing something there. As for permission, well that's something quite a few people these days are not troubling themselves with getting. After all, what could be the harm of doing some gardening there if whoever should be is so obviously not? It can't be so hard to do something better. That combination of creativity, optimism and mischief is at the heart of what drives many guerrilla gardeners, and the results can be remarkable.

People have been guerrilla gardening for years (there's even an obtuse reference to it in Matthew's Gospel), but in the past decade they've become much more visible. Whether as lone operatives, as I was to start with, or in organized groups, whether just for the joy of gardening or to make an explicit environmental statement, there is now a loose global network of guerrilla gardeners around the world. My role within the movement has become something like an accidental international spokesperson and rabble-rouser as my blog of activity in London got noticed and I began making connections with other guerrilla gardeners around the world. The guerrillas I meet usually tell stories of delight, of reaping far more than they expected when sowing. And they're not on the run. In most cases the landowners either don't care or don't know, and gradually the garden can become more formally recognized as the wider benefits are obvious and the fears recede.

There's probably a guerrilla garden not far from you: New York, Chicago, Berlin, Paris, Zurich, Amsterdam, London, Moscow — the locations read like the lists of outlets found on the windows of global retailers. But the form these gardens take varies much more than those clone stores. New York really is the big apple, the granddaddy of guerrilla gardens, where sizable derelict lots in the 1970s were transformed into community gardens by the Green Guerrillas, who today are a grown-up group providing advice to community gardeners. In Chicago the activity is more recent and the form more sporadic by the likes of Trowels on the Prowl, who plant up street corners and embrace the social and fun side by adopting pseudonyms. In Zurich, Maurice has scattered hollyhock seeds into the capacious open space around trees for nearly 30 years and made an unavoidable impact on the city during June and July. In London my pride is a pair of traffic islands in the middle of a dual carriageway intersection that we have mostly planted with lavender. This nature-friendly idyll also provides us with a cash crop, as we harvest the lavender and sell it in fragrant cushions to fund more planting. It's six years old now, looking better than ever, and while there's still no formal agreement or anything in writing to say we can continue, since our visit from the Duchess of Cornwall and a big friendly press pack last summer, we're pretty confident the battle has been won there now and we can garden carefree of the law. Having legitimacy from the royals was a bemusing development and slightly uncomfortable at first. I'd always assumed one day the local authority would just formalize what was informally tolerated anyway, as happened to guerrilla gardeners in New York and had already happened to me for the beds I first tended outside my high-rise home. But here was an HRH, a member of Team Royal, turning up instead; a far bigger authority keen to convey to onlookers that our activity was legitimate and impressively dismissive of my gently pedantic reminder to the royal staff that it actually wasn't authorized. (I suppose this kind of cheerful confidence is possible when you're in the team that actually, when it comes down to it, on paper owns the whole of the British Isles and 6,600 million acres across the globe.)

So by just being incessantly enthusiastic and obsessive about gardening the public realm, cheerfully belligerent about occasional obstacles and confident to trust that the media would look favorably upon the actions, I, with the help of other guerrilla gardeners, had secured some pretty satisfying chunks of south London for our pleasure as well as for all those who pondered upon it when passing by. [145]

I'm not sure how many of the seed bombs I have given away have been intentionally used as counter-urban weapons of life, even less sure how many of them have made it through a growing season; but the idea of the *seed bomb* is such a powerful metaphor that it deserves a quick instruction manual right here.

1) Get a load of soft clay, anything that can be rolled into balls and stay that way. The easiest way to get clay is from a pottery supplier. It comes as dust ready for mixing with water, and tends to come in sacks that will set you up in clay for a lot of seed bombing.
2) Get some compost, ideally some you have made yourself and put that, together with a load of seeds native to your area, into a bowl. (Avoid quick-growing grasses unless that is all you are using.) Alternatively, you can roll the compost ball around in some dry seeds so it has a crusty coating, which some seeds will like.
3) Take a small handful of clay and flatten it into a circle. Place a smaller amount of the compost/seed mix in the center, then form the clay around this mix into a tight ball.

4) You can throw the seed bombs right away or let them dry out a bit so they're cleaner to handle. As well as throwing them yourself, give them to all your friends and family with instructions to throw them anywhere that needs to be brought back to life.[146]

It only takes a few seconds to sabotage water sprinkler systems in public areas, especially golf courses. Try doing this at the same time as seeding drought-tolerant indigenous "weeds."

That final instruction is important; the vague nature of "anywhere that needs to be brought back to life" will exercise people's imaginations. For one person it will be the obscenely vast car park on the edge of town; for another it will be a vacant lot behind a security fence; for another it may be the "garden" of the neighbor obsessed with block paving; for yet another it may be the flat roof of a shopping mall. Seed bombs don't always work in practice, particularly if the environment is inhospitable and constantly changing, but for the person throwing them, that simple act of wanting a place to come back to life is a connection that has been made. Undermining the urban mindset may just be a case of giving people the chance to think for themselves.

Richard Mabey is the grandfather of wild food in Britain, and someone others look to for guidance in many other areas of ecology and natural heritage. There is something rather splendid about his approach to what constitutes a "weed," and not surprisingly his view deliberately contradicts that of the authorities who would rather anything not specifically planted for a purpose be kept down, preferably by chemical means.

> The development of cultivation was perhaps the single most crucial event in forming our modern notions of nature. From that point on the natural world could be divided into two conceptually different camps: those organisms contained, managed and bred for the benefit of humans, and those which are "wild", continuing to live in their own territories on, more or less, their own terms. Weeds occur when this tidy compartmentalisation breaks down. The wild gatecrashes our civilised domains, and the domesticated escapes and runs riot. Weeds vividly demonstrate that natural life — and the course of evolution itself — refuses to be constrained by our cultural concepts.[147]

In some parts of the USA and Canada it is illegal to grow vegetables in your front yard; or rather, it is not considered normal and therefore is in breach of various arcane zoning regulations put in place to ensure that everyone behaves the same. In effect, vegetables are treated the same way as any other "weed," because they are considered by those who like to play with power to be *in the wrong place.* A few people in the more tightly packed parts of our village grow the most amazing crops in their front gardens — some of the biggest leeks and turnips you have ever seen — and it would be unthinkable, and probably very foolish, for a council official to send them a letter requesting they turf over their source of fresh food. But it happens in some of the most "developed" parts of the world, which just goes to show that certain words should really not be taken seriously.

Regardless of whether you know the legality of *front-yard produce growing* in your area, I would strongly recommend you do it.[148] Not only is it a good use of space (many people have only front yards, if any yard at all) but it is a *visible* use of space. I have seen people stop and comment on the wonderful vegetables grown nearby; there is something going on here that is interesting and different. For every ten people who notice a front-yard crop, maybe one will seriously consider growing something, maybe somewhere even more visible. The numbers add up, especially as the area of ground turned over to produce increases and it becomes almost impossible to ignore what is going on. Here we have an example of something connecting at all sorts of different levels; engaging different people in different ways and having an outcome that is undeniably positive. Not only are people becoming more connected with the land and the source of their food, they are undermining the industrial system of food production and retailing. Not only are they undermining the industrial system of food production and retailing, they are becoming more resilient, and that is increasingly what we need to be, especially in the cities and suburbs that one day will stop being able to provide in more civilized ways.

And while you are at it, catch rainwater and use it in any way you can; dig a composting toilet, or at least make a compost heap that doubles as a *pissoire*; get some chickens (though watch out for foxes, the true rulers of the city); switch off the lights, and start getting used to the future. If you really plan on remaining in the city, then your concept of what comprises a "city" will have to change completely.

Maybe the idea of getting out of the cities before they collapse isn't entirely black and white — an apt term if ever we needed one to describe the current state of a crumbling and spontaneously blooming Detroit. Since the industrial heyday of Motown, the city has lurched its way down the economic staircase, coming to something of a tangled heap at the bottom. But it's only the "bottom" if you consider the deafening howl and reeking stench of full-throttle industrial production as being the "top" — the pinnacle of what we are told humanity should be aiming for. Halfway down the stairs was where Kermit's nephew, Robin, liked to sit, and for a young frog taking a break maybe that's fine; in the long term, though, maybe the bottom is a good place to start again:

> As you listen to the buzz of cicadas amongst the wild flowers and prairie that have reclaimed one-third of the city it is possible to feel you've travelled a thousand years into the future, and that amongst the ruins of Detroit lies a first pioneers map of the post-industrial future which awaits us all.[149]

Most of the white people have fled inner-city Detroit, headed for the suburbs and much further afield, perhaps to reinstate their urban succor. A large proportion of the non-white population, often much less able to make such a costly move, are forced to remain where they are. Ironically, in the absence of those who left, those who remain may be the ones that got the best of the deal. That's the thing about undermining; the solutions are never quite as obvious as people try to make out.

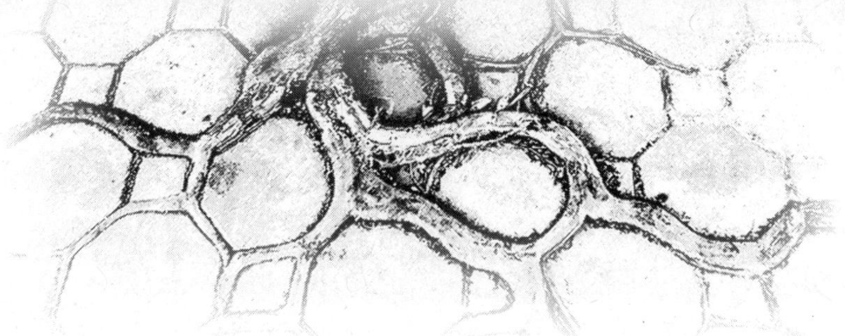

CHAPTER SEVEN

Real Activism

Lester R. Brown, one of the gurus of the modern mainstream environmental movement and head of the Earth Policy Institute (motto "Providing a Plan to Save Civilization"), has created a project called Plan B. In the book that explains the project, he writes,

> There is much that we do not know about the future. But one thing we do know is that business as usual, including our continuing failure to reverse the environmental trends undermining the world food economy, will not last for much longer. Massive change is inevitable. "The death of our civilization is no longer a theory or an academic possibility; it is the road we're on," says Peter Goldmark, current director of the climate program at the Environmental Defense Fund. Can we find another road before time runs out?
>
> Plan B is the alternative to business as usual. Its goal is to move the world from the current decline and collapse path onto a new path where food security can be restored and civilization can be sustained. The challenge is to build a new economy at wartime speed before we miss so many of nature's deadlines that the economic system begins to unravel.[150]

Essentially, Brown's "Plan B" is to mobilize the economic forces of Industrial Civilization (he cannot be talking about any other type) to protect the global ecology from further harm. So let me get this straight: he is saying we have to have a thriving economy in order to protect an environment

Exercise: You Are the Mainstream

Do you have a job with, volunteer for or belong to a mainstream environmental organization such as Friends of the Earth, the Sierra Club or the Nature Conservancy? Let's suppose, even if you are not, that you are a volunteer for such a group. For a few moments put yourself in that place, not as an Underminer but as a dyed-in-the-wool supporter ready to follow whatever orders are handed down from head office.[151] A new campaign is about to start, focusing on the greenhouse gas emissions of transport. How do you think that campaign will proceed, and in particular what do you think the main targets, tactics and desired outcomes will be?

that has been destroyed in order to sustain a thriving economy. This is the kind of thinking that has made the mainstream environmental movement the dangerous monster it is.

If you have made it this far through the book as an active participant, then I'm wondering how difficult it was to step back into the mainstream. Perhaps the phrase, "Focus on the reason" came into your head and you had to suppress the urge to consider the root causes of climate change. Certainly, for me, it wasn't easy to become that activist again. In normal conversation people refer to the "environmental movement," but really all they are talking about is business as usual, the continuation of the system that destroys all it surveys.

At best, a mainstream campaign to address human greenhouse gas emissions will raise awareness of the problems we face. It will never, of course, put them down to civilization alone, but that's a different kind of problem. In most cases actions and campaign work will simply allow businesses to reposition themselves in the market while giving campaigners some satisfaction of a "job well done" with perhaps more (of the same) work to do in the future. Often such campaigns make it possible for, or are even designed to allow, a destructive corporation or regime to look better, as they focus not on the causes of harm from an ecological perspective but from a market perspective.

I was recently speaking to a senior Greenpeace campaigner in the UK about a campaign of theirs to stop Volkswagen lobbying for a reduction in European Union emissions targets. The particular European target in question was a 30 percent cut in carbon emissions by 2020; this was being opposed by the industry, which had a preference for the slightly easier target of 20 percent by 2020. Both of these targets are woefully, suicidally inadequate. This is part of our conversation:

Keith: If we brought feedback loops into this — like the effects of methane hydrates, changes in ocean albedo, things like that — and actually turned round and said to Greenpeace, "Well, actually, the least we should be aiming for is a 100 percent reduction in emissions by 2030," do you think that's something that Greenpeace would support? [152]

GP: Er, no.

Keith: Why not?

GP: I mean, the thing is, 100 percent emissions [reduction] by 2030 would be better than 90 percent reductions by 2050. It would make us a lot safer. But we need to have some traction with corporations and governments.

Keith: So you're happy to work with corporations to get them to achieve a compromise aim — is that right?

GP: Well, it depends what you mean. If we had scientific evidence that said you need 100 percent reduction by 2030, and that's the minimum ...

Keith: Which there is.

GP: Well, like I said, it's all in probability bands. I mean, right now we've got — I don't know the numbers off the top of my head — but if we cut by a certain level by a certain time, that gives you a whatever percentage chance of avoiding runaway climate change. It might be the case that 100 percent cut in emissions by 2030 isn't enough because it would trigger feedback loops and it would be too late. It might be the case that you can go to 2040 and an 80 percent cut by then will be enough ... if you're lucky. So everything has gray edges — everything's fuzzy because we don't understand the climate well enough to say specific percentages by specific dates, giving specific outcomes.

Keith: But is that influenced by the fact that you're talking to corporations and you're trying to get, as you say, some kind of leverage with the corporations for them to change their behavior?

GP: Well, obviously we wouldn't bother asking a government or a company something which we knew there was no chance of them doing, because then we'd all just be wasting our time.

Keith: Well, if the corporations are not going to achieve anything like the cuts that you and me know are necessary, then why talk to corporations at all?

GP: That sounds a bit like an argument for just giving up.
Keith: No, it sounds like an argument for undermining the corporate system.
GP: Yeah, but that's a bigger and much more difficult job. [153]

Undermining the industrial system is anathema to the desires of the mainstream environmental and social movements that claim to speak for the Earth and humanity. You could be fooled into thinking that the people in such organizations are more enlightened than those in, say, an oil company or a political party, but from bitter experience I know it tends to be the other way round. The mainstream campaigner has been so indoctrinated in one particular course of action that alternatives are unthinkable, let alone unworkable. The groups that so many of us have up to now relied on to protect our interests are as much part of the problem as the corporations and governments they consistently let off the hook. Not only that, they are guilty of leading people to believe that by barely doing anything, great things can be achieved; the specter of hope rearing its ugly head, waiting to be taken off by whichever Underminer has the guts to make the first move.

The End of False Hope

If any one word represents the mainstream environmental movement, it is hope. As we saw in Chapter 2, hope is not merely a wish for good things to happen; it is a fundamental part of an entire, self-perpetuating belief system. This *false* hope (we will refer to it as just "Hope" for simplicity) allows the environmental mainstream to keep believing that something is being achieved in the absence of tangible progress. Therefore, if you undermine the idea of Hope, then you unlock the minds of people stuck in that self-perpetuating loop. If you undermine Hope, then real progress is possible in environmental and, by association, social activism.

So how can you undermine something as ethereal as Hope?

Imagine you are trying to undermine a well-established religion. You could perhaps, as many political activists tend to do, attack the leaders. This is not as fruitless as it may seem because, unlike a politician or business leader, religious leaders are often seen as spiritual links to, and even essential parts of, the roots of a religion. Thus, in undermining leadership, you must go beyond the person who is *in situ,* and *target the position of leader,* such that any person who fills the void will be similarly tainted. For the past few years the Roman Catholic church has been, more or less, doing this itself, with its sickening attitude to institutional child abuse. Therein lie many lessons.

More significantly, all religions, and almost all belief systems, have certain constituent parts that help to divide up the tasks necessary for undermining them:

- Mythology: the stories, sometimes ongoing, that explain the presence and workings of the belief system
- Symbols: the various artifacts that represent, either physically or spiritually what the belief system represents
- Doctrine: the rules by which the belief system is conducted

We can now start to disassemble the belief system upon which the mainstream environmental movement depends, in three easy chunks.

Task 1: Undermining the Mythology of Hope

Like all mythologies, the mythology of Hope is shrouded in mystery. It is not so much the presence of Hope that is a mystery, for as with anything that requires great courage, creating great change is bound to contain periods of suspension, where only time will determine the final outcome. What is a mystery is how Hope has become so embedded in the various environmental and social movements, to the extent that it has become the pre-eminent state: a sort of mass, slack-jawed ennui, where everyone sits around staring at the world's longest PowerPoint presentation or listening to an "inspirational" speaker who never comes to a conclusion. In effect, Hope derives from an absence of action, an inertness created from within and without. *Internally* it arises from the various movements, particularly the "environmental movement," being so self-referential: everyone reads everyone else's articles and books, then quotes from them, saying how great they are; they cheer whenever a group of people carries out some action, however trivial and ineffective, and promptly repeat the same meaningless trick; there are "gurus" who walk the mainstream path, carrying crowds of adoring, puppet-like fans in their wake. No surprise then that penetrating this bubble is just like telling any religious believer he is sadly deluded.

Externally, it is the simple fact that in the face, and the hands, of the industrial system, the environmental movement (and to a lesser extent Human Rights and other social movements) has achieved so pitifully little that Hope is almost all there is to hang on to. In effect, the Mythology of Hope is the environmental and social movements themselves, stuck in a cycle of failure.

To undermine this mythology, we need to *take away the ideas that (a) Hope is something worth having and (b) that it can achieve anything at all.* We are not talking about doing away with all discussion and debate, nor those things that have some genuine benefit for those who partake in them (meditation, for instance, can be an extremely powerful trigger) — we are talking about doing away with those things that *actively stifle* progress.

The second part is the easier part, so let's just start being honest. Much of the planet is in a ruined state, and no amount of "action" over the past 40 or 50 years — generally agreed to be the lifespan of the modern environmental movement — has made things any better. Since 1970, the year of the first Earth Day, a year that is bookended by the founding of Friends of the Earth (1969) and Greenpeace (1971), the following has happened:

- Global emissions of carbon dioxide have risen from 4,083 million tons to at least 9,000 million tons.
- Maximum Arctic sea ice area has dropped from 11 million km^2 to 9.5 million km^2.
- The deforested proportion of Amazonia in Brazil has risen from 2.5 percent to 18 percent.
- Global mean surface temperature has risen by 0.6°C.[154]

By these few measures alone, the mainstream environmental movement has been an abject failure. On top of this we have to look at the increasingly frenetic pace of civilized life, the gross levels of material consumption, the slavish adoration of money and any number of other indicators that show the industrial world becoming progressively more entrenched in its behavior, not less. This puts the lie to the claim that we are, as a society, far more "environmentally conscious" than ever before. What has really happened is that, as a society, we have become more aware of trivial matters, such as recycling, economical driving and adopting high-technology renewable energy, while becoming increasingly unaware of our place in, and impact on, the wider world. If that makes you as angry as it does me, then you will be keen to *undermine the belief in green trivia.*

Take the following list:

- recycling
- travel offsetting
- giving things to charity/thrift shops
- efficient driving

- tree planting
- turning off appliances

So, we have a list of things that, taken in isolation, seem to be okay in themselves. But now look at the list in a slightly different way:

- Every time you do the recycling and you think it's okay to generate waste, or buy things that are the cause of waste, you are greenwashing.
- Every flight you take for which you offset your emissions, use public transport to get to the airport or do some other act of servitude means you are greenwashing.
- Every piece of clothing or furniture you buy new and then take your old one to the thrift shop or sell it second hand means you are greenwashing.
- Every car journey you take during which you decide not to use the air conditioning or to brake less harshly to save fuel means you are greenwashing.
- Every tree you plant, while putting your money in a bank that makes money out of deforestation, means you are greenwashing.
- Every time you switch off an appliance, having bought then used that appliance prior to carrying out the switching off exercise, you are greenwashing.

This sounds rather unforgiving, but then why should we be forgiving of trivial acts that carry with them the weight of more damaging things? The list is obviously just a small sample of personal (and institutional, for it is just as happy at large scales) greenwashing, but it also makes it easy to undermine these various acts, all of which are actively being promoted by a large number of environmental NGOs at this very moment. By undermining any two of these acts of greenwashing, you will find you have pretty much found a way of undermining all forms of Green Trivia of the sort promoted by the mainstream environmental movement. For the sake of argument, let's choose the "switching appliances off" and "recycling" acts; you should, of course, choose your own two.

1) SWITCH WHAT OFF?

Here's a chance for some neat reverse psychology. I would like to create a character called Jenny Leaviton[155] who, in mainstream circles, would be considered a Bad Person. Jenny Leaviton is different, though, because although she has no qualms about leaving the odd light or radio on — *she has hardly anything to leave on.* Jenny is cool; she is a rebel because she decides what to do in her life, not what the establishment tells her to do. Hell, she even has a couple of ordinary light bulbs! Her equivalent down the road is Konnie Switchitoff[156] who religiously switches things off when she is not using them because there was a Department of Energy advert on her 42″ plasma television that showed rivers drying up if she didn't turn things off when they were not being used. Konnie has lots of appliances, and loves the winter sales, when she can buy more; not forgetting to sell all her old stuff second hand, because that's good too.

There are some very talented people out there: animators, film makers, musicians, artists, and other people who could take this message in the right direction, in a way subtle enough to make people realize that it's not whether you switch off, it's what you don't need to switch off that matters. Konnie is a full-fledged victim of the consumer culture. Jenny is liberated. Who do you want to be?

2) Don't Recycle

My younger daughter had to make a poster for school a few years ago. It was about recycling. Not surprisingly the poster didn't have any good things to say about recycling, and instead featured very heavily the word "Reduce." She is one savvy kid swimming in a sea of diluted good intentions; diluted by the system that wants to keep us contributing to the industrial economy. As a willing partner in the school system, the environmental mainstream has done a sterling job (joke!) in bringing the mantra of "The 3 Rs" to the children of the civilized world. Except it's *never* "3 Rs," it's always just

Recycle. Recycle. Recycle. Bloody Recycle. Recycling, as we all know is an energy intensive industrial process that assuages people's guilt about producing masses of waste from overconsumption.

The new message has to be that, taken as a part of the industrial system, recycling is a very bad thing. The word *"recycling" has to be struck from every single existing message* that includes any one of Reduce, Reuse and Repair (the missing 4th R). We could even add another "R" (as on the poster) that says just about everything that people of all ages should be doing, just like our new friend Jenny Leaviton.

Once you get under the skin of the trivia that the mainstream are putting out then you can start to *make inroads into the "goodness" of the mainstream environmental movement,* for if a movement isn't doing anything that makes things better, then how can it be good? Gird your loins here, especially if you operate within the movement itself, for we're going into territory that is normally sacrosanct to any who have ever called themselves "environmentalists." An understandable gut reaction is that portraying the environmental movement as impotent will be damaging for the environment; but we now know this is completely the opposite of what will happen. In reality, making the mainstream look bad will allow the more radical elements to show through — undiluted by greenwash and trivia.

As I write, another United Nations Climate Summit has ended with no agreements made, and nothing likely to be forthcoming except profits for those who can afford to go long on carbon. The NGOs, almost as one, are exclaiming their disappointment that nations could not agree to cut emissions, completely missing the point of civilization as being something that is bound to emit greenhouse gases at an increasing rate. So they rail and rant, expecting better, all the time achieving nothing because they are looking in the wrong direction (*towards the back of the cave*) while Underminers see the truth.

The environmental movement is as likely to change as governments and their corporate masters. This has to be made clear. They are no better than the institutions they declaim on a good day, and hold hands with on a bad one. Think of all the channels of communication crying out for some "enviro" to contact them, such as radio phone-ins and features, the corporate print media, the television news channels — think big. *Be that environmentalist* and say the very things you are not supposed to say. It's a long shot, but if it's not national or international you still have an excellent chance of penetrating the consciousness of local media and also impacting much of the grassroots.

A logical step further from pretending to work for mainstream groups is actually working for them, then turning the cards. It's easy to volunteer to work for a local group and get involved in small-scale public-facing activities like street stalls and leafleting. In my experience, though, because such activities are so ineffective, it is likely that telling the public the truth about campaigns (i.e., they are just making people think the NGOs are on the case, when they are not) will be even more ineffective. The real undermining as a volunteer is to be done in public meetings or helping out at industrial or political conferences. If you want to speak on behalf of the NGO itself at a conference, then you will almost certainly need to *already be working for that group:* trust takes a long time to build up. Once in a position of trust, though, the opportunities for telling both the people inside the Group (this is a way of removing the Veil of Ignorance in a specific context) and the public in general the truth about mainstream "activism" are considerable. If you want to stay on for a while, then you might be best concentrating on subtle messages or "accidental" slip-ups in press releases and speeches; but if you are already sick and tired of working for the Man, in the guise of an NGO, then you can be as blatant as you like:

> "At the beginning of this so-called 'Age of Environmental Awareness' there were people who wanted to change things and were prepared to fight to make that change happen. They were the pioneers — the battlers for whom compromise would remain a dirty word. It was not long before their uncompromising and truthful approach was subsumed and diluted in the formation of the modern Environmental Movement. The environmental organizations, such as the one I represent, claim to speak for the Earth and all life on it — the same organizations that willingly accept the ear of politicians and corporate powerhouses, and consider compromise and bargaining part of the way things have to be.
>
> "The truth is we've achieved nothing in the past 40 years as a movement. The current environmental movement is impotent, toothless and has never been a real threat to the industrial system. Our entreaties to governments and companies to pollute less and be greener have only created a culture of greenwash where they are able to get away with far more than if we had never existed. Essentially we do nothing that ordinary people would not have

> done anyway, and we prevent anything that resembles anarchy, illegal behavior or even that which might simply upset the status quo.
>
> "We now recognize our disgraceful and unacceptable behavior and want to hand over control of your destiny to you, the ordinary people who care about the world far more than any institution ever can. As of today [insert name of organization] is announcing a complete cessation of campaign operations. If we had realized up to now that all we have been doing is propping up the industrial system, then we would have stopped much sooner. Save your money and your support; you are far better off without us."

I feel a bit light-headed now.

You may have only one shot at this before being unceremoniously dumped, and you are unlikely to ever work for such a group in the future; but why would you want to work in the environmental mainstream if you consider them to be acting hypocritically? On the other hand, your bona fide newspaper article, or radio/television interview could completely change how the environmental mainstream is viewed by both the corporate and political world ("One of us") and those people who really want a future for humanity ("Not one of us").

An utterly expected effect of undermining the public image of mainstream NGOs will be to put the movement on the defensive. Of course they will be angry and try to deflect such criticism, but what will they be defending themselves against? In effect they will have to "defend" themselves not against the industrial system but against those of us making them look piss-poor. ("It's all lies — I mean, not all of it, but you see...") The old "successes" will be rolled out (to a crescendo of mocking) and, in a bizarre turn of events, the groups will end up attacking anyone more radical than themselves. Unfortunately for the mainstream, this will simply make the more radical views highly visible and undoubtedly attract some of the vast majority of people who exist outside of the movement's self-referential bubble.

Taking a peek online, can you imagine what this would look like on Facebook? Big ol' "green" blogs like Grist and Treehugger? Twitter will be trending #greenfight, and the idea that the mainstream environmental movement were always fighting the good fight will, at last, be blown out of the water.

Happy days indeed.

Task 2: Undermining the Symbols of Hope

Something that represents the idea of Hope more than anything else is Symbolic Action. I should probably put quotes around the word Action, but to anyone embroiled in the knotty decision over how many tea lights to take to the next vigil outside an oil company headquarters, setting out a pattern of candles really does constitute tough action. Bear that in mind while reading the following:

> Raimundo Francisco Belmiro dos Santos, a defender of the Amazon jungle, has requested urgent protection from the authorities in Brazil after reporting that a number of hired gunmen are looking for him, because landowners in the northern state of Pará have offered a 50,000 dollar contract for his death.
>
> Belmiro dos Santos is a 46-year-old "seringueiro" or rubber tapper who fears for his life and the lives of his family, after receiving numerous threats for his activism against the destruction of the Amazon jungle.
>
> "My life is really complicated today, because they have put a price on my head, and say that I will be killed before the end of the year," the activist told IPS [Inter Press Service] in an anguished voice by telephone from the Riozinho do Anfrísio reserve, where he lives.
>
> "I am fighting to defend life, the jungle, nature, and I can't live without protection anymore," Belmiro dos Santos, who is a married father of nine, told IPS.
>
> The latest threat came on Aug. 7, when an anonymous caller told the activist by telephone: "They are going to the reserve to kill you. If I was you, I wouldn't go back."
>
> But dos Santos says he will continue to return to his home.[157]

Meanwhile, in the USA, all sorts of "activists" are harping about how brave and determined they are, after having a sit-down "protest" at the Capitol building and being put in jail for a few hours:

> Fifty-two environmental activists were arrested Monday in front of the White House as part of an ongoing protest calling on the Obama administration to reject a permit for the 1,700-mile Keystone XL pipeline project, which would deliver Canada tar sands oil to refineries in Texas, and rather focus on developing

> clean energy. An estimated 2,000 people have signed up to hold sit-ins and commit other acts of civil disobedience outside the White House every day for the next two weeks — 162 have been arrested since Saturday.[158]

Much activism in Brazil is a battle between the destructive forces of Industrial Civilization and those who think there is more than one right way to live, often, in the case of those fighting for cultures and habitats that have been in existence for far longer than civilization ever will be, putting their lives on the line. In North America and Europe, the vast majority of so-called activists have accepted that Industrial Civilization is the only one right way to live, thus perpetuating the power of the system over those who are trying to defend some of the last truly wild places on Earth.

Wayne Grytting, author of the book *American Newspeak,* writes, "Tired tactics are a damn good sign that activists have retreated behind their own walls and have become weighed down with defensive armor, just like the bureaucrats they confront."[160] There is a striking polarity here, leading to the unpalatable, but inevitable conclusion that *mainstream campaigners have become at least partly culpable for the deaths of those who are truly defending the natural world.*

In the following short essay, I have reiterated some of the points already made in earlier chapters, but I feel that is necessary, for in order to undermine the world of Symbolic Action you really need to be sure what it is and why it is dangerous.

(Reproduced with permission.[159])

The Case Against Symbolic Action

First it is necessary to define what I mean by "Symbolic Action." Put simply, *it is an activity that does not create any tangible change in whatever the action is targeted toward.* Classic symbolic action includes petitioning, sit-ins, marches, occupations, lobbying, letter writing and many forms of direct action, including what the mainstream media, and many activists refer to as "violence." In general, symbolic actions do not break any "laws" (by which I mean legislation imposed by the system under which the action is taking place); arrests made are also, generally, symbolic, intended to demonstrate strength of authority, and rarely lead to conviction.

However, it is not so much a question of law-breaking; nor is it a question of the scale of the action or the methodology used: what matters is *whether change is achieved as a direct result of the action.* The definition of "success" of actions is a very loose currency in activist circles, particularly for mainstream NGOs and non-radical campaign groups. In very many cases we see success measured in terms of the size of a gathering, the number of politicians lobbied, the number of letters written or petitions signed, and so on. If the overall aim of a campaign is, for instance, to reduce carbon dioxide emissions or deforestation, then in no sense can such achievements even be considered successful, let alone have achieved genuine change. Change will have been achieved only when carbon dioxide emissions or deforestation have actually been reduced.

Non-symbolic action is that which does cause change. It does not matter whether laws are broken or not — though certainly in the case of achieving social/environmental change, almost by definition "laws" will have to be broken on the way to change taking place. It does not matter how large or small an action is, and it does not matter what form the action takes: what defines whether an action is symbolic or not is whether change happened as a result of that action. Furthermore you also have to decide whether your definition of "change" is something that is worth achieving or is simply playing into the hands of the system further down the line. An apparently non-symbolic action may end up being symbolic because it happened in the context of something contrary to, and greater than, the action originally carried out. For instance, a "successful" reduction in nuclear energy production may lead to an increase in coal energy production. Thus we have to add a further proviso to the definition of "symbolic": *an action is symbolic if it observes the same trajectory or actively serves the cause of that which it is trying to oppose.*

Context and the long view are critical in deciding whether an action is symbolic or not; however, we also have to ask the question: is there any point to symbolic action at all? As a tool for change then I would say "no"; others may disagree, in which case it is for those people to show where and when this change has ever happened. Their search will be long.

The next logical stage is to turn *awareness* into (non-symbolic) action, something the mainstream environmental movement have tried to convince us happens as if by magic. How many times have you spoken to someone recently and heard a line not unlike, "Well, people are so much more aware nowadays"?

Infuriating, isn't it?

The naive belief that awareness magically leads to change encapsulates the symbolism of Hope — that somehow by making people aware that the global ecology is going to hell in a handcart will actually cause them to change their ways, to fight back against the rapacious industrial system, to undermine the very core of the Culture of Maximum Harm. By *rejecting the notion that awareness automatically leads to change,* you create a powerful wall against Hope. Now, I have no problem with awareness per se, for without awareness change cannot happen; but that does not mean awareness actually creates change. That is a logical fallacy and one that has to be attacked at every possible opportunity, using every tool in your communications armory.

Another symbol of Hope much lauded by the mainstream is the petition. Those damn petitions are the bane of every hard-working activist, yet are held up as genuine evidence that change is happening. Petitions are like marches, only easier and with less wear to the soles of your shoes. They take many different forms, such as postcards, pre-written letters and emails, signature sheets and the latest monstrosity, the e-petition, so loved of groups like Avaaz.

This is how Avaaz sell themselves, without irony, and with some of the more revealing points highlighted:

> Avaaz — meaning "voice" in several European, Middle Eastern and Asian languages — launched in 2007 with a simple democratic mission: organize *citizens* of all nations to close the gap between the world we have and the world *most people everywhere* want.
>
> Avaaz empowers millions of people from all walks of life to *take action* on pressing global, regional and national issues,

> from corruption and poverty to conflict and climate change. Our model of internet organising allows thousands of individual efforts, however small, to be rapidly combined into a *powerful collective force.*[161]

How they create this "powerful collective force" is through a method of symbolic action called Clicktivism, described by Micah M. White as "the pollution of activism with the logic of consumerism." He goes on:

> What defines clicktivism is an obsession with metrics. Each link clicked and email opened is meticulously monitored. Subject lines are A/B tested and talking points focus-grouped. Clicktivists dilute their messages for mass appeal and make calls to action that are easy, insignificant and impotent. Their sole campaign objective is to inflate participation percentages, not to overthrow the status quo. In the end, social change is marketed like a brand of toilet paper.[162]

Avaaz's page of "successes" reads like a schoolboy dick-waving contest, in which sheer numbers of clicks are held up as engines of change, ignoring the multiplicity of campaigns that fail to achieve anywhere near the (already diluted) aims of the organizers, and especially ignoring the likelihood that things would probably have taken place without any Avaaz involvement at all. Denial is rife in the world of Clicktivism. We need to make this much more visible; but we also have to go way beyond that. "Awareness" in the world of mainstream activism is leading to nothing more tangible than a whole generation of Clicktivists and their cousins "Sign Ups" to organizations and, possibly the most benign of all, "Status Changes" *à la* Facebook or whatever social network is in vogue at the time.

So, how do you make people realize that clicking on a box is achieving nothing more than making them feel better? In his book *The Net Delusion,* Evgeny Morozov considered the hyperbole accompanying the growth of symbolic online campaigns ("slacktivism"):

> The danger that "slacktivism" poses in the context of authoritarian states is that it may give young people living there the wrong impression that another kind of politics — digital in nature but leading to real-world political change and the one underpinned entirely by virtual campaigns, online petitions, funny

> Photoshopped political cartoons, and angry tweets — is not only feasible but actually preferable to the ineffective, boring, risky, and, in most cases, outdated kind of politics practiced by the conventional oppositional movements in their countries. But despite one or two exceptions, this is hardly the case at all. If anything, the entertainment void filled by the Internet — the ability to escape the gruesome and boring political reality of authoritarianism — would make the next generation of protesters less likely to become part of traditional oppositional politics. *The urge to leave the old ways of doing politics behind is particularly strong in countries that have weak, ineffectual, and disorganized opposition movements;* often the impotence of such movements in their fight against the governments generates more anger among the young people than the governments' misdeeds.[163]

The phrase I have highlighted above is the key. *The more attractive offline movements are, the less tempting it is to join online ones.* Later in the chapter we will see how this might happen.

On the other side of the fence, we see great opportunities for directly attacking the online presence of not only the clicktivist campaign groups, but the mainstream's online presence in general. Of course, it is beyond most reasonable efforts to take down *all* the websites of even just the mass clicktivism brigade — but if Avaaz, for example, were to disappear overnight, those who had previously dedicated themselves to more concrete forms of activism might start to stir again. It is not beyond reasonable efforts to put in serious doubt the security claims of an organization that uses mass mailings. Avaaz claims, as of the end of 2011, to have (via a tedious counter) 10.5 million members worldwide. The political campaign group 38 Degrees claims 800,000 members in the UK alone.[164] How many of those "members" would feel tempted to get their names removed if even a *reported security breach* were to be made public?

In fact, I am not sure if the data held in these vast databases is private anyway; after all, if it is used for mass mailings to ramp up support for the next public campaign, does that qualify as private, personal information, or has it effectively been put in the public domain? Legal experts might want to consider that possibility next time a data grab is shared and the security of an online campaigning "force" terminally undermined.

Bill McKibben wrote a book called *The End of Nature.* It was interesting, quite enlightening in places, then right at the very end he put out an appeal for civilization to be preserved at all costs. He also wrote a book called *Hope: Human and Wild.* There is a theme developing here, especially when I bring out the specter of Bill's biggest project to date, an organization known as 350.org. This group runs campaigns based on symbolic action, and one of their most publicized has been Moving Planet, the website for which suggests ten ways to plan some kind of completely legal (e.g., "Organize ... permits for your route") symbolic event. Of particular interest among an almost wholly predictable list was this:

> 6. Invite your leaders
> If you want to make sure your leaders hear your demands, make sure you invite them out to your event! It's important to email an invitation, and call a few days later to follow up — do it early so their schedules haven't filled up. A few ideas for engaging your leader as a part of your event are a) asking them to speak in front of the crowd about their plans on climate change (so they have to say what they are or aren't doing publicly), or b) ask them to sign a pledge to take on your demands. This can work especially well for candidates who are seeking election who may promise things now that you can hold them accountable to later.[165]

This included a picture of people holding hands, presumably with their leaders. Now, I don't spot any irony here, not even any quotes around the word "leaders," so I can only assume that McKibben and his 350.org crew are being completely genuine — that is, they, contrary to the obvious absurdity of the ideas, really think that (a) hierarchy in society is an acceptable thing and (b) the people at the top of this hierarchy actually give a shit what ordinary people think, as opposed to the needs of the industrial economy.

There's little point me going over old ground here — I have covered hierarchy at length in Chapter 5, and I would expect you to be highly skeptical, if not outright damning, of any organization, individual or concept that gives *de facto* hierarchy the time of day.

Task 3: Undermining the Doctrine of Hope

These are the rules, the lodestone upon which the current environmental movement styles itself. It is made up of Wise Words, best-selling publications, oft-repeated sentiments, and a number of apparently binding axioms, such as the idea "We're all in it together" — implying that criticism is not acceptable and breaking ranks is a sign of failure. This sounds suspiciously like the way a corporation behaves, or perhaps a political party, and anyone who has spent time in the beating heart of an NGO will see the similarities.

The thing about true axioms is they are universally applicable, but from the point of view of a giant NGO such as WWF or the Sierra Club, axioms can be changed, depending on who is making the rules. As I write, it's heresy to suggest that businesses and environmental groups can't work together for a better future. It was once heresy to think they could work together.

As for sentiments and Wise Words, here's something you will have heard lots of: "Be the change you wish to see." Mahatma Gandhi, its author, was no saint, as several authors have been at pains to point out; and neither was he a dedicated proponent of peaceful action — his saboteur followers saw to that myth. And his phrase, above, is a pretty good one if taken in the right way: you want to see change? Then do something about it. All too often, though, this phrase has been taken as an excuse merely to change one's state of mind, without actually doing anything that is likely to bring about any other kind of change.

Any doctrine is made up of things that people have said and done and, in the words of the great Utah Phillips, those people have names and addresses — or at least they have names, those who have already left us. It's not so much the originators of the words who need to be undermined, as the way those words have been used and, in many cases, twisted for the benefit of the user. So, when I attack the phrase "Be the change you wish to see," I am most definitely taking to task those copywriters and poster designers who have completely failed to take into account the real meaning of and the potential ramifications of Being The Change.

Fuck it! I'm going to go further than that: if you use a phrase or saying and can't be bothered to understand what the words mean, let alone the context in which those words were laid down, then you have no right to use them.

I'm reminded of the original definition of Sustainable Development by the commission led by former Norwegian Prime Minister Gro Harlem Brundtland, which is precisely this:

> Sustainable development is development that meets the needs of the present without compromising the ability of future generations to meet their own needs.[166]

Taken completely out of context but with a careful and logical reading of the words, it is clear that any application of Sustainable Development cannot cause a net degradation of the natural environment and thus cannot allow anything like the current activity of Industrial Civilization to continue. For a few years I was happy to bandy around this definition, confident of its goodness. But read the rest of the commission's publication and it becomes clear that nothing suggested by the commission as part of a solution to the world's ills comes even close to its own definition of Sustainable Development. For a start, it takes the civilized concept of "development" at face value and makes a point of urging the need for economic growth above all other imperatives. The only sustainable thing that can be done with existing copies of this document is to burn them to keep warm, or perhaps line your clothes with the torn out pages!

The short undermining approach to this is to *challenge anything written or said by the environmental mainstream that claims to be immutable.* This goes back to Chapter 5, and the importance of Critical Thinking. So many times we are expected to accept what is said by the "great and the good" of the environmental movement as Gospel — I don't apologize for the religious imagery — and are given an extremely hard time when we challenge it. So many times we see the same phrases tacked onto materials or at the head of articles, yet we never think to challenge the significance of such words that have been lazily spewed into print.

There is no environmental Gospel.

Corporate Ties and Other Accessories

The vast majority of the supporters of large NGOs have little problem with corporations giving money to their favorite organizations. We know this because, almost without exception, the mainstream NGOs proudly display lists of sponsors on their websites, sponsors like BP, Cargill and Rio Tinto. These people are dangerous but not stupid.

Cory Morningstar, a tireless anti-symbolic environmental and political activist, recently took one particularly execrable project to task for all sorts of crimes against real action, including the now omnipresent corporate influence:

> [We should] take note of 350.org's latest adventure; that of SumOfUs (along with pro-war Avaaz and friends). In essence, SumOfUs are predominantly white, while "Some of Us" (Indians, Libyans, Africans, Chinese, etc.) are not! But not to worry — the

marginalized Americans, and in fact, all those marginalized, on the receiving end of the industrialized capitalist system, will soon find bliss in the new "worldwide movement" that will make capitalism ethical, fair and even compatible with the environment which it will protect! So while SumOfUs (strapline: "a movement

A Note on Conspiracy Theories

There doesn't seem to be an obvious place to put this, but as this section is about our "leaders" and the problem has yet to be addressed, then this would seem to be the best time to talk about conspiracy theories. First, definitions: a conspiracy is something that has been arranged between two or more parties without the knowledge of any other party — it's as simple as that. A conspiracy theory is thus anything that addresses a possible, as yet unproven, conspiracy. A conspiracy theorist is someone who specializes in conspiracy theories. All nice and simple so far. Now, a Conspiracy Theory (note the initial caps) is any conspiracy theory that is clearly bonkers; the capitals idea is mine, and it's the only way I can distinguish between a valid conspiracy theory ("The government are recording everything we do on the Internet," "Rail closures are the direct result of motor industry lobbying") and a bonkers Conspiracy Theory ("My skin complaint is called Morgellons and comes from Chemtrails," "Global Warming is just a way of getting us to buy more technology"). The vast majority of things I address in this book are neither; they are just facts, easily gleaned from research or logical analysis. Conspiracy Theories are a big problem because, like most (other) messages put out to keep us living in a particular way, they stop us seeing what is really going on. Why would it matter which religion controls the world's money markets if you knew that the world's money markets exist to control you, regardless of who controlled them? Why would it matter whether President X was a reptile if you knew that, regardless of species, the US president was just a figurehead for the all-destructive industrial system? Some very clever people indeed have become addicted to Conspiracy Theories and, indeed, some people who talk about Conspiracy Theories also speak a lot of sense — watch any video by David Icke, for instance, and you will see quite a lot of sense, followed by a lot of lizards. These people could be excellent Underminers, as could the people they are influencing, so we have to do what we can to *show up Conspiracy Theories as nonsense.* Chapter 5 should be helpful as this is just another Veil of Ignorance in operation, so if you are game for an intense battle of minds, then this could be one battle that results in a lot of freed minds, ready to battle against an even bigger target.

> of consumers, workers and shareholders speaking with one voice") will continue to "demand" and consume "ethical" iPads, "Some Of Us" must learn to accept their role and be satisfied with the 1 cent raise per pound or per day that SumOfUs is going to fight for! All while the planet burns. Apologies for the sarcasm — but the truth is that there is an underlying deep-rooted racism and classism humming along under the system (and this as 350.org with TckTckTck, Avaaz, Climate Action Network & friends grossly undermined Africa). I watched it again in Bolivia as 350.org fought to undermine the Bolivian Government. The arrogance is formidable. For clarification I do not consider myself and those who believe/defend 350.org as on the "same side". I don't consider 350.org and friends as part of the "environmental movement". Rather, I believe that 350.org and friends protects the system & keeps current power structures intact. I don't believe in an org. that was created/financed (1Sky) by the Clintons and the Rockefellers for obvious reasons. The only thing powerful that 350.org and friends build — is that of a brick wall to protect the very system destroying us.[167]

If we are to challenge the power of NGOs in their own backyard, we need to find something that will hurt both their public image and their bottom line. Some NGOs, such as the Nature Conservancy and WWF, are so heavily funded by corporations and corporate funds that a drop-off in supporter giving will have little impact on their turnover. On the surface, the bigger the NGO the harder it is to hurt. But don't be fooled into thinking that large NGOs should be left alone because of this. And just because an organization is relatively small, that doesn't mean it is not influential; in fact some of the smallest groups that can be very effective in changing the behavior of people on the ground are also some of most easily corrupted. The environmental movement is complex, but in terms of how it is organized, it can be broken largely into three areas, which helps the undermining process greatly:

1) Small community/non-hierarchical organizations and groups that are almost entirely self-funded and usually based around a single issue, such as an unwanted development. These are not usually a valid target for undermining unless there is strong evidence that they are being influenced in some way to work contrary to our best interests.

2) Organizations that are supporter-funded, though often having ties to businesses and special-interest groups. Sometimes they can be large, such as Greenpeace, but are generally smaller than the third type. Their importance lies in their influence over grassroots environmentalism, including quite radical groups and individuals (an assumption is made that radicals can be "turned" mainstream with effort), and as such are a severe impediment to the success of genuine community-based groups.
3) Organizations that are largely corporate and/or foundation funded, usually with close ties to special-interest groups and governments. Their income often runs into the tens or even hundreds of millions of dollars or equivalent, and they generally operate at a continental or global scale, with considerable influence on the political agenda. Given that they are heavily influenced by vested interests, such as energy companies or biotech firms, they provide a useful channel for these vested interests to influence public policy on a grand scale — in effect acting as a laundry service for dirty ideas.

So, for this section, we need to break up the targets into two camps: first, the organizations that depend heavily on their supporters for funding, and then the corporate-fed behemoths. One task will be assigned to each, although there will inevitably be crossover between the two.

Task 4: Exposing Corporate Ties

Insert contrary materials, such as flyers exposing a company or organization's activities, into the pages of reports, magazines and brochures.

For a long time I supported an organization I thought would be able to make a real difference; the Woodland Trust had been, and certainly for a considerable time after I joined, has been a true stalwart in the essential job of protecting, managing and replanting the native woodland of the UK. Its work on climate-related phenology has been second to none; it has been responsible for bringing doomed woodlands back from the brink of destruction and has re-established woodlands where once they had been. It has involved thousands of children in educational and practical work … the list goes on.

Then, a couple of years ago, it started ramping up the process of attracting corporate sponsors. It's not as though money was particularly tight — between 2001 and 2006 its total income steadily rose from just under £16 million to nearly £22 million, with no sign of any financial worries; but for whatever reason, perhaps because certain trustees deemed it "the right thing to do" the Trust started attempting to attract corporate funding in earnest. At the time of writing, the Woodland Trust has corporate partnerships with organizations as grossly inappropriate as Calor Gas, BP, Ronseal (Thompson), Tesco, Georgia Pacific and the UK Ministry of Defence. When Disney named a wood in return for sponsorship, my anger broke.

Remember what I said about personal motivation being a key factor in choosing what to undermine? Disney is one of those firms that encompass everything bad about the industrial consumer society, and a corporation I particularly loathe for the way it has polluted the upbringing of countless children. I felt I had no choice but to resign and write about it. But first I went about seeing how far I could push the Woodland Trust. As a "responsible" NGO, did it have a limit as to what it would ignore if funding was at stake?

Posing as a major logging company with a poor environmental record, I made and recorded a phone call to the corporate partnerships team, asking whether "we" could sponsor a large area of woodland with a substantial amount of money. The conversation was very positive, so I switched into confessional mode:

Me: I don't want to beat about the bush here — no pun intended — we're doing this because we want to appear to be a good company.

Woodland Trust: Yes.

Me: It is PR, I'll have to be perfectly honest with you.

WT: Yes, yes. That's fine, we're set up for that. You want promotion, we have people that can help, so yeah. What can I do for you now? Can I send you some information or do you want to go away and discuss...

Me: We would go away and discuss this; we're contacting a large number of charitable organizations in the environmental area as part of the portfolio. Some of them have been agreeable, some of them have been less agreeable, but it's horses for courses really.

WT: Yes. Well, is there anything else that I can help with?[168]

I blethered on for a bit about locations and questions about the Woodland Trust, but essentially the confession was in the bag. Clearly they would stop at nothing to get the money. *This recording went online,* followed up with a letter to the chief executive. The next year (2010) the Trust's corporate funding, both absolutely and as a percentage of total income, went down for the first time.[169] I suspect this was due to a change in policy, which is one outcome that is worth pursuing — after all, if an organization has less corporate funding, it is far less likely to be influenced by corporations and maybe even do some good.

The bigger game, though, is to hit hard those NGOs and Campaign Groups that are clearly practicing nothing but symbolism *and* are letting vested interests keep them that way. Earth Day is an event that has remained largely unchanged since its institutional founding in 1970, via the United Nations; it is little more than an observational period when we are supposed to think about what the planet means to us. Earth Day groups have sprung up all over the place as local focus points, and it seems that the event is getting bigger all the time. This would be a good thing if Earth Day wasn't such a mainstream and commercially polluted event.

That's not to say it has to be. Earth Day, trite as the term is, could be something that genuinely connects people with what it means to be human. The Earth Day Network purports to be an umbrella group, but in reality it is a large American NGO mainly focused on delivering its own programs based on "green economics" and other lies. Earth Day Groups, on the other hand, are very much at the grassroots of mainstream environmentalism and are far easier to take to task over their ties to the industrial and political systems. A quick tour of websites shows a huge range of affiliations and sponsors, ranging from small local businesses to major corporations, individual politicians to government offices and campaigns, local radio stations to media conglomerates — the contradictions are easy to spot, yet as long as there is support and money coming in, it seems that almost anything is acceptable. To my mind that is immoral. They are aiding and abetting the very active and entirely self-serving public relations efforts of whomever they are enlisting the support of. In this situation it is very easy to *tar the group accepting the endorsement/money with the same brush as the supporter.* Literally "tar" them if the supporter is involved in oil — no environmental group wants to be seen as reeking of pollutants in the public eye, even if in private they are happy to take money from the hand that harms.

Phone politicians, posing as company representatives and offering them funding in exchange for political favors. Record the conversations and if the politicians suggest impropriety, send the recordings anonymously to media outlets.

At first, you could gently advise the group(s) that their associations are not appropriate and you would very much like to see them change. If that doesn't do the trick, then you could give them fair warning that you are about to expose a particularly nasty practice of their supporter (or supporters) to a very wide audience. You don't even have to be able to do this, *the threat could be enough.* In the first instance ("Nice" Underminer), you would probably be taking the view that the group has some promise as a force for good — maybe it is a community-based group that wants to reconnect people with their landbase — and so give them some positive support in addition to the helpful advice. In the second instance ("Nasty" Underminer), it will probably have gone beyond that stage; there is still the chance of showing them the error of their ways, but if they reject your advice in favor of funding from bad places, then you can take the tough route — unless it is just one or two people taking the "any funding/support is good" line. That is an opportunity for *selective pruning;* yes, this will start to get personal and, yes, it might start to feel uncomfortable, but it can easily be justified if you feel that the benefits of the group continuing outweigh the singling out of individuals for undermining. Just don't get too personal; things have a habit of biting back if you aren't careful.

If you simply want to go down the exposure route, or have exhausted all other avenues and have no other option, then you will already have read more than enough here to know what to do, which seems like a good point to move onto bigger fish — the ones that really give environmentalism a bad name.

Task 5: Hitting the Big Boys

When I say "Big Boys" (the gender is accurate in most cases) I am talking about the kinds of organizations that are indistinguishable from multinational corporations. In fact they are multinational corporations in some cases. The names might not slip off the tongue so easily because, while these organizations often have a public face, it is their work in the background, influencing government policy and advising the business world how to finesse their brutal activities, that is more significant. Among these behemoths are the aforementioned Earth Day Network along with WWF, Sierra Club, United Nations Environment Programme (UNEP), The Nature Conservancy, The Climate Group, Earthwatch Institute and, biggest of them all, Conservation International. So let's take a quick look at how they behave, with an extract from Johann Hari's brilliant 2010 exposé "The Wrong Kind of Green":

> Environmental groups used to be funded largely by their members and wealthy individual supporters. They had only one goal:

to prevent environmental destruction. Their funds were small, but they played a crucial role in saving vast tracts of wilderness and in pushing into law strict rules forbidding air and water pollution. But Jay Hair — president of the National Wildlife Federation from 1981 to 1995 — was dissatisfied. He identified a huge new source of revenue: the worst polluters.

Hair found that the big oil and gas companies were happy to give money to conservation groups. Yes, they were destroying many of the world's pristine places. Yes, by the late 1980s it had become clear that they were dramatically destabilizing the climate — the very basis of life itself. But for Hair, that didn't make them the enemy; he said they sincerely wanted to right their wrongs and pay to preserve the environment. He began to suck millions from them, and in return his organization and others, like The Nature Conservancy (TNC), gave them awards for "environmental stewardship."

Companies like Shell and British Petroleum (BP) were delighted. They saw it as valuable "reputation insurance": every time they were criticized for their massive emissions of warming gases, or for being involved in the killing of dissidents who wanted oil funds to go to the local population, or an oil spill that had caused irreparable damage, they wheeled out their shiny green awards, purchased with "charitable" donations, to ward off the prospect of government regulation. At first, this behavior scandalized the environmental community. Hair was vehemently condemned as a sellout and a charlatan. But slowly, the other groups saw themselves shrink while the corporate-fattened groups swelled — so they, too, started to take the checks.

Christine MacDonald, an idealistic young environmentalist, discovered how deeply this cash had transformed these institutions when she started to work for Conservation International in 2006. She told me, "About a week or two after I started, I went to the big planning meeting of all the organization's media teams, and they started talking about this supposedly great new project they were running with BP. I had read in the newspaper the day before that the EPA [Environmental Protection Agency] had condemned BP for running the most polluting plant in the whole country.... But nobody in that meeting, or anywhere else in the organization, wanted to talk about it. It was a taboo. You

> weren't supposed to ask if BP was really green. They were 'helping' us, and that was it."
>
> She soon began to see — as she explains in her whistleblowing book *Green Inc.* — how this behavior has pervaded almost all the mainstream green organizations. To take just one example, when it was revealed that many of IKEA's dining room sets were made from trees ripped from endangered forests, the World Wildlife Fund leapt to the company's defense, saying — wrongly — that IKEA "can never guarantee" this won't happen. Is it a coincidence that WWF is a "marketing partner" with IKEA, and takes cash from the company?
>
> Likewise, the Sierra Club was approached in 2008 by the makers of Clorox bleach, who said that if the Club endorsed their new range of "green" household cleaners, they would give it a percentage of the sales. Executive director Carl Pope defended the move in an e-mail to members, in which he claimed that the organization had carried out a serious analysis of the cleaners to see if they were "truly superior." But it hadn't. The Club's Toxics Committee co-chair, Jessica Frohman, said, "We never approved the product line." Beyond asking a few questions, the committee had done nothing to confirm that the product line was greener than its competitors' or good for the environment in any way.
>
> The green groups defend their behavior by saying they are improving the behavior of the corporations. But as these stories show ... the addiction to corporate cash has changed the green groups at their core. As MacDonald says, "Not only do the largest conservation groups take money from companies deeply implicated in environmental crimes; they have become something like satellite PR offices for the corporations that support them."[170]

Industrial Civilization needs a healthy economy in order to exist, and so do environmental NGOs — not just to provide a source of funding but to ensure their corporate hierarchy and power base thrives. The Big Boys rely on it, and that makes them culpable. It makes them enemies of the very environment they pretend to care for. It is clear that without a "healthy" economy there can be no monolithic NGOs working the corporate and political world to grease their wheels. As long as there is a globalized, industrial economy, then these organizations will continue on their duplicitous, dangerous course, making ordinary people feel the world is in good hands. This must end.

This is potentially risky. You will not only be undermining major NGOs, you will also be undermining the credibility of the corporations that work with those organizations.

⁂

The powerful grip, both directly and by proxy, that these groups have on public opinion allows us to do a bit of reverse psychology, similar to one of the Black Friday ideas. You might have noticed that a number of activities described in this book go way beyond what most of the big NGOs are willing to do; but that doesn't mean these actions cannot be carried out *"on behalf of" such groups.* We are talking about the kinds of things they would not condone themselves but which would probably require the participation of large numbers of people, such as a mass locking of shopping malls or other facilities, the blocking of television or radio signals during advertising breaks, or sending provocative letters to hundreds of newspaper editors. The more closely the targets are to the NGO's corporate friends the better. How about threatening to barricade a few storage depots belonging to an oil company that works with the NGO that is purportedly "carrying out" the barricade?

If you can leave a relevant and obvious "signature" in the course of your action, such as branded stickers, headed paper or a digital image, then two advantages come into play: first, you are less likely to be found out and, second, it will force them to admit they would never do such a thing, thus undermining their own credentials as activists. The risk of this type of undermining depends on the action being carried out, but it is really only limited by your own imagination.

Now, let's consider a scathing but accurate image.

When I redesigned the Conservation International logo, I was looking to do something that fulfilled a number of criteria:

1) The redesigned logo had to make a simple, effective and easily understandable point to the extent that even the target could not question it.
2) It had to contain enough truth that it would be considered "fair use" under copyright law.
3) It had to look good — both professional and eye-catching (notice the falling monkey and half-sawn tree).

While pleased with the final result — produced, may I add, not with Photoshop but a much cheaper and less well-known software package — there was still the need to get it out into the public domain. And here's

the challenge: although I placed it on various websites, including my own and (for a short while) Wikipedia, it has not become common currency. Conservation International is not yet known as Corporation International. I don't have anything like all the answers, but I do know that such a logo — and there is no reason you shouldn't design one yourself — would play a big part in *undermining the Earth-friendly public image* of a major NGO.

I mentioned Wikipedia just now, and that's because there is little doubt that this online encyclopedia has become the *de facto* source of generic knowledge over the past few years, to such an extent that its own integrity is very, very carefully protected. I'm not one of those people who generally looks at Wikipedia and thinks, "That's completely wrong, it must be changed!" Part of the reason is that as a media form, wikis are supposed to be self-regulating, and the more people involved in the wiki — in general — the better the self-regulation. Okay, there are some wikis, like the infamous Conservapedia, that have such a bulk of prejudiced users that any attempt to correct information is doomed to failure (that said, it would be fun to try...), but in the main, a good wiki, such as Wikipedia, is going to end up about as balanced as it's possible to be in the context of Industrial Civilization. You can't really expect it to go against the tenets of the industrial system, but you can make it more objective. I like to call this "Wikicorrecting."

As an example, I stumbled across an article posted by an employee of either IBM or one of its PR firms.[171] The article in question was promoting the virtues of IBM's Green Computing and was a blatant advert. Simply by my marking the article with the appropriate "Speedy Deletion" tag — in this case **promo** — the article was deleted by an administrator, never to be seen again. One bit of greenwash consigned to the virtual dustbin. Of course, there is more to Undermining than just correcting obvious bias: what about exposing the real truth behind the corporate system? Yes, you can do it on Wikipedia, but you need to tread lightly:

> It is easy for a person to vandalize Wikipedia. Since anyone can edit any page, the possibility is always there. The vandal might add profanity or inappropriate images to a page, might erase all the content of a page, etc.
>
> However, there are tools that make it easy for the community to find and remove vandalism. There are also other tools available on Wikipedia to help corral users who are persistently destructive. For example:
>
> - It is easy for anyone who sees vandalism to revert pages back to a pre-vandalism state.
> - It is easy for any user to alert the rest of the Wikipedia community to vandalism that is in progress.
> - It is possible for an admin to block or ban users (or IP addresses) who are persistently destructive.
> - It is possible for an admin to protect a page temporarily to keep people from changing it.
> - It is possible for an admin to delete an inappropriate page.
>
> Tools like these make it easy for members of the community to quickly eliminate vandalism and prevent vandals from coming back.[172]

It's no good just steaming in with a rant as, certainly in the case of higher-profile pages, the changes will be undone. Stick to the following rules and you should be all right:

- Make sure the changes you make are evidence-based, referenced and written properly. Anything that suggests vandalism will be reverted. You could use terms like, "reinstating balance" in the change notes.
- Make subtle textual changes that alter the meaning of entries, undermining any positive image the company or organization may benefit from. Always mark changes as "This is a minor edit," and explain that it is for clarity. Avoid obvious trigger words like "pollution" or "destructive," even if it sacrifices clarity.
- Make changes to unwatched entries. From the point of view of an Underminer, the most useful Wikipedia page is "Most Watched Pages" (with "Pages with the Most Revisions" probably in second place) as it indicates those entries you cannot alter without comeback — the pages

you want to avoid. Also, look for the latest edit date of an entry you want to revise: if it is more than a year ago, then you should be able to get away with more nefarious changes, even subvertising, without the change being reverted.

In all cases, you should make changes either anonymously (for minor edits) or under a disposable alias, as you don't want to start getting a bad name for changing things.

Finally, and making an assumption that despite the Veil of Ignorance people would actually be pretty disgusted if they found out a major "environmental" NGO was corrupt from top to toe, it's time to go for the big corruption exposé. In March 2010, Christopher Booker, never a friend of the environmental mainstream but, ironically, a friend of those who wish to undermine the environmental mainstream, reported in *The Telegraph* on the amount of money WWF were likely to receive from the implementation of the REDD scheme. Essentially, a scheme that, WWF claims, protects forests was actually going to be a cash cow for the savvy investor, especially corporations that had no intention of reducing their actual emissions:

> If the world's largest, richest environmental campaigning group announced that it was playing a leading role in a scheme to preserve an area of the Amazon rainforest twice the size of Switzerland, many people might applaud, thinking this was just the kind of cause the WWF was set up to promote. Amazonia has long been near the top of the list of the world's environmental concerns, not just because it includes easily the largest and most bio-diverse area of rainforest on the planet, but because its billions of trees contain the world's largest land-based store of CO_2 — so any serious threat to the forest can be portrayed as a major contributor to global warming.
>
> If it then emerged, however, that a hidden agenda of the scheme to preserve this chunk of the forest was to allow the WWF and its partners to share the selling of carbon credits worth \$60 billion, to enable firms in the industrial world to carry on emitting CO_2 just as before, more than a few eyebrows might be raised. The idea is that credits representing the CO_2 locked into this particular area of jungle — so remote that it is not under

> any threat — should be sold on the international market, allowing thousands of companies in the developed world to buy their way out of having to restrict their carbon emissions. The net effect would simply be to make the WWF and its partners much richer while making no contribution to lowering overall CO_2 emissions.[173]

The attack on REDD, spearheaded by the campaigning group REDD-Monitor among others, was well underway before this article was written, but it is the big news stories that take something as fascinating as this from rumor and low-key exposure to widespread public awareness. The bad press has continued: despite the media reach of WWF and the United Nations Environment Programme (big supporters of REDD), the stories keep coming, with help from some outstanding journalism. REDD is now (as of early 2012) being reported as carrying out carbon offsetting in the form of owning the "non-destruction rights" to a piece of land that — now get this — belongs to someone else. So REDD is not only a way of profiteering from conservation but also something that is taking away the land rights of indigenous people in the name of "sustainability."

At the time of writing, REDD is foundering on the dry land of exposure; after more than three years there is still no sign of it getting underway, dealing WWF a killer blow to its money-making plans. And, trust me, there are many more examples of disgraceful, destructive corruption within the NGOs waiting to be revealed to a world very much skeptical of the motives of the environmental movement. It turns out that the very *skepticism generated by the corporate media and the political mainstream* may play a major part in undermining the mainstream environmental movement — and that will leave the way open for real change to take place.

What Activism Looks Like

It was October 2010, and a horribly self-congratulatory email came to me which made great capital of not much at all:

> Dear Friends,
>
> I don't quite believe it.
>
> I've been double-checking our numbers, and it's beginning to look like we might shoot past the total of events from last year's International Day of Climate Action. As I type this message, the counter is at 5203.

> You might remember that there were 5248 events in 181 countries last year, and you can watch the compilation video from that day for a reminder of just how beautiful it was. And how massive it was: CNN said that it was "most widespread day of political action in the planet's history." I was worried we couldn't top that for the Global Work Party on 10/10/10—in part because "experts" kept saying people were too discouraged after the failure of the UN climate talks in Copenhagen.
>
> But it's looking like "experts" were wrong, and this movement is more energized than ever. When we see our leaders failing, we want to show them how it's done....
>
> Apart from being one of quite a few people who expected nothing from the Copenhagen talks (except politicians talking about how to make more money), I couldn't work out what it was that the author didn't quite believe. Nothing had been achieved.

I wrote back:

> Well, that's nice xxx. And what has xxx achieved so far — and what is it likely to achieve? I'm talking real change not number of events, banners, signatures, petitions, participants…whatever — I'm talking real change.
> Keith

As is normally the case, I didn't get a response from the author — they are usually *far* too important to be involved in something as trivial as answering questions that don't get them big media coverage. I did get some response, though:

> Keith,
> What does real change look like to you?
> Thanks.

Which I thought was a really good question. It's one I've already answered in the section on symbolic action. But that leaves the equally good question, What does real activism look like to you? Okay, I could just say that it looks like undermining, or point to the fact that real activism is simply that which leads to change, but there is more here — it is about how activism actually presents itself to the ordinary person. In other words, if someone wants to move from being an ineffective activist to an effective activist, how does one make that move?

Task 6: Holding Hands with Activists

Back in August 2009 I found myself a little confused, not for the first time admittedly. I had just come back from a wonderful direct action and environmental information camp in the English Lake District, replete with thoughts of constructive anarchy and a future that we have to make our own, and I found the news full of London Climate Camp 2009 that was assembling at the scene of the 14th-century Peasant's Revolt, Blackheath in Southeast London. Wat Tyler would have approved of the location, but I wondered if he would have approved of the motivation.

I spoke to a fair number of people at the direct action camp who were intending to go to London Climate Camp, most of whom I would consider to be anarchists[174] and most of whom were pretty excited about going. This made me feel better about Climate Camp than I had in the past: they had no intention of watering down their ideas. But this was sorely tempered with the fact that many people who had attended Climate Camp the summer before were certainly not radical, and they spoke at length about the need to engage politicians and work to help corporations become greener.

Various national radio stations featured interviews from Climate Camp attendees, one of whom called himself "Oscar." (It might have been his real name.) Oscar found himself in the apparently uncomfortable position of having to defend actions that would potentially affect people's "legal right to work" (a presenter's words, not his). Unfortunately, rather than use this magnificent opportunity to decry the entire industrial capitalist machinery that is progressively destroying every aspect of the global ecosystem in the pursuit of profit, he proceeded to apologize to those people who would be affected, then talked weakly about the dangers of climate change.

> *During political or corporate interviews, make a nuisance of yourself, jumping up and down, holding up bits of paper with contrary messages, walking in front of the interviewee: in a public place there is nothing a broadcaster can do to stop you.*

It would be unfair of me to single out Oscar, but his words were deeply resonant of the environmental mainstream, not any radical form of environmental activism. I don't say this as an unqualified armchair observer: I have taken part in many actions on behalf of groups like Greenpeace, Campaign Against Climate Change, and Friends of the Earth, and I've seen f-all result from them, even the ones that appeared to be fairly radical at the time.

I decided to go to Climate Camp and take a brief look around the site, taking one of my daughters with me for the experience. The atmosphere was charged with anticipation, but at the same time I couldn't help thinking I had seen this all before — the stands, the leaflets, the video diaries, the endless lists of pre-arranged talks and workshops. There was certainly potential and some signs of more radical elements; but the overall sense was one of appeasing as many people as possible. I left with two feelings in my head (my daughter left with some leaflets), which at the time applied just to London Climate Camp but have subsequently turned out to apply to many other gatherings, including the burgeoning Occupy Movement and its many camps that started to spring up in 2011.

It seems that *at best,* they are places for people to meet, discuss the things that are upsetting and angering them and, for a good few of them, become radicalized against Industrial Civilization, understanding that nothing in the industrial system should be trusted or accepted as a way forward.

At worst, though, they reinforce the mainstream belief that it is possible to create change through existing means — political lobbying and campaigning, symbolic direct action (such as banner drops and office invasions) and so on — and so ensure that those people who might have become radicalized remain deeply entrenched in a "softly softly" mindset.

The Occupy camps and other such events that are on the edges of the mainstream have a much looser set of aims than more conventional activist gatherings, if they have any firm aims at all. How such gatherings pan out is down to a complex mix of goals, the people involved and the environment in which they operate. There is also another factor, and that is whether someone is prepared to guide such events in a more radical, yet completely rational direction. In many ways *these gatherings are crucibles for change:*[175] it just requires the right catalyst to start that change off. I have no doubt that some of the people attending these kinds of gatherings will already be radicals and anarchists, and they may help guide more mainstream activists toward actions that are more effective in undermining the industrial system, but we have to be careful with this assumption — there is a big gap between those who are ready and willing to create change, and those who are politely listening. Holding hands is a good analogy for the approach needed.

Set up local transmitting devices to broadcast pre-recorded anti-civilization messages on public frequencies.

Going right back to Chapter 1, the article I quoted by Paul Joseph Watson is instructive, as he sees anti-civilization ideas as terrorism, as do most politicians and corporate leaders. From experience I have found a great many environmental and social activists to have the same views, or at least feel such ideas to be unworkable or unnecessary. What needs to happen in order to (a) build up the number of potential Underminers and (b) help undermine the mainstream mindset, is to create a situation where *people decide Industrial Civilization is a bad thing on their own terms.* By that I am referring to a very important persuasive device. Remember when you were younger (or maybe this still happens to you) and someone older than you, say a parent, told you how to do something better than the way you were doing it. As a young rebel you would probably have objected to this — told them where to get off, maybe, or at least to let you do things your own way. Then, later on, maybe after a day or two, you needed to do the same thing and, lo and behold, you did it the way you had been told to, thinking — and here's the key — *it was your own idea.*

Can the idea of Industrial Civilization being a terrible thing take this course?

Yes, because you are not trying to brainwash anyone. Neither are you planting unwanted ideas in people's heads *Inception-style,* though that would be a cracking skill to have. Instead, we are simply creating a logical conclusion, leaving no doubt in the recipients' minds that what they previously believed was wrong, and what they now believe is obviously true, to the extent that it is their own belief. If it means buying a few cups of coffee, doing an extra round of dishwashing, helping erect the odd banner even if it might go a bit against your symbolic antipathy — all these things can bring people round to thinking that maybe you, with your undermining ideas, aren't some kind of freak after all. Maybe buying cups of coffee might be disingenuous, but it's not the same as getting them drunk or doping them — this is about acts of kindness that, even if not entirely altruistic, are being done for the right reasons. So get involved, be a friend, and show people who have potential how they can go a little bit further in the right direction and why it makes perfect sense to do so. If you have to, then give this chapter to them, and by the time they get to this point they might well want to do the same thing to someone else.

Building Real Movement

How do you build a movement that can create real change — a movement of Underminers? The first rule has to be that you cannot build a movement at all. Movements have to happen as and when they are needed. There are very good reasons for this, many of which have already been covered in the essay by Anonymous in Chapter 4. In essence, if something is worth doing and people are ready to do it, then it will be done. Removing the Veil of Ignorance is fundamental to allowing this experience to occur.

Another good reason for successful movements not being intentional is that, although this might imply nothing more than a high degree of planning, intentionality also implies many of the things that ensure failure: aims that are too rigid to adapt to changing situations, a predetermined hierarchy with the "founding members" given more power, an unwillingness to drop something and start all over again, a tendency toward growth and even empire-building by taking over other groups/movements. That is not to say that all movements that are not "organic" (for want of a better term) are bound to fail, but they can almost without exception be described as mainstream. We see this most vividly in the example of Greenpeace, which began as a radical, effective and spontaneous happening, and then turned into a top-down, inflexible organization that works only when its members decide to throw away the in-house rule book.[176]

The second rule of "building" a movement is related to scale. No successful movement has ever operated on a global scale, at least if you judge success as having caused a fundamental change. The "Arab Spring" uprisings mentioned earlier are usually portrayed as being the result of a large-scale movement desirous of political change across North Africa and the Middle East. In reality, setting aside the possibility of Western initiation, the uprisings in Tunisia, Egypt and Libya were local events that were inspired by other events but were very much in their own makeup. This localization effect can be observed throughout the history of popular uprising and social change in the context of, for instance, the Luddites in Victorian Britain, the racial equality movements in 1960s USA and the anti-slavery/abolitionist movements spanning the 19th and 20th centuries. Notably, none of these movements can be said to have been completely successful in any sense of the word for industrial oppression, racial inequality and capital slavery are all very much part of civilized life in the 21st century; however, without local, usually spontaneous disruption that antagonized and undermined the systems being fought against, change would have stopped before it started.

Al-Qaeda is not an "international terrorist network," as described by countless mainstream media organizations and government-sanctioned reports. If al-Qaeda is anything, it is a series of activities based upon an ideology. The success of al-Qaeda, if it is possible to judge success given that we may never know what the precise aims are, is predicated on its lack of formal structure: in a way it is irrelevant whether any such thing as al-Qaeda exists or not, for it is the mindset adopted by innumerable cells and individuals, likely inspired by actions carried out by other cells and individuals, that defines al-Qaeda above all else. Yet, most likely because governments have to impose a sense of fear upon civilized people to maintain power, we have retained the idea of al-Qaeda as a global organization to be feared, and countered using vast amounts of expensive technology and the lives of those who feel they are fighting for freedom. Regardless of what you may feel about the actions carried out by, on behalf of or perhaps in order to counter positive views of it, as a movement, al-Qaeda both succeeds and fails. Its successes[177] are because it *doesn't* operate as a global network but rather as a disparate scattering of people working for a single, if many-pronged purpose. Its failures are because it is seen as a global operation with a small number of powerful leaders, through which falsehood governments are able to restrict the freedoms of people even more than if such an impression did not exist.

So, with all that in mind, let's build a movement from scratch.

Task 7: Building a New Movement

Just let it happen.

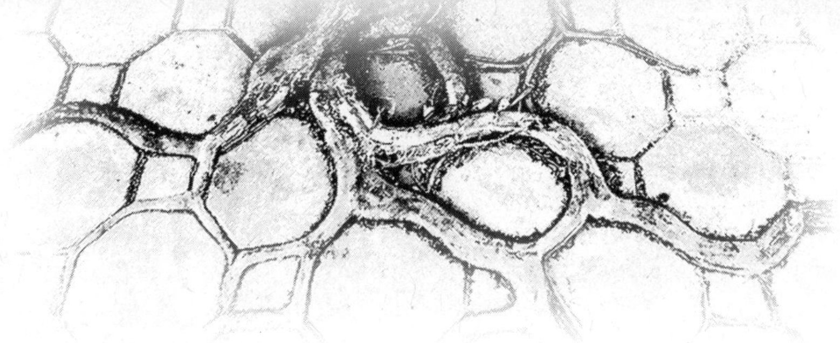

CHAPTER EIGHT

Recreating Community

COMMUNITY IS THE NATURAL STATE OF HUMAN BEINGS: dependent upon each other, working together to ensure the stability and success of whatever collective form we take. Community[178] is the antithesis of how civilization wants us to live. Sadly, as we seek the company and mutual assistance of others like us, this need is exploited by civilization to devastating effect. As we have seen throughout this book, the Veil of Ignorance places us in a position of dependency far removed from our natural state — instead chained to a system that only wants to take what we can give for the system's benefit. If we can learn to embrace genuine forms of community once again, then we not only remove the "need" for civilization that has been instilled in us, we create a situation that is far more resilient than any city, any government, any corporation and any civilization, however large and powerful.

> In a way, what you're saying is, "I'm going to take my toys and not play with you" — to the industrial masters; "I'm going to take my toys and go play with my neighbours, and my family, and the natural world that supports me."[179]

The future of humanity lies not with civilizations but with communities. We have to undermine the civilized idea that we can at once be homogenous, global citizens and atomized, selfish individuals. This chapter is about learning to live together once more.

What Isn't a Community?

One of my favorite spots as a child was a tree in the middle of a broken up asphalt parking area where my sister and I used to play imagination games and hunt for slowworms among the grass edges. It was a crappy spot that appeared, like so many other bits of "wasteland," to hold no pleasures, but we thought it was special and would head for it in preference to the municipal park that would take ten minutes to reach rather than a sharp sprint to the end of the road. The park was fine if we asked first and stayed together. The tree on the asphalt was within the limit our parents defined as "just round the corner," so we could visit it whenever we wished. Its closeness was part of its appeal: in a way that tree was ours. Friends from the houses along our little street used to come and play. Sometimes people we had never seen before came too, and they were made welcome. What made this place special was its proximity to our home; it was indeed an extension of our home, and anything that fell within that space was, by association, part of the community in which we played.

In summer holidays thousands of students from Northern Europe go to India, Thailand and Vietnam to experience something they then place on their Facebook and Flickr pages in the form of albums of joy — or perhaps gloating. I sometimes come across these, or others from American students in Machu Picchu, Australian students in London, X students in Y faraway place — all taking similar experiences and memories from somewhere the appeal of which seems to lie in its distance more than anything else. The saddest thing of all about these forays to faraway places is the lack of connection. There is a close relationship between community and connection. Community is, in its most basic sense, meaningful connection with other people. But it must be tangible — we have to "touch base" if we are to forge and strengthen links among people, just as our brains have to fire off messages along neurons if memories are to be made.

For some, these visits to strange lands with odd but invigorating cultures may be a moment of mental realignment, but most visitors are just observers in a place alien to them. Whether they are consciously trying to make connections with these ephemeral resting places is relevant because, unless you are prepared to make some kind of emotional investment in a place, in effect to make that place and nowhere else your home, then any sense of community you feel there is make-believe. Once you leave you cannot truthfully claim a connection to that place, as much as you might want to.

Like many things in this book, that probably sounds harsh, but think of it this way: community is intrinsically linked to survival, and few people would argue against survival as being dependent upon connections that run deep. You depend on others to help you, and others depend on you. You depend on the landbase that supports you and, in turn, the landbase depends on your connection with it and the connections of everyone else using that landbase, to ensure it is treated with respect and care. It follows that if you try to sustain more than one set of connections with somewhere you call "home," then those connections will be diluted.

Connections require perseverance and, more important, interdependence. Once you stop depending on something, that connection fades. Distance is fundamental to this. Say, for instance, a child has two homes because of a fragmented family. She stays with one biological parent every other weekend, but her life mostly revolves around the other parent and perhaps a stepparent. Close together these two places could reasonably both be called homes, and the area surrounding them might be considered a community. But think from the point of view of the child: the community around Home A might be the nearest street or two, some shops, a park or piece of waste ground, friends in those streets and maybe a grandparent or other relation. At Home B the community might be smaller depending on how many people the child knows and where she goes during that time. It is unlikely that the space between these two communities will be anything like as important, unless they intersect. The greater the distance between these homes, the less likely a contiguous community is to exist, and that is a problem for a child who needs to be rooted somewhere. Distance creates conflict between connections and can be a serious psychological burden.

Start referring to zoos as "animal prisons" and discourage children from attending anywhere that uses animals for profit. Take children on walks and show them real wildlife instead.

In an urban area a community might be just a couple of streets, but in a more rural area it might be wider, encompassing a couple of villages, only one of which has a shop or maybe a village hall. People might live in one village but have good friends in the other village that they regularly see, with the space in between having a river they fish in or a place they gather wood from, or maybe somewhere they do valuable work for someone. In most cases rural communities are larger than urban communities, and not just because of the density of people and services. Urban spaces are more atomized than places where the trappings of modern life are harder to come by, so urban connections tend to stay within a small area, sometimes even within four walls.

The important thing here is that beyond the point where you are not connected in a very real sense with something else, then any community that exists is not your community.

So what about *virtual* communities? We have perhaps been over the ephemeral nature of virtual connections enough, though such a huge emphasis is put on "connection" being possible through telecommunications alone by companies that want us as part of their consumer base, that a salutary reminder is needed. Eli Pariser in a recent talk[180] made it clear that this "fiction of community" is powerful, even when it quite obviously fails to deliver anything we would conventionally consider to be reality. We think we are connecting to important things when in fact most of our connections are being decided for us on the basis of automated, commercial decisions. How can we possibly maintain anything like real connections when we have no control over them?

In 2012, Facebook stands as the current apotheosis of the virtual "community" acting, as did MySpace, Bebo and others now fallen by the commercial wayside, in a manner that promises much but delivers only what is good for Facebook:

> Facebook is a living computer nightmare. Just as viruses took the advantages of sharing information on floppies and modems and revealed a devastating undercarriage to the whole process, making every computer transaction suspect … Facebook now stands as taking over a decade and a half of the dream of the World Wide Web and turning it into a miserable IT cube farm of pseudo human interaction, a bastardized form of email, of mailing lists, of photo albums, of friendship.
>
> The old saw is that people don't understand that Facebook doesn't consider the users their customers — they consider the advertisers their customers. Make no mistake, this is true ... but it implies that Facebook takes some sort of benign "let's keep humming along and use this big herd of moos to our advantage". But it doesn't. Facebook actively and constantly changes up the game, makes things more intrusive, couldn't give less of a shit about your identity, your worth, your culture, your knowledge, your humanity, or even the cohesive maintenance of what makes you, you.[181]

Facebook, or any other online environment, is not community. We should not trust online "communities" to deliver anything more that the immediate present along with a heap of corporate baggage. You will not find community down your Internet pipe, any more than you will find community in a crack den — that's perhaps taking dependency a little too far.

With this and the distance paradigm in mind, let's first try and dismantle something horrific. Then we can start the vital work of recreating something far more important to humanity.

Task 1: Killing the Myth of Global Community

This is not about reducing any concern humans have for each other — we are the same species, so to not care about another human, regardless of distance, would clearly be inhuman. Ironically, given how "connected" we are constantly urged to be, industrial history has demonstrated with hideous efficiency how inhuman civilized people can be. The same cannot be said for non-civilized humans.

Competition between non-civilized groups of people is not systematic in the same way as, say, ideological warfare or resource colonialism; nor does it deny the commonality between different groups of humans. What it does do, though, is to create a common bond *within* communities. The concept of Global Community (note caps) that is imposed upon us by the industrial system is something entirely different: the clue is in who or what this "Community" benefits.

Trade.

As with all situations that promise benefits to one of two sides, to get the true motivation you only have to ask, Who benefits most? In this case the Global Community phenomenon, as endorsed by Industrial Civilization, exists solely to make one party or other richer and/or more powerful. These parties are usually corporations or national governments but can be major religions, transnational organizations or certain powerful individuals. This is facilitated through increased trade among the different components of the Community that is being endorsed. Here is one example, and just one of potentially many ways to undermine that particular example.

The superstore chain Walmart takes great pride in flourishing its community credentials wherever its enormous presence lumbers up.[182] Awards for Good Citizens, sponsorship for local sports teams and "environmental" projects with local schools abound. This is just a tiny part of the countless other ways this and other superstore chains try to ingratiate themselves with the public. The idea that a 200,000-square-foot palace of consumption, forming a small part of a multi-billion dollar corporation, could be anything but catastrophic for a community is, of course, absurd; but we take the pill and convince ourselves that somehow this giant gray box sitting on the edge of town is beneficial to the place it is sucking the life out of. In the UK it is estimated by the New Economics Foundation that for every new job created by a supermarket, two jobs are lost in local food outlets.[183] Yet whenever a supermarket chain announces expansion, the mass media freely regurgitate the press pack that inevitably includes such phrases as: "We will be creating (x thousand) new jobs" and "This is good news for (x places about to be colonized)."

The fact that self-styled "neutral" media organizations (such as the BBC and CNN), along with local councils and other bodies supposed to represent the needs of ordinary people, embrace the *lies* of job creation and community integration so fully says a whole lot about where we are as a society. It is not just the Veil of Ignorance in operation that makes it possible for such lies to be promulgated and almost certainly believed by those who promulgate them, but also the relentless efforts of the retailers in making us swallow these lies, through repetition, powerful imagery and practical demonstrations of their community credentials.

The power of a simple sponsorship deal, for instance, is quite remarkable. This is approximately how it works:

1) The superstore's Community Team approaches various sports, arts and other social clubs offering sponsorship. (Sometimes it is the club that requests the sponsorship, but that doesn't matter — it has just saved the Community Team a job.)
2) A sponsorship deal is agreed that includes prominent display of the superstore's logo on clothing and/or premises, along with regular mentions in club materials, website and any other social media channels available.
3) The club gains a bit of money.
4) As a direct result of the advertising the superstore gains at least the equivalent back in retail sales in a very short time.
5) Because of the "support" given by the superstore, club members feel morally obliged to become loyal to the superstore, providing longer-term financial gains.
6) Also because of this "support," the superstore is perceived to be benefitting the community in some way, and thus is looked upon as a friend rather than a threat to the local area.

It is this last gain that is crucial to the superstore. If a company can be seen as a friend of the community, it notionally becomes part of that community. There are obvious benefits in competition terms with having a community on your side if you are a particular superstore chain, but that is as nothing compared to the wider benefits of being *part* of a community. Acceptance allows blind eyes to be turned to whatever misdemeanors the local branch, and by extension the entire corporation commits. People will actively defend the corporation too ("They were so good to us when they arrived; how can you not want them in your town?") because the corporation is part of their community.

From a few thousand sprinkles of sugar a Global Community can be established. And, I guess, by putting a bit of grit into that sugar, a Global Community can be undermined. From before the first opening of a superstore the sugaring will start, and that's by far the best time to undermine it; the earlier the better, though any time is a good time. A few well-placed letters in the local press, (fore)warning people of the assault on their minds and their communities would help, as would a similar mass-mailing to every club and society in the surrounding areas. However this wouldn't be as powerful as *an apparently direct approach from the company itself* in the form of a letter — see the bank letter in Chapter 6 as an example — introducing the superstore chain (shackle) to the community via the channels above. This letter should explain how important the success of the supermarket is to shareholders, and how becoming part of the community will ensure that success. Drop in a few phrases like "Traditional ideas of community are a thing of the past; caring for and looking out for each other are less important than making money," "We believe that trade is at the heart of the our Global Community" and "In return for the loyalty of your community we are prepared to offer some financial incentive to your club." The subtlety won't be lost to everyone. Make sure you letter-drop the clubs and societies before the press, just in case the company gets wind of it — chances are the letters will be read out at meetings and the damage will be done before the real approaches can start.

Faced with the might of an entire industry, it's tempting to just surrender whatever it is they are laying claim to and find something else to use instead. There are many, many precedents, and we have given away to the industrial system just about everything that defines us as humans, including our bodies. (What is a job other than the prostitution of ourselves for cash?) But there are other examples that suggest that maybe some of the most difficult battles are winnable, especially when it comes to words. I came across one prime capitulation in 2008 on the website of Nick Rosen. He had written that the word "green" had been so abused and manipulated by the corporate world that the only alternative was to use a different word with, perhaps, even more connection to the natural world. The word he chose was *brown*. This was feasible but problematic for two reasons:

1) The color brown has certain connotations that might not easily appeal in the same way that green does.
2) There is already a perfectly serviceable word in *green*.

My response to him was in the form of a second article which, to give Nick credit, he put straight on his website. This is the relevant part:

> I don't believe for a moment that the corporate world will let go of the word "green" without a fight, and I certainly have some sympathy with Nick in turning to our old friend "brown" — good old earthy brown, compost brown, manure brown, bark brown — but while brown is a colour you are far more likely to find in a woodland than in a shopping mall, it is not the only colour of life. In fact life has a host of different colours: the vivid reds that signify the fruits of autumn and the segment of sun as it disappears over the horizon; the warm oranges of so many flowers, pebbles and leaves; the wide blue of the sky and its reflected light in the oceans; the white of the brightest cloud and the firmest mushroom; but most of all the green of leaves, of algae, of plankton — the green that means photosynthesis, that means oxygen, that means life. Green is the reason we are here.
>
> No corporation is ever going to take that away from us — it can try, but I'm claiming it back from the bastards who haven't just stolen "green" for their own nefarious purposes, but are stealing the entire language from our lungs.[184]

No corporation is ever going to steal the word "community" from our lungs either. The word "community" doesn't have the same obviously negative and offensive connotations the word "queer" has when used by people outside of LGBT[185] communities, but in the hands of a corporation, the misuse of "community" is deeply offensive to those of us who know what real community is. Maybe, then, we can use some of the ideas that groups such as Queer Nation so brilliantly harnessed, to bring our beloved "community" back into the real world.

> The first instance of queer's public reclamation came from Queer Nation, an offspring of the AIDS activist group AIDS Coalition to Unleash Power (ACT-UP). Queer Nation was originally formed in 1990 in New York as a discussion group by several ACT-UP activists discontent with homophobia in AIDS activism and the invisibility of gays and lesbians within the movement. The group, originally comprised of members of ACT-UP, soon moved from discussion to the confrontational, direct, and action-oriented activism modeled after ACT-UP.
>
> This new coalition chose "Queer Nation" as its name because of its confrontational nature and marked distance from gay and lesbian. For a coalition committed to fighting homophobia and "queerbashing" through confrontation, queer, "the most popular vernacular term of abuse for homosexuals," was certainly an appropriate — perhaps perfect — choice. Rather than being a sign of internalized homophobia, queer highlights homophobia in order to fight it: "[Queer] is a way of reminding us how we are perceived by the rest of the world". To take up queer is at once to recognize and revolt against homophobia.
>
> Queers also publicly rejected the assimilationist tactics of gays and lesbians. Refusing to forge their existence within the heterosexual-homosexual polarity, queers chose to wage their war outside of the system. The goal was not to win heterosexual support or approval; therefore, their battle did not model a civil rights movement, struggling for equal rights for an oppressed minority.
>
> While linguistic reclamation may not produce clear victories, it does prove that the right of self-definition is a worthy cause for revolution. To appropriate the power of naming and reclaim the derogatory name that one never chose nor willed is to rebel against the speech of hate intended to injure. Linguistic reclamation is a courageous self emancipation that boldly moves from a tragic, painful past into a future full of uncertainty, full of doubt — and full of possibility.[186]

The growing numbers of people who would like, and frankly need, *the return of community to its rightful place* may be fighting an apparently impossible battle against the might of the corporate and political world. But the word "queer" as a form of identity is now most definitely the rightful property of those who were formerly abused with the very same epithet. Those who fight "impossible" battles can learn a lot from improbable victories.

Communities from the Ashes

When entire books, and bloody good ones at that, have been written about subjects, it's nice to be able to defer to them. As good as they are, these two books have not in any way entered the deeper consciousness of the civilized world. Had they done so then we would probably be looking at something quite different already.

The first book to read, and one that I will draw on later is Alastair McIntosh's *Soil and Soul*, an exploration of the nature of community, soul and spirit and the story of one fight against the industrial machine that can serve as a lesson for many future fights. The other book, one that is pertinent to this section, is *A Paradise Built in Hell* by Rebecca Solnit. This short extract takes us straight to the heart of the matter and provides many clues as to how communities may actually be used as a powerful weapon against the Culture of Maximum Harm:

> You don't have to subscribe to a political ideology, move to a commune, or join the guerrillas in the mountains; you wake up in a society suddenly transformed, and chances are good you will be part of that transformation in what you do, in whom you connect to, in how you feel. Something changes. Elites and authorities often fear the changes of disaster or anticipate that the change means chaos or destruction, or at least the undermining of the foundations of their power. So a power struggle often takes place in disaster — and real political and social change can result, from that struggle or from the new sense of self and society that emerges. Too, the elite often believe that if they themselves are not in control, the situation is out of control, and in their fear take repressive measures that become secondary disasters. But many others who don't hold radical ideas, don't believe in revolution, don't consciously desire profound social change find themselves in a transformed world leading a life they could not have imagined and rejoice in it.[187]

This takes a little explaining, which is why I recommend you at least read the compelling introduction to the book. In a nutshell, there is a myth about what happens when groups of civilized humans[188] are faced with disaster situations. That myth is what causes those in "authority" (usually those who have the most weapons) to prevent our natural community spirit from coming to the fore. Civilization fears lack of control, which is one reason why the word *anarchy* has so many negative connotations. A lack of authoritarian control leads people to pull together and deal with things in a far more equitable way. If equality reigns and, inevitably, people are able to connect with each other on a human level, then the Tools of Disconnection have failed. As we know, the industrial system relies on fear to keep us disconnected — fear of each other, fear of difference, fear of the system's own might — so it tries to impose fear at times of stress. Hell, it often creates disasters and makes people believe bad things are going to happen just to keep us scared. Through these means the status quo is reimposed.

As the book goes on to show, there is not a single case of a disaster-type situation in which humans have not mutually acted to make things better for themselves as a whole, *in the absence of authorities imposing control over the situation.* Now, I would add just one caveat to that, which Solnit doesn't emphasize, perhaps because the book would not have been published had she done so. The fact is, the fear felt by the elites that post-disaster changes will undermine their authority is fully justified. *The changes that take place after a disaster, which ordinary humans acting in communities cope so well with, completely undermine the authority of the industrial system.* Indeed these changes are so powerful that (say this quietly) they can even be the trigger for entirely new forms of society.

So, we know that communities emerge as a natural human response to crises. How these crises happen is, as Solnit's and as other recent examples have demonstrated, doesn't seem to matter. The important factor is a loss of authority and a need for a survival response to take place. In fact, that "survival" response need not necessarily be to a life-threatening situation. To take a small example, I remember power cuts and water shortages in the 1970s causing minor hardship, yet creating remarkable, spontaneous dialog and activity between neighbors, many of whom would never have dreamed of working together under normal conditions. Next time you are on public transport and something unexpected happens, see how people react in the absence of "authority" (such as a conductor) taking a lead. People talk, they open up, they plan — and then the train starts moving, and everyone returns to their little worlds again.

There is something rather exciting about the possibilities in this scenario — hold your horses for a second, though, because the second aspect of this, the return to normal, non-communicative, non-community activity, is also vital to consider. In her book *The Shock Doctrine,* Naomi Klein famously described a concept known as Disaster Capitalism as being synonymous with the "softening up" that torture is used for in working toward a state of mental compliance, but on a far larger scale:

> The shock doctrine mimics this process precisely.... The original disaster — the coup, the terrorist attack, the market meltdown, the war, the tsunami, the hurricane — puts the entire population into a state of collective shock. The falling bombs, the bursts of terror, the pounding winds serve to soften up whole societies much as the blaring music and blows in the torture cells soften up prisoners.[189]

While there is an element of pop psychology attached to this (Rebecca Solnit is a fierce critic of Klein's view that populations are so compliant in the face of disaster), there is also a great deal of truth in the historical events Klein documents, especially when — as Machiavelli so vitally pronounced upon in *The Prince* — there is something, such as a new regime, ready to fill the political void created by the disaster. Thus we must also address the problem of having this "void" filled with something other than our natural tendency to create communities.

Task 2: Creating the Disaster Community

Beware the backlash. This is something that wasn't explicitly discussed in Part One, but I don't think anyone will be surprised that for every undermining action there may be an equal and opposite reaction. I'm not talking about protecting against the reaction of the industrial systems of power in their defense, but rather the reactions of ordinary people who see themselves as civilized. Never is this truer than in the case of creating a situation, real or otherwise, where a community response is likely. Let's take a simple, localized example.

Suppose you were to somehow prevent food being distributed to a particularly aggressive supermarket on the edge of a town. Assuming there are no other food outlets available on the edge, the majority of regular customers will not try their hardest to seek other sources of food, but instead make it known how pissed off they are that the supermarket cannot supply their consumer needs. They will complain to staff, to management, to local politicians, to the media. Some people will seek out food sources in the middle of the town, giving much-needed funds to those shops sucked dry by the out-of-town supermarket, and some might decide not to buy the unnecessary items they normally would from the bloated selection in that superstore. Others, a few, might even consider — assuming the "crisis" carried on for a while — seeking out much more localized sources of food, sharing among neighbors, having potlucks and so on.

But the majority would react against whatever caused the crisis in the first place.[190] They might seek out the perpetrator, and certainly the system would apply whatever measures it could to make sure that perpetrator couldn't do it again. More insidiously, the attitude to the superstore might change. Yes, some might remain attached to whatever community efforts sprang up to deal with the situation, but others — probably the majority — will demand that such a thing is more strongly protected against in the future. As I say, this isn't the power structures protecting themselves, but the civilized population protecting the system it has become dependent upon. This is the backlash. You need to be prepared for it.

Some ideas will come in Task 3, but there is a much greater element of basic human psychology required here than will be considered later. In essence, *any disaster that initiates a community response must be complete enough for it not to cause a possibly more powerful backlash,* resulting in a worse situation than before. Completeness takes into account whether a disaster invokes enough community responses at a scale sufficient to cater for those affected by that disaster, bearing in mind that different people behave in different ways. This means that planning is absolutely critical for such a form of undermining. Backlash is far more likely where people feel or may actually have been harmed in some tangible way, making the "risk to others" rule particularly important to note. Even when people are not directly harmed, they may feel a sense of harm or even menace while a situation is unfolding. They will undoubtedly seek the protection of authorities, which is exactly the opposite of what we are trying to achieve. *There has to be a sense that this "disaster" is something good,* an opportunity for something better to emerge. Clearly a multi-faceted approach is vital if this is going to be achieved.

So, let's look at that supermarket food failure, but adding various elements that might make the backlash less meaningful, and the community response deeper and longer lasting. The following questions are all fundamental, and I have provided two sketch answers, though you will no doubt have your own. The third answer has been left blank as it is vital that an Underminer is able to apply general principles to a specific situation:

What are we trying to achieve?

A response through which people bring the purchase, distribution and production of their food to a community scale (say, within a 20-mile radius to start with). In addition this response will have various domino effects related to the increased level of dependency on people in the locality, including much improved social cohesion. Over time (probably a matter of weeks or months, depending on local availability) this will lead to a partial rejection of the industrial food system in favor of the local food network.

What are we trying to avoid?

Actual harm to others (hunger being a possibility, especially for the less socially mobile), perceived harm to others, entrenched reliance on the industrial food system as a result of existing dependence and perceived risks, and getting caught and punished.

How can each of these be avoided?

(This is for you to fill out — use the notes above if that helps).

How can the initial undermining be carried out?

Methods might include interfering with ordering systems/wiping data, breaking the supply chain at critical weak points, implying that orders have already been dispatched, preventing reception/stacking staff from reaching work, creating a health scare and many others.

Notice the obvious undermining is the last question to be considered. This is because it needs to take into account the problems above it. Obviously you have to decide whether such a thing is practicable in the first place; otherwise all that planning will be for nothing. But without the planning and all the contingencies in place, the most likely outcome is that you will end up as some kind of pathetic, truck-halting martyr that no one cares about except whether you spend two or ten years in jail. It may be that removing the risks is simply too difficult, and some other less risky action could have a similar outcome.

Such as just *pretending* the supermarket has run out of food.

You see, it is often possible to *create the perception of a disaster without actually creating the disaster itself.* Not only is such an approach less risky, and thus more likely to be carried out on a larger scale and also more likely to be repeated, but there is far less chance of a backlash.

> FREETOWN: At least 200 people were killed when a trench collapsed at an unofficial gold mine in Sierra Leone, the West

> African country's Ministry of Mineral Resources said on Friday.
>
> "Over 200 gold miners were killed when a ... trench dug by the miners collapsed," a ministry spokesman said.
>
> Unofficial gold mining is common in Africa where miners usually have no professional training or equipment and often dig by hand. Accidents are frequent at the sites, which do not meet safety standards found at professionally engineered mines.
>
> "A forty feet (12 meters) pit was dug out to mine gold," a senior police source said. "Hundreds of [miners] entered the pit, and when it collapsed it trapped them."
>
> Children as young as 13 were working in the mine when it caved in, police said, adding that around 20 people escaped. Officials from the resources ministry were en route to the scene of the disaster on Friday, the ministry spokesman said.[191]

The "disaster" was possibly a communications failure, but more likely a hoax. If we assume it was a hoax of some kind, then its origins could easily be traced to the appalling working conditions of diamond and gold miners in Sierra Leone and an attempt to expose this. Certainly that background was picked up by the mainstream press when the hoax was exposed. The next day The Associated Press syndicated the following to nearly 200 news outlets: "Mining accidents are common in Africa's unregulated artisanal mines, where poor villagers use crude instruments and their bare hands to dig through the dirt. Sierra Leone — the country upon which the film 'Blood Diamond' is based — has many diamond and gold mines." People forget about hoaxes quicker than tangible events; they may even laugh about them. But they may also get the point the hoax was trying to make.

However, not everyone is taken in by a hoax, and the return to "normality" is going to be significantly quicker than if something genuine is unfolding. You will struggle to find anything reported more than a couple of days after the "mine collapse." One can immediately return to a *perceived lack* of something, but one can't immediately return to something if it is no longer there.

Memories of great storms and whiteouts are speckled throughout the anecdotal history of the area in which my family lives. A "once in living memory" period of snow took over our village in February 2010. People talk of the local Co-operative store being staffless until a brave person managed to trudge miles to open up. Soup deliveries were widespread, and the elderly in particular were checked up on regularly to make sure they were warm and fed. Long conversations and frequent laughter were endemic, alongside the fallen guttering and immovable cars. Supplies of wood and other necessities were made available within micro-communities of individual roads and groups of houses.

We missed this event by a couple of months, but more bitter and soft white weather was to come the following November and into December, leading to a spontaneous outbreak of sledding. For the week that school buses were canceled and schools were closed, the hill down to the public golf course (for once a beauteous thing) was awash with people of all ages, me included, risking at least a limb for a short downhill thrill — again and again, on sleds, compost bags, backsides and, most memorably, an inflatable mattress that eventually became a tattered but still exciting addendum to the great community downhill experience. People were happy to hand over responsibility of their precious offspring to near-strangers, and there is little doubt that the week when school was closed and the slope was open was a wonderful time for the community to become stronger. Of course no one can make it snow, but there are other ways of keeping people at home to enjoy each other's company.[192]

Soon after this, the council changed the policy. No longer would a lack of transport be an impediment to school attendance — the local schools would simply admit everyone within walking distance, and every school staff member would have to "check in" on pain of unemployment. The school system, you see, doesn't see learning about each other to be educational. And free time to experience pure joy is wasted time. I guess next time the snow comes down someone had better see to it that the local school is snowed in too.

Here's a more hypothetical example, but one that still relates to real-life events. All across our area, and probably near you as well, there are music events, live theatre, interesting talks, workshops and demonstrations of practical skills, clubs and societies doing their best to bring people together with common interests. All of them, almost without exception struggle to bring in more than a tiny proportion of the people who live even round the corner. Okay, not every event is of interest to a great number of people, but the only reason most of these things keep going is because of community grants (for once not an anachronism) and sponsorship. People stay away, and it's not, strictly speaking, because of the overused term "apathy" — it's because most people are staring at a screen of some form or another. We have often semi-joked that if someone were to cut off the television signal on the last Friday of the month, then our local music club would be bursting at the seams — and it probably would.[193] But this goes deeper: as was discussed way back, the presence of so-called "connecting" elements of technology, with television being the classic one-way communication, are incredibly potent forces in keeping people disconnected from the real world and, most pertinent to this section, from each other. The Human Community is a victim of technology, and so it follows that *in the absence of television, the Internet and, to a lesser extent, radio and mobile phones, the Human Community would flourish* as it did prior to the mass adoption of these things.

One critical element of this is the lack of risk to the people affected by any technological shutdown. Sure, there are examples where people have been saved from possible harm or even death by the intervention of communications technology. Equally so, there are examples where communications technology has led directly to deaths. But we are talking about what are essentially entertainment media here — I wouldn't, for instance, ever advocate interfering with emergency communications equipment as the immediate risk to life is too high to justify; but television, the Internet and especially entertainment websites, commercial radio and instant messaging are certainly ripe for intervention in the name of recreating community.

When I was speaking to a friend about this concept, he said something that brought me sharply back to sickening reality: "We are already in a disaster situation." If you are sensitive to world events, then it's impossible to ignore the fact that we are already in a disaster scenario, whether that be in the form of climate change, food scarcity, habitat destruction, environmental toxification or any other horrors we currently face. Yet we are not acting as though this is the case. So, to paraphrase my friend's follow-up comment: "How do you help people feel the disaster that is already upon them?"

In any disaster, people are our first priority. For instance, despite my love of non-human animals I struggle to take reports of dogs and horses washed away by floods as seriously as those reporting on human casualties. Some people, washed out by the tide of civilized humanity would prefer to spend time with non-human animals, and I can understand that; but if we are trying to understand the minds of the civilized, then we need to accept that civilized people care for other civilized people — a bit. Non-civilized people, regardless of culture, will also seek to protect the human before the non-human, leading to the unavoidable conclusion that whether operating on base instincts or at a highly filtered cultural level, *the most effective way to make people feel a disaster is to emphasize the human impact.*

That's not quite enough to get through, though. The Indian Ocean tsunami of 2004 was a disaster that few people can comprehend in anything but purely mathematical terms. A quarter of a million people killed by a wave and its aftereffects is just too many for one mind to deal with: a quarter of a million human beings is, to put it in its crudest terms, a mass of people. As Wendell Berry so eloquently stated in a 2012 lecture,

> To hear of a thousand deaths in war is terrible, and we "know" that it is. But as it registers on our hearts, it is not more terrible than one death fully imagined. The economic hardship of one farm family, if they are our neighbors, affects us more painfully than pages of statistics on the decline of the farm population. I can be heartstruck by grief and a kind of compassion at the sight of one gulley (and by shame if I caused it myself), but, conservationist though I am, I am not nearly so upset by an accounting of the tons of plowland sediment borne by the Mississippi River.[194]

We cannot separate the individuals from the mass at vast human scales. Loss becomes personalized only at far smaller scales — at community scales, such as when a village is buried by a landslide or a family is killed in a house fire. Such small, yet tragic events affect us in ways that *belie* their apparent scale. It follows then that *the most effective way to make people feel a disaster is to emphasize the human impact at a scale we can easily comprehend.*

But there is still something missing. That phrase returns: *what matters, is what matters to us.* What matters to us is our fellow human beings; what matters to us more is the human beings who matter most to us. Rightly or wrongly, we value those who are most like us, whether in terms of cultural beliefs, genetic similarity or personal experience. It rocks you to the core when someone you love dies. The raw human emotions that come from a close loss are unequivocal. That kind of loss lies at the root of community cohesion. It also lies at the root of helping people feel the disaster that is unfolding at this very moment.

The most effective way to make people feel a disaster is to emphasize the human impact at a scale we can easily comprehend upon those we most care about.

I don't think there is any need to go into the mechanics of this, but I must emphasize that this is anything but an excuse to cause hurt deliberately. What has to happen is a concerted focusing of minds upon those events that actually mean something to people, as a catalyst for change. Whether referring to a disaster that has happened, one that is happening at present or one that may happen in the future, if we are to garner any kind of effective response to it, then we have to allow those we are engaging with to feel its impact at a personal level. It has to be *their* disaster, and they have to feel as though they can do something about it.

Task 3: Protecting Communities

Let's broaden this out a bit. The post-disaster community could be the result of real, engineered or imaginary disasters. To be honest there is little to distinguish the first two types: as Naomi Klein showed in *The Shock Doctrine,* a disaster engineered to provide a platform for some new regime is a real disaster in all but name. On the other hand something coming from the hands of an Underminer is engineered only in the eyes of the system it threatens. As far as the negative impact on the human population is concerned, the disaster is imaginary. Underminers never seek to cause harm.

Whatever the cause, and whatever the extent of the community that emerges in the period during and immediately following the disaster, we still have a community. As long as the emergent community is genuinely organic, then there is little reason to doubt its legitimacy, and nothing to prevent its ongoing success in the absence of external forces. The problem is that a hell of a lot of powerful external forces are determined that any such community cannot be allowed to exist. Industrial Civilization is, of course, the overarching force, but below this level we can identify a lot of discrete groups:

- armed forces
- police and other civilian enforcement
- political leaders
- corporate interests
- retail, entertainment, travel and other related distractions
- mainstream media outlets
- well-meaning but pro-civilization NGOs and charities
- other, unaffected civilized people

Notice the transition from the obvious and direct to the less obvious and apparently less direct. When there is a disaster of any type, the first impulse of any agency of civilized society is to impose "normality" upon the affected population. This happens at all levels. As I said earlier, the civilized idea of what is normal, is utterly, sickeningly *abnormal.* Civilized people are damaged, physically and mentally, to the extent that from within the confines of that bubble of normality the communities that emerge from disaster are considered by almost all of us to be abnormal — quaint at best, dangerous at worst. If we accept this, then we are never going to be able to re-establish our natural state.

Eric Weiner, in *The Geography of Bliss*, provides a clue to one of the most powerful tools we can use against this reimposition of the bloody status quo:

> Necessity may be the mother of invention, but interdependence is the mother of affection. We humans need one another, so we cooperate — for purely selfish reasons at first. At some point, though, the needing fades and all that remains is the cooperation. We help other people because we can, or because it makes us feel good, not because we're counting on some future payback. There is a word for this: love.[195]

Before anyone accuses me of falling into some cloying, symbolic trap, I have to emphasize that the idea of love as a defense against the forces of destruction does not belie its human, or indeed its most basic biological, origins. The warm, soft embrace that shows we care is just one outward expression of something that has its roots in the deepest of protective instincts, best described by Derrick Jensen thus:

> I disagree that love implies pacifism, and I think that mother grizzly bears will back me up on this one. I grew up in the country, and in my life I have been attacked by mother horses, cows, dogs, cats, chickens, geese, hawks, eagles, hummingbirds, spiders, mice who thought I was attacking their babies. And if a mother mouse will attack someone six thousand times her size, and win, what the hell's wrong with us? I realize that [mainstream activists] are right when they say that ... what we need is more love. And we do, we need to love ourselves. We need to love ourselves enough so we don't have to put up with this shit. We need to love ourselves enough that we say "No more." We need to love ourselves enough to say, "You are not going to do this to me, or to those I love."[196]

If you love, then you will resist threats to your community, your friends, your family and yourself. If you do not resist in the face of such threats, then you do not love. There is no doubt that building any kind of community, whether in relative security or as a response to some major event, takes a great deal of effort, time and patience. If you and those you care about have put so much of themselves into creating something better than went before, then of course you would resist efforts to damage it. Wouldn't you? Put love into the equation and it becomes a no-brainer. It takes little additional effort to *express your love for your community.* That love can be expressed in many joyful ways, such as celebratory gatherings (parties, festivals, meet-ups), the physical reinforcement of community identity (sign-making, tree planting, Beating-the-Bounds or Common Riding events, song and storytelling, or even myth creation) or building self-reliance and resilience, something that will be discussed later. That love for your community, when shared, is amplified — it creates a bond and a shield from interference. This is not just about defending your patch, though, as Eric Weiner says, "At some point ... the needing fades and all that remains is cooperation."

If storytelling is your thing, then start creating your own versions of fairy tales, with the stars of industrialization taking the "baddie" roles, and turning civilized "morality" on its head, casting Underminers and other traditional "wrong-doers" as heroes. The better the story the more likely it is to become part of the new counter-culture.

Protecting another community from attack, whether it is something new or something that's has existed for a very long time, is also a vital, if morally complex, undermining task. Upon hearing of a community elsewhere threatened by external forces, be that an indigenous tribe on the verge of destruction from commercial loggers or a town where a superstore chain wishes to site its latest "job creation" scheme, the response seems obvious enough. But don't forget, your efforts are also a form of external interference. Unless you know the full story, you might end up making things worse. So, first you need to find out what is being done by the affected community in their own defense, whether they actually need help and what, if anything, you can do to help. Too many times so-called relief efforts have ended up playing into the hands of those who want to destroy communities, and in very many cases those "relief" efforts may actually be the greatest threat to the community. Witness the multiple corporate, missionary and US-led political incursions that took place following the, possibly industry-triggered, 2010 earthquake in Haiti. This was perhaps best embodied by the Heritage Foundation's Jim Roberts, who stated, "In addition to providing immediate humanitarian assistance, the US response to the tragic earthquake in Haiti offers opportunities to re-shape Haiti's long-dysfunctional government and economy as well as to improve the public image of the United States in the region."[197]

Some groups, such as Survival International, the London Mining Network and Intercontinental Cry, manage to keep involvement at arm's length while trying their best to keep news channels open and information as objective as possible. Survival's work as an advocacy group is most definitely via mainstream channels, and often using symbolic methods. In contrast to this, a glance at its website makes it horrifically clear where work is needed to protect some of the last remaining pure tribal communities and also those that are seeking to reassert their independence. That should be the motivation. Direct and relentless, if non-lethal, attacks on those parties carrying out such abominations seem perfectly justified; although in truth, unless the root causes (i.e., industrial civilization and its market forces) are undermined as well, then such point efforts will seem like pissing in the wind.

With that said, we should never feel impotent, and certainly not alone, in the face of others' problems. *Carrying the world's burdens on one pair of shoulders is bound to crush you,* when undermining should be an uplifting experience. And yes, we are still undermining. In our efforts to build communities and protect them, we are undoubtedly undermining the civilized dream in our own patch of home — not just building the communities but also creating ways of living within those communities that the system desperately wants us to avoid.

New Ways to Live

We're going to take a look at a few aspects of the many elements of community living, and at how we can use undermining to help these elements become more attractive to others. Specifically I am going to focus on three areas that affect us all, and three completely different ways of looking at them. These three areas are economics, schooling and work. All three have already been discussed at some length, but now they need to be seen in the context of community living.

You will almost certainly be able to identify more areas and their alternatives, and in doing so carry out your own analysis of how undermining can assist in their establishment as key elements of peoples' lives.

Task 4: Embracing the Vernacular Economy

Two chapters back the concept of bartering was introduced as a method of undermining the cash economy. That point still stands and, for most civilized situations, bartering is the most practical starting point in both understanding the folly of the cash economy and creating a workable alternative. In the context of a community, however, bartering is one segment of a much wider view, that of a "vernacular economy," which Alastair McIntosh describes vividly in *Soil and Soul,* with reference to his Hebridean upbringing (the emphasis below is mine):

> At the deepest level of care [the first "pillar"] is **mutuality.** As the owner of a fishing boat, let's say, I will give you fish because I have plenty and you have need. It would be nice if you could give me some eggs in return, but only if you are able to do so. If you can't, because you are too sick, too old, or just a bit feckless, somebody else will see that I have eggs.... Now my giving you fish comes from a *sense of obligation,* because we are mutually part of the community. Likewise your giving me eggs. And *nobody keeps a formal score of things* because the village economy is centred around seeing that everybody has sufficient.
>
> Let's move on to the second pillar of the vernacular economy: **reciprocity**. Here I catch the fish and you, let's say, still produce eggs. I agree to give you fish if you keep me in eggs. However, in this conditionality we measure only the function and not the degree of our sharing. If the fishing is bad, you still give me eggs. If the hens are moulting and therefore not laying well, I still give you fish.... Usually in a vernacular society, relationships will be reciprocal when people are fit and of an economically active age, but *mutuality comes into play as a safety net* when they are unable to care for themselves.
>
> The third vernacular pillar — and we're starting to see a spectrum of economic understanding emerge here — is **exchange** or **barter**. Here the principles of measurement that lie behind cash economies drop into place. In a barter system, I give you, say, one fish in exchange for three eggs. In other words, goods and services have a price fixed in terms of

Give away produce and other homemade foods that you have a surplus of, even to people you barely know, rather than throw it away.

> other goods and services. Goodwill is no longer the primary driving mechanism, but we are still sufficiently connected to each other for the economy to be personalised. The immediacy of exchange means that, most of the time, *we can see where our produce is coming from and we know who makes it.*
>
> The problem with barter is its rigidity. If I have fish to trade but I don't want your eggs, we cannot do business. That is where, fourthly, **cash** enters the equation. It lubricates between supply and demand for goods and services. Money is, at its most primitive, just an accounting system. It records our obligations to each other using banknotes and other bills of exchange as IOUs. These are given legitimacy, normally, by a government bank in which people have confidence. The confidence demands faith. The focus of such faith however, has turned away from an immediate relationship with a home community and a local place.[198]

It's interesting to note that in Chapter 6, when I introduced barter as a means of undermining, the concept possibly seemed radical, at least in the context of the capital economy. Now see what we have. Barter is relegated to Division 3 and ideas of reciprocity and mutuality, in the context of real community, seem normal.

The phrase "nobody keeps a formal score of things" is the turning point. When we barter, we expect something in return, and that implies a lack of trust. The key to taking things to the next level is using the cushion of community as a means of establishing that trust. If someone I do work for doesn't have anything to barter and doesn't insist on paying cash, then I will see if there is anything they might be able to do for me in the future, such as a job in return or some produce when it is in season. That usually works fine for friends and family, but for others it is only within a community that this reciprocal arrangement can work as an ongoing way of doing things. On the other hand, the simple act of making reciprocal arrangements with people you do not know enough to ordinarily trust is enough to create at least a sense of goodness, and probably some connection that would not have been there had the transaction been completed at the point of action. To put it another way: if you don't hang up a telephone call you leave a connection open.

Undermining with such a simple act is more powerful than you might think. Not only are you undermining the capital economy both practically and as a belief system, you are also *chipping away at the intrinsic lack of trust that civilization breeds into people.* Bizarrely, we are taught to trust figures of authority, such as police officers and religious leaders, and institutions such as governments and banks (that vouchsafe banknotes then collapse when they are under pressure!), but we are not meant to trust each other as ordinary people. If we can re-establish that individual trust, then the connections that bind communities together become exceptionally strong.

In fact, the vernacular economy goes far beyond the trade of services and items. What about more fixed things, such as land? Not many of us have anything we would confidently call "a piece of land," and certainly the vast majority of land in the civilized world is in the hands (at least on paper) of a very few institutions and individuals. In Scotland the extremes of land ownership are laid bare.

- One quarter is owned by 66 landowners in estates of 30,700 acres and larger.
- One third is owned by 120 landowners in estates of 21,000 acres and larger.
- One half is owned by 343 landowners in estates of 7,500 acres and larger.
- Two thirds is owned by 1252 landowners in estates of 1,200 acres and larger.
- So two thirds of Scotland is owned by one four thousandth of the people![199]

On the other hand, Scottish law allows for communities of less than 10,000 people to buy land as a collective responsibility, something that Alastair McIntosh can take part credit for as a result of his incredible work with the Isle of Eigg Trust (another reason you should read *Soil and Soul* in full). That this right hasn't yet been successfully executed by more than a handful of community groups is in part due to Scotland having such a high level of inherited land "ownership" (a.k.a. theft from its original users), but there is at least the seed of an idea inherent in such a law, and from small seeds can grow wonderful things.

On a smaller scale, those who do have something we might describe as "a piece of land" might be persuaded *to share it for the good of the community.* Chef and writer Hugh Fearnley-Wittingstall started an online project called Landshare off the back of a request from some potential growers who were struggling to find a place to cultivate. The project is by no means unique, but it does have a lot of media coverage behind it, as well as being relatively unsullied by corporate "partners," making it a pretty good model for something that could easily be taken offline and continued on a more local scale.[200] All you need is a notice board and a contact list, then with a few words across the grapevine see what comes up. Just off the top of my head I can picture half a dozen gardens a trowel's throw away (ouch!) that would benefit both the landholder and other people in a flourishing mutual relationship.

Related to this is the idea of *mapping your local area* for potential growing and sharing space, as well as foraging and other practical uses. This really is not as complex as it sounds. You obviously need some kind of map, and also the guts to talk to your neighbors, but by now that should be a joyful challenge. Even if your neighbors are not willing to share, the simple act of pointing out space that has the potential for growing, or making the most of (I have lost count of the number of apples and plums that are left to rot when they could be harvested), might be enough to start your neighbor doing something in the direction of self-sufficiency. On the foraging side, obviously you don't want everyone stripping the hedgerows of everything edible, especially if it means other animals going hungry, but again a little knowledge can reforge a connection that most people have lost — that of enjoying the natural bounty offered up on your doorstep.

Then there is the small matter of taking back land that was once ours to share.

> We: peaceful people, declare our intention to go and cultivate the disused land of this island; to build dwellings and live together in common by the sweat of our brows.
>
> We have one call: every person in this country and the world should have the right to live on the disused land, to grow food and to build a shelter. This right should apply whether you have money or not. We say that no country can be considered free, until this right is available to all.
>
> With our current system in crisis we need a radically different way of growing our communities. We call on the government and all landowners to let those who are willing, make good use of the disused land. Land that is currently held from us by force. By our actions, we seek to show how we can live without destroying the planet or ourselves. Free from the yoke of debt and rent, our labors can be directed to the benefit of all.

Exercise: Trust Someone

This is easy to do, but for many people difficult to imagine doing. Choose something you are thinking of selling, and give it away instead. It has to be something that is yours to give away, and it must also be something that you would definitely have been able to sell for cash rather than something you might normally have just given away to, say, a thrift shop. For example, if you have a manual profession, then do a job for someone for nothing, or if you are selling something at a shop you own, or at a yard/garage sale or perhaps on eBay, then give it away. But the deal is that the person to whom you are giving that thing needs to know that at some time in the future it would be nice if he or she could do the same for you. It should also be someone who lives close enough to you so that you effectively share a community. The point is you are trusting someone to make good on a promise and thus making a connection with that person. You could also ask the person to do the same for someone else, in turn making another connection. There are many variations on this idea, all of them in some way undermining the idea that we have to have some kind of guarantee before we are prepared to give something to or do something for someone. Don't think about whether you will get something in return. This is also about changing the way you feel about such arrangements and if things don't happen then you can always try again.

> Though we may be oppressed for our actions, we will strive to remain peaceful. But we are committed to our cause and will not cease from our efforts until we have achieved our goal.[201]

This was not written back in the time of the Enclosures, or the Baronies stealing land by force from the common people of Europe. It was written in 2012 by a group called Diggers 2012, styling themselves as a new generation of True Levellers. Gerrard Winstanley would know exactly what they are talking about, having been the driving force behind the original Diggers in 17th-century Surrey, England. Motivated by a powerful religious belief, Winstanley looked upon the situation in the land where he lived and declared it should once again be common. This extract from his statement *The True Levellers Standard Advanced: Or, The State of Community Opened, and Presented to the Sons of Men* is a direct challenge to all landowners who hold power by force, taking their lead from the monarch whose power was claimed to be of Divine Right. Clearly there was more than a simple demand for land going on behind Winstanley's eyes, as righteous as such a claim was: the statement was predicated on the very same Divine Right by which land was taken from the people. In short, the Master's Tools were going to be used to dismantle the Master's House.

> The Work we are going about is this, To dig up Georges-Hill and the waste Ground thereabouts, and to Sow Corn, and to eat our bread together by the sweat of our brows.
>
> And the First Reason is this, That we may work in righteousness, and lay the Foundation of making the Earth a Common Treasury for All, both Rich and Poor, That every one that is born in the land, may be fed by the Earth his Mother that brought him forth, according to the Reason that rules in the Creation. Not Inclosing any part into any particular hand, but all as one man, working together, and feeding together as Sons of one Father, members of one Family....
>
> And that this Civil Propriety is the Curse, is manifest thus, Those that Buy and Sell Land, and are landlords, have got it either by Oppression, or Murther, or Theft; and all landlords lives in the breach of the Seventh and Eighth Commandements, Thous shalt not steal, nor kill.
>
> First by their Oppression. They have by their subtle imaginary and covetous wit, got the plain-hearted poor, or yonger Brethren to work for them, for small wages, and by their work have got a great increase; for the poor by their labour lifts up Tyrants to rule over them; or else by their covetous wit, they have out-reached the plain-hearted in Buying and Selling, and thereby inriched themselves, but impoverished others: or else by their subtile wit, having been a lifter up into places of Trust, have inforced people to pay Money for a Publick use, but have divided much of it into their private purses; and so have got it by Oppression.
>
> Then Secondly for Murther; They have by subtile wit and power, pretended to preserve a people in safety by the power of the Sword; and what by large Pay, much Free-quarter, and other Booties, which they call their own, they get much Monies, and with this they buy Land, and become landlords; and if once Landlords, then they rise to be Justices, Rulers, and State Governours, as experience shewes: But all this is but a bloudy and subtile Theevery, countenanced by a Law that Covetousness

> made; and is a breach of the Seventh Commandement, Thou shalt not kill.
>
> And likewise Thirdly a breach of the Eighth Commandement, Thou shalt not steal; but these landlords have thus stoln the Earth from their fellow Creatures, that have an equal share with them, by the Law of Reason and Creation, as well as they.[202]

If this were written today, not a word would need to be changed; indeed the archaic spellings could be mistaken for text-speak! In civilization nothing stays still, and nothing changes.

Winstanley and his colleagues set up camp on St George's Hill and made a strident effort to grow food in the face of physical and legal onslaughts from the land's "owners." Four months later the group had been driven off under threat of attack from the army — they were behaving illegally and so the system decided Something Had to be Done. Some of these Diggers moved to other sites, and other groups sprang up around England to persist for a short while. Sadly the movement died in 1651, crushed under the yoke of civilized hierarchy.

It seems the time for the Diggers is here again, and this time both morality and numbers are on our side.

What about things we consider to be more ethereal, such as ideas? When I took *Time's Up!* to its publisher, apart from being delighted to have it accepted, I also insisted the intellectual property remained mine to share as I wished. The publisher had the rights over the sold-as-printed version,[203] but otherwise the words were mine to distribute as I saw fit, to the extent that this was written into the contract:

> The Author hereby grants the Publishers the exclusive licence of printing and publishing the said Work during the period of copyright in volume and serial form in all languages throughout the world and also the exclusive licence to assign or licence such rights to others subject to the conditions following, on the understanding that the Author may post the text online under Copyleft terms.

As far as I know this clause is unique in publishing circles. It shouldn't be. Ideas are for sharing, as any *good* scientist will tell you. Copyleft is a great, and to most people amusing, word that in itself can spark off all sorts of discussions. It does what it says on the tin: you can't keep something to yourself; *you have to allow others to copy it.* The terms I attach to my online work are in the form of a Creative Commons license, which allows anyone to copy, edit and redistribute the work, as long as it is appropriately credited, is not passed off as someone else's work and, most important, no one makes any money out of it. This idea is almost endemic in the world of computer software, best exhibited by the Open Source Initiative, which regulates the distribution of non-proprietary software across the world to ensure compliance with a set of standards designed specifically to benefit the user rather than any commercial interests. For space reasons some more technical sections have been taken out:

> Open source doesn't just mean access to the source code. The distribution terms of open-source software must comply with the following criteria:
>
> 1. Free Redistribution
>
>   The license shall not restrict any party from selling or giving away the software.... The license shall not require a royalty or other fee for such sale.
>
> 2. Source Code
>
>   The program must include source code, and must allow distribution in source code as well as compiled form. Where some form of a product is not distributed with source code, there must be a well-publicized means of obtaining the source code for no more than a reasonable reproduction cost preferably, downloading via the Internet without charge....
>
> 3. Derived Works
>
>   The license must allow modifications and derived works, and must allow them to be distributed under the same terms as the license of the original software....
>
> 5. No Discrimination Against Persons or Groups
>
>   The license must not discriminate against any person or group of persons.
>
> 6. No Discrimination Against Fields of Endeavor
>
>   The license must not restrict anyone from making use of the program in a specific field of endeavor. For example, it may

not restrict the program from being used in a business, or from being used for genetic research.

7. Distribution of License
   The rights attached to the program must apply to all to whom the program is redistributed without the need for execution of an additional license by those parties....
10. License Must Be Technology-Neutral
   No provision of the license may be predicated on any individual technology or style of interface.[204]

I don't know how uncomfortable you feel about clause 6, but after an initial "oh" I realized that this encapsulates the entire spirit of Open Source. You create something, you give it away, you don't interfere. Just like the person you trusted to give something back to you in return for your free item or service, as a programmer, an author, a musician, an artist or any other creator of intellectual matter, you are trusting the recipient to not misuse that trust you have granted. If they do then, hey-ho, that's the civilized world for you, but overall you are taking part in something far bigger: the return of mutuality to the world.

Task 5: Unschooling

Unschooling may be right near the front of the queue for building strong, resilient communities — certainly it's near the start of our lives — but it needs to be feasible, continuous and more attractive than the alternatives.

So, what is Unschooling?

Self-evidently, it is not schooling; it is far more constructive than that, being a philosophy as well as a practical way of doing things differently. Idzie Desmarais, a self-described "lifelong learner" from Quebec, who has (almost) never been to school, provides three definitions on her blog "I'm Unschooled. Yes, I Can Write":

> I feel like several different explanations, all equally accurate, just from different angles, are in order:
>
> **Version #1**: Unschooling (usually considered a type of homeschooling) is student directed learning, which means the child or teen learns whatever they want, whenever they want. Learning is entirely interest driven, not dictated or directed by an external curriculum, by teachers, or by parents. For an unschooler, life is their classroom.

> **Version #2:** Unschooling requires a paradigm shift, one in which you must stop looking at the world as a series of occurrences/ resources/experiences etc. that can be learned from, and a series that can't. The world doesn't divide neatly into different subjects, and you can't tell right from the outset what a seemingly unimportant question, interest, or TV show obsession will lead to. I learn from: wandering, wondering, listening, reading, watching, discussing, running, writing, daydreaming, searching, researching, meditating, hibernating, playing, creating, growing, doing, helping, and everything else that comprises the day to day happenings of my life.
>
> **Version #3:** Unschooling, at its heart, is nothing more complicated or simple than the realization that life and learning are not two separate things. And when you realize that living and learning are inseparable, it all starts to truly make sense.[205]

This is a very personal version of what Unschooling means, but the subjectivity makes sense in that Unschooling doesn't prescribe just one way of doing things. Unlike the one-size-fits-all curriculum and model of learning offered by national school systems, Unschooling recognizes that there is no one right way to learn. Just as there is no one right way to live.

It's also worth asking the question, How is this different from Homeschooling? to which there is a similar array of answers offered by practitioners but with one key distinction. Unlike Unschooling (sometimes called Home Educating), Homeschooling still legitimizes the bulk of national/state curriculum guidance, except that guidance is applied in a different setting. This is important, as Homeschooling has historically been used as a way of imposing other, often just as damaging beliefs, upon children, such as fundamentalist religious teaching. It goes without saying that Homeschooling is a far more "acceptable" thing to the state than Unschooling.

Unlike Homeschooling, Unschooling is not an ideology, it is an *absence* of ideology. Thus it undermines the industrial system in two ways:

1) There is an inherently uncivilized methodology involved, eschewing formal structures, hierarchy, timetables and such life-wasting things as career goals and narrow academic syllabi. Children are not taught the "importance" of these things, and so never accept them as normal.
2) It is centered on communities rather than institutions. Unschooling requires support from others in order to provide the range of interest,

activities and wisdom that is enriching to the learners (and educators) involved. As such, without at least a knowledge community it cannot exist; and without a real, human community it cannot thrive.

In Chapter 5, we looked at Knowledge Sharing as a way of countering the school system. Implicit in this was that the people involved had not (yet) removed themselves from the school system. We are now moving toward something that can stand on its own. Both strands are required: undermining the school system from within, and providing alternatives from without. By providing an Unschooling environment in the communities in which we live, we can really help people struggling over the decision whether to withdraw from formal schooling. *The more people Unschool, the stronger these communities become, and the more attractive Unschooling and community life become to others.*

I cannot leave this section without citing Erica Goldson. You might recognize her name; she is certainly a hero of mine. In 2010 Erica carried out an audacious act of undermining under the noses of the very people, and in the grounds of the very institution, she was undermining. A valedictorian speech, also known as a dux speech in some countries, is a farewell address given by the most notable student or students in an "educational" establishment at the time of their leaving. Erica Goldson's valedictorian speech was ice-cold, calculated and cracked open the myth that institutional learning is to the benefit of most individuals and society as a whole. Certainly it is of benefit to the system as a whole, but as this part of the speech demonstrates, the benefit stops there:

> Here I am in a world guided by fear, a world suppressing the uniqueness that lies inside each of us, a world where we can either acquiesce to the inhuman nonsense of corporatism and materialism or insist on change. We are not enlivened by an educational system that clandestinely sets us up for jobs that could be automated, for work that need not be done, for enslavement without fervency for meaningful achievement. We have no choices in life when money is our motivational force. Our motivational force ought to be passion, but this is lost from the moment we step into a system that trains us, rather than inspires us.
>
> We are more than robotic bookshelves, conditioned to blurt out facts we were taught in school. We are all very special, every human on this planet is so special, so aren't we all deserving of

> something better, of using our minds for innovation, rather than memorization; for creativity, rather than futile activity; for rumination rather than stagnation? We are not here to get a degree, to then get a job, so we can consume industry-approved placation after placation. There is more, and more still.
>
> The saddest part is that the majority of students don't have the opportunity to reflect as I did. The majority of students are put through the same brainwashing techniques in order to create a complacent labor force working in the interests of large corporations and secretive government, and worst of all, they are completely unaware of it. I will never be able to turn back these 18 years. I can't run away to another country with an education system meant to enlighten rather than condition. This part of my life is over, and I want to make sure that no other child will have his or her potential suppressed by powers meant to exploit and control. We are human beings. We are thinkers, dreamers, explorers, artists, writers, engineers. We are anything we want to be — but only if we have an educational system that supports us rather than holds us down. A tree can grow, but only if its roots are given a healthy foundation.[206]

Watched by her peers, the staff of Coxsackie-Athens High School in New York, millions of people via YouTube and countless others via news reports and bloggers worldwide, Goldson demonstrated the importance of two of the key tools in the Underminers Toolbox: Communication and Creativity. As a one-time event, this was notable; as a regular occurrence in such events, this will be a major disruptor to a school system that celebrates rote learning and obedience. More than that, though, is the continuity the speech provided to those who were prepared to listen. Just before the extract above, Goldson made the comment: "A worker is someone who is trapped within repetition — a slave of the system set up before him."

Communities are places of learning, but they are also places of work. Walking away from your job, as I suggested earlier, is stage one. Walking into something better is stage two.

Task 6: Enjoying Real Work

While working to undermine the Job Culture, we will need to turn what was once considered mundane work into something we all do, not just because it is necessary to the community but also because we want to do these

Exercise: Unpaid Work

For a short while, write down or think of all the unpaid things you do for yourself and for others in a typical day. Everything, however small and insignificant, should be included. Be sure to include things you do while in a place of paid work that are not part of your formal job description. I can guarantee you will be surprised at the number.

Don't do any unpaid work at all for any commercial organization. Discourage others from doing so too.

things. There are countless individual acts of work that you and I do every day for ourselves, without which we would not be able to live with any semblance of purpose or dignity. A person who needs round-the-clock care depends upon the acts of others, and to some extent we all depend upon the acts of others whether directly or indirectly. For the most part, these acts are unpaid. Yes, even in a culture driven by the desire for wealth and status, the vast majority of acts — acts we can truthfully call *useful work* — are not rewarded by anything civil society would consider to be of value. We do them because they are part of ordinary life; part of being a good person.

You might think some of these are trivial, such as waking someone up in the morning or making lunch for yourself, but their value in comparison with the things most people do in their *job* of work is far greater in terms of how much they contribute to normal living. In a society that doesn't actually need money to exist, a paid job has no significance. Survival, on the other hand, often requires damn hard work, as well as the kinds of tasks that many of us would consider unacceptable. Dealing with the shit of one baby is pretty easy for a parent; dealing with the shit of a whole community is much harder, and messier! So as civilized people we have turned such tasks over to slaves, human slaves that may or may not be paid, or machines built and run using rapidly depleting materials that cause massive environmental degradation. Either way, we don't have to do these tasks ourselves, and the moment they threaten to intrude on our lives we recoil in horror.

There is nothing horrific about dealing with shit; just learn to do it properly, as a family and as a community. The same goes for all the other tasks that are required to live a normal life. Some of them are dull; some of them are messy; and some of them are back-breaking hard. All of them are essential and we have to learn to once again accept them, however much mental realignment this requires. To be frank, though, the second time you ever change a child's diaper is nowhere near as stomach-turning as the first; eventually it even becomes *enjoyable*, because you learn to accept this as an essential part of caring for that child. Can we do the same for every task we do?

By turning the mundane into the enjoyable you can bring people together in surprising ways. I was tempted to place Bob Black's seminal essay, "The Abolition of Work" in Chapter 6, and there are important lessons there for bringing down the Job Culture, but as a way of undermining the perception of drudgery that essential tasks carry in civilized society, I can't think of a better way than *turning work into play:*

> What I really want to see is work turned into play. A first step is to discard the notions of a "job" and an "occupation." Even activities that already have some ludic content lose most of it by being reduced to jobs which certain people, and only those people are forced to do to the exclusion of all else. Is it not odd that farm workers toil painfully in the fields while their air-conditioned masters go home every weekend and putter about in their gardens? Under a system of permanent revelry, we will witness the Golden Age of the dilettante which will put the Renaissance to shame. There won't be any more jobs, just things to do and people to do them.
>
> The secret of turning work into play, as Charles Fourier demonstrated, is to arrange useful activities to take advantage of whatever it is that various people at various times in fact enjoy doing. To make it possible for some people to do the things they could enjoy it will be enough just to eradicate the irrationalities and distortions which afflict these activities when they are reduced to work. I, for instance, would enjoy doing some (not too much) teaching, but I don't want coerced students and I don't care to suck up to pathetic pedants for tenure.
>
> Second, there are some things that people like to do from time to time, but not for too long, and certainly not all the time. You might enjoy baby-sitting for a few hours in order to share the company of kids, but not as much as their parents do. The parents meanwhile, profoundly appreciate the time to themselves that you free up for them, although they'd get fretful if parted from their progeny for too long. These differences among individuals are what make a life of free play possible. The same principle

> applies to many other areas of activity, especially the primal ones. Thus many people enjoy cooking when they can practice it seriously at their leisure, but not when they're just fueling up human bodies for work.
>
> Third — other things being equal — some things that are unsatisfying if done by yourself or in unpleasant surroundings or at the orders of an overlord are enjoyable, at least for a while, if these circumstances are changed. This is probably true, to some extent, of all work. People deploy their otherwise wasted ingenuity to make a game of the least inviting drudge-jobs as best they can. Activities that appeal to some people don't always appeal to all others, but everyone at least potentially has a variety of interests and an interest in variety.[207]

What we are looking at here is not just making mundane work enjoyable in itself, but doing these things in a way that works collectively — essentially, *sharing the load.* Take the example of digging a garden to plant onions. Three people "share" the work. One digs over the soil, removing stones and other unwanted matter, and creating a tilth in which to plant; another follows on, planting the onion sets in rows, covering them and watering them; another makes the tea. In order of enjoyment, you would probably say that for a sizable patch of land, the Tea Maker has it best and the Digger has it worst. But the Tea Maker gets no exercise beyond stirring and pouring, whereas the Digger is getting a large dose of life-affirming physical activity. The Planter, somewhere in the middle, doesn't exert as much physical effort, but is doing something equally mundane as the Digger, so maybe the Planter has it worst. Or the Tea Maker. What if these roles were regularly swapped; say, for one round of tea at a time? Everyone shares in the drudgery, the rest and the physical labor. Everyone also shares in the end product — a task well done and a feeling of solidarity.

Taking a lead from the few remaining, truly connected indigenous tribes, we can see quite clearly that enjoyment and laughter are not only desirable but essential to cohesiveness. In *Don't Sleep, There Are Snakes,* his beautiful and revealing exploration of the lives of one Amazonian tribe, Daniel Everett observed with civilized astonishment how much the Pirahã laugh, before realizing that they *have* to laugh:

> Pirahãs laugh about everything. They laugh at their own misfortune: when someone's hut blows over in a rainstorm, the

> occupants laugh more loudly than anyone. They laugh when they catch a lot of fish. They laugh when they catch no fish. They laugh when they're full and they laugh when they're hungry. When they're sober they are never demanding or rude. Since my first night among them I have been impressed with their patience, their happiness, and their kindness. This pervasive happiness is hard to explain, though I believe that the Pirahãs are so confident and secure in their ability to handle anything that their environment throws at them that they can enjoy whatever comes their way. This is not at all because their lives are easy, but because they are good at what they do.[208]

Working together, playing together, eating together, sleeping together. These are things we do as families as a matter of course. In larger groups, we struggle far more with these kinds of things. Yet the Pirahã have no problem at all with this level of collective intimacy, largely because that is how they survive, and have always survived.

If we are to move forward as communities, then we have to learn to do more things together rather than continue to exist in the atomized state that civilization recommends. Yes, of course there is a great joy to be had in the spirit of competition, and I would never wish to deny anyone that. I play a bit of cricket and run against other people from time to time, as well as skimming stones as far and as many times as I can to try and impress my children. (It still works!) That's all fine, and is good for the soul as well as the mind and body, and little things like that often help bring people together rather than push them away. They, along with so many other things such as growing food, cooking, making shelters and fire, and perhaps learning to play a musical instrument, help us *understand the nature of success and failure* better than any academic study ever could.

It sounds perverse, but failure and success are two sides of a very thin coin, and far closer to each other than their opposition suggests. We learn from our own and others' failures, just as we learn from our own and others' successes. We also take pity and pride in these things, picking others up and also congratulating them. This mutual struggle between success and failure is the kind of competition the industrial world doesn't want. This is the kind of competition that is healthy and an essential part of the human spirit.

So, we work together, and we compete together, and we grow stronger with every new day. We need to because, like the Pirahã, *we will have to face up to the challenges of a rapidly changing world.* If we can undermine civilization in time, then the real world will still be there in all its bounty and all its rawness. Whether we undermine the civilized killing machine or not, we will be at some point be exposed to the real world. Communities who know how to work together will be able to make far more of what the real world has to offer than those who don't.

Looking After Numbers One, Two, Three ...

I'm not suggesting that nothing good ever came out of civilization.

There is a regular argument I see against anti-civilization views that goes something like: How would you be able to type this kind of thing or be able to do any of the other neat things you do from day to day without civilization? It's a spurious argument that takes its cue from Creationists, who claim (among other things) that we must have been designed by a supreme being, otherwise how could we be the center of the (our) universe. Such pro-civilization arguments place civilization at the center of everything, aggrandize technology in particular, and almost always fail to acknowledge there being any other ways to live.

Despite all this, civilized people have brought about some good things, or at least things we would really struggle to now do without[209] — for instance, anatomical knowledge and general surgery, sanitation and food hygiene, a certain level of rationalism that challenges superstition (although that last one could be my civilized brain having panic attacks about religious fundamentalism) and, not least, the knowledge of what types of human behavior should be avoided. There aren't many other really useful things civilization gives us that other cultures might benefit from. And even then, the presence of these things in other cultures could result in the loss of things that make that culture what it is. Who am I, or any person living in the civilized world, to say what another culture needs or doesn't need?

But the same doesn't apply for a culture that is *coming out of civilization.* The fact is that certain key systems will need to persist for a while as civilization is undermined and carefully brought down or, in the absence of this, collapses with brutal consequences. Control or collapse: you can have one or the other, but I know which one I would prefer. So while things are coming down we will almost certainly need some kind of healthcare provision, food distribution network, perhaps an energy grid for a while but certainly a way of getting forms of energy to where they are needed, and probably some localized form of security if only to keep the soldiers and other enforcers out. As Underminers we need to be acutely aware of those things which, at least in the short term, could cause net harm should they collapse or be taken down.

Ironically it may be a key role of Underminers to ensure that, while obsolete and downright harmful things such as global money markets and mass entertainment/advertising are being removed, *underlying structures that support more important systems are protected while they are needed.* Come to think of it, this is not so ironic considering it is the normal behavior of governments to siphon as many resources as possible away from important services — such as emergency healthcare and basic social provision for those with very low incomes — into the coffers of shareholders and private investors. Underminers and those who fight against extreme poverty and for basic welfare are ideologically pretty close.

Beyond such easily identified post-civilization needs, we then have to consider what is to be established in the longer term. We know we need communities to take us forward, but how can those communities best provide for themselves? One way of looking at this is through the eyes of Abraham Maslow, whose classic "Hierarchy of Needs" still has great relevance, despite many attempts to challenge and update it. One update that is worth noting, however, is that of Douglas Kenrick et al., who took the original hierarchy and applied the order in which humans typically acquire these needs.[210] What is important is they still acknowledged the usefulness of Maslow's own work, placing the two structures next to each other, as the diagram shows.

You might be wondering what such a discussion is doing in a chapter dedicated to communities. The answer is "everything." As I stated at the

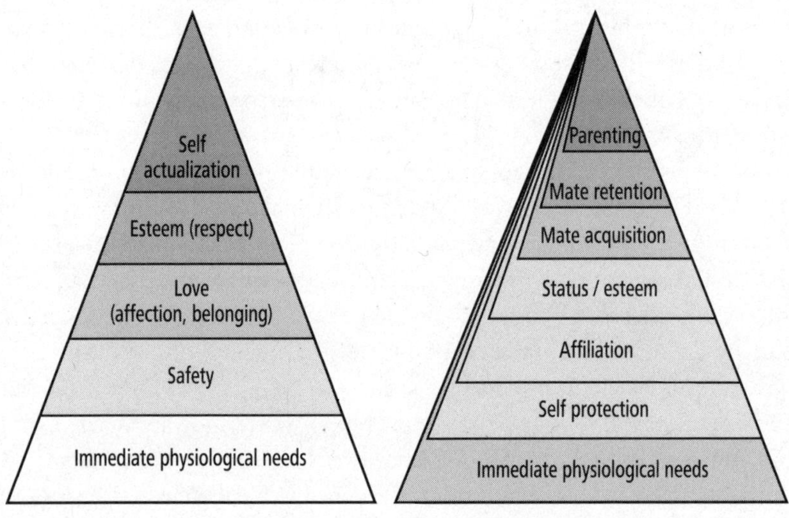

beginning of the chapter, *community is the natural state of human beings: dependent upon each other, working together to ensure the stability and success of whatever collective form we take.* Any discussion that encompasses the needs of humans moving forward is, by its very nature, a discussion about communities. Without community, all we are talking about is survival, and nothing else.

I don't know about you, but I don't fancy a world where surviving day by day is the only thing of any worth. Ask anyone who has lived a truly connected existence whether all they cared about was being alive and you would get a host of different answers, all of them including one or more other reasons to be alive and to truly savor what it means to be human. Maslow puts this very well:

> These basic goals are related to each other, being arranged in a hierarchy of prepotency. This means that the most prepotent goal will monopolize consciousness and will tend of itself to organize the recruitment of the various capacities of the organism. The less prepotent needs are minimized, even forgotten or denied. But when a need is fairly well satisfied, the next prepotent ("higher") need emerges, in turn to dominate the conscious life and to serve as the center of organization of behaviour.[211]

So, while basic survival is the predominant motive other, more distinctly human behaviors are pushed to the edge until survival becomes more routine than urgent. At this point the next most fundamental need is something that can be described as "affiliation" or "belongingness." A cheerleader for civilization would consider this to be less important than status within society, but from both the above studies and countless observations of basic human need in crisis, it is the collective instinct that overrides everything but raw survival. And, even then, it really isn't possible for the vast majority of people, civilized or not, to survive long-term without the help of others. The extraordinary, and extremely rare, stories of people going off into the wild and surviving for more than a few weeks (three minutes without air, three days without water, three weeks without food) attest to the need for something more organized and cooperative.

Let's pause for breath and consider the words of Carolyn Baker again before plunging headfirst into the process of envisaging a community that is prepared for (almost) anything. More than anyone, Baker acknowledges that any major change can hurt, but by preparing for its inevitability, that hurt can be a powerful force for rejuvenation:

> Community does not happen as a result of process groups and dialog circles. While these tools may be valuable in many respects, they cannot take us where soul is calling us. Only soul can take us there, and it will do by pulling us down into the darkness where we encounter loss and pain and where we can "commune" with other suffering souls through poetry, story, ritual, song, celebration and creating beauty. In communing in this way and through these eruptions of community out of soul, we find an "unintentional" community that may be more solidifying than anything we could have tried to make happen.[212]

Carving a spoon provides a good analogy for real community: just as you must find the object within the wood, rather than imposing a form upon it, any community you are part of should be an organic coming together of people, not some die-cast model of perfection.

Task 7: Building the Community Toolbox

To undermine the "need" people have for the industrial system, we need to give them the knowledge through which that need disappears. The range of necessary knowledge is vast and, as anyone who attempts to "go it alone" will realize, is not the domain of any one person. In any group of people, though, there is a *knowledge base* upon which others can draw and learn from.

Near the beginning of Chapter 5 is a task called Creating Resilient Individuals which, toward the end, focuses on Knowledge Sharing. Although this is ostensibly about liberating the developing mind from the grip of the school system, it is the start of a vital learning experience that can be widened to encompass entire communities and people of all ages. Knowledge, in the case of communities, starts with the most basic of needs and works through all of the skills that a community requires for resilient, cohesive and long-lasting existence. While by no means definitive — nothing intentionally written down could ever be definitive — *A Rewilding Community Toolbox* takes a brave stab at covering all the major areas of learning by which a community could at least come out of civilization relatively strong and intact.

The term "rewilding" is important (notably, it's absent from my spell-checker) and deserves definition. One of its most notable proponents is Peter Bauer, a.k.a. Urban Scout, whose book *Rewild or Die* is worth reading. Bauer carefully reviewed the various ideas around rewilding and concluded that a new definition was necessary that would stand on its own. I believe his definition also defines very many of the goals of undermining:

> *Rewild,* verb; to foster and maintain a sustainable way of life through hunter-gatherer-gardener social and economical systems; including, but not limited to, the encouragement of social, physical, spiritual, mental and environmental biodiversity and the prevention and undoing of social, physical, spiritual, mental and environmental domestication and enslavement.[213]

A Rewilding Community Toolbox clearly observes the outcomes of long-term rewilding. Rather than me regurgitating the entire contents here, you can find it by following the reference in the endnote. I have also placed a copy on the *Underminers* website. The main headings, listed below in alphabetical order, are useful in themselves as a way of building discrete learning "packages" for the community. I have added "immediacy" descriptions to each to help with this, but obviously knowledge acquisition is an ongoing process, it never ends:

- Aquaculture [medium term, use in a matter of months]
- Bug Foraging & Cultivation [short term, use in a matter of weeks]
- Clothing [short term]
- Communications, Signaling & Encryption [short term]
- Containers [short term]
- Depaving [medium/long term, use in a matter of months/years]
- Emergency Preparedness [immediate, use prior to and immediately after event]
- Empowerment — Psychology, Creativity, Learning, Critical Thinking & Planning [immediate/short term]
- Fasteners — Cordage & Glue [short term]
- Field Dressing Animals [short term]
- Fire [immediate]
- Fishing [short term]

- Food — Preparation & Cooking [immediate]
- Food — Preservation [short/medium term]
- Food & Water Storage [short term]
- Foraging Wild Plants [short term]
- Frugality [medium term]
- Fungiculture [medium term]
- Health Care — Exercise & Fitness [short/medium term]
- Health Care — First Aid & Medicine [immediate/short term]
- Health Care — Hygiene, Sanitation & Dentistry [immediate]
- Health Care — Mental Health [immediate/short term]
- Health Care — Nutrition [short term]
- Heating & Cooling [short term]
- Horticulture & Food Foresting [medium term]
- Hunting & Tracking [short term]
- Micro-Livestock [medium term]
- Self-Defense & Security [short term]
- Shelters [immediate/short term]
- Social Skills — Sociability, Consensus, Negotiation, & Conflict Resolution [short term]
- Trapping [short term]
- Travel — Movement, Navigation, Time-Telling, Measuring, Weather Forecasting [short term]
- Water [immediate]

The real joy of the Toolbox is that it doesn't give you "Everything you need to know about..." Instead it outlines the main topic areas and allows for local knowledge to fill the not insignificant gaps. The guide has the following advice for users:

> Take stock of what you already know, and any relevant skill-sharing or supplies you can access. Mark in at least 2 different ways: one for things you know conceptually or through witnessing, and one for things you know through your own practice. Classify skills for personal relevance, accessibility of locations or materials, and effort required, highlighting or underlining the easiest-with-the-highest-impact. Start with "Empowerment" then prioritize by immediacy to survival.
>
> If you have a small group (or even a pair) of like-minded folks, divide the skills into "things everyone should know" and

> "things at least one should know for now", and from there divvy it up and practice. Once people become competent they should teach others, as specialization breeds dependency and fragility. You don't need to know every little thing, but everyone should know the basics. Start with the minimum in each area, make a routine, and practice diligently. Practicing in pairs or small groups will help make the learning more fun and more reliable. Start a local skill-sharing group if possible. It takes time, support, and humbly learning from failures before one becomes competent. Enjoy! [214]

The idea of starting with "Empowerment" rather than practical bushcraft-type skills mirrors the vital need to remove the Veil of Ignorance before assuming people are ready to take responsibility for their own destinies and communities. The rest of the advice is just damn good sense. Enjoy! Indeed. This should be an enjoyable process, otherwise how can you even consider sustaining intensive learning over a long period of time?

A lot of circles are closing here. Enjoyment has to be part of learning, and learning has to be a replacement for the industrial schooling system. One method of bringing indoctrinated people back to a connected state is with Forest Schools, one form of Outdoor Education. This approach is not just about being in a specific environment (woodland, tidal zone, wide-open space, etc.) but applying a tried and trusted methodology that is being adopted not just by groups of liberated people but even by institutions that are undoubtedly going to be undermined by such a style of learning.

In essence, Outdoor Education/Forest School is a cooperative learning experience that uses a combination of practical teaching (e.g., fire making, shelter building, tracking), artistic expression (e.g., storytelling, natural arts, music making), playing all sorts of games — especially "wide games" that encourage exploration — and "down time." These activities encourage both cooperation and personal development, and they all take place in an environment that is as far removed from the civilized world as is practicable. Over time — and it can take a few days — the mixture of fun and serious activities, cooperation and the uncivilized environment cause a fundamental shift in what is normal. The shift is tangible and long term. If anything, it is not the skills that are important but that other, less obvious effect in shifting the participants' mindsets away from "civilization good" to "wild good."

Unbreakable Bonds

Stories are the glue that holds communities together. In the form of yarns, songs, poems and other expressions of human vocal creativity, stories are far more than just retellings of what happened to whom; they encapsulate the very soul of a society. It is through stories that histories are maintained. It is through stories that lessons are learned. It is through stories that vital knowledge is transferred, from generation to generation, changing with the teller and the time but always maintaining the essence of what needs to be conveyed. There is nothing that cannot be encapsulated in some form of storytelling, and thus it is possible to contain an entire culture within the medium of the story.

It will come as no surprise that the more civilized a society becomes the less important that society regards storytelling. One could suggest that civilized people don't "need" stories any more as everything is now recordable, re-playable and able to be held in some archived form for later recall. But that reduces the vibrant, human nature of the story down to mere data. Once you do that, then the story no longer has any real meaning — with stories, more so than perhaps any other thing, the medium is the message.

We have lost the ability to tell stories as we have acquired stuff, and even the writing down of stories damages their cohesive effect. It was high romantic and recorder of folk tales, Sir Walter Scott who observed, and may have helped instigate the loss of, the oral tradition in the Scottish Borderlands.

> When he heard my mother sing [the ballad of Old Maitlan'] he was quite satisfied, and I remember he asked her if she thought it had ever been printed, and her answer was, "Oo, na, na, sir, it was never printed i' the world, for my' brothers an' me learned it frae auld Andrew Moor, an' he learned it, an' mony mae, frae ane auld Baby Mettlin, that was housekeeper to the first laird o' Tushilaw."
>
> "Then that must be a very auld story, indeed, Margaret," said he.
>
> "Ay, it is that! It is an auld story! But mair nor that, except George Warton and James Steward, there was never ane o' my sangs prentit till ye prentit them yourself, an' ye hae spoilt them a'thegither. They war made for singing, an' no for reading; and they're neither right spelled nor right setten down."[215]

A rough translation of the last paragraph, for non-Scots speakers, is, "Yes, that's true. It's an old story! But more than that, apart from George

Warton and James Steward, there were never any of my songs printed until you printed them yourself, and you have spoiled them altogether. They were made for singing and not for reading; and they're neither spelled right nor set down right." James Hogg, the interviewer, passes over Margaret's astute and forbidding observation as one would expect of a documenter of high art, but at least the observation remains — a stain on the pages of every book that claims primacy over the remembered word and tune.

Should we be so harsh about every "collector" of poems, songs and tales? There is something to be said for preserving that which may be lost forever as a culture takes its leave of the Oral Tradition; but there is a huge difference between a smash-and-grab approach to collection and using the act of collection as just part of preserving the traditions of a culture. Unless the tradition itself is maintained, nurtured and encouraged from within, free of the destructive influences of the civilized world, then "collection" is no better than theft.

It is worth noting that any efforts to recreate and sustain the tradition of storytelling may help protect existing traditions simply because the same things that are melting that vital glue are in operation wherever civilization plies its trade.

Task 8: Telling Stories

One of my greatest pleasures as a father of two is to read to my children, and when I read out loud I don't just say the words. My intention is to create worlds in the heads of the listener; so the like of *Lord of The Rings*, the *Harry Potter* series and the entire canon of Douglas Adams has been shared evening by evening, sometimes a single book taking months of careful teasing out. Needless to say my impersonations of Gollum, Gandalf and Professor McGonagall are awesome! I would love to be able to pass tales on through memory alone, for it is through memory that storytelling really has its power. I believe there is nothing to match the summoning of a good campfire story as a demonstration of the power of words.

What I *can* do from memory is sing songs.

However you best retain and then pass on words is how you can best *undermine the unwritten law that anything of value has to have a physical form.* I believe the first step to reinstating the oral tradition as the predominant form of knowledge transfer is to learn

> *Offer to run nature talks and foraging workshops for schools; during the events, tell the children about the real world vs. the commercial world.*

for yourself in the (non-physical) form you are most comfortable with. The second step is to pass that on to others, so they can decide for themselves whether that is the form by which they wish to use that knowledge. But it is not just the content you need to pass on, that is for later; far more important is passing on the pleasure that comes from retelling that content in whatever form works for you. *The environment in which that retelling takes place* is most definitely part of this, which is one reason the campfire story holds a powerful symbolism for many people. Recently, just out of curiosity, I started asking friends whether they are a Fire, Water, Air or Earth person. (I am, despite my claims not to be a latent pyromaniac, most definitely a Fire person.) The "elements," unlike such spurious symbolism as zodiac signs, contain more than a mere metaphor as to the way a person connects with the real world: I connect strongly with the act of making and maintaining a life-giving fire. Other people experience no greater pleasure than to swim in wild places, or to work the earth to grow food, or to stand on a precipice with the wind tousling their hair. These are real connections, and if you can learn *how* people best connect, then you can create the environment by which the greatest pleasure can be gained through any act — in this case, receiving, and learning how to retell a story. This lesson holds for all forms of teaching/learning, inspiring/being inspired, loving/being loved.

The other part to creating a pleasurable experience is by *exuding the pleasure* you get from the act of telling. You can liken it to the difference between giving a presentation with the aid of PowerPoint slides and a script and giving a presentation with no visual aids or prompts. The former is *bound* to be stilted and mechanistic and will exude little in the way of energy. Compare this to the freedom (and for many people, admittedly a little fear) allowed by the crutch-free approach. Yes, there is no support evident, but the effect of having nothing to hold you changes how the audience receives the presentation — in a way, they become your support, and this shared experience further enhances the act of telling. Storytelling has to be a *shared experience,* for it is through sharing that communities become strong.

What is emerging is the sense of two difference spaces: outside the community and within the community. Within the community is not to the exclusion of all that is outside, but it is within this space that the vast majority of what matters takes place. Outside the community, at least at first, is likely to be the civilized world that doesn't want strong communities to exist. Storytelling helps to create this dichotomy for the benefit of everyone within the nascent community. Go and share.

Susan Maushart documented a wonderful "experiment" (as she referred to it) in which she banned all screen-based forms of communication from the house she and her three children occupied. What transpired was a period of almost boundless creativity within the four walls, accompanied by an unalloyed period of real communication that had been almost absent from the family in the presence of electronic gadgetry. Maushart makes the point late in the book *The Winter of Our Disconnect* (a title, I assume, chosen as much for its irony as for its Shakespearean overtones) that, of course, books are as a much a disconnecting form of communication as are smart phones, but the real point of the "experiment" was to see what effect the absence of the *currently favored* forms of communication would have on the household. The passage that holds most relevance for this section is an apparently remarkable outbreak of singing, as if this were some alien, inhuman happening:

> And then, pulling into the driveway, I hear funny sounds coming from the living room. And voices. Loud voices. Loud male voices. My heart lurches in my chest. I don't have a cell phone anymore, so there's no way anyone can contact me while I'm out. Up to now, I've been fine with that. In fact, I've been ecstatic with that. But at this moment...? I race to the open front door and that's when I see it. I stand there in shock, my mouth as round as a laser disc.
>
> It's a bunch of kids, five of them, around the piano.
>
> They. Are. Singing.
>
> "What's next on the agenda, dudes? A taffy pull?" is what I'm thinking but don't dare say. If they are sleepwalking in another decade, far be it from me to disturb them. This, I realize, as I practically tip-toe to my bedroom, strenuously feigning nonchalance, is the moment I've been waiting for. Doing homework, sure. Reading and listening to music, absolutely. Practicing saxophone, cooking meals, sleeping and eating better — all of that has been extremely gratifying. At times verging on the magical, even. But it's this above all else — this, what would you call it? Connecting? One to the other, in real time and space, in three dimensions, and with all five senses ablaze....[216]

For such an eye-opening experience, the book ends on a distressing note, but not it seems for the author or, apparently, her children. They return to their gadgets with unbridled pleasure as though nothing had changed at all. Maybe it was all the homework.

More seriously, the most likely reason the "experiment" ended in such ignominy is because there remain a host of Tools of Disconnection trying to keep such simple and vital pleasures as storytelling, playing games and just being together in the same place from ever happening. If we take the phrase "the medium is the message" in this context, it is clear that anything that promotes physical media, whether that be an iPad, a television or a book, as more desirable than vocal communication is a Tool of Disconnection acting against the glue of community. Thus, we currently have myriad forms of information transferal all clamoring for our attention and actively trying to obsolete the previous incarnation for, above all, commercial reasons; and all the time giving ordinary human communication a serious kicking. Hark back to previous chapters and there are many ideas on how to *reverse this mass distraction from the real world* — they are as relevant here as anywhere else.

Task 9: Bringing Families Together

There is a special kind of community we need to finally consider, a type of community that naturally points toward the subject of the next chapter. It is family. Many people remain close to their biological families; others, an increasing number, suffer from the pain of familial breakup and disintegration. Some people, and I know a few, feel happier to be without the family they were born into, although I am convinced that, given the opportunity, all of us would rather be part of a loving family than not.

Family does not have to be the biological type. Many families consist of a mix of biologically close members in human terms — what we would conventionally call "relatives" — and those who have been brought together by other events than birth. Stepsisters, foster children, second cousins, great uncles, close friends, even neighbors who are there when you need them are all potential family members.

The only definition of family I can really think of that suits is "a group of people who voluntarily spend and enjoy more time together than they do with the surrounding community." I suppose, ultimately, it's the genetic bonds that call the shots, but that is not always the case, and such thinking is a little disingenuous to those groupings that have far tighter bonds than many "real" families. We have friends who we consider as much part, if not more a part, of our family than many people we are biologically related to. We love them and treasure them as part of our family and, perhaps, they feel the same about us.

The point I am trying to make is that *you* know who your family is.

And knowing who your family is really matters when it comes to knowing who you can depend on in hard times. This is going to be a very short Task, but a crucial one in determining how we approach an uncertain future, and how we tackle those things that test us in the groups of people we are closest to. Sharon Astyk sums it up beautifully in her book *Depletion and Abundance,* a work I consider to be essential reading:

> No matter how maddening they are, no matter how frustrated you are, no matter how difficult moving in together is, no matter how close the quarters or stressful the situation, these people are your tribe. It is in some ways easy not to love and appreciate the people who are always there, especially when you sometimes wish they would be elsewhere. It is also worth noting, however, that the world is not full of people who will share their homes with you, add water to their soup so your husband can eat, rock your child through a nightmare to let you sleep, give you the coat from their backs and the bread from their table, and say, in a thousand words and gestures, "You are one of us." If you have such people in your lives, treasure them.[217]

Treasure your family; treasure your friends; treasure your community — and nurture them all. When times get tough, and when things look like they are truly beyond your control, a *strong connection with the people you hold dear can be more powerful than anything that seeks to break those connections apart.*

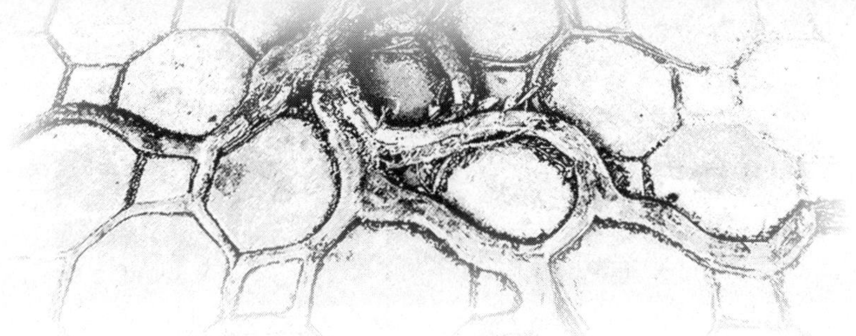

CHAPTER NINE

Reclaiming Ourselves

THERE IS ONE MORE THING TO DEAL WITH. Over the past decade I have encountered many damaged souls — people who have suffered the ravages of too much knowledge and, in many cases, huge mental capacity for processing this knowledge. A head full of worry without an escape route invariably leads to breakdown.

Through this book I have sought to provide many psychological, and tangible, escape routes in the form of productive actions within our grasp. Thus, for every new ice shelf that slips into the ocean we can do something that will reduce the burden on the burning sky; for every indigenous tribe sucked into the vacuum of civilized life we can do something that rescues civil society from the machine; for every habitat razed by industry we can do something that rewilds lands sitting on the precipice. *By taking positive steps to undermine the system we can remove the torment of knowing the truth.*

Impotence creates despair, which leads to denial, which leads to acceptance, the most dangerous state of all. In the civilized world the Kübler-Ross model of bereavement is powerfully analogous to how we deal with all sorts of stressful events. The way to break out of it is not to grieve for what may be lost, but to leave this linear pathway and create something that has numerous outcomes.

Paul Kingsnorth, former road protestor and now a working writer and social organizer, has chosen a pathway that seems to belie what many would consider constructive action but which a true Underminer will recognize as another form of resistance:

> I withdraw from the campaigning and the marching, I withdraw from the arguing and the talked-up necessity and all of the false assumptions. I withdraw from the words. I am leaving. I am going to go out walking.
>
> I am leaving on a pilgrimage to find what I left behind in the jungles and by the cold campfires and in the parts of my head and my heart that I have been skirting around because I have been busy fragmenting the world in order to save it; busy believing it is mine to save. I am going to listen to the wind and see what it tells me, or whether it tells me anything at all. You see, it turns out that I have more time than I thought. I will follow the songlines and see what they sing to me and maybe, one day, I might even come back. And if I am very lucky I might bring with me a harvest of fresh tales, which I can scatter like apple seeds across this tired and angry land.[218]

This encompasses many lessons, including the need to find our own time and space away from the pressure of civilization, the caustic elements that erode our sense of what is important. Of course, Paul speaks in metaphor as well as the physical. Just having the strength to say "Enough!" and thus reclaiming a little bit of ourselves from the rush of civilized life is a small victory, and one that can pay huge dividends if the outcome is renewed strength to work for what is right.

The following tasks take three aspects of what we have lost by living in the civilized world — personal time, personal space and our sense of belonging — and suggest a smattering of ways in which we can reclaim that which we have lost, and which we may not even know is ours to find. By no means do these tasks alone fulfill the deep need for personal liberation we all have, but I think that by at least engaging with the challenges at hand we can begin to see chinks of light beyond the cloying dark of the industrial world.

Task 1: Give Yourself Time

The number of phrases and words related to time is simply astonishing. The number of lives damaged and limited by the artificial constraints set on our use of time even more so. There is a divisiveness that illuminates the gulf between our natural sense of time as related to the pulses and rhythms of celestial bodies and the civilized use of timing devices that create synthetic order in our lives. We feel sleepy as the sun sets, whatever the time of year, yet the demands of the civilized world and in particular the clash between the natural darkness and artificial light take us through that barrier and into a world we never evolved to occupy in a fully awakened state. A. Roger Ekirch describes a fascinating corollary to this in his magnificent book *At Day's Close:*

> Until the close of the early modern era, Western Europeans on most evenings experienced two major intervals of sleep bridged by up to an hour or more of quiet wakefulness. The initial interval of slumber was usually referred to as "first sleep" or, less often "first nap" or "dead sleep" [in many languages]. The succeeding interval of sleep was called "second" or "morning" sleep, whereas the intervening period of wakefulness bore no name, other than the generic term "watch" or "watching".
>
> Although in some descriptions a neighbor's quarrel or a barking dog woke people prematurely from their initial sleep, the vast weight of surviving evidence indicates that awakening naturally was routine, not the consequence of disturbed or fitful slumber. There is every reason to believe that segmented sleep, such as many wild animals exhibit, had long been the natural pattern of our slumber before the modern age, with a provenance as old as humankind.[219]

BEEP-BEEP-BEEP-BEEP!!

It is a curse of the modern age that most of us have to be told, sometimes by other people, but more usually by machines, when to wake. If we sleep when our bodies tell us, then we will wake early, in plenty of time to see the sun rise. We may even wake in the night to experience a half-consciousness that bears more resemblance to a meditative state than full wakefulness. If we follow our bodies' natural rhythms, then sadly for the commercial world, we will have to miss the many things that late nights offer, such as television, 24-hour shopping or endless periods browsing the Internet. Fortunately for us, we will then have early mornings in which to use the incredible energy that seems to accompany those who listen to their internal rhythms.

Turning this almost revelatory stance into practical undermining is not easy if you are still the slave of whatever civilized routine has been imposed upon you, whether that is your job of work, another day spent in Mind Prison or having to cater for others who insist you help them deal with the timetable imposed upon them. Can you claw back that time at least to give you moments that are truly yours? The first step is to note everything you have some element of control over and which you can change. The three examples of commercial time theft above are obvious limitations, but there are plenty more where you can decide *not to waste your own time doing what you aren't forced to do.*

By doing so you regain valuable time to make constructive use of, and you are much more likely to be able to shift your life patterns away from the civilized norm. Try gaining back 150 breaths of stolen time (maybe 10 minutes in the civilized vernacular) and use it in a better way, perhaps taking a short walk, tending to a vegetable patch or talking to a neighbor face to face. That can be every day for seven days, or maybe five or ten if you like — why conform? Then take back another 150 breaths a day and widen your ambitions. Share what you are doing; make it a fun thing to do. If you are a "normal" civilized person, then you will rapidly encounter what seems like an immovable obstacle, such as work shifts, commuting time, school lessons or domestic duties. The first three have already been addressed, and they are tough nuts to crack from a personal point of view if you are still living a civilized life among other civilized people. Go back to Chapter 6 and you will find you are closer to liberation than you think.

On the latter point, there are easy ways of cutting into those tasks we feel are absolutely vital at home. Most obviously, do we really need to do all the things we do? How dusty is "dusty" and how clean is "clean"? It's all relative, but as aesthetic standards change so do expectations of what level of tidiness and cleanliness is acceptable. I appreciate the work our household spiders carry out, so am more than happy to have a few webs around. I also don't think that cleaning a toilet just once a week, unless absolutely necessary, is evidence of terminal hygiene breakdown. As for keeping a lawn, if you really want to, then accept that these things grow and they don't have to be shorn to within a millimeter of every inhabitant's life. Less work equals more time. Unless we are talking about the civilized perception of domestic appliances, in which case prepare for this quotation from a very robust study of work in the modern household:

> Our overall conclusion is that owning domestic technology rarely reduces unpaid household work. Indeed, in some cases owning appliances marginally increases the time spent on the relevant task. The concept of rising standards implies a greater quantity or quality of domestic production — for example, more

> or better meals, cleaner clothes and more attractive gardens. In other words, the appliances are used to increase output and not to save labour time.[220]

But there's even more to the failure of appliances to save time than that. How do you pay for these appliances that are meant to bring liberty to the domestic god(dess)? By spending time going to work and earning the money, of course.

There is no doubt that the removal of open fires from homes has massively reduced the presence of particulates coating every surface, but that doesn't mean vacuum cleaners have by the same principle removed the drudgery from domestic life. Hard floors can be swept with brooms; carpets cannot. The introduction of the vacuum cleaner made fitted carpets a desirable item — you couldn't hang them out to beat them so you had to have a vacuum cleaner (or at least a carpet sweeper), and because vacuum cleaners were available people filled their homes with fitted carpets. And dust mites. It's hardly worth me mentioning the dishwasher, but it's such a classic example of the myth of domestic "liberation" that you really have to marvel over the power of the culture that makes us believe rinsing, then loading, then waiting an hour, then unloading and usually hand-drying, and then putting away far more items of crockery and cutlery than we would have ever used had we hand-washed, is actually saving us any time at all.

Simplify your life. With each fewer item of domestic automation, you return to a more self-determined level of work. Having no washing machine may equal less-white whites and a lot of heavy scrubbing, but think of the number of times you wash clothes compared to how often you need to wash them, and as for the size of your wardrobe... It's not an easy thing, but it is so liberating in a way Hoover and GM never imagined we could be thinking.

As for the minutiae of timekeeping itself, I am indebted to my Scottish friends for introducing me to the phrase "the back of" as in "I'll be 'round the back of 10." Translated this means "I'll be there sometime just past 10 o'clock although it might be later depending on what I have to do before that, but I'm sure you won't mind because life isn't about keeping to a rock-solid schedule." My personal goal in my occasional computer/bartering work is to start being vague about when I'll be there, not for any malicious reason but simply because I am fed up with having to rely on an artificial timepiece to tell me when I have to do something. My wife is blessed with a remarkable body-clock so she can tell clock time to within a few minutes. I asked her how she does this and was intrigued to learn that she consciously tunes in to whatever time feels right, rather than seeing a row of digits in her head. We might not all be able to home in on the exact time — not that we should have to — but we all seem to know when it's about to rain because that's a natural ability that has genuine practical use even in the civilized world. Cast off our watches (and phones) and it takes very little time to "tune in" to how far along its diurnal path the Earth has rotated, and what point in our wakefulness cycle we are currently at.

I can't see such principles being readily accepted in the world of commerce, where time is money and money is the meaning of life, but that's one more reason why the commercial world is completely incompatible with human beings. We have only a finite time to spend on this world, with the people we love, doing the things that are truly important. Who gave anyone the right to steal that time away from us?

Task 2: Give Yourself Space

More than half of all human beings on Earth now live in urban areas (cities, towns and other high-population-density zones).[221] In the so-called "developed" world, the furnace of industrial civilization, this rises to around 80 percent. Imagine that. Four-fifths of the people in the parts of the world considered to be wealthy and developed, living cheek-by-jowl with barely enough room to grow a few carrots, let alone enough room to be self-sufficient or able to connect with the natural world on which we totally depend.

No wonder we feel hemmed in and controlled. No wonder it is so easy to ensure that civilized people live in a predetermined manner, at a predetermined pace, casting predetermined votes and spending predetermined amounts of money on the things that keep us living our predetermined lives. We are that tiger, pacing the cage, knowing our place and rarely tempted to escape even when the door is left ajar.

While the end of the city settlement has to be one of the ultimate aims of Undermining, we also need to accept that the vast majority of people aren't leaving just yet. Bearing in mind also what I said in Chapter 6 about the post-urban landscape being a land of future possibilities, finding ways through which we can feel alive, connected and determined to create change within the limited space we have may be doubly beneficial. Not only can we undermine the urban malaise created by a lack of physical and mental space, we may also find ways to make the most of what remains once the infrastructure has taken its last filthy belch.

The wind is blowing hard, and the trees are bending down low, the air rushing across their branches, dragging leaves and blossom into the sky. The early summer grass, soaked in the thick drizzle falling in an urgent slant, ripples and chases with the gusts. A blackbird announces its territory, darting across the patch of green before being pulled askew by a fresh blast of air, still vocalizing urgently. A family of humans are scattered through their house: one on a laptop, another immersed in a Nintendo game, the third goggling at the television that finds its market and homes in on the hypnotized viewer. The humans barely hear the wind, let alone feel its embrace, as it caresses the side of the house and cuts around, leaving eddies of detritus dancing at the foot of the solid walls.

The trees and the grass and the blackbird feel the warmth of the sun as the wind drops and the clouds fracture like an ancient lace shawl. The atmosphere is thick with post-rain smells that rise from the soil, and the music of nature fills the sky in a celebration of continued life. The humans feel nothing different: they carry on living their civilized, disconnected lives.

This is normal. The walls and windows, the high fences and concrete yards, the inner barriers that lock out the real world and focus upon our latest acquisitions — all of this is symptomatic of the urban existence. Imagine if those barriers could be broken down.

In the glass of the window that shields me from the world outside, I see the image of a tree, blowing in the breeze, and wonder what the air tastes like. I open the window and feel the cool air touch my face as the soft rain patters on the sill and wets the floor in tiny circles of darkness — difference. A sudden gust brings a litter of flora across the threshold that dances in the spaces and falls upon my feet — beauty. The blackbird sits on a swaying branch and tells its story in a burst of sublime avian music that pushes back the noise of the traffic below — joy.

John Muir was fully aware of the power of the outdoors, and especially wilderness, in changing the way we view the world. As one of the earliest and most influential Underminers, his view of civilization resonates even more today than it did more than a century ago:

> Thousands of tired, nerve-shaken, over-civilized people are beginning to find out that going to the mountains is going home;

> that wildness is a necessity; and that mountain parks and reservations are useful not only as fountains of timber and irrigating rivers, but as fountains of life. Awakening from the stupefying effects of the vice of over-industry and the deadly apathy of luxury, they are trying as best they can to mix and enrich their own little ongoings with those of Nature, and to get rid of rust and disease.[222]

This quotation is not a naive, hopeful attempt to coax people out into the wild; it actually demonstrates knowledge of the cathartic power of exposure to the real world, the power of connection that only now is being shown as a scientifically demonstrable fact. Of course we don't need science to tell us that connection is a powerful therapy for good, but it doesn't do any harm to see what is self-evident backed up by research. A groundbreaking study led by Roger Ulrich in 1991, and since repeated by others, found a close correlation between rates of stress recovery and exposure to natural settings.

> The results strongly support the conclusion that [stress recovery] was faster and more complete when subjects were exposed to the natural settings rather than the various urban environments.... The quickness of recovery during the nature conditions raises the possibility that these laboratory findings might be found to apply in many real contexts characterized by short-term contacts with nature. In urbanized countries, the great majority of encounters with nature elements probably are short episodes lasting only several seconds or a few minutes. Common types of nature contacts for urbanities may include, for example, viewing trees through a window in a workplace or residence, lunching in a park, or driving through an urban fringe area where roadsides are undeveloped.[223]

It would be fair to say that stressfulness is the normal state of the civilized urban dweller; certainly urbanization is far removed from our natural origins, and the continual "needs" we have imposed upon us by the forces of commerce are nothing if not continual stressors. Thus, it seems that *simply exposing an urban dweller to elements of the real world may be enough to create deep and resonant connections.* You can do this for yourself. You need a little time, and of course you now have more, but you don't have to go far. The real world exists not just in wide-open skies, mountains, rivers and forests but in the small spaces between the grotesque and the immovable.

Walk out of the door and keep walking until you find somewhere that belongs to you; places you feel a connection to. They don't need to be the green, flowing, sun-kissed or rain-washed perfection the explorer seeks — just the brush of a low branch upon your arm or the softness of a patch of ground that has escaped the ravages of urbanization.

A "sit spot" is a place where you are both in touch with the natural world and also safe enough to feel comfortable remaining there. On the outdoor learning sessions I help out with, we encourage people to find their own sit spots so they can take time out from whatever they are doing or just be alone with their thoughts. It can be anywhere they like, so long as it is special to that person — in a tree, amid a clump of bracken fern, on a mossy log, sprawled across a patch of grass.

Anywhere that makes a connection.

It is but a matter of time and energy between finding a sit spot and finding a life elsewhere, tilt-shifted from the horrors of imperialism. Guy McPherson, author of the influential *Nature Bats Last* website, holds the title "Emeritus Professor" at the University of Arizona. For the past three years he has achieved something far more tangible than any illustrious academic career. He has become as near to self-sufficient as he dare, and he has found a location that provides him with a peace he could never have achieved while in academia.

Exercise: Find Your Sit Spot

You have 30 minutes. Go for a short walk.

Somewhere out there is a place more special to you than anywhere else in the vicinity. You may already know about it, at least in the back of your mind. When you reach it, then use it in whatever way helps you to connect with the real world. It might mean closing your eyes or lying down. In my case it means taking off my glasses and using my other senses more acutely. However you connect then don't force it; just let it happen. Then come back again.

This is your sit spot. For 30 days go back to that place and do the same, or maybe something else that connects you in a different way. The important thing is that you make a connection with that small place that is important to you, and by doing so you take yourself away from the stresses and pressures of whatever ails you.[224]

A Life Out of Empire

BY GUY MCPHERSON

As I look out the picture windows of the mud hut on an overcast morning during early spring, snow-capped mountains in the nearby wilderness provide a stunning backdrop to the last few sandhill cranes in the small valley I occupy. The cranes are among the last to leave their winter home before heading north for an Idaho summer. They remind me that some things are worth supreme sacrifices. Some things are worth dying for, the living planet included.

It's not at all clear that my decision to abandon the empire was the right one. I know it will extend my life when the ongoing economic collapse is complete, and I know it is the morally appropriate decision (as if a dozen people in the industrialized world give a damn about morality). But Albert Einstein seems mistaken, at least in this case: "Setting an example is not the main means of influencing others, it is the only means."

My own example has generated plenty of scorn, but essentially no influence. On the other hand, the imperialism of living in the city and teaching at a university has rewards that extend well beyond the monetary realm. I miss working with young people every hour of every day. I miss comforting the downtrodden, notably in facilities of incarceration where I taught for several years, every day. And I miss afflicting the comfortable, notably hard-hearted university administrators, at least weekly.

So I sit in my rural home, alternately staring at the screen of empire and staring out the window into timeless beauty. I contemplate the timing of imperial collapse and the implications for the tattered remains of the living planet. Half a century into an insignificant life seesawing between service and self-absorption, I wonder, as always, what to do. My heart, heavy as the unbroken clouds overhead, threatens to break when I think about what we've done in pursuit of progress.

Spring's resplendence lies ahead, with its promise of renewal. Is there world enough, and time? Will we yet find a way to destroy a lineage 45 million years old, or will the haunting call of the sandhill crane make it through the bottleneck of human industry?

Now that I'm retired from the academic life — or rather, now that I've departed the academy in disgust and despair — I no longer spend time in my swivel chair, dispensing information on the telephone or tending to the tender young psyche of an overwrought twenty-something. Nonetheless, my days are entertaining, if only to me, and therefore worth sharing with others.

After putting on my cleanest dirty shirt — one never knows when a neighbor might drop by, after all — I fire up the laptop, respond to a half-dozen email messages, and ignore the list of back-stretching and -strengthening exercises on the table.

Maybe tomorrow, when I have more time. No, that won't work: I have visitors tomorrow and the next day, taking a quick tour of the property to view the arrangements we've made. The tea has been steeping while I read and respond, and now I drink it while plowing through a breakfast of cold cereal and piece of fresh fruit as I skim the morning's counterculture news and commentary. I peek over the computer screen as the sky turns pink, then azure, in the span of a few minutes.

Walking slowly to pick up the hay, I am reminded how pathetic was my attempt at construction on my first-ever awning. It keeps the hay dry, for now, but insufficient pitch and long-abused tin cause the roof to leak, thus prematurely rotting the boards.

I chuckle as I open the door to the goat pen, an old bed frame I found on the property. After placing the hay into the hand-made manger and filling the water buckets, I release Lillian and Ellie from the insulated goat shed I constructed. Lillian bleats anxiously, knowing she is about to get a quart of grain and relief from her full udder. Ellie, the barrel-shaped three-month-old kid, runs between and then jumps onto the straw bales in the small paddock.

Crossing the driveway, I step into the 15-year-old mobile home and check the temperature in the kitchen: 42 F, a few degrees warmer than outside. I arrange the quart jars, durable coffee filter, and funnel for easy pouring when I have a full bucket of milk, then grab the milking pail and wander back to Lillian. The aches and pains are giving way to an easy gait and appreciation for another beautifully verdant day.

I recall last week's visitors, a gaggle of university students. After talking for hours about economic collapse, including lights out in the empire and no water coming through the taps, I was extolling the virtues of living in a "third-world" country with rainwater harvesting and hand-dug wells. A very fit, 20-year-old woman asked for clarification about the wells: "They really dig them by hand?"

I explained that I move as much dirt in an average weekend as required to dig a 20-foot well. Tears welled up, and she turned away. Economic collapse is fun to talk about, until it becomes personal. And for most people, the personal nature of physical labor is no fun at all.

In the goat shed, I marvel at Lillian's calm disposition and take quick note of her condition. Her toenails need trimmed, so I'll get Carol to help with that when she comes back from a week-long visit to the northern half of the state. I marvel, too, at my ability and willingness to tend barnyard animals. I'm feeling good about my new skills despite the criticism from beyond the property. When my parents visited a few months ago, my dad — a product of his culture, steeped in societal economic growth and individual financial success — made a point to watch and comment: "I never thought one of my kids would be reduced to milking a goat."

Two quarts this morning, same as usual. It's stacking up in the fridge, so I'll have to make cheese tomorrow or the next day. I'm partial to Parmesan, but I'll check the inventory of hard cheeses in the root cellar to make sure we have similar amounts of Parmesan, cheddar, and Monterey Jack. Chevre, mozzarella, and ricotta need to be eaten quickly, and I won't take time to cook a decent meal based on either of the latter two during the next week.

The milk goes into the freezer for an hour as I let the ducks and chickens out of their respective houses. They'll range free all day, the ingenious ducks spending most of their time in the irrigation ditch adjacent to the property they discovered after living here only a year.

I water the seedlings in the garden. The carrots and peas are just emerging, so they need a light shower twice daily. The citrus trees seem to perk up every time I shower their leaves, so I hit them every time I walk past.

Today's big task is construction. The still-tender ribs I broke last month working on a similar project remind me to work deliberately as I attach an awning to the cargo container in the northwest corner of the property. We'll want to store bales of hay and straw and, when we can no longer obtain bales of either, stacks of hay from the peanuts in two large gardens. In time, peanuts will feed us and the goats, as well as improving the soil.

The frame is finished at 1:00 p.m., but only after I pummel my left thumb with a poorly aimed hammer several hundred times, walk back and forth between the stack of lumber and the new awning too many times to count, and nearly fall off the roof. I guess the ribs aren't a sufficient reminder. I'm thirsty, hot, and tired, and it's time for lunch.

A handful of aspirin later I'm back at the awning, misguided hammer in hand. After a surprisingly smooth afternoon characterized by few bruises and no blood, I complete the awning. I've covered the frame with plywood, tarpaper, and tin on an afternoon with temperatures in the mid-80s. Sweating and sore, I barely have time to hand-water the large garden behind the mobile home, trying not to notice how badly the beds need weeded, before my evening encounter with Lillian. Were Carol here today, the goats would have been walked a couple times, with special attention to the abundant weeds on the east end of the property.

Distracting Ellie with a little grain in her own bucket, I close the door to the goat shed and Lillian steps up on the stanchion I built to ease the milking operation. I apply bag balm after I finish milking her, give Ellie a pat on the head, and head to the mobile home to strain the milk into two more quart jars.

Supper is the same as lunch: rice and beans left over from last night's supper. A quick shower removes the first layer of grime before I put the goats into their lion-proof shed, lock the chickens into their skunk-proof coop, and herd the ducks into their raccoon-proof house. The setting sun sets the sky afire before unleashing the Milky Way.

One more round with the imperial screen of death allows me to catch up with a couple dozen email messages while viewing the latest dire news about the ecological collapse we're bringing to every corner of the globe. A cup of herbal tea to wash down more aspirin, a few pages of Nietzsche in the silence of the straw-bale house, and I tumble into bed. Sleep comes slowly and poorly, as it has since the summer of 1979 when I last logged six consecutive hours of sleep. Even then, my nagging subconscious was trying to tell me something about the empire wasn't quite right. [225]

Remember, this chapter is about you. Sharing your experiences for the benefit of others transfers that "you" to someone else, but this undermining has to be a personal endeavor, for only by battling your own demons can you truly be liberated from the civilized mindset. There are many aspects to personal liberation, and we have touched on only two of the fundamentals: time and space. So many others, such as language, culture, a sense of belonging and the absolutely vital element of being at peace with yourself, are tied up in the next task.

Task 3: Find Yourself

We are raised, as citizens in the industrial world, to believe there is a single mode of fulfillment that will hold us in good stead from birth to death. We must never question it; we must never challenge it; we must only identify with it. Carolyn Baker describes this crisis of identity in her book *Sacred Demise:*

> Civilization's toxicity has fostered the illusion that one is, for example, a professional person with money in the bank, a secure mortgage, a good credit rating, a healthy body and mind, raising healthy children who will grow up to become successful like oneself, and that when one retires one will be well taken care of. If that has become our identity, and if we don't look deeper, we won't discover who we really are.[226]

At the root of the loss and agitation every civilized person feels is a question, a question so simple that the answer surely must be self-evident just by its asking. Yet eons of mindtime and reams of pulp-print have been expended by some of the finest minds civilization has vomited from its blandness on this very question, with no usable answer emerging. The reason there is no usable answer is because the wrong person is being asked the question.

You need to ask *yourself* the question.

"Who am I?"

No one can ask it, and certainly no one can answer it, on your behalf. But I can give you a hand if you want. In August 2009 I carried out something similar, at least on a superficial level, because I was feeling rudderless and ungrounded, stuck in a place I didn't want to be. The key to restoring my sense of self was to *find an identity that I could relate to at a very real and personal level.* Discovering an identity allowed me to resist whatever label civilization wished to impose upon me, as Baker has alluded to above. More basically, it seems that *without identity we are less human.* The evidence for this is compelling: identity from the dawn of humanity is written across the ground, the walls and the artifacts of everyone who has ever been part of a tribe or close community. The tongues of countless people have spoken, and still try to speak in myriad different languages, dialects and accents. The way we have dressed, the way we have expressed ourselves, the way we have made our lives different in subtle and deliberate ways shouts of the need for an identity, a commonality in our local culture that enhances the success of each group that shares that identity.

At the time, this is what I wrote about my personal journey:

> I was born in England and I have lived here all my life. I love this country as a place, and I am content to root myself in the soil from which its life emerges. I have, very recently, also realised that a large part of what I write and speak about is rooted in Anarchy; the simple and natural concept that there is no place for arbitrary authority nor a self-selected hierarchy — the kind that the political and corporate milieu utilise to ensure we remain good Consumers. In that sense, Anarchist is the antithesis of Consumer, and I know which identity I am more comfortable with.
>
> There are many other pieces for me to find; some of them may shuffle around and some may come and go over time, but at least I am now able to choose my identity for myself. That is a wonderful thing, one that we owe it to ourselves to fight for.[227]

I had no idea how prescient this would become. Only four months after writing this, we made a family decision to move to the Scottish Borders.

The move had a number of very practical causes, but the actual decision to relocate to a specific place with its unique setting and culture was most definitely heartfelt. It just seemed *right.* Less than 12 months after identifying as an English Anarchist I felt like a Borderer.

Other parts of my identity are falling into place. I have become more of a listener than a talker, more of a community person than an individual, more tolerant of others' different views from my own, and even able to walk past a group of teenagers with a sense of collective need rather than urban fear. They are not the whole picture by any means, but all of these do signify a journey that is still taking place at a very elemental level.

It may be you are not in a position to identify with anything in the same way; I am certainly lucky to have become settled in such a way that there is something I can attach myself to. But that's surely not the point. I initially searched for an identity as a way of excising myself from the mentally draining position I was in, not to reinforce a positive experience. The power of identity in undermining lies in its value as a recuperative force. *Even if you can attach yourself to "only" one thread of genuine goodness in your current existence, that is one more thread than civilization permits most people.* Surely that, in itself, is worth the effort. And, of course, once you have that single thread, then you can trace it to others with which you can start to weave something that is truly your own.

Where Did Your Soul Go?

There is a moment in Joseph Conrad's incredible novella *Heart of Darkness* where the storyteller, Marlow, bares his raw soul. A heap of junk, masquerading as a boat, clatters past a group of drumming, crying, wailing forest

people on the bank. ("Cursing us, praying to us, welcoming us?") At that moment the story takes a pivotal jerk toward a vivid realization that maybe the civilized world is just a thin veneer, created to keep us disconnected from the world from which we came and to which our soul still belongs:

> We were cut off from the comprehension of our surroundings; we glided past like phantoms, wondering and secretly appalled, as sane men would be before an enthusiastic outbreak in a madhouse. We could not understand because we were too far and could not remember; because we were travelling in the night of first ages, of those ages that are gone, leaving hardly a sign — and no memories.
>
> The earth seemed unearthly. We are accustomed to look upon the shackled form of a conquered monster, but there — there you could look at a thing monstrous and free. It was unearthly, and the men were — No, they were not inhuman. Well, you know, that was the worst of it — this suspicion of their not being inhuman. It would come slowly to one ... if you were man enough you would admit to yourself that there was in you just the faintest trace of a response to the terrible frankness of that noise, a dim suspicion of there being a meaning in it which you — you so remote from the night of first ages — could comprehend.[228]

Soul is a strange beast. It has been corrupted in its definition by the established organized religions of the West, which insist that it is some kind of post-partum entity that ascends to heaven or descends to hell, whatever they are. Soul is both less definable but more accessible than any religious doctrine would have us believe.

However you view the idea of soul, there is no getting away from it that to be connected to the Real World, and thus burn all traces of the Tools of Disconnection, requires something beyond the material. Whether that connection manifests itself in your mind, or even outside of your material self, it is something we have grown increasingly unfamiliar with in the industrial culture. It is no coincidence that *materialism* is analogous with Industrial Civilization. Soul, on the other hand, requires the opposite of materialism. It is the intangible sense of otherness that fills the space between our physical self and everything else in the Real World. It is the sense of closeness. It is what creates genuine need and beneficence. It is love. It is all of the things for which there is no physical explanation, but which we know exist.

And, as civilized people, it is what we are missing.

Of all the undermining we have encountered, *finding your soul* is the least tangible yet perhaps the most fundamental of tasks. I cannot tell you how to find it, but it's there somewhere. When you have found it, you will know, I promise.

We set out on this great project with the aim of undermining the Tools of Disconnection, of removing the things that prevent us from connecting with the Real World. Maybe the act of finding your soul is impossible without first removing that which keeps us disconnected; maybe it is not possible to start undermining the Tools of Disconnection without first making that fundamental step in discovering the true nature of connection. I don't know.

Maybe it doesn't matter. Maybe all of these things just happen when they need to happen. We are all different: some of us can be connected while still wirelessly attached to broadband routers; some of us can help build wonderful communities while still holding down destructive jobs; some of us can be dismantling the corporate machine while buying our weekly food at their nearest globe-spanning supermarket. At some point we will need to accept that some of these things will be no more, while some of them will become commonplace. I suspect you know this and are already preparing for when it will become reality ... with your help

We are the Underminers, and this is our time.

Epilogue: A Last Toast to the Old World

WE WANTED TO TAKE THE TRAIN, but the train wasn't there. "Canceled Forever," someone had scrawled across the board that had once announced engineering works.

Walk? An epic journey south if we had no other choice; but the guy in the taxi was alive after all, just snoozing between rides. He admitted the sleeps had been getting longer, but could be persuaded to drive to Brighton for a bottle of sloe gin and some aged chocolate.

We drove into what could have once been any day in Anytown, except for the uncanny silence. Back in the Civilized Time the long hill between the railway station and the esplanade had shuddered with traffic: now, as we made our delicate way down the cracking asphalt it felt for the first time as though nature was winning through. Clumps of daisies poked up between paving slabs. Buddleia loomed down from window sills, prising apart the cement, and turning the light-etched walls into a pretty purple picture. Clouds of insects were preyed upon by the birds that criss-crossed the chasm between the moss-dressed buildings.

We both stopped at the unlit traffic lights, more out of habit than anything else; there was still a part of me that urged a crowd of strangers to appear from some side street or emerge, laden with bags, from the now dusty and subdued shopping center off to the right.

Of course we had to do the walk: the driver had given us an odd look when we asked him to drop us off at the station, but by that time the car had been running on air. He knew some "people" over in Kemptown who would be able to top him up again; we only knew that we had to retrace our steps for the last time.

Beyond that lay uniqueness.

You can do anything if you set your mind to it — cider in this case. Trees keep growing and apples keep falling: squeeze enough of them, let them sit for a while and.... People used to drink cheap, refrigerated lager, and keep drinking it until they fought or fell down. There was a lot to get angry about, but eventually The Machine did most of the work itself; we just cut a few of the strings.

There's still plenty of plastic around, though — behind a door round the back of the Wetherspoons pub was an unopened pack of disposable tumblers. We took three, just in case, then crossed the road to the seafront and tumbled onto the beach.

We sit on the shingle as it breathes in the sea. Incoming: each wave is absorbed by the honeycombed voids between the grains ... a second's embrace before the water seeps back into the sea.

Whoosh ... shhhh ... whoosh ... shhhh ...

Incessant but random. Sometimes a larger wave strikes the shore, rushing upward, bestriding the hollows and touching the tips of our toes.

Tiny bubbles sparkle like glass beads rising up the sandy-yellow liquid in our cups. As they burst, minute puffs of moisture expand and settle down onto the surface of the cider, mirroring the sea froth at our feet.

We look at each other and push our cups together, gently buckling, and toast everything we left behind that was good. Through her tears I can't help but notice a glint, and then her face opens into a daylight smile.

"It's finished, isn't it? All the bad stuff."

"Probably," I reply.

Did we deserve another chance? Perhaps not.

As we crunch our way toward Shoreham she points at the smokestack on the old coal-fired power station: idle. Dormant? Extinct?

The wind pushes some pebbles across our path, and in the sky the starlings shake their ephemeral blanket over the setting sun.

"Let's chase it," she says.

So we run.

Notes and References

All references are correct at the time of publishing. Notes are written to supplement the text, and are integral to the content of *Underminers,* only excluded from the main text for the sake of readability. Full links are available at www.underminers.org.

1 Acetaminophen/Tylenol
2 James U. McNeal. *The Kids Market: Myths & Realities.* Paramount, 1999.
3 Paul Joseph Watson. "Eugenicist Gunman Exposes Dark Side of the Environmentalist Cult." Prison Planet website, prisonplanet.com (accessed October 2010).
4 Keith Farnish. *Time's Up! An Uncivilized Solution to a Global Crisis.* Green Books, 2009. Also published as "A Matter of Scale" at amatterofscale.com.
5 To avoid accusations of self-promotion, I must emphasize that all of my writing is available *free of charge* online. (See, for instance, amatterofscale.com and theearthblog.org.) I just want to avoid repeating myself too much in this book.
6 Screenplay extract from *What a Way To Go: Life at the End Of Empire,* courtesy of T.S. Bennett, whatawaytogomovie.com.
7 As someone who is cognizant of scientific method, and a critic of anyone who tries to make financial capital from that for which there is no empirical evidence, I understand this sounds hypocritical; but I am also aware that our capacity to know something in the absence of detailed analysis is perhaps the root of our development of scientific understanding. Civilization has just formalized what humans have been doing since the origins of our species. And I also subscribe fully to evolutionary theory, in case you were wondering.
8 Sir Walter Scott. *The Lay of the Last Minstrel: A Poem.* Longman & Co, 1805.
9 Economic growth is ubiquitous in civilization: we will come to that later.
10 Some of this text is derived from Carolyn Baker, *Sacred Demise: Walking the Spiritual Path of Industrial Civilization's Collapse,* iUniverse, 2009,

and *Navigating the Coming Chaos: A Handbook for Inner Transition,* draft manuscript.

11 Kent Mountford. "Price of wholesale destruction of woods for shopping mall is no bargain." *Chesapeake Bay Journal,* September 2006.

12 Raymond de Young. "Restoring Mental Vitality in an Endangered World: Reflections on the Benefits of Walking." *Ecopsychology* (2)1, March 2010.

13 Keith Farnish. "Anger Is Good." The Earth Blog, 2010: earth-blog.bravejournal.com (accessed November 2010).

14 In reality, there is often little to separate government policy and the work of NGOs, and all NGOs — which, significantly have to be formally registered as such, whether as a non-profit or a charity — have their basis in the industrial system. Examples of environmental NGOs include Conservation International, Greenpeace, Sierra Club, Friends of the Earth, RAN, WWF and the very many public interest research group (PIRG) type of organizations.

15 Sometimes known as "laws," although as you will see later on, the idea of what constitutes a law is usually determined by the system that enforces power rather than through any valid agreement of what is right or wrong.

16 For a brilliant exegesis of the myths of Mammon and Moloch, read chapter 11 of *Soil and Soul* by Alastair McIntosh (2001, Aurum).

17 The term "Business Leader" injects false authority into figures whose primary motivation is to create wealth for themselves. However, as the primary motivation for the industrial machine is to create wealth for a selected few, then that authority is tangible: thus when a Business Leader is wheeled out in front of the media you *are* hearing from authority in the civilized world.

18 Leviticus 26, verses 14–16 , 27, 30, Holy Bible, New Living Translation, 2004.

19 Derrick Jensen. *Endgame. Volume I: The Problem of Civilization.* Seven Stories Press, 2006.

20 "If those below damage the property of those above, those above may kill or otherwise destroy the lives of those below. This is called justice." This is part of the fifth Premise from Derrick Jensen, *Endgame* (see above). The previous reference quoted the fourth Premise.

21 John Taylor Gatto. *Dumbing Us Down: The Hidden Curriculum of Compulsory Schooling.* New Society Publishers, 2005. This is a superb book and critical reading for anyone who wishes to understand more about the nature of the school system.

22 Ronald Reagan. Remarks to citizens in Hambach, Federal Republic of Germany. Accessed via the Ronald Reagan Presidential Library Archive, University of Texas, reagan.utexas.edu/ (accessed September 2011).

23 "Obama acceptance speech in full." *The Guardian,* November 2008, guardian.co.uk (accessed September 2011).

24 Paul Kingnorth and George Monbiot. "Is there any point in fighting to stave off industrial apocalypse?" *The Guardian,* August 2009, guardian.co.uk (accessed February 2011).

25 This "simile" is better described as an allegory, and indeed in many texts the passage in question is referred to as "The Allegory of the Cave." The translation

used here, however, is more faithful to the original. Excerpts are from Plato tr. Desmond Lee, *The Republic,* Penguin Classics, 2003.

26 Ibid.

27 "World Death Rate Holding Steady At 100 Percent." *The Onion,* theonion.com (accessed February 2011).

28 A. Rosalie David and Michael R. Zimmerman. "Cancer: an old disease, a new disease or something in between?" *Nature Reviews Cancer* 10, 728–733 (October 2010). Of this paper, the lead author states, "In industrialised societies, cancer is second only to cardiovascular disease as a cause of death. But in ancient times, it was extremely rare. *There is nothing in the natural environment that can cause cancer.* So it has to be a man-made disease, down to pollution and changes to our diet and lifestyle.... The important thing about our study is that it gives a historical perspective to this disease. We can make very clear statements on the cancer rates in societies because we have a full overview. We have looked at millennia, not one hundred years, and have masses of data." (manchester.ac.uk: accessed February 2011).

29 An apt term considering the Western Enlightenment period was both a concerted effort to unchain society from the strictures of the mediaeval church and to proclaim civilization as the philosophical and artistic savior of humanity.

30 This is a compilation of two essays by CrimethInc. Ex-Workers' Collective: "There is a Difference Between Life and Survival" and "Indulge...& Undermine" (crimethinc.com, both accessed October 2011). Reproduced with permission. The CrimethInc. website is a superb collection of literature, essays and thoughts on a wide range of subjects related to combating exploitation.

31 I'm now expecting this to appear on various websites as "clear evidence" of a desire to assassinate certain world leaders. Yeah, sounds like a great idea — I'll start digging my grave now.

32 Except for perhaps basic intelligence, which cannot be attained by effort any more than additional adult height can.

33 Sun Tzu (translated by Lionel Giles). *The Art Of War.* 1910.

34 There are parallels between this list and the general layout of the second part of this book, and Donella Meadows' classic essay, "Leverage Points: Places to Intervene in a System" (sustainabilityinstitute.org, accessed October 2011). The latter essay is recommended reading for all *Underminers,* providing as it does a neat summary of the differences between the types of targets that are worth pursuing and those that may have only very limited impact if undermined. I must hasten to add that the structure of Underminers was not inspired by Meadows' essay in any way — at least not consciously — but it seems to turn out in life that if two or more people have the same ideas spontaneously, then maybe there is something in it.

35 *Ozymandius' Sabotage and Direct Action Handbook.* Available from Reach Out Publications' online archive (reachoutpub.com) and various other locations.

36 The undermining of an individual is fraught with legal traps and may also be morally unsound. An individual may "represent" something that needs undermining, but the person is rarely the thing that actually needs undermining. In

many cases an individual may simply be a corporate martyr, such as a head of PR, resulting not only in wasted time and effort but in sabotaging an individual who really didn't deserve to be undermined, however poor his career decisions. In short, individuals are rarely fair game — rarely, but not never.

37 Nicky Hager in *Battling Big Business,* ed. Eveline Lubbers. Common Courage Press, 2002. *Secrets and Lies* refers to the 1999 book by Nicky Hager and Bob Burton, a masterpiece of investigative journalism.

38 There is always the option of rapid-state hypnotism, if someone is prepared to go to those lengths. Failing that, a session in make-up and a good hairdresser might be sufficient.

39 Podjobs are those that, in the spirit of Scott Adams's Dilbert, don't actually lead to an improvement in the lot of humanity, or even have any part in the production of anything tangible. A real job might be making wooden boxes for neighbors to store apples in; the Podjob equivalent would be advertising the same boxes to a global market or calculating the relative benefits of different colored boxes on a consumer's lifestyle.

40 Global urban population growth between 2000 and 2010 was 64 million people per year according to the United Nations Department of Economic and Social Affairs (esa.un.org/unup). Urbanization is the most obvious indicator of civilized living and industrial dominance, but even this is a conservative estimate for it does not include the millions of people subject to creeping industrialization and cultural homogenization as a result of religious, educational and aid programs, along with the removal and alteration of their indigenous habitats in the name of development.

41 It is the victims who should decide whether they have been harmed by something, not someone on their behalf, and then only after some time has passed, ideally after the effects of the undermining have been seen. It may be that they don't feel they have been harmed after all.

42 I have sometimes been asked why I don't get depressed, given the subjects I deal with on a daily basis and the worries I have, particularly for the future of my family. The reason I give is that I am doing something to combat the cause of that potential depression; being proactive, not getting caught in a cycle of angst and worry, is a very powerful anti-depressant, certainly in my case. Undermining may be just the thing for some people who are feeling helpless.

43 I am probably being overcautious in statements such as "expose your person to danger." As you will see in Part Two, the vast majority — in terms of absolute numbers of individual tasks — of undermining is low risk, so the entire section discussing personal risk may seem over the top. However, make no mistake, once you have become an Underminer in however small a way, then you will become hooked. Not just because of the intrigue and mischief that most people like to dabble in from time to time but because of the undeniable joy in knowing you are part of something that is absolutely right. At some point you may wish to move onto higher-risk activities, and it is for that reason that I make serious points about collective and personal risk.

44 In the mid-2000s Scientology groups managed to influence the results of Internet search engines such as Google and Yahoo! to ensure that websites critical of their activities rarely showed up in search queries. This has since been countered, for the time being at least.

45 A "troll" is a person who makes comments or posts media purely to incite a reaction.

46 Generally refers to members of Internet forums that purport to be liberal and innovative but do not reflect that in their operation (e.g., banning people for offensive posts, overly heavy moderation, etc.)

47 This essay was constructed from a range of contributions by people who support and consider themselves to be part of Anonymous. Views were provided on request, except for one piece that was referred to by a contributor, written by him/her at an earlier date. By its nature the essay cannot reflect the complete range of viewpoints within the Anonymous community; however, the range of views, some of them opposing, does reflect a fair cross-section of those who occupy this mindset.

48 John Young. "FBI Visits Cryptome." 2003, cryptome.org (accessed April 2011).

49 See, for instance, Security Culture: A Handbook for Activists, available at deep-green resistance.org/wp-content/uploads/2011/04/security-culture.pdf (accessed December 2012).

50 Feral Faun. "Feral Revolution" in *Against Civilization,* ed. John Zerzan. Feral House, 2005.

51 I just did a quick dictionary check on the word "convey" to see if there was something more appropriate and there seems to be an Underminer operating in Thesaurus Central. The synonyms were: send, forward, impart, communicate, contaminate and infect. Spooky!

52 I use the term "Australian" simply because this is what it is referred to in Australian schools. The vast bulk of history in this region is, of course, prior to the Australian nation ever existing.

53 keepschoolssafe.org (accessed August 2011).

54 I will come to Unschooling later. It is a vital thing to acknowledge, but not something that can be achieved on any scale without a powerful community in place to support it.

55 John Taylor Gatto. *Dumbing Us Down: The Hidden Curriculum of Compulsory Schooling.* New Society Publishers, 2005.

56 Various models are available from TV-B-Gone or Adafruit Industries, and various other "gadget" outlets, sometimes advertised as joke products. Fun they may be, but a joke they are not. Building the high-powered version was actually the first time I had soldered anything, and it worked first time! Undermining is not just about removing the Tools of Disconnection, it's about gaining a load of useful skills too.

57 Naomi Klein. *No Logo.* Flamingo, 2001.

58 The word "bargain" should be in quotes because unless you intended to buy something in the first place it can be a bargain only if it is free. When you are encouraged to buy something that you were not intending to buy, then

however cheap something is, it is not a bargain. You have been lied to.

59 An early concept of this book was to use a series of real-life case studies to assist Underminers create their own strategies. This is useful up to a point, but it is an example of inductive thinking in that you can generalize based on specifics. This could be dangerous, giving people a false sense of security. So instead I wrote two chapters giving general processes and rules upon which specific undermining tasks can be based. While a number of real-life examples are used, and reinvention is not always necessary, the emphasis in Part Two is thus on working out your own strategies for undermining, helping ensure that you can take responsibility for your actions for better and worse.

60 BBC News. "Shell annual profits double to $18.6bn." bbc.co.uk (accessed June 2011).

61 BBC News. "Bupa profits fall amid tough times in key markets." www.bbc.co.uk (accessed June 2011).

62 Partial transcript of "The Love Police vs. The Propaganda Pushers" (British Election Special) from youtube.com/watch?v=cko7BImRAfQ (accessed April 2013).

63 Andrew Sparrow. "Sept 11: 'a good day to bury bad news." *Daily Telegraph*, October 10, 2001.

64 I know this section is full of technical details, but Underminers are often specialists in particular fields — experience that can be extremely useful across the board. Therefore I have no intention of dumbing-down the text just because some book retailer says I should be appealing to a wider audience. In this case, "number masking" might just be a case of calling Reception and asking to be transferred; but in practice it is a lot safer to (a) use a number not associated with you; (b) use the appropriate "mask" prefix that a telephone provider usually offers; and (c) go via Reception.

65 Philip Verwimp. "Machetes and Firearms: The Organisation of Massacres in Rwanda." *Journal of Peace Research* (2006), 43, 5–22.

66 Full title: *Her Majesty* Elizabeth the Second, by the Grace of God, of the United Kingdom of Great Britain and Northern Ireland, and of Her other Realms and Territories, Queen, Head of the Commonwealth, Defender of the Faith.

67 Debrett's. "How to Address The Queen." debretts.com (accessed June 2011).

68 I use the term "police officer" and "policeman/policewoman" interchangeably here, but in some jurisdictions there is a distinction, with police officer implying an official of a corporation (a state, an incorporated police force, a private force, etc.) and policeman/policewoman implying someone who only deals in Common Law. Rarely in civil society are the two considered as separate roles.

69 "Chinese Cultural Connection: Chinese values and the search for culture-free dimensions of culture." *Journal of Cross-Cultural Psychology*. 1987, 18, 143–164.

70 BBC *Nationwide*, May 1983.

71 Egalitarianism differs slightly from anarchism, in that anarchy is predominantly a rejection of hierarchy, whereas egalitarianism describes a more general way of doing things in a fair and equitable manner. In practice, where

things are equitable and there is no hierarchy, there are unlikely to be any *de facto* leaders.

72 Richard Borshay Lee. "Eating Christmas in The Kalahari." *Natural History*, December 1969. Note, there are all sorts of anecdotal stories of such instances, but the history of colonialism has ensured they are largely modern, with older examples of such human behavior being struck from history.

73 Peter Gray. "How Hunter-Gatherers Maintained Their Egalitarian Ways: Three Complementary Theories." psychologytoday.com (accessed July 2011).

74 Riane Eisler. *The Real Wealth of Nations*. Berrett Koehler, 2007.

75 Bear in mind that shit is also of genuine practical use, as described in *The Humanure Handbook* (humanurehandbook.com, 2005) and, to further defend myself against accusations of misuse, this refers to excrement in its raw, floaty state — not something to be enjoyed!

76 Insert name of latest A-list fashion victim here.

77 Keith Farnish. "The Problem With...Civilization." The Earth Blog, 2008, earth-blog.bravejournal.com, (accessed August 2011).

78 To be found at, respectively, eff.org and article19.org.

79 "1971 Year in Review: The Pentagon Papers." UPI, upi.com (accessed August 2011).

80 Note that "system" in this context does not necessarily mean computer system; it could be anything that has a structure that enables information to be processed in some way, be that word of mouth and ideas, physical documents or electronic data.

81 One very good example, the dead-letter box, is described well in "How to set up and use a dead-letter box...", originally published by Spy & Counterspy, republished at www.ncmilitia.org/spycounterspy (accessed September 2011).

82 Joshua Hammer. "The Death of Rachel Corrie." *Mother Jones*, 2003, motherjones.com (accessed September 2011).

83 Billboard Liberation Front. "The Art and Science of Billboard Improvement." destructables.org (accessed September 2011).

84 There may be exceptions, for instance, bartering with ready commodities such as gold or copper, but these still have to pass through some kind of filter prior to being accepted as currency. So if you barter with a kilo of coffee beans, they have no agreed value in the capitalist system until the beans have been formally graded, and even then the price would change depending on the *market value* of that particular type of bean.

85 "Tax Responsibilities of Bartering Participants." IRS, irs.gov (accessed September 2011).

86 There used to be a wonderful hardware store in our village, but it closed down before we moved there. It wasn't so much a lack of custom that caused it to close as the suppliers insisting in their mass-market mindset that no one was allowed to order less than 1,000 of anything small, and less than a dozen of anything large. So it was capitalism that closed the local shop down. I would love to get something going again — maybe a weekly hardware stall in the village hall run by one of the nearby stores.

87 Bernard London. *Ending the Depression Through Planned Obsolescence.* 1932. Quoted in "Consumer Society Made to Break." Adbusters, 2008, adbusters.org (accessed September 2011).

88 The Yes Men. "New York Times Special Edition." November 12, 2008, theyesmen.org (accessed September 2011).

89 It was Wednesday, October, 5, 2011, but putting dates in books is terribly clunky.

90 Ana Salote is the author of one of my favorite children's books, *Tree Talk* (Speaking Tree, 2007), a wonderful tale of disconnection and reconnection that left me in tears — and might do the same to you.

91 Taken from Dubit Insider FAQ, dubitinsider.com (accessed October 2011). Dubit, a leader in social marketing, was recently cited in a number of UK media reports for its practice of using paid teenagers to infiltrate school and other peer groups for commercial purposes.

92 Julia Finch and Zoe Wood. "Superdry fashion label sees profits almost triple." *The Guardian*, July 15, 2010, guardian.co.uk (accessed October 2011).

93 There are other types of corporation, such as in the UK where "corporation" more commonly means a body created by royal statute and the term "company" is more usual to describe profit-making entities, but in the case of this book, a corporation is a profit-making business.

94 George Carlin. "Back In Town." HBO Special first broadcast in 1996. Extract is from a segment titled "Why I Don't Vote."

95 The Bible and Qur'an seem to make a special point of casting moneylenders into the deepest pits of hell, with frequent mention of the word "usury" (the charging of interest on a loan) in particular. This extract from The Bible is typical:

> 1 Look! The LORD is about to destroy the earth and make it a vast wasteland.
> He devastates the surface of the earth and scatters the people. 2 Priests and
> laypeople, servants and masters, maids and mistresses, buyers and sellers,
> lenders and borrowers, bankers and debtors—none will be spared. 3 The
> earth will be completely emptied and looted. The LORD has spoken!
>
> (Isaiah 24, verses 1–3, Holy Bible, New Living Translation, 2004.)

The Qur'an is even more scathing:

> Those who consume interest cannot stand [on the Day of Resurrection] except as one stands who is being beaten by Satan into insanity. That is because they say, "Trade is [just] like interest." But Allah has permitted trade and has forbidden interest. So whoever has received an admonition from his Lord and desists may have what is past, and his affair rests with God. But whoever returns to [dealing in interest or usury] — those are the companions of the Fire; they will abide eternally therein.
>
> (Surat Al-Baqarah 2:275, Qur'an, Sahih International Translation.)

96 "Will US Consumer Debt Reduction Cripple the Recovery?" McKinsey & Company, 2009, mckinsey.com (accessed October 2011). Short answer: Yes.

97 *The Daily Telegraph,* October 5, 2011, telegraph.co.uk (accessed October 2011).

98 Ibid.
99 Ibid: "The comment sparked concern among retailers and economists, with the British Retail Consortium warning that urging people to 'retrench' was 'at odds with promoting growth'. The Institute for Public Policy Research think-tank said that if consumers took the PM at his word, the UK economy would be 'in real trouble', shrinking significantly over the years to come."
100 Saul Alinsky. *Rules for Radicals*. Random House, 1971.
101 A large part of this section derives from an article titled "Throwing off the Shackles of Debt" by Sharon Astyk, Guy McPherson, Dave Pollard and Keith Farnish (thesietch.org/mysietch/keith, accessed October 2011). This was a collaborative work made all the more powerful by the four different versions, customized for the authors' individual websites.
102 Scott Pierpoint. "Disobeying the Banks: An Interview with Enric Duran." Institute for Anarchist Studies, anarchist-studies.org (accessed January 2012).
103 "Australian coal miners predict at least $3/mt hit from new carbon tax." Platts, platts.com (accessed October 2011).
104 Mick Whale. "As BAE threatens cuts... Fight for Jobs!" The Socialist, socialistparty.org.uk (accessed October 2011).
105 The Invisible Committee. The Coming Insurrection. MIT Press/Semiotext(e): *À force, on a compris ceci : ce n'est pas l'économie qui est en crise, c'est l'économie qui est la crise; ce n'est pas le travail qui manque, c'est le travail qui est en trop. En France, on fait des pieds et des mains pour grimper dans la hiérarchie, mais on se flatte en privé de n'en ficher pas une. On reste jusqu'à dix heures du soir au boulot quand on est débordé, mais on n'a jamais eu de scrupule à voler de-ci de-là du matériel de bureau, ou à ponctionner dans les stocks de la boîte des pièces détachées qu'à l'occasion on revend. On déteste les patrons, mais on veut à tout prix être employé. Avoir un travail est un honneur, et travailler une marque de servilité. Bref : le parfait tableau clinique de l'hystérie. L'horreur du travail est moins dans le travail lui-même que dans le ravage méthodique, depuis des siècles, de tout ce qui n'est pas lui: familiarités de quartier, de métier, de village, de lutte, de parenté, attachement à des lieux, à des êtres, à des saisons, à des façons de faire et de parler.* Also available for download at tarnac9.wordpress.com/texts/the-coming-insurrection/ (accessed October 2011).
106 Keith Farnish. "What If ...We Stopped Using Money?" earth-blog.bravejournal.com (accessed October 2011).
107 *Weekly World News*, October 24, 1989, quoted in Martin Sprouse. *Sabotage In the American Workplace*. AK Press, 1992.
108 Ibid.
109 Global Strike 2011 (globalstrike2011.blogspot.com, accessed October 2011). The project was perhaps doomed to failure, partly because the context was wrong — people wanted to hang onto to their jobs so were loath to strike — but mainly because there wasn't sufficient coverage. Had this converged with the growth of the Occupy Movement in late 2011, it would perhaps have formed a rallying point for a lot of people. This demonstrates the importance of context with large-scale undermining.

110 Personal communication.

111 Stephen Moss. "Why the spoon-billed sandpiper's luck might change." *The Guardian,* October 16, 2011, guardian.co.uk/environment (accessed October 2011).

112 Martin Hickman. "The guilty secrets of palm oil: Are you unwittingly contributing to the devastation of the rain forests?" *The Independent*, May 2, 2009, independent.co.uk/environment (accessed October 2011).

113 John Vidal. "Nigeria's agony dwarfs the Gulf oil spill. The US and Europe ignore it." *The Guardian*, May 30, 2011, guardian.co.uk/world (accessed October 2011).

114 Anti-terrorism Act 2008, justice.gc.ca (accessed October 2011).

115 Consumer Confidence Index, The Conference Board, conference-board.org (accessed October 2011).

116 James McWhinney. "Understanding the Consumer Confidence Index." Investopedia, investopedia.com (accessed October 2011).

117 Barbara Sibbald. "Estimates of flu-related deaths rise with new statistical models." *CMAJ* March 18, 2003 vol. 168 no. 6.

118 "The Economic Impact of SARS." CBC News Online, July 8, 2003, cbc.ca (accessed October 2011).

119 British Member of Parliament Peter Viggers infamously charged the cost of a duck house to his expenses, one of the more notorious but by no means the worst abuse uncovered by journalists in 2009.

120 The 3–5 percent figure is a widely recognized measure of the level of growth required for a company or national economy to remain viable; any less and things start to become tricky for the institution, leading to job cuts, further borrowing and potential takeover/collapse. Ratings information derived from Philippe Jorion and Gaiyan Zhang, "Information Effects of Bond Rating Changes: The Role of the Rating Prior to the Announcement." *Journal of Fixed Income,* Spring 2007, vol. 16, no. 4.

121 Anna Politkovskaya. "Poisoned by Putin." *The Guardian,* September 9, 2004, guardian.co.uk (accessed October 2011).

122 Feel free to sue me; I await a detailed investigation.

123 Personal transcript of a recording from *The Richard Bacon Show,* broadcast on BBC Radio 5Live, October 6, 2011 (recording available at guardian.co.uk, accessed October 2011).

124 "National Pudding Week." 72point media, 72point.com (accessed November 2011). The range of press releases lapped up by the gutter press is astonishing. This company's "Coverage" page is full of wonderful lessons in how to get your fake story into the press or onto high profile blogs. I particularly liked the paragraph in a press release about a shopping mall, that went: "Spending time with girlfriends and hitting the shops, or stopping for a coffee and a chat, can lift a woman's mood and I certainly believe in the phrase 'what we can't solve in real life, we can solve through retail therapy.'" FFS! The phrase quoted was just made up by the PR company, as was the entire quote; yet four national newspapers published all or part of this piece of PR-puff. The same company

also happen to run a "proper" news service, which is just as easy to duplicate if you have the right contacts.

125 The Real News. "Ralph Nader speaks on an Obama presidency" (therealnews.com, accessed December 2011).

126 Peter Preston. "War, what is it good for?" *The Observer*, October 7, 2001.

127 Andrew Marr. *My Trade.* Macmillan, 2004, p.112.

128 Dan Sabbah. "Pay of top Guardian Media Group executives published." *The Guardian,* August 1, 2011, guardian.co.uk (accessed December 2011).

129 "Once more with feeling." *The Guardian,* September 2, 2005, guardian.co.uk (accessed December 2011).

130 Ibid.

131 John Pilger. "Once again, war is prime time and journalism's role is taboo." johnpilger.com (accessed December 2011).

132 "Power, not oil, Mr Greenspan." *The Sunday Times,* September 16, 2007.

133 "Melting Ice Sheets and Media Contradictions: An Exchange with George Monbiot of the Guardian." Media Lens, medialens.org (accessed December 2011).

134 Email, June 25, 2007.

135 George Monbiot. "The editorials urge us to cut emissions, but the ads tell a very different story." *The Guardian,* August 14, 2007, guardian.co.uk (accessed December 2011).

136 Siobhain Butterworth. "Open door — The readers' editor on ... the contradiction between what we say and the ads we run." *The Guardian,* October 29, 2007, guardian.co.uk (accessed December 2011).

137 Ibid.

138 From "Local Hero," Warner Brothers, 1983, directed by Bill Forsyth. Get hold of a copy immediately; you won't regret it.

139 Derrick Jensen. *Endgame, Volume II: Resistance.* Seven Stories Press, 2006.

140 Lawrence J. Saha. "Dictatorship 101: killing the internet plays into the hands of revolutionaries." theconversation.edu.au (accessed November 2011).

141 Dave Pollard. "Living Disconnected." howtosavetheworld.ca (accessed November 2011).

142 It could be considered ironic that this was written on a Facebook "wall," but we return to the question of the Master's Tools and using what we currently have to the best of our abilities. It's clear that this person has little to fear from the Internet being a thing of the past.

143 Maps like this are readily available from the websites of almost every telecommunications provider. You have to be careful not to directly associate such maps with undermining actions, but on the other hand if you know where to get the information, it doesn't have to be explicitly associated with an action. I would recommend also using WikiLeaks and the Cablesearch engine to find more information that is now in the public domain.

144 "BlackBerry BBM, email downed in epic FAIL" and "RIM: 'Faulty switch took out faulty-switch-proof network.'" The Register, theregister.co.uk (accessed November 2011).

145 Richard Reynolds is the author of *On Guerrilla Gardening* (Bloomsbury, 2009) and blogs regularly at the Guerrilla Gardening hub, guerrillagardening.org.

146 This concept has been developed and refined across the civilized world by all sorts of people, ending up in a fluke of convergent memevolution as products you can buy off the shelf (known as "Boms" to calm the nerves of the paranoid) that are almost identical to the version you can produce yourself just by following this guide. Richard Reynolds kindly finessed some of the details for me.

147 Richard Mabey. *Weeds.* Profile Books, 2010.

148 For non-US speakers, a "yard" is a small garden or lawn. For US speakers, a "yard" in many other countries is called a "garden," whether it is cultivated for produce or flowers or not.

149 Julien Temple. "Detroit: The Last Days." guardian.co.uk (accessed February 2012). The movie *Requiem for Detroit,* about which this article is written, is well worth seeing.

150 Lester R. Brown. *Plan B 4.0: Mobilizing to Save Civilization.* Earth Policy Institute, 2009.

151 In case anyone has any illusions as to the contrary, ENGOs (Environmental Non-Governmental Organizations) such as Greenpeace (in Europe and North America), WWF and the Sierra Club are no less of a hierarchy than any other corporations. In their normal operation, a group of high-level policy-makers decide on the campaigns well in advance, drawing up strategies and drafting campaign materials such that ordinary supporters and volunteers have almost no room for maneuver. If you don't follow the campaign strategy, and even the precise text handed down from above, then you don't represent that group, and most likely you will be asked to leave.

152 This is a widely cited figure for highly industrialized nations for the stabilization of global temperature rise, not some scare story picked out of the air.

153 The conversation took place, and was recorded in the public interest, on June 28, 2011. It was a long conversation and it turns out that, many years earlier, I had worked with the person I was talking to. The conversation ended with him asking me to send him a formal proposal that could be considered by the campaign team. Despite sending a few chapters of this very book and a summary, and requesting feedback twice more, I never received a response. This is known in the trade as "stonewalling," which is an attempt at making the other party give up through the act of silence. It didn't work.

154 Figures from, in order: (1) derived and extrapolated from CDIAC. "Global CO_2 Emissions from Fossil-Fuel Burning, Cement Manufacture, and Gas Flaring: 1751–2008"; (2) C. Kinnard, C.M. Zdanowicz, R. Koerner and D.A. Fisher. "A changing Arctic Seasonal ice zone — observations from 1870–2003 and possible oceanographic Consequences." *Geophysical Research Letters* 35, 2008; (3) INPE/FAO, quoted in "Calculating Deforestation Figures for the Amazon," (rainforests.mongabay.com, accessed December 2011); (4) GISS. "Global Land-Ocean Temperature Index (C) (Anomaly with Base: 1951-1980)" (data.giss.nasa.gov, accessed December 2011).

155 I love a good pun. Jenny=Gene=Generator.

156 Konnie = Consumer. Sorry.

157 Fabíola Ortiz. "Rainforest activist asks for protection after death threats." *The Guardian*, August 31, 2011, guardian.co.uk (accessed December 2011).

158 Democracy Now. "Over 160 Arrested in Ongoing Civil Disobedience Against Keystone XL Tar Sands Oil Pipeline." democracynow.org (accessed December 2011).

159 Stephanie McMillan. "Code Red." stephaniemcmillan.org. Reproduced with permission from the illustrator. Stephanie is a wonderfully observant cartoonist and illustrator, whose insights often reveal far more about the failure of the environmental mainstream than any amount of text ever can.

160 Wayne Grytting. *American Newspeak*. New Society, 2002.

161 Avaaz. "About Us." avaaz.org (accessed December 2011).

162 Micah M. White. "Activism After Clicktivism." Adbusters, adbusters.org (accessed December 2011).

163 Evgeny Morozov. *The Net Delusion: The Dark Side of Internet Freedom*. PublicAffairs, 2011.

164 The word "member" seems to have very loose currency and can mean things as diverse as someone who has signed up with a subscription fee, someone who has filled in a petition or someone who has just clicked "like" on Facebook. A far cry from the active participation the word suggests.

165 "How to plan your event." moving-planet.org/plan (accessed January 2012).

166 *Our Common Future*. World Commission on Environment and Development, 1983, un-documents.net (accessed January 2012).

167 This was part of an ongoing online discussion, partly informed by Cory's article "SumOfUs are Corporate Whores | Some of Us are Not." wrongkindofgreen.org (accessed April 2012).

168 You can hear the entire phone call at archive.org/details/WoodlandTrustAcceptDubiousCorporateSponsorship (accessed June 2012).

169 "Woodland Trust Report and Accounts 2010." woodlandtrust.org.uk (accessed January 2012).

170 Johann Hari. "The Wrong Kind of Green." *The Nation*, 2010, thenation.com (accessed January 2012).

171 You can check this by looking at the article history and comparing contributors' names with those working for the organization itself, or by comparing IP addresses to their registered networks.

172 "Vandalism and Edit Wars." How Stuff Works, computer.howstuffworks.com (accessed January 2012).

173 Christopher Booker. "WWF hopes to find $60 billion growing on trees." *The Telegraph*, telegraph.co.uk (accessed January 2012).

174 "Anarchist" simply means "one who has no leaders": any other definition must be taken with a big pinch of salt. There are lots of different anarchist subgroups, but any group that does not embrace the idea of there not being a *de facto* leadership structure cannot be regarded as anarchist, however fashionable it may be to use the term.

175 Much like the fashionable coffee houses of 19th-century London, and almost certainly the back rooms of pubs now. Revolution can be fomented in all sorts of places.

176 Which is almost never, and which Greenpeace Inc., or whatever formal title a national group goes by, immediately disowns even though — and maybe because — it is successful in a non-symbolic way.

177 Just because you don't agree with something, or because something may directly impact upon you, does not mean it cannot be a success for someone else. One person's "act of terrorism" is another person's "victory for freedom." I use the term "success" very much in that sense.

178 When referring to a community that includes only humans, the term "Human Community" is more accurate, but when including connections with other living organisms, then the term "Community" is best used, as an analogy for Ecosystem. Obviously that makes the civilized definition of the term utterly absurd.

179 Janaia Donaldson. Peak Moment, quotation from *Time's Up! An Uncivilized Conversation.* wordpress.peakmoment.tv (accessed March 2012).

180 Eli Pariser. "Beware online 'filter bubbles.'" TED Talks, ted.com/talks (accessed March 2012).

181 Jason Scott. "Facefacts." ascii.textfiles.com (accessed March 2012).

182 See the execrable walmartcommunity.com/ for lots of examples.

183 "Markets create twice as many jobs as supermarkets and food is half the price." New Economics Foundation, neweconomics.org (accessed April 2012).

184 The last sentence is a nod to one of the greatest living English lyricists, Andy Partridge of XTC.

185 LGBT (lesbian, gay, bisexual, transsexual) is useful shorthand for individual people and groups falling outside the "norms" prescribed by societies rooted in, usually, Judeo-Christian-Muslim religious beliefs.

186 Robin Brontsema. "A Queer Revolution: Reconceptualizing the Debate Over Linguistic Reclamation." *Colorado Research in Linguistics,* Volume 17 (2004).

187 Rebecca Solnit. *A Paradise Built in Hell.* Penguin, 2009.

188 Although "civilized humans" and "citizens" can and should be used interchangeably, for some reason, probably cultural, even the most radical American writers sometimes use the word "citizen" to denote ordinary people whatever their culture. I make a point of telling them this, to little effect. On a related point, I think the differentiation between "civilian" and "military" is useful in many cases, though again I tend to avoid using the former word.

189 Naomi Klein. *The Shock Doctrine.* Penguin, 2007.

190 The words "disaster" and "crisis" are not completely synonymous. A disaster is more akin to the event itself, whereas the crisis is the outcome of the disaster, and normally associated with the human response to the disaster. Sometimes it's convenient to use the word "crisis" when referring to something at a smaller scale, such as an localized event. Context is important.

191 "At least 200 killed as mine collapses in the Bo district of Sierra Leone." *The Statesman,* March 20, 2012. thestatesmen.net (accessed May 2012).

192 Oil tanker or refinery strikes and blockades spring to mind.

193 Sadly the music club partially succumbed to lack of numbers, and no longer runs monthly.

194 Wendell Berry. "Lecture: It All Turns on Affection." National Endowment for Humanities, 2012, neh.gov (accessed May 2012). Thanks to Tim Bennett for the pointer.

195 Eric Wiener. *The Geography of Bliss.* Black Swan, 2008.

196 Derrick Jensen. *Now This War Has Two Sides.* Audio recording — PM Press, 2008.

197 The statement was quickly removed when it was widely publicized by activists, but there is a good report on the immediate aftermath at "Heritage Foundation Covers Up Its Opportunistic Hopes in Haiti," January 14, 2011, governmentalityblog.com (accessed May 2012).

198 Alastair McIntosh. *Soil and Soul: People Versus Corporate Power.* Aurum Press, 2001.

199 Ed Iglehart. "Territory, Property, Sovereignty & Democracy in Scotland — A Brief Philosophical Examination." tipiglen.co.uk (accessed May 2012).

200 For more information see landshare.net (accessed June 2012).

201 "About." diggers2012.wordpress.com (accessed June 2012).

202 Gerrard Winstanley, William Everard, Richard Goodgroome, John Palmer, Thomas Starre, John South, William Hoggrill, John Courton, Robert Sawyer, William Taylor, Thomas Eder, Christopher Clifford, Henry Bickerstaffe, John Barker. *The True Levellers Standard Advanced: The State of Community Opened, and Presented to the Sons of Men.* John Taylor, &c., 1649. strecorsoc.org (accessed June 2012).

203 As opposed to *A Matter of Scale*, the original manuscript of which I still have complete control over, including for free print distribution.

204 Open Source Initiative. "The Open Source Definition." opensource.org (accessed May 2012).

205 Idzie Desmarais. "New to this blog? New to Unschooling? Read this!" yes-i-can-write.blogspot.co.uk (accessed May 2012).

206 Erica Goldson. "Here I Stand." America via Erica, americaviaerica.blogspot.co.uk (accessed June 2012).

207 Bob Black. "The Abolition of Work." zpub.com (accessed February 2012).

208 Daniel Everett. *Don't Sleep, There Are Snakes — Life and Language in the Amazonian Jungle.* Profile Books, 2008.

209 You could argue that this is inevitable, given that civilized people are human beings, and civilization is — fortunately — not quite powerful enough to wash away all traces of humanity .

210 Douglas T. Kenrick, Vladas Griskevicius, Steven L. Neuberg and Mark Schaller. "Renovating the Pyramid of Needs: Contemporary Extensions Built Upon Ancient Foundations." *Perspectives on Psychological Science* 2010 5: 292, carlsonschool.umn.edu (accessed June 2012).

211 A. H. Maslow. "A Theory of Human Motivation." *Psychological Review,* 1943, 50, 370–396, psychclassics.yorku.ca (accessed June 2012).

212 Carolyn Baker. *Navigating the Coming Chaos: A Handbook for Inner Transition.* iUniverse, 2011.
213 Urban Scout. *Rewild or Die.* Urban Scout LLC, 2008.
214 Nikanoru. *A Rewilding Community Toolbox.* guymcpherson.com/wp-content/uploads/2012/02/A-Rewilding-Community-Toolbox-V.pdf (accessed July 2012) or underminers.org.
215 James Hogg. "My First Interview with Walter Scott." *Edinburgh Literary Journal,* June 27, 1829, 51–52, spenserians.cath.vt.edu (accessed July 2012).
216 Susan Maushart. *The Winter of Our Disconnect.* Profile Books, 2011.
217 Sharon Astyk. *Depletion and Abundance.* New Society, 2008.
218 Paul Kingsnorth. "Confessions of a Recovering Environmentalist." *Orion Magazine,* January/February 2012, orionmagazine.org (accessed August 2012).
219 A. Roger Ekirch. *At Day's Close: A History of Nighttime.* Weidenfeld & Nicolson, 2005.
220 Michael Bittman, James Mahmud Rice and Judy Wajcman. "Appliances and their impact: the ownership of domestic technology and time spent on household work." *The British Journal of Sociology,* 55 (3), 2004.
221 United Nations Department of Economic and Social Affairs/Population Division. *World Urbanization Prospects: The 2011 Revision.* esa.un.org/unup (accessed August 2012).
222 John Muir. *Our National Parks.* The Riverside Press, 1901, available at sierraclub.org/john_muir_exhibit (accessed August 2012).
223 Roger S. Ulrich et al. "Stress Recovery During Exposure to Urban and Natural Elements." *J. Env. Psych.* 11, 1991.
224 You might find it useful to read the experiences of others who have taken this "30 Day Sit Spot Challenge." See wildernessawareness.ning.com/group/sitspot/forum.
225 This is a specially edited extract from Guy R. McPherson, *Walking Away from Empire: A Personal Journey,* Publish American, 2011. I highly recommend Guy's writing as an antidote to those who pretend we can buy our way out of the global crisis and that collapse is just scaremongering.
226 Carolyn Baker. *Sacred Demise: Walking the Spiritual Path of Industrial Civilization's Collapse.* 2009, iUniverse.
227 Keith Farnish. "Finding my Identity." The Earth Blog, 2009, earth-blog.bravejournal.com (accessed August 2012).
228 Joseph Conrad. *Heart of Darkness.* Penguin Classics, 1985 (orig. 1902).

Index

About the Author

KEITH FARNISH IS A FATHER, a writer, a thinker, a grower, a baker, a maker, a talker and a listener. He helps run various groups and clubs in his village, is a bit of a computer geek, and generally makes life difficult for corporations and governments.

New Society Publishers

ENVIRONMENTAL BENEFITS STATEMENT

New Society Publishers has chosen to produce this book on recycled paper made with **100% post consumer waste,** processed chlorine free, and old growth free.

For every 5,000 books printed, New Society saves the following resources:[1]

38	Trees
3,436	Pounds of Solid Waste
3,781	Gallons of Water
4,931	Kilowatt Hours of Electricity
6,246	Pounds of Greenhouse Gases
27	Pounds of HAPs, VOCs, and AOX Combined
9	Cubic Yards of Landfill Space

[1]Environmental benefits are calculated based on research done by the Environmental Defense Fund and other members of the Paper Task Force who study the environmental impacts of the paper industry.